JONATHAN
STURGES

Merchant of Old New York
Rev. Ed.

JONATHAN
STURGES

Merchant of Old New York
Rev. Ed.

———⨝———

ROBIN McPHILLIPS

Gems of History Publishing, LLC

ISBN 978-0-99830379-0-5

LCCN 2018914286

Printed in the United States of America.

Gems of History Publishing, LLC 33 Office Park Road A-151, Hilton Head Island, SC 29928

Front cover: U.S. Treasury building, 1860s, "Popular Series of American Views," Library of Congress, https://www.loc.gov/item/2017649880/ (accessed April 9, 2018); Durand, Asher B., *Jonathan Sturges*, c. 1840, accession no. 1977.342.1, Metropolitan Museum of Art, New York, NY. http://www.metmuseum.org/collection/the- collection-online/search/10791 (accessed November 14, 2014)

CONTENTS

Acknowledgements

So many people and institutions aided in the research and compiling of this six-year project. Foremost, I must thank Mary Bullard Rousseau, may she rest in peace, and her daughters. Mary "Polly" Roessler and Helene "Lenie" Epifano. They are an inspiration as they fight to sustain the legacy of Jonathan Sturges and his 1840 country home in Fairfield, Connecticut. Without their encouragement and support, this project would not have had the same personal insight and detail. Also, I would like to thank their extended family, Fargo Rousseau and David Sturges, for their ongoing familial input to *Jonathan Sturges—Merchant of Old New York*.

Mary Rousseau[1], Mary with Judge Sturges Gavel in Library[2]

Special thanks go to the staff of the Fairfield Museum and History Center, and especially to its Library Director, Dr. Elizabeth Rose, who expertly assisted and guided me in accessing pertinent Sturges family documents, artifacts and other reference material. Heartfelt thanks go to the Morgan Library and Archives who put a priority on preserving the largest collection of Jonathan Sturges family documents, letters, photographs, and other relics, and regard him as a Morgan family member. Research access to this collection was absolutely critical in putting a voice to the various Sturges and Osborn family members. The New York Historical Society and the Princeton University Library, who also house many Osborn and Sturges family documents, were all so generous in providing access to their archives.

I would also like to extend special thanks to Dr. David Levine of the Hospital for Special Surgery (HSS) in New York. His book on the history of the hospital, and his personal involvement in aiding my research into the hospital archives, helped me understand Jonathan and his family's role in founding the forerunner of HSS, the New York Society of the Ruptured and Crippled. Additional thanks goes to Arlene Shaner, reference librarian at the New York Academy of Medicine, Center for the History of Medicine and Public Health, for her help in directing me to those reference materials telling the history of the hospitals that Jonathan founded, as well as Virginia Osborn's Bellevue Nurse Training School. New York National Academy Museum and School curator Diana Thompson provided the insight on the portrait of Jonathan Sturges commissioned and owned by the museum. Lisa Schoblasky, Chicago Newberry Library, provided helpful aid in researching information in the archives of the Illinois Central Railroad.

I extend my gratitude to Anita Prentice who, along with her husband Nat, are the current residents of William and Virginia Osborn's former residence Wing-and-Wing in Garrison, New York. Her family insight, the many family pictures provided, and the tour she arranged with the knowledgeable Castle Rock caretaker, Chip Marks, were all key to illustrating the Sturges-Osborn legacy.

Deep appreciation goes to the many readers and editors of the multiple drafts of the manuscript, including, Don Weise, whose thoughtful and professional editing helped provide some needed framework for the story; the Rousseau/Roessler/Sturges family who provided unique family knowledge; Michael Brennan, Louise McCormick, Ellie Berghausen, Casey Vanderveer, Mary McNeill; my daughter and son, Kelly Anderson and James McPhillips; and many other friends and associates who have encouraged me and helped edit and round out the accuracy and readability of the book.

As I started researching this book, little did I know that it would be a six-year labor of love. I attribute the patience and tenacity that was required to complete this project to my mother Dixie Curtis, one of the strongest women I know, and my father John LeBlanc, who would not deem a task complete until it was done to a high standard. Last I would like to thank my husband Tom, whose patience, support and love was critical to the project as I put in thousands upon thousands of hours of writing and researching over many years. His reading and rereading of the book, and hundreds of hours of genealogy work on the Sturges family, has helped the story immeasurably in getting to the end. Thanks to all and enjoy the book!

INTRODUCTION

Jonathan Sturges—Merchant of Old New York

Jonathan Sturges was laid to rest in his hometown of Fairfield, Connecticut, in early December 1874. His wife, children, grandchildren and extended family, including former son-in-law J.P. Morgan, held a small, intimate family religious service at his home in New York City. Later that day at the Dutch Reformed Presbyterian Church on Fifth Avenue, a packed crowd assembled to honor the beloved man of business, philanthropy and faith. A distinguished panel of no less than seven clergymen presided at his service. Friends, high society, pillars of business, art and politics, and those in their threadbare Sunday-best clothes, all took hat in hand to grieve the death of Jonathan Sturges, a man of whom it was said "never made an enemy."[1] Junius Morgan and William Cullen Bryant were among his distinguished pallbearers. This prodigious Civil War Union supporter, founder of railroads and hospitals, pioneering American art patron, champion of the poor and beleaguered, and merchant of a committed Christian faith, had become fatally ill after attending a church conference in Philadelphia.

At his death, Jonathan Sturges was a stalwart of a bygone era, one of the old guard of merchants who built their reputation on the pillars of integrity, dependability, and tenacious commitment. By the time of the Civil War, these noble men were making their exit as the infamous speculators, corrupt civic leaders and ruthless industrialists, were taking main stage and amassing extraordinary wealth. His life was closely intertwined with many of the period's notable names and personalities of the era such as Vanderbilt, Belmont, Roosevelt and Astor; politicians Tweed, Calhoun, Webster, Lincoln and Tilden; Generals Scott, McClellan and Grant; men of the arts Bryant, Longfellow, Morse, Greeley, Cole, Durand, Bancroft; as well as Jenny Lind and Gen. Tom Thumb, among many others.

Jonathan Sturges—Merchant of Old New York is a saga of a young nation and the development of its infrastructure, economy, and charitable safety nets for its impoverished citizens—all through the lens of one of the relatively small circle of influential New York businessmen who significantly impacted national politics and the country's march to world economic prominence. This is the extraordinary story of *Jonathan Sturges—Merchant of Old New York*.

JONATHAN
STURGES

Merchant of Old New York

ONE

Jonathan's Early Life and Pioneering Old English Ancestors

Mr. Sturges, in early life, struggled with poverty, his only capital being his own sterling character and qualities.

—*Rev. Atwater*

Jonathan Sturges's many and varied accomplishments, and the values he embraced, stemmed from his upbringing in Connecticut, in one of the oldest of New England towns, rich in Old English Protestant traditions. These ancestral roots and traditions formed the basis for his life and were well represented by the Sturges crest and motto, Esse Quam Videri, meaning "to be, rather than to seem." It is a Latin term from Cicero's essay on friendship: "Few are those who wish to be endowed with virtue, rather than to seem so"—a theme that personified Jonathan's life of probity and integrity.[a]

The story of Jonathan's pioneering ancestors is a case history in the settling and eventual independence of the United States. Born in 1802, Jonathan Sturges grew up in Southport, a Mill River hamlet of Fairfield, Connecticut, the American ancestral home of his English forefathers. Roger Ludlow, of the Massachusetts Bay Colony, founded the town in 1639 with a few dozen settlers. Both Jonathan's father (Barnabas Sturges) and mother (Mary Sturges) descended from John Sturges, one of the early settlers of Fairfield. Sturges joined the settlement in 1650 and married Deborah Barlow, whose family had also just emigrated from England. He became a town selectman and a wealthy man with land holdings of an estimated 774 acres, and was a well-

---

a The motto Esse Quam Videri is shared by forty-six other Great Britain/Ireland families and North Carolina.

respected leader of the community, not only in Fairfield, but within Connecticut.

Barnabas descended from the oldest son of John Sturges, the first Jonathan Sturges (b.1650), who inherited the Sturges homestead and was the great-grandfather of the Honorable Judge Jonathan Sturges. The Judge was a man of national prominence—a Founding Father, member of the Sons of Liberty in the American Revolution, a Connecticut Supreme Court Justice, represented Connecticut at the Constitutional Convention, and was a congressman during the first and second federal Congresses. Jonathan's father, Barnabas Sturges, was the Judge's son.

Patriarchal Genealogy Chart

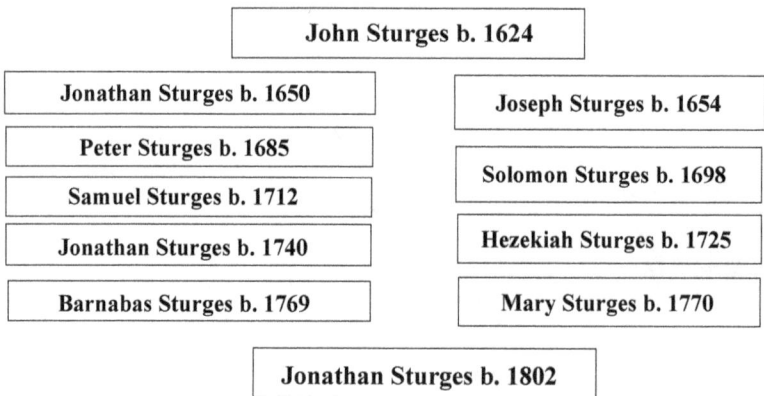

John Sturges b. 1624

Jonathan Sturges b. 1650	Joseph Sturges b. 1654
Peter Sturges b. 1685	Solomon Sturges b. 1698
Samuel Sturges b. 1712	
Jonathan Sturges b. 1740	Hezekiah Sturges b. 1725
Barnabas Sturges b. 1769	Mary Sturges b. 1770

Jonathan Sturges b. 1802

Jonathan's mother, Mary Sturges, descended from John Sturges' son Joseph (1654-1728). Joseph, a farmer who lived his whole life in Fairfield, participated in the 1692 dunking of Mercy Disborow in Edward's Pond,[b] as part of an infamous witch trial held there in 1692.[1] A guilty verdict was rendered by the governor and Mercy was sentenced to death but pardoned when more thoughtful heads prevailed. Joseph's son Solomon Sturges (1698–1779), Mary's grandfather, was a man of prominence in Fairfield and owned a homestead in the coastal Mill Plain area, near the Old Post Road, close to where Jonathan's country home still stands today. Solomon's home, near the Judge's home on the historical Post Road, was among the many houses

---

b Edwards Pond was a small body of water in the Fairfield town green area (now just a noticeable depression in the ground) and is widely known locally as the witch's pond, although this is the only record of its use in this way. Dunking (buoyancy thought to be a rejection of baptismal water) by this time was not given credibility by the courts.

burned in the attack on Fairfield by the British in July 1779, when this eighty-year-old man was shot and mercilessly bayoneted. Solomon's son, Mary Sturges's father, Hezekiah Sturges, was a captain in the Revolutionary War militia. Her family's house was also destroyed in this attack when Mary was nine years old. This pioneering and revolutionary family history coupled with a hardworking, religiously based life, instilled in Jonathan a strong work ethic and an abiding loyalty to country, family and faith.

Barnabas Lothrop Sturges and Mary Sturges married in 1791. In his early adult life, Barnabas was a coastal trader; however, he had his share of misfortune. Barnabas built his first ship for trading, stocked with valuable goods, likely sailing to the West Indies. Somewhere on the ship's first voyage in the late 1790s, the French seized his vessel.[2] It is a common misconception that the War of 1812 was America's first military conflict as a sovereign nation. However, several years before the clash with Britain, the United States engaged in a naval war with France. The United States signed Jay's Treaty in 1794, resolving maritime and trade issues that had lingered since the Revolutionary War and had threatened war between Great Britain and the United States. However, it directly conflicted with the 1778 Treaty of Alliance and Commerce with France, when America discontinued debt payments to the French, owed for their assistance in the Revolutionary War. They felt betrayed, and in response, the French began seizing U.S. merchant ships in 1795. Captain Sturges' ship became a casualty of this Quasi-War that ended with the Treaty of Mortefontaine in September 1800. This loss would have been a significant setback for Barnabas and notionally where he started to struggle financially.

In 1797, Barnabas bought a house and land in Fairfield from his father. The original home, built about 1784, overlooked the beautiful Mill River harbor, an area known as a center of shipping, commerce, and farms. Barnabas built a new home about 1800, across from this original home and the coastal highway (now Harbor Road) that was forged in 1790. Jonathan was the first child born to Barnabas and Mary in their new home on the Mill River. In total they had four girls and two boys: Mary Ann (b.1792), Lothrop Lewis (b.1794), Deborah Lewis (b.1796), Lucretia (b.1798) Jonathan (b.1802) and Abigail Dimon (b.1805). This Mill River section of town, now known as Southport, was where the Sasqua Indians lived in the early days and where Jonathan spent his young life being schooled in this Protestant Land of Steady Habits, a term first coined in the early 1800s for

Barnabas Sturges House and Southport Harbor c. 1830s[3]

Connecticut's predictable aristocratic governance and Congregational Church dominance.

Following family tradition, Jonathan was baptized in the Fairfield's Congregationalist Christ's Church on May 2, 1802[c] only two decades after the Revolutionary War.[4] This time period was the era of the Second Great Awakening in America, a revival of religious fervor, increasing church enrollments, and a broadening of the number of Christian denominations beyond the Congregationalist and Anglican churches of Jonathan's youth. This included Methodists, Baptists, Unitarians, and Presbyterians—a religious awakening he would embrace in adulthood.

The church served as the center of social life in this era and attendance was expected, even compulsory, and residents risked being fined for non-attendance. Attendees, many of whom traveled long distances, brought foot stoves with hot coals to warm their feet during cold weather, and also their lunch, inevitably dropping crumbs and attracting the "church mice."[d] In this era of a fledgling national infrastructure and few newspapers, it was church services, house raisings, militia drills and other such community events that brought the people together and allowed the men to debate the issues of the state and nation. Tea parties, husking bees, and sewing circles,

---

[c] Barnabas and Mary were officially admitted to the Congregational Church just before his birth on March 7, 1802.

[d] This may be the mouse's only meal of the week, inspiring the saying, "poor as a church mouse"

allowed women to share recipes, fashions, family news, and other ideas on raising children and running households.

These community gatherings became an opportunity for the young people to mingle. Reverend Frank Child, a local minister, noted, "The larger freedom of these gatherings made them happily convenient for those significant and delicious love passes which were not congenial to the parlor, when the parents and small children were close at hand to note each telltale look, word, act."[5] Child, a founder of the Fairfield Historical Society, wrote of house raisings in Fairfield during the early 1800s:

> When a building was to be raised, it was considered a community affair. It is a fact that often the assembled citizens did more than raise the building; we have it recorded that on many an occasion they "raised Cain" as well. For these good people were nothing if not hospitable on such days. Happy thing was it for the town, if no more than one leg was broken, or rib crushed, or head smashed, by a fall from some dizzy height.[6]

Fairfield's population rose from 3,725 in 1800 to 4,125 in 1810, because of the increased activity in the maritime trade at the Black Rock and Mill River wharves, much of it from New York, Boston, and Wilmington, North Carolina.[7] With this increased maritime commerce, it could be surmised that Barnabas prospered enough to overcome the loss of his ship, but still his family was not considered affluent. In the 1810 census, only the immediate family lived in their home: Barnabas, Mary, and their six children.[8] Although many families in Fairfield housed live-in domestic servants, including slaves, Jonathan's family had none. This supports a picture of a modest family lifestyle. A local minister and contemporary of Jonathan's in Fairfield, Reverend Atwater, commenting in 1874 on Jonathan's upbringing, further clarified this picture as he said, "Mr. Sturges, in early life, struggled with poverty, his only capital being his own sterling character and qualities."[9]

As there is no family journal or cache of letters from Jonathan's formative years, his early experiences must be surmised by the reminiscences of Mary early in their marriage, sparse reminiscences from Jonathan himself, newspaper reports and their extended family and friends later in life. In a well-publicized retirement dinner speech by Jonathan in 1868 (Appendix IV), he recounted lessons he received from his grandfather as a youth in Fairfield:

One of the first lessons I received was in 1813, when I was eleven years of age. My grandfather had collected a fine flock of merino sheep, which were cherished during the War of 1812-15. I was a shepherd boy whose business was to watch the sheep in the fields. A boy who was more fond of his books than of sheep was sent with me, but he left the work to me, while he lay in the shade and read his books. I finally complained of this to the old gentleman. I shall never forget his benevolent smile as he replied: "Never you mind; if you watch the sheep, you will have the sheep." I thought to myself what does the old gentleman mean? Then I thought of my Sunday lesson: "Thou hast been faithful over a few things, will make thee ruler over many things." Then I understood it: "Never you mind who else neglects his duty; be you faithful and you will have your reward." I do not think it will take many lads as long as I did to understand this proverb.[10]

Barnabas Lothrop Sturges House, c. 1800[e]

During this time, the town had an official sheep master who was responsible for the safety of the sheep, applying brands and cultivating ample quality grasses in the common areas. Until 1750, the land on the Mill River where Jonathan's father built his house was common land for sheep grazing. It was typical to assign boys ten to fourteen to watch the community sheep herd while their fathers and older brothers tended to the daily chores around the farm. Jonathan

[e] The 534 Harbor Road home which Captain Barnabas Lothrop Sturges built in 1800 (picture taken in the 1970s prior to architectural modernization that took place, modifying its appearance).

also presumably attended school at the Fairfield Academy (an institution which his grandfather founded and was a trustee), at least until the age of thirteen when young scholars either had to end their formal education or look elsewhere for schooling or private tutors. From the journal of Jonathan Bulkley, a leading citizen in the Mill River area of town, it is seen that thirteen-year-old Jonathan Sturges was under the tutelage of Mr. Haul:

> Friday, March 10th, 1815, Mr. Haul of Weston has this day had his pub-
> lic exhibition 30 scholars who performed to the admiration of the whole
> audience, which was very large, Mrs. Pike's house was crowded and what
> was most laughable was that Jonathan Sturges and Burritt [sic] Sherwood
> acted the part of negro slaves and they did extremely well, the scholars and
> the young people had a ball in the evening.[11]

While Jonathan was attending school and watching the sheep, the town fathers and the governor were occupied with fighting the War of 1812. Fort Union, Black Rock, and Fort Defense, at the mouth of the Mill River in South-port Harbor, were fortified with local militia. Jonathan's brother Lothrop was a private in Sergeant Osborn's Connecticut Militia. Jeremiah Sturges, his cousin, led the organization of The First Company of Defensive Independent Volun-teers and was Captain of the company.[12] At Jeremiah Sturges' urging, a pow-der house[f] was established in 1814 on land provided by Levi Jennings inland, between the two forts. The young boys of the town, including Jonathan, would have observed these war preparations and militia activities with much interest, with many of their friends and family participating.

Fairfield had been experiencing an economic recovery after the destruction of the Revolutionary War. However, the war and blockade between 1812 and 1815 was a significant blow to coastal trade, forcing ports to close and ships to remain in port. Many merchants lost everything. Barnabas Sturges' business would also have been affected, along with the fortunes of his family. The U.S. government relied heavily on tariffs and the federal treasury suffered. Jonathan's future wife later commented on the effect of the war on her family. As they moved from Connecticut to Fredericksburg, Virginia, the war went in to full effect. "My father had expected to make his arrangements in Fredericksburg and remove us all by water in the spring. This was at an end, our ports were all closed, and all

---

f The remnants of which still exist today on the grounds of Fairfield's Tomlinson Middle School.

travel and all transportation of merchandise was overland by stages running day and night, and long, covered baggage wagons."[13]

As a respected and accomplished family, the Sturgeses were acquainted with most of the political and civic leaders in the region. In Jonathan's youth, the county courthouse in Fairfield brought many influential lawyers and politicians to its doors, including Roger Minot Sherman, Jr. (Connecticut Assembly), Jonathan's Uncle Lewis B. Sturges (U.S. Representative 1805–1817), and Gideon Tomlinson (Governor, Congressman, and U.S. Senator for Connecticut) who all lived in and practiced law in Fairfield. The family and the town gravitated toward the Federalist Party which espoused the continued leadership of the well-to-do, established families. Jonathan had in his possession at his death (probably passed down from his father Barnabas or grandfather) an 1805 manifesto that warned of a great threat of the rising opposition political party in Connecticut—the "godless" Democratic-Republican party.[14] The Federalists opposed the War of 1812, seeing it as a ploy by President Madison to aid Napoleon.

The memoirs of Jonathan's first cousin Solomon Sturges provide a lens into family life in Fairfield in the early 1800s. Born in 1796, just six years before Jonathan, Solomon recalled a typical Sturges family gathering, where it easily could have been Jonathan narrating:

> There was an enormous chimney in the center of the house, the whole west side of which was occupied by the kitchen, fireplace and the oven at the north end of it... I would take a seat upon a stool within one of the jambs of the fireplace...Then the exploits of the Revolutionary War would be rehearsed. All the men had participated in one battle or another; some fierce encounter by land or water. How many skirmishes with the Tories that came over from Long Island on whaleboats! What one did not know or recollect, another one would. My mother and sisters would be busy at various household employments. When nothing more important... the spinning wheels were brought forward...My father kept a flock of sheep, the wool from which was manufactured in the family and furnished our winter clothing. Flax was a staple product and its preparation and manufacture into linen was no small part of the winter employment of the household...Industry and frugality were the order of the day.[15]

The home fire burned perpetually to provide for heat and cooking. If the fire extinguished, it would need to be reignited with the frustrating flint and rock technique, or with coals obtained from distant neighbors. Flax was a bountiful crop for Fairfield and hundreds of tons were harvested each year and exported to England and the West Indies. Everyday needs were locally procured through a barter process, rendering metal or paper money scarce, and necessarily hoarded to pay taxes or other official fees. This life of industry, frugality, faith, service to country, and the importance of community, became the foundation for his perspective on life and the conduct of his business. His father's failures in business motivated Jonathan and his brother to apply themselves and do better—they had little choice.

TWO

Mary Pemberton Cady and Jonathan's Early Years in Business

He would go down to the great metropolis, fling himself with enthusiasm into the work, and make a fortune and a name that rendered him conspicuous in the land.

—*Rev. Child*

While Jonathan was growing up in Fairfield, his future wife, Mary Cady was born to her parents Ebenezer and Elizabeth Smith Cady on New Year's Eve, 1806 in New London, Connecticut.[a] Her father, Ebenezer Cady, in partnership with a gentleman by the name of Samuel Green, was editor of the *New London Gazette*.[b] Green family members were among the earliest of Connecticut newspaper dynasties, dating their start in the business as early as 1755. Ebenezer's mother, Joanna, was from the distinguished Pemberton family of Boston, one of whom was the founder of Princeton University. Ebenezer's wife, Mary's mother, was the former Elizabeth Smith of New London, Connecticut.

The Cadys lived in New London until Ebenezer failed in his business there. He took a position as an editor at the *Intelligencer* in Fredericksburg, Virginia, with Samuel Green's brother Timothy, who also owned the *Virginia Herald*. When Ebenezer left in 1812, the family stayed behind until living arrangements could be settled for the family in Fredericksburg and Mrs. Cady could travel.[1] She was in New London recovering from the birth of Mary's sister, Elizabeth, while Mary stayed with her grandmother in Plainfield, Connecticut. Mrs. Cady followed to Plainfield when she and the

---

a   Mary Sturges wrote an important memoir of her early life, up until the Civil War. It is largely a factual, personal and remarkable accounting of Mary's early life providing much of the basis for the history of family events.

b   Ben Franklin was an early investor in the *Connecticut Gazette*, which became the *New London Gazette* in 1763.

baby were both able. However, Congress declared war on Great Britain in June 1812, and it would be years before the family could reunite.

Working in Fredericksburg, Ebenezer bided his time until his family could join him. Like the Sturges family in Fairfield, "He (Cady) was a strong Federalist, and politics ran so high at one time he had to sleep in his office in Fredericksburg with his pistols by his side, often being threatened with tar and feathers."[2] Although not supportive of the war, Ebenezer was in the Fredericksburg militia, as Mary explained:

> After the burning of the Capitol at Washington, young men were drafted from the towns on the Rappahannock and Potomac into service; those from Fredericksburg were commanded by Major Byrd Willis.... My father used to relate many funny things of their life in camp. They were three months in their tents, had several false alarms, but never saw the enemy.[3]

In 1814, Mr. Cady returned to collect his family and escort them to Fredericksburg. With travel by sea still not an option, he engaged a private coach out of New London to transport his family to Virginia via a coastal land route. They spent the first night in Guilford, Connecticut, and their second night in Fairfield, at the Knapp Tavern on the old Post Road, coincidentally in the same town where Jonathan lived, although they were not yet acquainted.[c]

The traveling party stopped next in Rye, New York, just over the Connecticut border near Long Island Sound, then through to New York City, Jersey City, Trenton, Philadelphia, and Baltimore. According to Mary, "Sometimes the passengers would have to stop and assist in prying the stage out of the mud with rails."[4] On their route they came upon 10,000 troops camping near Bladensburg, Maryland, and in Washington they drove to the Capitol and came upon the destruction that the British had wrought on that area of the city. They witnessed firsthand the damage to the Capitol building. "My father stopped, and we all got out. I looked at the scene of destruction. I remember the marks of fire on the mahogany stair-railings and the broken marble mantels in the small rooms, and the general battered appearance of things."[5] The party stopped overnight in Alexandria before continuing on and arriving at Fredericksburg, a total journey from Connecticut Mary estimated to be sixteen to eighteen days.[6]

---

[c] Knapp Tavern burned down in the early 1830s.

Not yet having received their household goods from New London, the Cadys boarded with a local family, the Peacocks, for the winter. They were renting just one bedroom for the entire family. The Peacocks also had three slave boys living in one of the upper rooms. Mary witnessed one of the small boys getting whipped for selling his cap, an early exposure to that "peculiar institution" that would in her lifetime so affect the fortunes of the country.

Also imprinted in Mary's mind during those days in Fredericksburg was her experience with medical treatments. During the early nineteenth century, remedies and procedures were more guesswork than proven science and often harmful. During that 1815 winter, Mary's little sister Elizabeth became ill, and her life was threatened by aggressive and irresponsible treatment. The doctor (a drinking man) weighed out a white powder for Mrs. Cady to administer to Elizabeth. In the morning they discovered he had given them powder magnesia, instead of calomel, which could have poisoned her.[7] The Cadys called the doctor one last time in 1817 during the illness of her two-year-old sister Frances. Mary lamented of the doctor's destructive treatments:

> It was here that my little sister sickened and died. We had a physician this time who was not a drinking man and was very kind and attentive; but the treatment was something fearful to think of in this enlightened age. She was taken with spasms; calomel was administered, and a blister put on the back of her neck. It seemed weeks that the little creature laid in suffering. A blister on the breast was the next thing, and then as the brain seemed affected, the top of the head was shaved, and another applied to it.[8]

Soon after, Mary and her sister Elizabeth were sick with bilious fever, but Ebenezer Cady refused to call a physician, relying instead on natural treatments and rest, and they fared better than those with the same sickness that received treatment from a doctor. These primitive therapies, and other similar experiences, shaped both Mary and Jonathan's views regarding medicine and predisposed them toward active support of more holistic or homeopathic remedies throughout their lives.

Jonathan's brother Lothrop was already starting his career in the merchant trade and had a home in the Sasco Neck area of Fairfield. There was an eventful barn-raising for him in June 1814, chronicled by local diarist Jonathan Bulkley.[9] About 1816, Lothrop departed Fairfield and moved to Fredericksburg with his brother-in-law Thaddeus Bennet, husband of Jonathan's sister Deborah.

Lothrop was in business with his uncle, Josiah Sturges, a shipping merchant in New York. In February 1817, Jonathan wrote to Lothrop, declaring that he would like to be a merchant's clerk, apologizing that his writing was not that of a merchant clerk yet, but he promised to work on it.[10] In 1818, Lothrop summoned Jonathan to join him. About this time, Mary's father resigned his editorship in Fredericksburg and opened a grocery business there. Ebenezer became acquainted with Lothrop. One fateful day, Lothrop accompanied Ebenezer home and brought with him his younger brother Jonathan:[11]

> There was some business connection between him (Mr. Cady) and Mr. Sturges, and when he returned home with my aunt, he brought back with him my future husband, then a rather small-sized youth in his seventeenth year. He became a clerk in the concern and boarded in our family. This was the beginning of my acquaintance with my husband, and we had a good many pleasant times together. I think, however, his clerkship did not amount to much, as it was decided he should return home to Fairfield in the month of March. I never saw him again until six years after.[12]

About three years passed between the time Jonathan left Fredericksburg and his employment in New York. There is little evidence of his life during this time. One letter in September 1819 infers that he was living with a family by the name of Williams, at an unknown location, and was engaged in farming. An anecdotal story from an 1872 obituary suggests Jonathan was at one point an apprentice tailor:

> Noah Thorp Pike was seventy-two years old when he died in June last, worth nearly half a million dollars. He came to New York from Plainfield, Conn., forty years ago, with only fifty cents in his pocket. He worked on the same bench with Jonathan Sturges, the millionaire, as a journeyman tailor, in Fairfield.[13]

In about 1819 or 1820, Jonathan's father Barnabas failed in his business. Although there is no record of the exact circumstances, in later years Henry C. Sturges, his grandson, wrote that Barnabas had lost everything through speculation. Land records show that Barnabas signed over his land and home at Mill River in November 1820 to Hezekiah Sturges, his brother. Jonathan and his siblings could count on no help from Barnabas in their start in life. His father's misfortune, and the ultimate loss of the family home, profoundly influenced Jonathan's trademark conservative approach to business the rest of his life.

With his father's fortunes diminished, Jonathan needed to become self-sufficient. Various reports of his initial job search in New York City trace his arrival between 1821 and 1823. It is surmised that Lothrop relocated from Fredericksburg to New York sometime late in 1821 or 1822, and it's likely that Jonathan's search coincided with Lothrop's move or occurred just after. In Jonathan's retirement speech in January 1868, he spoke of having "habits of forty-five years" and he also spoke of a business practice in his firm being in place "since 1822." This all suggests that it was probably mid to late 1822 when he arrived in New York.

Departing for the big city to seek their vocation in life was a common occurrence among the young men of the rural areas of New England after the War of 1812. The family business and land would often pass only to the oldest son. If a son wasn't the oldest, or otherwise not able to make a living off the land, he might seek an apprenticeship either in a trade or in a merchant house. Reverend Child, a historian and friend of Jonathan's, wrote of this phenomenon:

> When any son of these old and respected families yearned for richer pastures and dreamed of grander scenes, he had simply to push a little farther in a suburban direction and he came to New York. So, it occurred that time after time, when the home, the academy, nature, and society here in Fairfield had done their best to equip the boy, he would go down to the great metropolis, fling himself with enthusiasm into the work, and make a fortune and a name that rendered him conspicuous in the land.[14]

During the first half of the nineteenth century, the merchant class was arguably the most respected occupation in New York City, if not the country. This profession offered many attractions for determined young men who were ready and able to apply themselves and follow the mentoring of experienced merchants. These early merchants were reputed to be the most industrious, of the highest integrity and the most engaged in the affairs of the community. The American Tract Society, a national publisher of religious materials, of which Jonathan was an early supporter, published the "Rules for the Christian Merchant, Mechanic, &c" [sic] (Appendix III). Jonathan and his future boss were ultimately influenced by the guidelines in this 1830s publication. It was general knowledge who the most prosperous merchants were and where they lived. Joseph Alfred Scoville wrote several versions of his book and directory, *The Old Merchants of New York*, a who's who of its day. Scoville celebrated the profession and provided a short biography and an estimated wealth for the most substantial merchants of the City:

> A glorious occupation on this continent is that of a merchant! He has no superior. There is no class of citizens that excel, or even equal him, except it be editors… The clergymen, in this city, never get on and become very great, very good, or very popular, until they can spot in their congregation audiences fifty or a hundred extensive merchants.[15]

When New York merchants held a public meeting, it was reported nationally. They were routinely consulted by the state and federal governments on matters of banking and business. They were the conduits for world trade and were paying the high tariffs, and consequently the bills of the nation. These were the men who were developing the capital and business networks that would build the country's infrastructure and fuel the industrial age. Jonathan was destined to take his place among them.

An anecdote from the *Youth Companion* describes a fateful interlude Jonathan had on his first full day in the city after arriving on a Saturday night, searching for a Sabbath refuge:

> He found the old Wall Street house of worship near Broadway. He stood on the doorstep while the gay throng passed in. The grandeur of the place appealed to him. Robert Lennox[d] a prominent member of the church, was always interested in young men. He saw the rustic lad and went up and spoke to him. "Are you a stranger in the city? Yes Sir, I arrived last night. So, you came at once to the house of God? Would you like a seat? I would." The bashful lad was ushered in to Mr. Lennox's own pew. The next morning, he [Jonathan] sought out a dealer in sail-cloth. He wanted credit for a little canvas. "Did I not see you in Mr. Lennox's pew yesterday," said the merchant. "I don't know whose pew I sat in, but a kind gentleman gave me a seat." "Well lad, that was Mr. Lennox, and it is no common honor to be asked to sit in his pew. I will trust any boy with goods who has had that honor conferred upon him." To the day of his death Mr. Sturges said that his success dated from that Sunday.[16]

---

d Robert Lennox (1759–1839) a wealthy Scottish merchant and large land owner in New York City, father of James Lennox, later an associate of Jonathan's and a prolific philanthropist and fellow founder of Presbyterian Hospital.

Jonathan was a particularly determined example of the young men of New England who went to the big city to seek their fortunes. He showed this tenacity by literally going door to door in the waterfront area of New York City asking for an opportunity. One day he fatefully knocked on the door of the merchant firm Reed & Lee.

Luman Reed came to New York City from the upstate Catskills area where he had been engaged in the produce and freight business. He worked for his father for two summers, rafting logs down the river and serving as a ship captain for freight. While there, he enjoyed the beautiful scenery and developed an appreciation for the beauty of the Catskills. During the War of 1812, he set up a partnership with a Mr. Hall, also of the Catskills. Hall died of a fever in 1817, and Reed joined with his brother-in-law, Roswell Reed, of Coxsackie, New York, to form R. & L. Reed. They rented a four-story building at 125 Front Street, where the wholesale tea and coffee traders and other grocers had coalesced. Luman was the visible front man for the firm.

Next door at number 127 was the firm Leavitt and Lee (David Leavitt and David Lee), a similar grocery house. The two partnerships dissolved in 1821 and then merged as Reed and Lee. Reed's nephew George Barker later recalled, "Lee was a New Englander, and brought New England business to the firm; Reed went after new business in the South and West and was the go-getter partner and head of the firm."[17] Now one firm, but still with two separate entrances, the stage was set for Jonathan to come knocking—twice. Mary Rousseau, Jonathan's great-granddaughter, told the family story:

> Jonathan arrived in New York and...started knocking on doors at the waterfront businesses. One of those doors belonged to Luman Reed. He knocked, Reed answered, "I'm sorry I'm unable to hire you." So, Jonathan continued down the street and knocked at the next door. Reed answered again and announced to Jonathan, "Anyone who has the determination to knock twice at the same establishment I feel inclined to hire."[18]

Frank Leslie's *Sunday Magazine* told an amusing version of this first meeting with Luman Reed:

> Clothed in his simple country garb, and yet with the inherent bearing of a gentleman, he followed out his plan of taking each business house in the street, up one side and down the other...The establishment of Reed & Lee had two doors, and the young applicant entered one and came out the

other in his fruitless jaunts up Front Street. He had not observed this, and regarding the house from the other side on his journey down, he thought he had missed one place where he might have applied. He hurried to recross, entered, and presented the formula of inquiry so diligently plied all the forenoon. "Why, no, my young man," was the answer, "we do not need any more help. You've been in here once before, this morning." The visitor apologized, and was about to withdraw, explaining how he happened to call the second time. Mr. Reed now asked him what his expectations in regard to salary would be, say, for a year. "I should not expect much the first year," was the reply. "Well," said Mr. Reed, "I'll make you two offers, either one of which, if you like, you can accept, and remain in my establishment. I'll give you a hundred dollars the first year, and the same the second; or, I'll give you fifty dollars the first year, and two hundred the second. Which will you take?" "I'll take a hundred the first year, sir," was the prompt reply. "Well, what is your reason for this decision, rather than the alternative?" asked Mr. Reed. "I might die the first year, sir," was the direct answer. The merchant was pleased, and the young man was engaged, and so Mr. Sturges entered upon a career which he was destined to adorn.[19]

Reed admired the young man's determined, straight-forward, conservative approach, and he would never regret this decision. Over the years, Reed and Jonathan developed a deep mutual affection and respect, like father and son. Some accounts of their relationship even erroneously referred to Jonathan as Reed's son-in-law.

During the challenging business environment that Jonathan entered, tariffs were as much as 97% of the total revenue for the federal treasury, with high tariffs on tea weighing heavily on trade. Credit and capital became scarce. If one possessed adequate capital, and could overcome the ever-present risk of weather disasters, price fluctuations, and privateering, up to a 300% profit was possible. However, merchants could easily go bankrupt if they either lost cargo or the price of tea plummeted while a shipment was en route. John Jacob Astor was particularly successful in the China trade in this way, as was Jonathan's brother Lothrop who made his mark in this business starting in the late 1820s.

Reed and Lee survived these tight credit markets, reportedly due to Reed's emphasis on diversifying and developing trade from the South and West (today's Midwest) United States. The firm pressed on to benefit from the opening of the Erie Canal in 1825, a pivotal development for New York and the national economy. The canal created a water transport system from Lake Erie through Albany, connecting to the Hudson River and New York's harbor. Goods were coming faster and cheaper than ever before, much of it passing through New York for further shipment to the world. At the inception of the canal, New York City was only the fifth largest port by volume in the United States, behind New Orleans, Boston, Philadelphia, and Baltimore. Within twenty-five years, it was by far the busiest port on the East Coast.

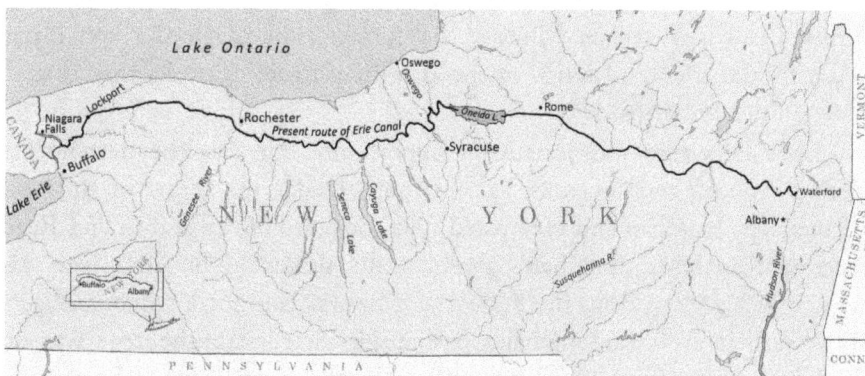

Route of the Erie Canal [20]

In 1825, Reed and Lee expanded, renting the building at 123 Front Street in addition to 125 and 127 Front Street. This made for a new establishment that comprised four adjoining four-storied warehouses and office space. In 1827, Charles Hempsted, the firm's former head clerk, was added as a partner, and the firm became Reed, Lee and Hempsted.

Reed was reputed to be an honest, industrious and forthright mentor, who treated his clerks well. John Durand, Jr., brother of A.B. Durand, the noted Hudson River School artist, worked at the firm for a short time. He pointed out that Luman Reed emphasized sagacity, promptness, self-reliance and strict discipline in his training of subordinates, along with a sincere concern for their interests and welfare.[21] He also established a three-story boarding house for his clerks' comfort, convenience, and well-being, just across the street from their warehouses, although there is no evidence that Jonathan boarded there. Scoville observed, "Mr. Reed always paid his clerks good salaries, and he made excellent merchants of them."[22] If a clerk showed promise, they received more responsibility and the best ones became partners or left to start their own firms, some becoming very successful.

Lee retired in 1828, supposedly due to the ongoing loss of his sight. George Barker, Reed's nephew, noted that Lee was the introvert of the firm and Reed the more social front man. However, at some point, a distance developed between them, a bad chemistry that contributed to a breakup. When Lee left, Reed paid for his share of the partnership very liberally, and the firm of Reed, Lee and Hempsted dissolved by mutual consent. Unfortunately for Reed, Lee did not retire as he had led Reed to believe, and he started the competing firm of Lee, Dater, and Miller at nearby 161 Front Street. Lee's new partner Miller was a former clerk of Reed's, and Dater was a former client, all much to the chagrin of Reed.[e] A rivalry then ensued between the two firms.

Lee's departure was Jonathan's opportunity. He was the next-in-line clerk promoted and taken in as a partner. Under the terms of the new partnership, Jonathan and Hempsted split one-third of the profits, and Reed received two-thirds. Jonathan's share of the profits in his first year was $5,000—a big jump from the $100 a year he was paid for his first year, just six years before. With Jonathan's partnership now established, he was on solid financial ground and setup well to marry and establish a household. He didn't wait long and went no further than a young lady he'd known since he was seventeen.

---

[e] Miller retired about 1852 to a life of directorships including the Erie Railroad Co. After a few years he shifted his responsibilities to his ambitious son-in-law Jay Gould, often being his surety for his business dealings, and setting the stage for an epic robber baron railroad securities battle between Gould and Commodore Vanderbilt.

THREE

Marriage and a Coastal Journey
Through America's Primitive South

I certainly should not have married him as I did, had I not felt assured
that he was an improvable man in the points in which I considered him
deficient.

—*Mary Cady Sturges*

Mary Pemberton Cady was a devout Presbyterian and a long-time Sunday
school teacher by the summer of 1825, performing various teaching and tu-
toring services and living with her family in Fredericksburg. This placed her
at a remarkable historical event. That summer, General Lafayette, France's
American Revolutionary war hero, visited the United States and made a farewell tour. This included a visit to Fredericksburg, to pay his respects to
Robert Lewis, George Washington's nephew, who had served as Washington's private secretary. Mary was excited and fascinated by Lafayette's visit
and was one of a party of young ladies who welcomed him and bid him a
final farewell. She noted a family historical coincidence:

> I have always felt that this visit of Lafayette to America was one of the
> wonderful and beautiful things in history, especially when I remember that
> as a youth of nineteen he was greeted in our little village of Plainfield by
> our grandmothers. I specially remember that Grandmother Eaton used to
> tell about the time that the French army were encamped at Plainfield—one
> division of officers at her house. She asked a fair young man who stood
> near her to point out the Marquis Lafayette, when he made her a low bow,
> announcing himself as the man.[1]

Mary and her family were on their way to Plainfield when they stopped
in New York to pay a visit to Lothrop Sturges and his wife, the former Jane

Curry, at 16½ Cheapside in New York City.² Ebenezer stayed in New York to explore a business opportunity. The rest of the Cady family returned to Fredericksburg after their visit to Plainfield, but in 1826 the family, except Mary, left Fredericksburg to join Ebenezer who was staying at the home of her mother's uncle, Lemuel Smith. He had accepted employment with Jonathan's brother-in-law, William Lockwood (husband of Jonathan's sister Mary Ann). Mary Cady remained in Fredericksburg for a time, boarding with a French teacher to finish out her term teaching at the Union Academy through July. Just before she left, a joyous event occurred:

> There was a famous wedding in our circle of friends. The daughter of Robert S. Lewis, (Washington's nephew) was married to George Washington Bassett, the grand-nephew of Martha Washington, a wealthy planter, and a splendid specimen of the Virginia gentleman of that period. He came in his coach with four superb horses and a train of servants, and it was a regular gala time in our little town. As they were to make a bridal trip to Saratoga Springs, and neither of them had ever made the Northern journey, they were very glad to escort me for the sake of my experience, and I was only too glad to have such good company.³

After her arrival in New York City, Mary set about the important task of affiliating with a church. After visiting a few churches, the Cady family applied for membership to St. Johns on Varick Street, a Trinity Episcopal Church, ministered by Dr. Cox. Mary became a Sunday school teacher and joined the choir. Her uncle became a representative to the New York General Assembly as a Tammany Hall candidate and entertained many guests. Among the frequent guests that the Cadys and Smiths hosted was the young merchant clerk, Jonathan Sturges.

In 1827, Jonathan's parents, Barnabas and Mary, were living in Manlius, New York. Local diarist Jonathan Bulkley noted them leaving in a loaded wagon from the Mill River/Southport area of Fairfield, on a Monday in May 1823, for a new life in New York.⁴ Barnabas was forced to give up their home in Southport to pay debts from his business failures. His brother Hezekiah assumed his outstanding debt, and in return he received Barnabas's share of any future inheritance from his father.

Manlius, near Syracuse, is where Barnabas's sister, Priscilla, and his brother-in-law, Stephen Ely, kept a sheep farm. Barnabas and family had become nothing more than hired hands when Priscilla Ely, Jonathan's aunt, passed away in 1826. It was time for Barnabas, Mary, Lucretia and Abigail to move on. Jonathan leased a house for Barnabas and family to live at 53 Pine Street in New York City about 1827, and he boarded out rooms there to bachelor clerks in the area. Jonathan's mother cooked, and the boarding house arrangement was profitable for Jonathan for several years, until his mother's health became frail.[5] He seemed to get no help in the care of his parents and sisters from his brother Lothrop, who had just established the shipping business Doane and Sturges with Philo Doane at 39 Peck-Slip.

Meanwhile, Mary and her family lived near the corner of North Moore and Greenwich Streets. Ebenezer was a merchant on Wall Street, albeit struggling to sustain his firm.[6] In 1828, Ebenezer Cady became ill and had to close his business. He moved back to Plainfield hoping fresh air would hasten a recovery, he died soon after arriving in late February 1828, likely losing the will to live. He was only forty-four years old. His fascinating diary reflects a depressed soul constantly searching for schemes that would relieve his economic difficulties and lamenting his many failures and poor judgment. Undeniably, for every Jonathan Sturges, there were countless more Ebenezer Cady and Barnabas Sturges sagas of failure in this presumptive era of opportunity.

Lothrop received the news of Ebenezer's death and was the bearer of the sad tidings to the family. Jonathan volunteered to escort Mary and her family to Plainfield. They accepted his escort services and went via a packet ship to New London and a hack[a] to Plainfield. Jonathan had developed an abiding affection for Mary and after the funeral he took the opportunity at the family gathering to declare his intentions. Jonathan confided in Mary's Aunt Olivia, only to hear from her that there was a young navy military man with whom Mary was corresponding. This took him by surprise and Jonathan felt he had no time to lose. He proposed to Mary quoting the following sonnet:

> Oh! give me no sway o'er the powers unseen,
> But a human heart where my own may lean,
> A friend, one tender and faithful friend,
> Whose thoughts' free current with mine may blend,
> And leaving not either on earth alone,
> Bid the bright calm close of our lives be one![7]

---

a Horse-drawn carriage for hire

After hearing of Jonathan's discussion with her aunt and receiving his heartfelt appeal for her hand in marriage, the realities of life told Mary that continuing a serious relationship with the naval man would take her away from her family. She broke off the "affair" and accepted the proposal of the financially stable, local family friend, Jonathan Sturges.

Perhaps in explanation of the early romantic insecurity that Jonathan would convey in future letters to his wife, Mary wrote in her memoir of her marriage:

> There is no important event in my life where I can trace the leading hand of my Heavenly Father more clearly than in my marriage, so entirely was I turned aside from all my preconceived and romantic ideas and led into the sober and practical realities of life. Before I left Plainfield, my good aunt had opened to me her interview with Mr. Sturges, which gave me a new and more exalted view of him than I had ever had before and gave me a confidence in his character and a conviction of his true and <u>disinterested love</u>[b] for me, which I had never before known…my engagement to Mr. Sturges was formed, but was kept very quiet, as was the fashion in those days.[8]

Andrew Jackson was elected the seventh President of the United States on December 3, 1828, and on Christmas day the Reverend Dr. Cox married Jonathan Sturges and Mary Pemberton Cady.[9] In his practical way, it was the only day Jonathan felt he could spare time away from work. His groomsmen were his partner, Charles Hempsted, William Roe, a clerk in the firm (and future partner), and another friend, Mr. Bush. Mary's bridesmaids were her sister Elizabeth, Jonathan's sister Abigail, and a friend, Miss Noble. Mary noted that Mr. Ketchum (possibly Morris) also attended, and it was he who found the ring baked into the wedding cake, foretelling as the tradition went, that he would be the next to marry—and he was in fact the next one of the attendees to marry. They lived with Mary's mother until March, when they moved to Pine Street with Jonathan's parents. However, soon they found a separate home at 57 Beaver Street to start their life together.[10] Interestingly, Luman Reed lived in this same house early in his marriage and he would often stop by after work to dine with the young couple.[11]

---

[b] Disinterested love is a religious term attributed to St. Francis de Sales meaning a loving attraction to a person or thing only because of the love of God; giving without caring for self.

In a letter to Jonathan in the early 1830s, Mary illustrated her habit of referring to Jonathan in the third person and expounds on the fact that he wasn't what she had in her imagination as her ideal mate.

I will frankly acknowledge that I feel myself far more comfortable to give my children correct views of the world than I ever could have been, had I been united to such a man as my "youthful imagination" painted as most desirable of a husband. You, I believe my husband, to be just the one I needed—but I certainly should not have married him [Jonathan] as I did, had I not felt pretty well assured that he was an improvable [sic] man in the points in which I considered him deficient.[12]

Early in their marriage, Mary coaxed Jonathan to become more proficient in the literary world (perhaps one of those traits she saw in her ideal husband). She resorted to flattery in a letter to him where she said, "I think my husband has a mind which would have been equally superior in the literary world had that been the course marked."[13] Mary further gently suggested that he could help enlighten both her and the children if he became more well-read. Jonathan's marriage to Mary was certainly fortuitous, and it could be said that his interest and standing in the fine arts circles, and his active interest in the furtherance of education for all, was at least partially due to his well-chosen life alliance.

On Tuesday, February 9, 1830, Jonathan and Mary were blessed with their first child, a daughter, Virginia. Mary's mother and two sisters-in-law, Abby and Lucretia, came to help. Jonathan's niece Lucretia Bennet also came to live with them to help with the baby. They tried to live simply and frugally, well within their means. Mary sewed much of their own clothing and always sought the best value for their needs. These thrifty ways gave them comfort in the coming decade, which held many trials for their family and for Jonathan's firm.

Jonathan's parents left the Pine Street boarding house about this time and moved to a house on Duane Street, where an older couple boarded with them. However, the arrangement lasted for only about a year when Barnabas's health failed, and they and Jonathan's sisters relocated to Allen Street, on the upper east side of New York.

In March 1830, Jonathan again advanced in the firm when Charles Hempsted died of scarlet fever. Reed did not have another candidate for partner, so Jonathan became Reed's sole partner—now allotted a full one-third of the profits from the newly formed partnership, Reed & Sturges. Reed's early instincts and Jonathan's tenacity and hard work had been rewarded.

In June, Mary's uncle, Lemuel Smith, passed away and Mary began spending summers with her Plainfield family, enjoying the country air, family, friends, and having help with childcare. This would begin a long record of correspondence between Jonathan and Mary during these summer separations. Some of their most intimate thoughts were expressed in these letters. While Mary and baby Virginia visited Plainfield in 1831, she wrote, "Oh my dearest, here and here only I do not open my heart to you, often my heart is full to bursting, when I have longed to tell you all its sweet thoughts, and a fear of dishonoring…has held me back."[14] Unfortunately for Mary's longing heart, her letters were delayed, and she received a stark, mean letter from Jonathan, a quick temper on display. Wounded, Mary responded:

> How should I begin to answer your cruel letter sent the day before yesterday? I took the letter, opened it and glared at the blank page (with money inserted)! My heart bounded. I thought, I shall see my husband on the next stage and this letter is to give me notice. I can tell you of tears suppressed because I had not "solitude" to indulge them…I waited impatiently for all to retire to rest that I might sit down alone to converse with my, shall I say, unjust husband. I feel as though he might have attributed my silence to unkindness. But one thing my dearest I say of you, never send money when you feel so, and I hope not again. I almost would have said; does he think my heart is to be bought—or does he mean to hurt me? …I think we can account for the irregularity of our letters, the mail through this place is but a small one, and letters from here at the distribution office in Stratford can be sent different routes which makes a difference.[15]

In following correspondence things between them appear to be smoothed over and she attempts to "improve" him once again:

> I know there is a feeling common to men of the world…A feeling that shrinks from even appearing in presence of others to care as much for their wives as anyone else. I do not believe this appearance of indifference ever really raises a man in the estimation of man, and it certainly lowers him in the eyes of our sex. But kind looks such as I have seen, that language that are good substitutes for any expression of kindness, which even at parting in the presence of others, may appear ill-timed.[16]

He apparently took heed of Mary's pointers at the end of their next reunion as she reported to him, "I have no complaints to make of your farewell. It seemed like a husband farewell, and that is all I ever want."[17]

In another very intimate letter she wrote: "… [may our love] be like the holy fire, which the vestals of old guarded and kept constantly burning, feeding and replenishing it with constant watchfulness and care.…may we continually cherish the sacred flame of conjugal love, keeping it alive by every means in our power and adding to it such fuel as it needs where it languishes."[18] Just after the visit of her husband to her and the children in July 1834, she continued in this vein. "Conjugal love is a plant…this plant is so important to the happiness of both. I believe my husband feels this perhaps more now that we are a season separated."[19] These intimate emotions were recorded throughout their marriage and many separations over their lives. Sometimes they were understated or over-expressed, but their love appeared to be true.

Illustrating the standard and accepted role of the wife and mother in the 1830s, in an August 1831 letter Mary wrote, "I can truly say, I do most sincerely 'love', 'revere', and desire to 'obey', Yes! I never would desire to have that word struck out of my part."[20] Days later she wrote, "You know of my principle notion that a woman's love increased after marriage and experience has taught me the justice of this notion."[21] This was a positive development in their relationship as it had evolved from an initial perception of her marriage as a "sober reality," to a bond of deep love.

These letters document examples of lengthy stays in the country away from her lonely husband. Although she missed Jonathan, Mary wanted no part of raising the children solely in the city, even if it meant physical and emotional separations from him. In August 1834 she wrote, "You ask if I enjoy myself. I do so very much. I love to walk, to ride, to enjoy the pure air and fresh vegetables, the corn is now fine…Your company is all I wish for."[22]

Like their love of life in the country, they valued a faith-based education for all their children. Their letters were peppered with mention of their latest literary pursuits and they delighted in reading aloud to each other. In her memoir, Mary wrote of the winter of 1829–1830:

I think my little sister was rather lonely the first season she spent with me, our household was so quiet; but she says she well remembers hurrying through her lessons (for she was a great student) in order to hear my husband read Shakespeare aloud. This he did in the winter evenings, while I had to ply the needle busily, so as to keep everything in order.[23]

Writing in 1831, Mary addressed the children's religious training. In a previous letter, Jonathan had put the onus on Mary to take the lead in this area of their lives. Mary preferred a unity of effort. "Shall we indeed 'hand in hand' train up our offspring 'in the way in which they should go?' This comprehends a great deal, are they to be trained for the glory of God in two worlds, that while living or dying they may be happy.... how important my dearest that we should be entirely united."[24]

Jonathan continued to care for his mother and father, who were becoming increasingly dependent due to failing health. Jonathan's relationship with his father was probably trying and difficult. After Barnabas' failures in Southport, Barnabas, his mother, and sisters became dependent on one family member or another. Jonathan revealed his ill-regard toward his father in a letter he later wrote to Mary: "I am not partial to the name of B. L. Sturges. If the name was to be perpetuated, I think it will have to come better from one of the sons. I hope I shall not let the feeling show itself toward the 'heir apparent' only I don't like it—that is all. If he honors the name, I shall like him, if not, an indifferent name would not be as likely to throw me into spasms whenever I see him."[25] Jonathan's mother had taken Barnabas back to the old homestead in Fairfield (Jonathan's Uncle Dimon's home), where he died on September 28, 1831. After Barnabas' death, Jonathan's mother, and sisters, moved back to New York City.[26]

About this time, Mary and Jonathan moved from their Beaver Street home to another rental home at 30 Whitehall and Pearl Street,[c] which was about one block from the Battery at the south end of Manhattan. Although Mary thought the house "contracted and uncomfortable,"[27] there was a wonderful large park at the Battery with the Castle Garden Theater,[d] and they enjoyed this new vibrant location. However, as the summer of 1832 approached, a deadly epidemic was advancing toward New York.

Coming from Europe, the cholera first appeared in Canada, then the Lake Champlain area of New York and southward with its black wave of death.[28] It

---

c Interestingly, the house in 2017 was a four-story building in the middle of two eighteen-story high-rise buildings.

d Castle Garden became the immigration processing center in 1855. It had been converted from the old Castle Clinton, a fort from the past, which was last active for the War between 1812 and 1815.

arrived in New York City in early June 1832. Many used the disease to promote the strict enforcement of Sabbath laws, including the prohibition of alcohol sales on Sundays. One doctor's published assessment of the causes of cholera noted that the "better classes" and temperate individuals were faring better in the epidemic, and that "the local causes [of the cholera] are in crowded, ill ventilated and filthy habitations...the individual susceptibilities have been owing to intemperance in the use of intoxicating drinks, licentious habits, imprudence in eating."[29]

Most who could afford to leave the city left. As the disease progressed, one house after another closed, until they could see lights glimmering in only a few houses on each street in an evening.[30] Public places were closed or had limited hours as described by an assistant to the painter Asher B. Durand: "There is no business doing here...except that done by Cholera, Doctors, Undertakers Coffin makers, etc.... Our bustling city now wears a most gloomy & desolate aspect—one may take a walk up and down Broadway and scarce meet a soul."[31]

The Sturges family had a similar response. Mary's mother and two sisters went to Plainfield. Jonathan's sisters Abigail, Lucretia and Mary Ann and her family went to Glastonbury where relatives lived. Deborah Bennet went back to Fairfield. Lothrop and his family went to Madison, Connecticut, where he was building a ship. Young Lucretia Bennet and brother Josiah, who was working for Reed & Sturges, stayed in New York with Mary and Jonathan. They limited their family exposure to a maid and a washerwoman who came two days a week. Despite precautions, Virginia contracted cholera, but recovered within a short time. The *New York Times* estimated: "The epidemic left 3,515 dead out of a population of 250,000. An equivalent death toll in today's city of eight million [2008] would exceed 100,000."[32]

The disease subsided by the end of the summer. Residents flowed back into the city and were socializing again although the medical authorities remained ignorant of the cause.[e] For fresh air, Mary started taking riding lessons at Col. John Roulston's famous riding school on the designated ladies riding day. Luman Reed, who had been ill and in the country before the cholera hit, returned to the city and moved into his beautiful new house at 13 Greenwich Street in July 1832. Scoville noted that the house was the wonder of its day:

---

[e] The cause of cholera did not come to light until 1854 when a London physician, John Snow, sometimes called the father of epidemiology, asserted that it was brackish water from local water pumps that was carrying the virus.

Within the house, he built a gallery on the third floor for his art collection and was open to the public once a week:[33] The doors were of solid mahogany. He had a gallery of paintings in the upper story. It was considered superior to any in the city of New York. The marble was the purest Italian. The mahogany was the old, I think, costly St. Domingo, now so rare…"[34]

After riding out the cholera epidemic, Reed suggested a business trip South for Jonathan. Mary accompanied him for part of the trip and she later noted, "It will be remembered that this was the season that 'Nullification' was first attempted in South Carolina, and our President, General Jackson, ordered the gun-boats into Charleston harbor to bombard the city if anything of the kind was persisted in."[35]

This was a tenuous time in the country's history. In the fall of 1831, the Nat Turner slave rebellion heightened the South's sensitivity to the fragile nature of slavery as an institution. Also, in November 1832, South Carolina declared the Tariff Laws of 1828 and 1832 (adversely affecting the cotton trade) to be null and void within the sovereign state of South Carolina, and further that should the government try to collect the taxes, the state resolved to withdraw from the Union. Vice President John Calhoun from South Carolina was a leader of this movement. President Jackson acted decisively, sending General Winfield Scott to shore up fortifications at Fort Moultrie in Charleston and rotate out officers deemed sympathetic with the "nullifiers." After Congress authorized the use of force to deal with the nullification question, Henry Clay and Calhoun led successful negotiations to work out a more moderate compromise tariff. Crisis averted; the nullification legislation was repealed. However, this was an early move toward secession in answer to laws not deemed fair to Southern interests. This was the volatile political environment into which Jonathan and Mary ventured that winter of 1832 to 1833.

The available prevailing options for travel were boat, coach, cart, and other horse-drawn means of transportation, and often a circuitous route. Mary relates in her memoir:

At this day, we can have very little idea of the toil of travel then… [there were] important changes in the mode of travel since I made my last journey from Virginia: The Camden and Amboy Railway had been built, but the cars were drawn by horses: We took the steamboat from New York to Amboy, as formerly—the cars to Camden, and the steamboat to Philadelphia.[36]

However, they did get a taste of a pivotal new way of traveling. The locomotive steam engine was just being put in to service in relatively short runs of track. Peter Cooper had built the Tom Thumb locomotive in 1830 for general cargo and passenger carrying purposes, and it pulled the cars on the first route built in the Baltimore area. On this 1832 trip, Jonathan and Mary traveled on this earliest of train routes, a definite technological wonder of its time compared to other available forms of transportation. Local historians outlined the pioneering railroad route:

> The New Castle and Frenchtown Railroad, which for sixteen miles ran a nearly straight course from New Castle, on the Delaware River, to Frenchtown, Maryland, on the Elk River at the head of the Chesapeake Bay. As a result, travelers from Philadelphia, the financial capital, heading for Washington, the political capitol, would take a steamboat down the Delaware River to New Castle where they would board the train to Frenchtown…It was among the first railroads in the United States.[37]

After the railroad trip to Frenchtown, they had to revert to stagecoach to Washington and steamboat down the Potomac River. After one final coach ride, they arrived at Fredericksburg, Virginia. Four months pregnant, Mary did not go farther with Jonathan, but instead stayed there with friends. Jonathan continued his journey through Virginia, North Carolina, and on to Charleston, South Carolina, and back, providing for a historically significant travelogue.[38]

His journey could be likened to that of an early day hitchhiker, not knowing if or when his next transportation might materialize. From Fredericksburg, he traveled to Richmond and then, after meeting with business contacts, spent the night in Norfolk. In the morning, the stage driver woke him up to depart at 7:00 a.m. The traveling party started off with eight passengers, stopping for breakfast, then headed through Portsmouth and the Great Dismal Swamp Canal at Deep Creek that was "filled with boats and small sloops."

The party next reached the Virginia-North Carolina border where they stopped to change horses, then on to Elizabeth City and through many other North Carolina towns including Edenton, on steamboat across the Albemarle Sound to Plymouth, Washington and New Bern. One segment of their travel was through a thickly wooded area of pines. There they stopped by a school to water the horses and allow the passengers to get out and stretch their legs. The children were singing a Portuguese hymn inside the school, but soon appeared outside to stare at the stage passengers. "They stood wide eyed…

mouths wide open with a vacant stare…these sons of the pine swamps," Jonathan mused. At New Bern he labeled it the "land of turpentine and tar" (staples harvested from the vast pine tree resources) and deemed it a most pleasant place. On the next leg to Wilmington, they passed the large, beautiful River Oaks, where Jonathan saw a troubling sight. It was the gallows "where they hung the Negroes who were engaged in the insurrection last year, also several high posts where they stuck the heads of the ringleaders after they were executed."[39] This was an outcome of the Nat Turner Rebellion in September 1831, when suspected conspirators were pursued, jailed, tried, and hung.

Jonathan was not born into an abolitionist family and his extended family (uncles, cousins, grandfather) owned slaves, albeit in small numbers, although his grandfather was an early advocate of emancipation. In 1779, Judge Jonathan Sturges was the author of a petition to the Connecticut General Assembly on behalf of two slaves from Fairfield named Prince and Prime. This eventually unsuccessful petition requested the abolishment of slavery in Connecticut, under the "unalienable right" of liberty, during the colonies' own struggle for independence.[f] Also, as a Congressman from Fairfield, the Judge cast one of only seven nay votes against passage of the Fugitive Slave Act of 1793, and the only nay vote from Connecticut. This act directed local state authorities to aid in the seizure and return of escaped slaves to their owners across state lines and imposed penalties on anyone who aided their flight.

The stage left the next morning heading for Smithville, N.C.[g] Reporting to the stage office at Smithville, Jonathan learned that the next transportation was two days away. After berating the stage manager for poor contract performance and resolving to ensure the termination of his mail contract, he found a dwelling for two days and warmed to the place. He described this area near the junction of Cape Fear Inlet and the Atlantic Ocean as "a mere collection of sand banks, there is a little fort and a few U.S. soldiers." Securing tavern accommodations, he found "a fire and a comfortable bed…there is nothing wanting but the clams to make this as interesting a place as Coney Island."[40]

The stage left Smithville Thursday evening, December 20, where Jonathan's seat was open to the elements. Stage ticket prices were set based on an inside or outside price. Although he took an inside seat when he could, on this

---

f In 1784, Connecticut embraced gradual emancipation, declaring that any child of slaves born after March 1, 1784 would be freed on their 21st (women) or 25th (men) birthday. Older slaves were not freed by law until 1848.

g Now known as Southport on Cape Fear.

trip he was seated outside, cold and miserable. They changed horses along the way and then were driven by a boy of about fourteen for twenty-two miles overnight. When they went into a house to warm up and eat, he was so cold he wrote Mary, "I can hardly find my mouth." Reaching Georgetown, they boarded the ferry at eight o'clock to leave North Carolina and made their way to Charleston, South Carolina. Arriving there on December 22, 1832. Jonathan sent instructions to Mary to be ready to depart between January 7 and 15, when he thought he might arrive back in Fredericksburg. He was concerned about getting through before the Potomac River froze.

On his return trip north in winter conditions, travel became truly arduous. There was one segment of the trip he would never forget. On January 4, his stage reached Fayetteville, North Carolina, then moved onward through a steady rain to a small town called Lewisburg. There he was advised that the next available transportation for days was a two-wheeled, open mail cart going to Petersburg, Virginia, a trip of 110 miles.[41] Although he had refused such transportation before, Jonathan was eager to get back to Mary and boarded the cart. "We rode this way for 25 miles with every jolt seeming as if it would take your breath away. The rain beat in upon us so that we were soon wet through." Arriving at Warrenton, N.C., two of the passengers opted to wait for other transportation, but Jonathan and two other determined travelers went on in the mail cart. "The wind now blew hard and directly in our faces, it got cold, and the rain turned to sleet. I was...in fact miserable...I now reflected that I was wrong to expose my health so much that I might get sick on the road and cause my dear wife much more anxiety than I should do by stopping and not arriving as soon as she expected me." This was the last letter on a long and tough road up and down the Eastern seaboard, documenting the hardships that Jonathan and his fellow merchants suffered to maintain distant business relationships in that era.

On a more poignant note, while Jonathan was in Charleston, Mary was traveling via steamboat. On Christmas Day, their anniversary, the steamboat stopped at a place in Virginia. That evening she wrote to Jonathan, reflecting intimately on their marriage and wedding night:

> I wish you could just stop in and sleep with me tonight. I assure you that you would meet a different reception from the one I gave you four years ago this night. ... I do not doubt that you have thoughts of the anniversary of our union, and perhaps wished that you would be with me. ...I feel it is good for us...to review the past...and to form new resolve for the future.

When I look back on my married life I see many failures, both in judgment and even in <u>known</u> duty, and on this day all I can do is to ask my beloved to forgive me. I desire solemnly to renew the vow which I made four years since, to "love, honor and obey" him who is indeed my heart's chosen. When I sit down and reflect on…our general unity of thought and feeling which exists, I wonder how it is that even an unkind word passes between us, but then I know how actually hasty and thoughtless I am…I must and will resolve to receive reproof from my husband…and not allow my quick temper to rise when he tells me my faults.[42]

After reuniting in Fredericksburg, they started back home to New York, but the frozen Rappahannock and Potomac rivers hindered their progress, requiring detours, digging stages out of the mud, and alternate transportation. Arriving in Washington at Gadsby's Inn, Mary recalled: "We stayed there for ten days, going daily to the House of Representatives, hearing Daniel Webster, John Q. Adams and John Calhoun."[43] Jonathan's life would coincidentally intersect with Webster, Adams, and Calhoun, in politics, art and death.

After their visit to Washington, Jonathan and Mary made their way back to New York, glad to be home and in their own bed. The threat of the river freezing, muddy roads on rainy nights, riding on open mail carts in the cold, driving rain, unpredictable connecting transportation, sparse meal options, washed out bridges, etc., all paint a picture of a skeletal infrastructure in 1830s America, including more populated areas such as the District of Columbia. The young country badly needed a transportation network that would tie together the far-flung states and territories within its borders. Just one decade later, Jonathan would become one of those visionaries who would do his part to build the infrastructure of the young nation.

FOUR

Death of Luman Reed—
Art Patronage—A Country Home

I never will consent to have my children brought up entirely in the city. It
is not in the nature of things.

—Jonathan Sturges

After their travels South, Jonathan became an early adopter of a revolution in
everyday carriages. In a book documenting the history of carriage transport, he
is highlighted as an early owner of a Rockaway carriage which included
wooden springs and a top. His experience with topless transports no doubt
motivated him to pursue and purchase this more commodious and weather
protecting carriage for his family. His early adoption of new technology
would somewhat surprisingly be a theme through his life including being one
of the early users of gas lights and plumbing in his own home.

Jonathan and Mary needed to find a new place to live and Luman Reed
was intent on having them move near him. He recommended a three-story
home on his street, but even though Jonathan was considered wealthy by that
time, in their very frugal way they opted for a smaller two-story home nearby
at 28 Greenwich Street. There was a river running behind their new house,
separated only by a road, and they were close to the Battery and the Atlantic
Garden House,[a] a place for couples to socialize and listen to music.[1] The
music often drifted over to the Reed and Sturges homes. As Scoville recalled, "For years Mr. Reed enjoyed the luxury of listening to the choice music in
the summertime, and witnessing hundreds of couples who, at one time, made
it a place of regular resort to get their ice cream and talk sweet things."[2]

---

[a] Formerly the Burns Coffee House, built on the site of the Kings Arms Tavern, where George
Washington headquartered during the Revolutionary War.

Atlantic Garden House, c. 1859[3]

Jonathan and Mary enjoyed their Greenwich Street residence and stayed there eleven years, with four children being born there. They hosted many evenings singing and playing old Presbyterian music in the privacy of their home. Mary encouraged Jonathan to master the flute, and she trained with a voice teacher. Luman Reed and other friends joined them in their home for these evenings. They, in turn, frequented Reed's growing gallery of art in his splendid home, cultivating Jonathan's growing appreciation of and interest in art and American artists.[4] Reed opened his gallery once a week to the public, per the European model of collectors.

Before the 1830s, there were scant efforts to develop native art and artists. There were no professional standards or training to distinguish sign painters from portrait painters. They were both called artists. Additionally, it was impractical to study the great works of art, when most of these paintings were in Europe, and although a patron system had fueled artists in Europe for centuries, such a support network had not yet developed in the United States.

There has been much written about Reed and Jonathan as important patrons for Hudson River School landscape artists, one of the first recognized "schools" of American art. Jonathan was an extraordinary businessman, civic leader, and philanthropist, but his most noted legacy was arguably his art patronage. From the late 1820s to his death, Reed, one of the early art patrons, mentored Jonathan and opened many doors into two of the seven schools of the fine arts,[b] painting and literature, setting the stage for Jonathan to become a household name in that sphere of influence in the nineteenth century.

---

b Architecture, sculpture, painting, music, literature, dance, theater (later cinema)

Eager to show their sophisticated taste, the nouveau riche American art collectors directed their interest and money to the art of the Grand Master painters of Europe. Typically, an art agent would be retained to connect with artists and art collectors in Europe and either purchase or commission works of art. Reed started his "Old World" collection in this way around 1832 with an assortment of engravings, most representing the work of Italian, Dutch, and Flemish painters, favoring paintings that told a story. He also bought a few pictures that were misrepresented as old Master renderings. Mary Sturges recalled Reed's start in art collecting:

> Mr. Reed's first essay was with Michael Paff, the principal "old picture" dealer of that period in New York. A few old pictures were purchased, but Mr. Reed had too much intuitive good sense to be taken in by such "old pictures" as were on sale at that period of our country's history, and he soon began to look around among our own artists, sought their personal acquaintance, examined their works and purchased with great good taste and judgment. Thomas Cole had just returned from Europe, and one of his Italian studies, a large picture, now in the Historical Society,[c] was one of the first pictures purchased by Mr. Reed for his collection.[5]

Reed was one of the first art patrons to build his collection around American art, and especially those paintings that captured the landscape of his youth in the Catskills, making native art fashionable. Reed and then Jonathan became friends with and patrons of some of the best American artists of the time, including Thomas Cole, William Sidney Mount, Asher B. Durand, Thomas P. Rossiter, Charles Ingham, and George Flagg.

Reflecting on this period where American art was in its infancy, Jonathan said, "I did not see or hear much of pictures or artists until about the year 1826," and further noted, "Up to the year 1828, I am not aware that there was a school of landscape art in this country."[6] It was probably the Sketch Club through which Reed introduced Jonathan to the New York fine arts community, sometime around 1830. This was a gathering of artists, writers and art patrons that met over the winter in member's homes, including Reed and Jonathan's homes. Reed, Jonathan, editor and poet William Cullen Bryant, artists Cole, Durand, Henry Inman, Charles Ingham, Samuel F.B.

---

[c] This first commission for Reed was *Italian Scene Composition,* influenced by the artistry of Claude Lorrain.

Morse,[d] and author James Fenimore Cooper, among others, formed a close-knit group who gathered to promote the arts and socialize.[e] An arts historian noted:

> [The] short-lived Bread and Cheese Club [was] founded by Cooper in 1822. It was succeeded by the Sketch Club, whose early members included Bryant, Cole, Durand, Morse and Verplanck, as well as several nouveau-riche "amateurs", men who dabbled in the arts and were eyed as patrons. Members were notified of the weekly meetings by means of cryptic messages in the press "C.I. pr. ov. t. c. 69 Franklin," appearing in The Evening Post on April 8, 1830, signified a gathering at Ingham's residence—which aroused public suspicions that the society was actually a gambling club. Although the first hour of a meeting was given to impromptu sketching, camaraderie was probably more important to members; once, the assembled group attempted to raise a ghost, and on another evening of particularly inclement weather, "there was no drawing but of corks."[7]

It is interesting to note that Jonathan's close friend, the famous poet William Cullen Bryant, was the editor of the Evening Post from 1829 until his death in 1878. He was also a founder of the Sketch Club and was likely placing newspaper club meeting messages. A Sketch Club meeting announcement placed in the *Evening Post*, illustrates the example mentioned above:

Evening Post, April 8, 1830[8]

John L. Benson was a guest at one meeting at General Cummings' home in the 1840s, where Jonathan was in attendance. Benson describes the proceedings:

---

d   Samuel F. B. Morse, an accomplished artist, was also the inventor of the Morse code.

e   It has been reported that a final reunion of the original Sketch Club, which had long since morphed in to The Century Association, took place in 1872, two years before Jonathan's death.

At these meetings, the artists and literary men were kept ignorant of the subject that was to engage their attention and genius, until it was announced by the host, when pens and pencils would work vigorously for exactly one hour. At the end of that period all productions, artistic or literary, finished or unfinished, was gathered up by the host. These in groups, were distributed by lot at the end of the year. On the evening in question the members were seated at a large, well-lighted table with working materials ready for action. At precisely eight o'clock General Cummings touched a bell and said, "Raising the Wind." Edmonds, I think, sketched a colored boy raising the wind by vigorously blowing a fire with a bellows... (others produced) poetical products.[9]

Jonathan remembered these sketch sessions in a look back:

It was an interesting study to watch the workings of each mind...on one occasion the subject was "Just in Time." One artist drew a bull in chase of a boy who had just time to catch the top of a board fence and draw himself up out of reach of the bull's horns. Another drew a poor half-starved fellow entering a room just as a family are seated for a smoking dinner...Mount [William Sydney] with his irresistible propensity for humor represented the angel lifting the old man clear of the boat (in an ocean of eternity, oars of self-reliance gone) by the collar while the devil was stretching his arms after him, and sure enough the angel was just in time to save the old man.[10]

At another gathering, Jonathan became a peacemaker between Asher Durand and Charles Ingham. A disagreement had occurred over an issue at the artist-led National Academy of Design. Ingham and Durand, who was president of the Academy, had exchanged harsh words and hard feelings prevailed, whereupon these good friends stopped speaking with each other for several months. Daniel Huntington related Jonathan's effort to heal their rift:

Jonathan Sturges was a sincere friend of both men. He was pained at this estrangement. He determined to reconcile them. At a meeting of the Sketch Club at his house, when all were gathered at the supper-table, the guests being in genial spirits (the champagne flowing), Mr. Sturges said, "Mr. Durand—Mr. Ingham, shake hands and be friends for my sake." Durand replied, "I'll be glad to do so," and gave his hand to Ingham, who shook it warmly, saying; "It gives me great pleasure," and the two were ever after good friends. "Blessed are the peacemakers, for they shall be called the children of God."[11]

As the Industrial Revolution grew and wealth spread among a growing number of successful businessmen, a cache of discretionary funds became available for such philanthropic endeavors. These emerging patrons sponsored artists to travel to the great museums of Europe to view and absorb the painting styles, and to "copy" the great paintings. These copies often ended up in the personal collection of the patron who funded the trip. At times, there were so many artists at such places as the Louvre copying paintings that it was hard for museum visitors to move through.

The American Academy of Fine Artistry in the United States Arts (AAFA), chartered in 1808, was one of the earliest art promotion organizations in America. Soon a few accomplished artists, such as John Trumbull and Washington Allston, became associated with the AAFA, and by 1816 it had a decent gallery of paintings and sculptures originating in Europe. However, a small group of wealthy patrons dominated the board and the education and advancement of native artists was not a priority. Local artists requested to use the AAFA's assets to study and develop their skills, but the Academy offered little cooperation. It had become scarcely more than an elite collector's group.

Scorned by the AAFA, these young artists formed their own drawing associations, such as the Sketch Club in the 1820s, and then in a formal and concerted effort they established the National Academy of Design (NAD). Informal meetings started in 1825 and their charter was formalized in 1828. The bulk of the artist community threw their support to the artist-led NAD. Membership consisted of many of the same artists and patrons connected with the Sketch Club, including Asher B. Durand, Samuel B. Morse and Thomas Cole, who were among the founders.

The NAD focused on the education and promotion of native artists. Modeled after London's Royal Academy, its declared mission was to "Promote the fine arts in America through instruction and exhibition."[12] Reed became an honorary member of the NAD in 1834 and Jonathan in 1837.[13] There was talk of merging the AAFA and the NAD, but the American Academy board, led by painter John Trumbull from 1817 to 1836, was unsympathetic to the artists' needs for education and mentoring. This decision proved to be a fatal blow to the AAFA and it eventually disbanded in 1841 for lack of support by the art community.[14]

Gaining prominence in the art world, Jonathan likewise gained an elite standing in the business community. On July 1, 1834, the New York Chamber of Commerce, easily the most esteemed business forum in the country, selected Jonathan at the young age of thirty-two for membership. The Chamber's meetings, recommendations, and resolutions drew national attention and had the ear of the federal government.

Now that Jonathan was secure in business and reputation, he had the means and time to establish a "country seat" in his hometown. According to Mary's *Reminiscences*, in the spring of 1835, Jonathan purchased from cousin Hezekiah Sturges[f] the homestead that had belonged to his maternal uncle, Dimon Sturges, at the Mill Plain area of Fairfield, and established his mother and sister there.[15] The collective land the descendants of John Sturges owned in Fairfield was immense. At its height in the early nineteenth century, the main body of land in the extended family approached one thousand acres, bounded from the Mill River eastward, southward near where the turn-pike (I-95) now runs, and northward through the vicinity of the current Osborn Hill area. Westward boundaries were less defined, but they included areas west of Mill Plain Road, a main north-south travel artery through Fairfield.

Jonathan delighted in returning to the restful country environment of his youth and being close to his many cousins and family members. Mary and the children spent summers in Fairfield, and these respites away from the city would be a recurring theme for the rest of their lives, with Jonathan coming out as many weekends as possible on the scheduled packet ships. He and Mary kept a written correspondence going during the week. Over many years Jonathan revealed his insecurities and thoughts of loneliness as he re-mained in the city, including his lack of confidence regarding his wife's af-fection for him. He became particularly irritated if she didn't promptly answer.

Their first letters to each other, from their new summer home in Fairfield in 1835, revealed intimate feelings and priorities for their family. In one letter, Jonathan and the children were visiting, while Mary recovered from the birth of their daughter Amelia in New York. He had something of an epiphany regarding the priceless value of escape to the country:

---

[f] Hezekiah Sturges was the executor of the Dimon Sturges estate.

I wish you could just walk in and take a peep at this moment, surrounded by the stillness of country Sabbath. The little ones laid asleep—little son[g] lies at my foot, his head resting on his little hand and the rest of him on the floor. It is really refreshing to my mind to be set far from…the city. Every moment seems to restore that elasticity of mind, which we almost lose from such constant application, as we have in the city. We could not be situated better than we are here to recommit ourselves both body and mind. …I never will consent to have my children brought up entirely in the city. It is not in the nature of things, but that their feelings should be formed by art and not more by nature. I envy every moment I spend here…soon we will have plenty of sweet corn, fine pears…I'm inclined to have you stay here until the middle of September. I could come up every week.[16]

Jonathan was a partner at a leading wholesale grocery business, specializing in the spice, tea and coffee trade. He rarely mentioned his business activities in these letters, only as an explanation when the demands took him from his family. Jonathan felt a strong responsibility to stay vigilant and meet his commitments, but family and church were his priority. This watchfulness was warranted, as his firm was tested again and again through upheavals in the tea and coffee trade, and through firsthand experience of a historic catastrophe in Manhattan.

In 1830, the United States government decreased the duties on tea, making it more affordable. In parallel, the tea trading volume increased and the introduction of the clipper ship, first built in the United States, cut the voyage times in half. Between the clipper ships, the new steamships, and an increased number of tea producers, the cost of tea became depressed. "I think it was during this year (1830) that there was revulsion in the tea market, and they lost heavily. It was at this time my husband said to me, if things do not soon take a turn, we will break up housekeeping for a little while, and board. But things did 'turn', and we were never obliged to do this. Of course, we lived very quietly and inexpensively."[17]

Reed and Jonathan's conservative business approach allowed them to have a solid financial footing and the luxury of being able to support their favorite philanthropic causes, such as their mutual interest in the arts. Reed had become partial to the work of Asher B. Durand (formerly a noted engraver of paintings). He commissioned a series of paintings with Durand to capture the likenesses

g Frederick b. 1833.

of all seven United States presidents to donate to a worthy museum. The series was to include live sittings and copies of existing portraits of deceased presidents. Reed wrote several letters to Jonathan from Boston in June 1834, where he was facilitating a sitting with former president John Q. Adams. Reed's correspondence conveyed an intimacy with Jonathan and a mutual passion for the task at hand, as a father would write to a son. Reed described having been to visit the former president: "The Hon. J.Q. Adams was much pleased with my visit. He is to sit for Durand tomorrow with which Mr. D is much pleased."[18] In March 1835, he captured the image of President [Andrew] Jackson. Durand told his wife: "I have had a great deal of trouble in painting the President...had to wait ten days upon arrival to get a sitting. The General has been part of the time in a pretty good humor, but sometimes he gets his dander up and smokes his pipe prodigiously!"[19]

Reed had also tried to get permission for Durand to copy Gilbert Stuart's portraits of General and Mrs. Washington from the Boston Athenaeum. He had been to the Reading Room at the Athenaeum and saw several Stuart portraits and noted that some of them were very good, but "he cannot paint as well as Durand...females in general are crude and painted in a careless manner... Stuart is overrated!" Durand became in high demand in Boston, as he says, "I've never been so busy in my life as I have been since I've been here." Reed declared that Durand "will be a great man among us in his way to a certainty."[20]

The next year, in June 1835, Reed returned to Boston, to visit the art galleries and to further Durand's projects, and he wrote several letters to Jonathan in early June. The first portrait painted of Adams in 1834 was not acceptable to him and Durand was there to get a better likeness.[21] Adams requested that Durand also paint his grandchild (Georgianna Frances Adams, completed in 1835) and another portrait of himself. Reed was still working on getting permission for Durand to copy the Stuart portrait and to paint Washington Allston, a renowned poet, painter and uncle of the painter George Flagg, for whom he and Jonathan would later become patrons.

While there, Durand had received another commission, from Mrs. C.A. Davis of Boston, to paint Edward Everett. Everett was a Congressman from Massachusetts until 1835, one of the most famous orators of his time (later the forgotten keynote speaker at the Gettysburg Cemetery dedication, who spoke for two hours before Lincoln). He became Governor in 1836, then Ambassador to England and Secretary of State. In July 1835, Reed told Jonathan, "Mr. Allen writes me that Durand has returned and tells me that his portrait of Everett is the best he has done. I do not know where the man will end if he keeps going and improving in this way. I presume you will have him at your children before the week is out, he will do them justice beyond all doubt."[22] Durand completed a portrait of Jonathan's children Virginia and Frederick sometime in 1835.[h] Reed donated the seven presidential portraits to the Museum and Library in the Navy Yard, Brooklyn, keeping copies for his own gallery.[i]

A.B. Durand—(left) *Luman Reed* c. 1835[23] and *Frederick and Virginia Sturge*s c. 1835[24]

Reed had thirty-four paintings by American artists at the time of his death. All but one painting was by Cole, Durand, William Sidney Mount, or George Whiting Flagg.[25] Reed's crowning achievement as a patron was his commission of a set of paintings by Thomas Cole, considered a founder of the Hudson River Art School, called *Course of Empire* in 1833. Cole had sketched his concept of a series of paintings depicting the rise and fall of an empire and Luman Reed commissioned the paintings for the sum of $5,000. This *Course of Empire* first series of paintings included: *Savage State, Pastoral State, The Consummation of Empire, Destruction, and Desolation.*[j] They depict the course that an empire might take from its dawning to its end. Reed did not

---

h The portrait of Frederick and Virginia is in the possession of the descendants of Frederick Sturges.
i When the U.S. Naval Lyceum closed in Brooklyn in 1888, the collection was transferred to the U.S. Naval Academy Museum in Annapolis, Maryland.
j The Course of Empire series is resident at the New York Historical Society, New York, NY.

live to see the series finished, but his legacy was intact, and the completed product was a triumph for Thomas Cole and American art. Jonathan noted a curious coincidence, in his "Reminiscences of Art" article for the *Crayon* art periodical, regarding Cole's three series of paintings. After Reed's commission for the *Course of Empire*, which he never saw finished, Samuel Ward commissioned *The Voyage of Life* [k] and died before those paintings completed. Cole then started on *The Cross and World* [l] on his own with no commission, and he did not live to finish the last series.[26] After the death of Reed, Jonathan became a major patron of Cole.

Other than his art patronage activities, Reed sat on no boards or committees and was not active in politics or other philanthropic activities, nor was he known to be an evangelical man. His political leanings were with the Democratic party, with an affinity for President Jackson its standard-bearer, and a distaste for the politics of Webster and Clay. In 1831, Reed and his daughters visited President Jackson at the presidential mansion, whereupon Jackson gave each daughter a rose.[27]

Reed took a public stance only as an art patron, but in 1835, he took a one-time public, yet cautious, stance on the question of slavery. Typically, during the mid-nineteenth century in New York City, when an issue raised the interest and emotions of leading citizens, a public meeting was called, and resolutions were put forward, with the most prominent supporters being made honorary vice presidents, for the credibility and stature that their name gave to the cause. Local newspapers gave prime coverage to these resolutions and they gained national media attention. At such a meeting, entitled "Public Meeting of the Citizens" on August 27, 1835, chaired by New York Mayor C.P. White, Luman Reed was a "vice president" of the gathering and they resolved that the country should take a legislative, non-reactionary approach to abolishing slavery:

> We hold that the citizens of the North have no political right to interfere with the slavery of the southern states, nor moral right, under any circumstances to adopt violent or aggressive measures for the purpose of abolishing it...We recommend a resort to such constitutional legislation that might meet the exigency of the case and remove the evil.[28]

---

k *The Voyage of Life* series is resident at the Chrysler Museum of Art, Norfolk, VA.

l The study for *The Cross and the World* is held by the Brooklyn Museum, Brooklyn, NY.

Reed was winding down his career in the 1830s and increasingly confident in Jonathan's ability to manage the business—Jonathan taking the active lead by about 1834. He was showing little interest in getting back to work during his trip to Boston. "I won't be home until the latter part of next week unless I'm wanted. I have not fixed on a day to leave here and as you say, 'you are calm as a drummer's morning,' I see no necessity to be in a hurry to getaway."[29] A number of reports refer to him retiring as early as 1832, at age forty-eight.

Jonathan and his firm had been very busy during the cholera epidemic of 1832—many businessmen limited their trading to the most established import houses such as Reed and Sturges. In 1834, China closed its ports to foreign, vessels and the East India Company in England lost their monopoly on the tea trade in Britain, which created competition all around the world. Markets were opening worldwide to meet the demands, including Kenya, India, Indonesia, Japan, and Taiwan. The competitive environment drove down prices further and bred races between clipper ships to arrive in port first to sell their tea.[30]

Report Date	Company Assets	Company Stock held by Jonathan	Quarterly payments to Jonathan
Sep 1833	$845,223.65	$48,874.48	$12,722.98
Dec 1833	$792,929.00	$48,874.48	$644.92
Feb 1834	$655,746.85	$48,874.48	$15,243.69
Jun 1834	$788,385.81	$68,162.12	$16,047.48
Sep 1834	$677,942.03	$68,162.12	$16,918.06
Dec 1834	$822,514.40	$68,162.12	$17,913.72
Feb 1835	$693,335.11	$68,162.12	$19,935.37
Jun 1835	$1,008,159.82	$98,801.11	$23,285.01
Sep 1835	$941,896.03	$98,801.11	$211,207.18
Dec 1835	$958,503.66	$98,801.11	$25,586.28

Table Data from Reed and Sturges Account Books[31]

The business had been increasing in profits year by year. An analysis of the account books of Reed and Sturges for 1833-1835 showed a profit increase for the business from $100,000 in 1833 to $200,000 in 1834 to $300,000 for 1835.[m] Combined net worth of the firm was over $950,000 in 1835. Capital reserves and payments credited to Jonathan increased, while payments to Reed declined.

---

[m] Analysis performed by Kenneth Williams, accountant, Burlington, Massachusetts.

One setback occurred in December 1833, probably reflecting the contraction in the tea market and a building of reserves. However, in September 1835 he received a $211,000 payout following a significant increase in the firm's assets that year. This was a huge payment, perhaps a bonus for taking the lead in the business, or previous conservative retention of capital by the firm. Regardless, he was a significantly wealthier man. The firm soon had their business acumen and instincts put to the test by a trying calamity that destroyed the greater part of lower Manhattan—a disaster known as The Great Fire of 1835.

The Sturges family was at home when the city alarm bell rang. It was December 16, 1835, a bitterly cold and windy Wednesday night in New York City. Historian Robert McNamara described the discovery of the fire, about three blocks from the Reed and Sturges warehouse:

> Approaching the corner of Pearl Street and Exchange Place [and Wall Street], the watchman realized the interior of a five-story warehouse was in flames. He sounded alarms, and various volunteer fire companies began to respond. The situation was perilous. The neighborhood of the fire was packed with hundreds of warehouses…that held a concentration of some of the most expensive goods on earth, including fine silks, lace, glassware, coffee, teas, liquors, chemicals, and musical instruments.[32]

The firemen's attempt to respond was frustrated by freezing water in the hydrant pipes, high winds, and the closeness of buildings, which encouraged the rapid spread of the fire. Mary Sturges described Jonathan's response:

> The children were all in bed, and my husband had been playing on the flute, when we heard the alarm bell on the City Hall strike. My husband set the flute up in the corner, and said, "There is fire! I must go and see where it is." It was about nine o'clock. My sister and myself sat on, but very soon found by the light outside, that the fire was spreading with fearful rapidity…We sat wearily on, till it seemed as if the heavens were in a blaze. We could hear the roar of the fire, and noise of wagons conveying goods to places of safety. At two o'clock, a quick step and a ring at the door, one of the clerks came to tell us that the books of the firm had been brought over to Mr. Reed's house opposite, as the stores were in great danger, but were not burned yet…. I was awakened by my husband coming into the room. The day had dawned. He was at the iron chest getting out insurance policies. He said they

were removing goods on to vessels, drawing them out into the stream, and taking a marine insurance...The insurance companies of the time were, I think, nearly all ruined.[33]

The Great Fire Of New York—December 17, 1835[34]

The northernmost point of the fire was at Wall Street. The impressive Merchant Exchange was destroyed in the fire, along with most of the commercial district of New York. Most businesses held fire insurance, but with the mass destruction the insurance companies were insolvent, unable to pay out the tremendous number of claims. Many businesses went bankrupt.

Jonathan and Luman Reed's response to the fire was innovative, impressive, and solidified the firm's reputation as being one of the most dependable in the city. There was still a concern that the fire would restart, fire insurance was hard to find, and fire-fighting companies' capabilities had been diminished by the significant toll the fire had taken on their equipment. Reed and Sturges took decisive steps to secure their valuable goods. They moved their most expensive cargoes such as tea, coffee, spices, and foreign liquor stores to a chartered schooner within one day and bought marine insurance. They kept their goods on board until three weeks later when they could get fire insurance from abroad. The newspapers lauded Reed and Jonathan's decisive action and they earned the universal respect of the business community.

Unlike many of their competitors, Reed and Sturges possessed their full warehouse of goods to sell, and the unstrained finances to stock their shelves and provide for customers. Other businesses who suffered major losses survived by receiving aid from the federal government and from the Erie Canal authority. This enabled commerce in Manhattan to continue, albeit in a tough, cautious credit environment, although the credit of Reed and Sturges was golden.

In February 1836, the firm became Reed, Sturges & Co., adding Reed's nephew, George Barker, and William Roe as partners, but that partnership was short-lived. In May 1836, Luman Reed became very ill, and the doctors were called. As illustrated by accounts of treatments from Mary's youth, the medicine practiced in those days was often aggressive and harmful. Twenty years later methods had changed little. The technique of bleeding or "blood-letting" was still in wide use during much of the 1800s and was a standard way of treating diseases where they had no other answer or cure. It relied on the ancient concept that the body was a balance of "four humors: blood, yellow bile, black bile, and phlegm[n]... A proper and evenly balanced mixture of the humors characterized health of body and mind; an imperfect balance resulted in disease."[35] According to Reed's close friend A.B. Durand, he had been suffering from remittent fever with inflammation of the liver. Reed's sickness followed a very similar path to Mary Sturges' young sister over twenty years before. Mary related Reed's suffering:

> His physicians belonged to the old heroic class. The disease did not yield, the more violent it became, the more severe the treatment. My husband would come in with a sad face, and say, "They have bled him again today, and he is no better." I went in to see him once; he was much wasted, and gasped out, "Oh! Mrs. Sturges, I'm a poor, weak creature." And at last the morning came when the doctors were gathered around him in consultation, and he dropped away...saying the trouble went to the heart; but years after, Mrs. Reed describing his illness, said, "And so they killed him."[36]

He died June 7, 1836. Jonathan, and Reed's son-in-law Dudley B. Fuller, were the executors for Reed's estate, and his final resting place was a vault in New York City's Second Street Cemetery.[37]

Jonathan took the loss of Luman Reed hard, as one would grieve the loss of a close relative. Reed had been a friend, mentor, and a father-like figure, more so than his own father. He carried the mantle forward for Reed in the business and in the art world, while blazing his own path as an activist in civic, business, faith-based, and philanthropic pursuits.

Jonathan had been mentored by a stalwart of the merchant community and schooled in the most conservative of business approaches. Now the lead partner

---

[n] The humors were associated with the four elements (air, fire, earth, and water), which in turn were paired with one of the qualities (hot, cold, dry, and moist).

and mentor for his firm, he became the example by which the junior partners and clerks would be judged. Embracing the American Tract Society's rules for merchants to live by (Appendix III), in 1838, Jonathan wrote to his wife summering in Fairfield. Invoking Rule #10 he said: "my compliments to Mr. [illegible] and say I always keep my engagements with men and I never allow a man to break his promise to me but once."[38]

After the death of the founding partner, Jonathan attended to reorganizing the business. Except for the merger with Lee, the firm had a long history of promoting from within its ranks. After Reed's death, Jonathan became the senior partner, and the new partnership, Sturges, Roe & Barker was formed, with George Barker and William Roe. When Reed passed away, the firm needed to settle his share with his family. Reed's capital in the firm had been decreasing as he took a less active role in the business, but it was important to ensure adequate capital was retained for operations. Mary Sturges described the business of settling with the Reed's heirs. "The articles of partnership provided that three years should be allowed for the settlement of the business in case of the death of any of the partners. I will just say here, at the end of that time the business was entirely settled up and the capital paid over to the heirs."[39]

The firm was thriving, and Jonathan's income was growing. As Mary commented in her *Reminiscences*, "Happily for us, we had lived in a very quiet, inexpensive way. This had enabled my husband to accumulate a much larger capital than was generally supposed."[40] These increasing discretionary funds enabled him to invest in other varied business pursuits and further his philanthropic causes. Starting with the transformational effect the Erie Canal had on business and trade in the country and the burgeoning technological advances, the opportunities were many and varied or those with funds to invest, and New York City was the de facto financial capital of the country where 25% of millionaires lived. Jonathan Sturges was in the right time and place to take advantage of these emerging opportunities. However, first he and others would have to suffer the detrimental actions of the populist Jackson administration.

With the re-election of "Old Hickory," Andrew Jackson, the Northeast-led banking system of the United States was dismantled. Jackson was determined to break up the federal banking network that he viewed as monopolistic and unfair to the Western and Southern regions of the United States. He first funneled treasury funds to private banks to undermine the federal government's central bank, the Second Bank of the United States

He then vetoed the renewal of the charter of the Second Bank in 1836, creating a void in the nation's ability to regulate banks, the money supply, and investment resources.

To fill the void, private banks were chartered by state legislatures, all minting their own notes that worked like checks drawn on an account. With an increasing number of unique notes in the market and varying levels of credibility, these bank notes became prone to frequent counterfeiting, and it was difficult to exchange them for the universal form of currency known as specie,° of which each bank kept a reserve. It was also hard to control the amount of specie in reserve as it was the primary currency used in overseas transactions and increasingly hoarded. Due to the growing lack of confidence in the banking system, and a contraction of specie available on the market, banks suspended specie redemptions for paper money to its depositors on May 10, 1837. In a final ill-conceived move, the Jackson administration redistributed specie reserves away from the financial center of the country, in favor of Western and Southern banks, and the financial Panic of 1837 ensued.

In a very public rise in Jonathan's business stature, he was named secretary for a gathering of New York City merchants in 1838, where they deliberated on the national management of specie reserves. They provided the Jackson administration with a "Memorial"ᴾ of recommendations that advocated bringing reserves back in to New York banks.[41] These actions, among others, resulted in the reversal of the distribution, and banks resumed specie payments to customers a year later.

However, the void created in the investment market by this crisis and a lack of bank funds to invest, was an invitation to private individuals and investor groups to become major players in financing new ventures. In 1839, Jonathan became one of these private investors, who took a leap into the banking business. Early in his life, borrowing money was perceived as a weakness, a precursor to failure, even a moral failing. However, his thinking and national business trends had evolved to the point that lending money had become more profitable for some merchants than their primary business. Jonathan started on a large stage, becoming a founding director of one of the

---

o The currency used by all banks and the government's primary form of fiduciary was known as "specie." It was a bimetallic coinage system that consisted of various sizes and weights of silver and metal coins

p "Memorials" were petitions that offered a group's opinion or suggestion pertaining to certain policy issues being debated, usually sent to Congress by men whose names were respected and well-known to the public.

largest and most important lending banks in the history of the country, the National Bank of Commerce. A bank history described the original incorporators:

> The eighteen original associates included twelve prominent Merchants, two Lawyers, two men of affairs and two bankers. The names of these merchants were closely linked with inspiring a period of American commerce which was then at its height; names such as Gracie, Minturn, Carow, Donaldson, Sturges, Whitney, Stevens, and Russell. Their industry had helped to send our merchant marine to all quarters of the world.[42]

Jonathan and the board of directors solicited general subscriptions for the new bank starting in 1839.[q] The original capital of the Bank of Commerce, located at the corner of Nassau and Queen Street,[r] was $5,000,000. The bank's mission was to infuse new capital into a depressed economy. Working with the Secretary of the Treasury, the bank became the depository for receipts from the New York Customs House, a primary source of government income. By 1856, the bank held deposits of $10,000,000, becoming the largest and most substantial bank of the nineteenth century.

Now that Jonathan was the senior partner in his firm, and a powerful director of a leading national bank, it was time for him to savor the fruits of his labor and build a country retreat in his hometown that he had dreamt of building for some time.

---

[q] The Bank of Commerce became a National Bank in 1865 with the new banking laws passed in Congress during the Civil War. The Bank of Commerce was a party to many mergers over time. Among its mergers were with the National Union Bank of New York in 1900, reverting to the Bank of Commerce name again in 1929, and part of the J.P. Morgan Chase banking empire in 2004.

[r] This land had been previously owned and sold in 1790 by Aaron Burr, Thomas Jefferson's vice president and the slayer of Alexander Hamilton, the country's original Secretary of the Treasury, in an "honorable" duel.

FIVE

Summer Cottage—An 1830s Relationship— Saving the Reed Legacy

My husband immediately employed an English architect, Mr. Joseph C. Wells, to draw plans for a new house

—Mary Cady Sturges

The Sturges family had been enjoying the countryside, and the company of extended family at the old Dimon Sturges homestead they purchased in 1835. Jonathan and his family cultivated a farm with an orchard, kitchen gardens, and livestock, and enjoyed the clamming and fishing in Long Island Sound. In early 1836, Jonathan bought a house in Fairfield for his widowed sister Deborah Bennet and her family. Her husband Thaddeus had died in December 1820. Mary and Hattie Bennet became teachers and as Mary Sturges reminisced, "Mary opened a little private school, in which Hattie assisted her, and their life in Fairfield was a far happier and healthful one than it could possibly be in New York."[1]

Mary Sturges and children spent most of the summertime in Fairfield Jonathan's work and commitments in the city prevented longer stays but on one of his visits, in July 1836, he brought with him the artist Asher B. Durand This was around the time Jonathan gave one of his first commissions to Durand for a landscape composition. He was no doubt eager to share with him his treasured country home, but also to reassure him that could count on his support in the wake of the death of Luman Reed, Durand's close friend and devoted patron.

While Mary was at the country home, Jonathan wrote from New York about family, friends, and his thoughts on raising the children. In one of these letters, he expressed concern to Mary regarding the family's Sabbath activities:

[It] has long been my views that our children should be kept under our instruction on the Sabbath at home and that less business should be done out of doors, religious business if you please. I consider the tendency of so much being done on the Sabbath as being to give it more the character of a business day than was intended…has tended more than anything else to do away with that veneration for the day…. I wish you to reflect upon the subject because sometimes I think you view it differently and I consider it of importance to our children that you should take the same view of it that I do.[2]

Mary responded three days later, but Jonathan still felt that she did not understand:

I do not believe that I alluded to the manner in which we spend our Sabbath. I speak of the general mannerism at this time and expressed my dissatisfaction of it and my fears that you approved of it, although out of respect perhaps to my wishes you did not enter into all the schemes of the day…. I was afraid you did not look upon them as evils, neither do the great mass of the peoples…. perhaps you expect too much from me and do not consider the importance of quiet reflection on Sabbath for myself.[3]

This continuing discussion of reverence for the Sabbath personifies Jonathan's lifetime dedication to reserving the day for religious pursuits and quiet reflection. He would, to his dying day, be a staunch supporter of Sabbath laws, including prohibiting alcoholic sales and amusements on Sunday.

Alone in New York in 1836, Jonathan grudgingly underwent a "cupping" procedure for recurrent bouts of pain in his side.[4] Cupping is a homeopathic or Eastern medicine procedure that uses a cup made of pottery, bamboo, bronze, or sometimes a cow horn. It could be a dry cupping, or a wet cupping which requires an incision, drawing blood from the area. The cupping device is heated and pressed against the skin to take the oxygen out of the enclosed area. When it cools, it contracts, causing a sucking effect which draws blood to the area to promote healing. There was the additional risk of the hot cup causing burns where the cup met the skin. Jonathan described his experience: "I had the operation of cupping performed on my side last night and am keeping house today as it's unpleasant. I feel released from the pain in my side and think I will be better for the operation."[5] With his belief in less invasive procedures, it is likely he chose the dry procedure.

As we have seen in communications between Jonathan and Mary, letter writing in the nineteenth century was an important and integral means of communicating. If one received a personal letter, the receiver was expected to reply within a day or two if possible, despite the undependable mail delivery schedules. Mary's sister Elizabeth was taking care of Jonathan in early September in New York, but he was lonely and not feeling well. He had a cold and had just taken some catnip tea.[a] Jonathan's usual salutation to Mary was, "To My Dear Wife," but this letter in September, addressed very coldly to "Mrs. Sturges," admonished her, "I won't call you by a more familiar name. I'm determined I won't give you [illegible] such a naughty woman and such a bad correspondent. You don't deserve to hear from me and all this work is because you have not written me…. If scolding would do any good I would try it, but I give it up and hope you will write me as soon as you get this and tell me how Aunt Eunice is and all the Fairfield folks."[6]

The next year, in May 1837, Mary was seven months pregnant with their fourth child, Edward. This was during the Panic of 1837, an issue of which he was engaged in addressing at a national level throughout his life—the national banking system. Jonathan related his financial worries: "Our affairs will require all my vigil, after the month of August I hope to be relieved from such close watching. There is a kind of stupid [illegible] relief in the market which is not encouraging to me. I shall not feel easy until I am nearly out of debt…as you see my letters are always a true index of my feelings."[7]

In his loneliness in New York City, he seemed to have written these letters in solitude to clear his head, sometimes throwing them out and starting again or rambling on with senseless thoughts. He would often show a longing to be with her, but also an insecurity about Mary's love for him. However, a June 1837 letter displayed only contentment with the fullness of his life with Mary:

> I can hardly tell you it was truly grateful to my feelings to read it [a letter from Mary]. [It] had that calmness of feeling and thought, which in my estimation is the greatest ornament to the woman and Christian…it is the morning of the Sabbath and thanks to our parents and New England [?] we have been taught to collect our wandering thoughts on the morning of that day that all may be calm…. I can truly say that without the calmness of this day my present life would be that of a Slave. I fully agree with you that our happiest hours are not spent in childhood… There is not a day nor an hour that I do not see you in my mind's eye watching your little flock

---

[a] Catnip tea is another homeopathic or herbal cure still used today. It has a relaxing effect, full of vitamins and minerals, sometimes used for the common cold and flu, migraines, stomach cramps and other digestive issues.

on the green or starting for school and I am free to say I then feel a glow of delight which in childhood or in <u>single</u> manhood I never knew.[8]

The next summer, in July 1838, Jonathan again poured out his deep affection for Mary:

> I don't suppose you will understand the feeling when I tell you that I take great satisfaction not often experienced when I read that part of your letter telling me how disappointed you were that the warm weather didn't bring you to me on Saturday....I did not want anyone to see me reading that part of the letter. Can you guess why?... Let me tell you it won't be the warm weather that brings me. You know I have rode [sic] through snowstorms in a mail cart before now because my mind was bent on being in a certain place!—no fear of a man that will do that with decent treatment, with so much kindness as I receive, the thing is doubly secure...Your letter has made me want to see you, there is no use in concealing it. I don't think you will take advantage of it and get fancy again. If you do I can just come away again, that's all.[9]

Later, Jonathan lamented to her about being home all alone the night before. He wrote a bunch of "nonsense" to her, but only so she "would love me more" but adds "consider yourself saved."[10] He quoted Thomas Jefferson, who remarked about Roger Sherman,[b] a Connecticut signer of the Declaration of Independence from Fairfield, "There is a man who never said a foolish thing in his life." Then he seems to justify his ramblings by saying, "Sir Walter said, 'the greatest pleasure in writing is to write first what comes to your pen.'" He begged her for a more intimate response, that he "should sometimes get a letter from you that should inform me of the state of your feelings."[11]

In another correspondence, he confesses to Mary that she is superior to him in "mental accomplishments," conceding that she had more advantages in this area of her life. He considered it a risky experiment to marry such an educated wife, as he had been told that it was a disadvantage to do so, but then declared that he "should not have been satisfied with anything short of what I have in my wife."

---

[b] Roger Sherman was the only person to sign all four United States founding documents; the Continental Association, the Declaration of Independence, the Articles of Confederation, and the Constitution.

Jonathan loved and respected Mary, but also felt she should defer to his wishes. In one missive, he entered a relationship minefield in any era, pointing out flaws and expecting contrition:

> You will recall a conversation which took place while I was in Plainfield. Mother recommended that we tell each other our faults in a spirit of love. I should consider it a dangerous course that however willing we might be to [illegible] one fault generally, we should not be apt to receive it with humility when told of any fault in particular...This spirit first showed itself in our first parents, when Eve had erred, she was not better for it, until she had placed her husband in the same situation...just confess that you have not done right, and you are resolved to do differently....I wish you to reexamine all your letters and see in which of these you have acknowledged your errors without attempting the kind of justification I speak of. I think you will be struck with the justness of my remark.[12]

These intimate exchanges were also very illustrative of the time not only in their relationship, but of life in the first half of the nineteenth century, including bathing practices of the day. There was no plumbing installed in any houses in this era and for most people for the entire century. As a result, the communal baths could get very crowded. Although hard to imagine today, in the summer in New York City there were busy bathing areas in both the East and Hudson Rivers around Manhattan. Jonathan described his bathing regimen; "Saturday we went to the new bath on Broadway—soft water in one pipe, but so hot you have to use 'two-fifths Manhattan.' One advantage after a soaking is you can let out the hard water and let in 'soft' to rinse off with. I did so and found it first rate."[13]

Jonathan's mother died in 1840. His sister Lucretia, who had been their mother's caregiver, was distraught and felt adrift after her mother's death. Jonathan and Mary made it clear to Lucretia that she would always have a home with them; as Mary recalled, "She was, of course, most lovingly received by my friends. I drove with her all about the country, and she finally returned home strengthened and refreshed, and ready to take up a new life with us and our family; and she took charge of the housekeeping in the country that summer."[14] With Lucretia in Fairfield, they could look forward to a constant and welcoming family presence.

Jonathan's Mother Mary Sturges c. 1834-1835

Jonathan made a commitment to himself that the old Dimon Sturges homestead, his current country home, would not be torn down until his mother passed away.[15] She had an emotional attachment to this home, which had been the family homestead for many years. After her passing, Jonathan eagerly set out to build his new country retreat on the same site. To start the process, Jonathan employed an English architect, Mr. Joseph C. Wells, to draw plans for a new house. Mary had a bedroom added on to Jonathan's sister Deborah's house for them to stay while the new house was being built. They used materials from the old house to build the bedroom. She told Jonathan that sixty dollars is what it would cost to add on the bedroom and that is what it cost![16] Mary enjoyed the process of building their country home, which included a traditional community house-raising:

> My husband purchased the Sherwood place across the road, which is now Fred's, and the old house which then stood there was used as a workshop for the carpenters all winter. The cellars were dug and built in October, and the house raised during the excitement of the campaign for the election of Harrison. At that time a "raising" was a great affair, and the neighbors all gathered to assist, and the raising supper was served in the old house...The winter was a favorable one. The house was finished, ready for putting in of pantries and drawers the first of April...Mr. Wells procured for us an English gardener to layout the grounds, Mr. Atkinson.[17]

Atkinson had worked for Morris Ketchum at his large estate known as Hoka- num off Cross Highway in Westport, and Jonathan built a small home for his use on the grounds across from the main home on Mill Plain Road.

Construction of the Cottage was completed in 1840. A National Historic Landmark, the Cottage is a wonderful specimen of Early American Gothic Revival architecture and is thought to be Wells's first commission after arriv- ing in the United States. Joseph Wells was one of the thirteen founding members of the American Institute of Architects, which included the legend- ary architect Richard Morris Hunt. He became known for building Gothic Revival homes in the greater New York area, such as Roseland Cottage in Woodstock, Connecticut. Wells designed Roseland in 1846 for New York businessman, abolitionist, and *Independent* publisher Henry C. Bowen and it is now a museum and National Historic Landmark.

Gardener's Cottage c. 1840[18][c] Jonathan Sturges Cottage c. 1840[19] Roseland Cottage c. 1846[20]

While Jonathan was in New York, and Mary traversing between there and Fairfield, young Virginia went to stay with her grandmother and Aunt Elizabeth in Plainfield, Connecticut, for the summer of 1840, to attend a school for girls taught by a Miss Pierce. That first summer, ten-year-old Virginia wrote many letters home to her mother, but neglected to direct her letters to, or ask after, her father. After Mary requested that she remedy the situation, Virginia's dutiful letter resulted in a scolding by Jonathan:

> I was complaining to Mother the day before that you did not write to me nor so much as mention me in your letters and I felt quite hurt that you should apparently think so little about me. It is true you wrote me once as you said, "in obedience" to your mother's commands and as it did not appear to be a free will offering I concluded I would wait until you write again. It would seem that I had done you some injustice, so I hasten to make amends by writing you a "little" letter. There are some things in your

---

[c] The Sturges-Atkinson Gardener's Cottage was torn down by 2017.

letter which I perhaps ought to correct as being if not ungrammatical, at least inelegant, upon the whole I think you have done very well. [21]

Presentable composition and penmanship was a trait that Jonathan and Mary emphasized and reinforced in their children. Aunt Elizabeth added her own critical assessment in one of Virginia's letters, "…you have here a specimen of her own unaided composition…though you can see by what she has written above that she has not progressed much."[22]

By 1840, the better families had moved away from their Greenwich Street neighborhood. The proliferation of boarding houses in lower Manhattan spread north and pushed the affluent to more uptown areas. It had been an upscale neighborhood that included the Schermerhorns. In *Mrs. Astor's New York* (Mrs. Astor was born Carolyn Schermerhorn), the author wrote:

> Memories of living near Bowling Green, of taking childhood walks on the Battery, and having a garden like those described in accounts of colonial New York, gave Caroline Schermerhorn a proprietary sense that the history of the city and its great growth in her lifetime was truly a living part of her family's history. A few representatives of the Old Yankee and Knickerbocker families (Ferdinand Suydam, Stephen Whitney, Jonathan Sturges, Jonathan Goodhue) remained on lower Greenwich Street, Bowling Green and Whitehall, but by the 1850s, only a few elderly residents were left to remember the social prestige of the city's first aristocratic neighborhood.[23]

In 1841, Mary had her fifth child, Arthur. With their growing family, Jonathan's increasing prominence and wealth, and the changing demographics of the neighborhood, they decided to move uptown. In 1843, Jonathan found a property at 45 Murray Street, about a block and a half from City Hall. The land, where a church had been torn down, bordered on the Columbia College campus and was divided into four lots.[d] "My husband bought one of these lots; Moses H. Grinnell, two; and a Pearl Street merchant, the fourth. Mr. Grinnell afterwards changed his mind and moved further uptown. My husband took Mr. Grinnell's lots at the price which they all paid, $6,000."[24] With the three lots, Jonathan built three houses on Murray Street. He sold one to David Hale, the editor of the Journal of Commerce and one to his nephew Josiah Bennet who had just married. Joseph Wells designed the three homes and

---

[d] Columbia College street boundaries were Murray (north), Barclay (south), Church (west) and Broadway (east).

and superintended the building activity between the fall of 1843 and the spring of 1844.[25] The Sturges family loved the area and their friends including the Aspinwall, Grinnell (Henry) and Mason families, who also lived in the neighborhood. With the college providing airy, open land, they enjoyed the country-like atmosphere, with prevailing brownstone homes, and social circles that included college officers and professors.

The collegiate atmosphere provided many social opportunities to debate the topics of the day with professors and the nearby politicians and administrators at City Hall. Jonathan never ran for office, but he became increasingly active in politics and other civil affairs as a fundraiser and an active public voice. By the 1840s, the political landscape in New York had been transforming for the last two decades. City government had been controlled by the wealthy of the city since its beginning. However, starting in the 1820s, the right to vote became a reality for all white men, when property ownership and income requirements were eliminated. As the population grew, fueled by the large influx of Irish, German, and other European immigrants from 1830 onward, the demographics and voting power in New York City shifted gradually in favor of the working class. This explosive increase in new immigrant arrivals, and the expanded voting base in the city, fed and emboldened the populist Tammany Hall political organization. Founded in the late 1780s, Tammany had steadily gained strength, and by 1850 it was the dominating political force in New York City. The mayoral election was a prime example of this swing in voting power. Until 1834, the state government and then the city council appointed the mayor. Then the city elected the mayor by popular vote for the first time.[e] This was in the early years of the dominant two-party system in the country, when the parties were the Democrats (Jacksonian Democrats) and Whigs.

Jonathan and his fellow merchants and businessmen, responded to this populist movement around 1840 by forming public alliances, clubs, ad hoc groups, and associations—pooling resources to influence the outcome of elections. Jonathan was named a vice president at such an ad hoc gathering in September 1840, featuring politician and orator Daniel Webster. This meeting at the Merchant Exchange was in support of the Whig presidential candidates Harrison and Tyler, running against the incumbent Martin Van Buren. He lectured on the evils of the currency and bank policy

---

[e] Excepting one historic occurrence in 1689, Cornelius Van Wyck Lawrence became the first popularly elected mayor, and he was, not surprisingly, a merchant.

still in place from the Jackson administration that was depressing the credit markets and exasperating East Coast capitalists. He found an enthusiastic audience.[26]

The Whig ticket, Harrison and Tyler, won the election. However, Harrison became ill, died within a month of taking office and Tyler, a Virginian and a former Democrat, became president. A states-rights advocate, he generally disagreed with the Whig's domestic agenda and was irreverently referred to as "His Accidency" or "His Ascendancy." Prompted by Senator Henry Clay, most of Tyler's cabinet resigned in September 1841 to press him to resign, after his second veto of a Whig, Clay-sponsored bill that would have created a national bank. After the resignations, Tyler did not reverse his position or resign. Instead he dug in and appointed his states-rights colleagues to cabinet positions. After these September events, the Whigs ejected Tyler from the party and he became a man without a party, one of the least effective presidents in history. Banking reform had to wait until Tyler's term was completed.

Continuing in Reed's footsteps, Jonathan became a leading art patron for Hudson River Art School painters. One of the first artists he reached out to after Reed's death was Asher B. Durand. In the mold of old Europe patrons, he provided the financial means for Durand to tour Europe, viewing, copying and doing studies of classic paintings. In return, Durand kept Jonathan apprised of his activities and travels. One of Durand's first letters from London was typical of many he wrote to Jonathan describing his travels and observations, and his comparison of current standards in America to painting quality and technique of the Old Masters. In June 1840, Durand raved about a Claude Lorrain (aka Claude) painting. "*Seaport with Embarkation of St. Ursula* [c.1641],...realizes my expectations. The water is exceedingly fine, the trees on the right beautiful and true, the distant architecture and the vessels absorb the morning light...the foreground architecture is not all I'd wish."[27] About London's Royal Academy he wrote:

> The majority of portraits are not much better than our own, and the few that are superior are far below what I would conceive to be the standard of elevated portraiture...and in landscape...the general aim seems to be the attainment of brilliant and striking effects, in light & dark and color, the calm and quiet loneliness of nature, rich without crudeness and brilliance without glare, subdued and modest aspect, attractive without dazzling, impressive but not startling.[28]

A.B. Durand—(left) *Jonathan Sturges,* c. 1840[29] *Amelia and Edward Sturges* c. 1840[30]

Durand traveled from London to Paris, Belgium, Holland, Germany, Switzerland, Naples, Florence, and Rome. For part of this trip he traveled in the company of fellow artists Thomas Prichard Rossiter, John Casilear, and John Kensett. In Paris, Durand painted a copy of Gabriel Metsu's *Soldier Visiting a Young Woman* which Jonathan obtained after Durand returned.[31] Durand was in awe of Switzerland's beauty, and in October 1840 he wrote, "...if you see our dear friend Cole tell him to sell what he has, to mortgage his estate, like Don Quixote, collect together all his substance, and with his beloved wife and children, set off for once for Switzerland....could any possible circumstances produce a willingness to repatriate myself...Switzerland would be the place."[32] While there, Durand painted the landscape *Cottage on the Lake of Thun, Switzerland* for Jonathan.[33] He left Europe the end of June 1841, returning to the United States in July with renewed energy and inspiration, and produced many paintings, primarily in the portrait and landscape genre, including paintings of Jonathan and his family. The 1840 portrait of Jonathan's children, Amelia (b.1835) and Edward (b.1837) was a gift to Jonathan in appreciation for sponsoring his trip.[f]

In 1837, in one of his early commissions, Jonathan engaged Thomas Cole to paint a landscape of the Hudson Valley and Catskill Mountains area. He expressed his vision to Cole, "I shall be happy to possess a picture showing what

---

[f] In 2014 the painting resided in the Director's office of the Pierpont Morgan Library and Museum in New York.

the Valley of the Catskill was before the art of 'modern improvement' found a footing here. I think of it often and can imagine what your feelings are when you see the beauties of nature swept away by avarice. We are truly a destructive people."[34] This painting was the landscape *View on the Catskill—Early Autumn*,[g] capturing the raw beauty of the Catskills, before railroad construction marred the landscape.

Thomas Cole, *View on the Catskill—Early Autumn*, c. 1837[35]

The Apollo Association for the Promotion of the Fine Arts in the United States was incorporated in New York in May 1840. Its goal was the cultivation and diffusion of fine arts appreciation, and the encouragement, promotion, and development of native artists.[36] The Apollo immediately overextended itself by running costly art shows and funding a permanent art gallery. In 1841, the board brought in Jonathan Sturges, Charles Leupp and William C. Bryant as managers, where upon they eliminated the costly overhead, improved their financial footing, increased subscriptions, and righted the ship.[37]

Apollo subscribers paid five dollars a year and received free admission to exhibitions throughout the year. In 1843, Jonathan lent his copy of William Sydney Mount's *Farmer's Nooning* to engrave and provide copies for subscribers.[38]

---

[g] Now at the Metropolitan Museum of Art in New York City.

Farmers Nooning is one of Mount's most acclaimed works. An art historian noted that his depiction of African-Americans, "is rendered in a detailed, naturalistic manner, in vivid contrast to the racist caricature of African-Americans found in many genre paintings."[39] Jonathan purchased this 20" by 24" size painting from Mount for $270 in 1836.

W.S. Mount, *Farmers Nooning,* c. 1836[40]

In December 1843, the Apollo Association took on a more national approach and the name changed to the American Art-Union for the Promotion of Fine Arts in the United States. Jonathan served on the Board of Management from 1843-1846.[41] The board featured many of the men that were forefront in the arts community in New York City which, besides Jonathan and Bryant, included Francis Edmonds, Prosper Wetmore, Charles Leupp, William Hoppin, Benjamin Winthrop, Marshall Roberts, Richard Demilli and George Allen.[42] Their management efforts were a success and, "In 1849, the best year of the Art-Union,[h] there were 18,960 subscribers, and the receipts were $96,300."[43] However, after Jonathan's departure, because of poor management, problems with a lottery they had relied on to bring in funds, and a waning interest in the general concept of an Art Union, it dissolved in 1852.

Jonathan's partnership of Sturges, Roe and Barker dissolved on February 1, 1841. Reed's nephew George Barker[i] left the firm. Jonathan's nephew, Josiah Bennet, a clerk in the firm, became a partner; Benjamin Arnold became

---

[h] George Barker wrote a lengthy "Reminiscence" on the life of Luman Reed and the Reed and Sturges merchant firm. Although overloaded with prose and flowery commentary, it provides an important insight into Reed's life.

head bookkeeper; and the firm became Sturges, Roe and Co.[44] Then just a year later, Roe withdrew from the firm and Benjamin Arnold rose to partner, the company becoming Sturges, Bennet & Co.[45]

Jonathan resigned his directorship with the Bank of Commerce in 1843,[46] a significant position to vacate, but with his many business and philanthropic causes it also gave him more time to take on an emerging challenge to save his mentor's legacy. Seven years after Reed's death, the Reed family still owned his home on Greenwich Street with its extraordinary gallery of collectible art. However, in February 1843, the family put the house up for sale. The advertisement read: "The lot is 30 feet front and rear, and 100 feet deep...is unsurpassed, if equaled, by any in the city, in the substantial character of its construction...It is finished with the heating apparatus, gas, and water fixtures bathing room, etc."[47] The house languished on the market, probably due to the changing demographic of the neighborhood. One year later, the house was scheduled to be auctioned on February 11, and the art, shells, and mineral collection were to be sold separately.[48] The home sold to Amos Eno, a dry-goods merchant, for $20,000. Jonathan had assumed the family would keep Reed's collection, so the intention to sell announced in the same advertisement was a surprise. Reed was an important mentor and friend and Jonathan later reminisced about the unique atmosphere created at Reed's home, "What a mingling there was of artists such as Morse, Cole, Weir, Inman, Durant, etc. with literary men such as J. Fenimore Cooper, Washington Irving and Bryant, and I cannot imagine anything better calculated to fire the genius of young artists than such gatherings."[49]

Due to a void of art museums in the United States for collectors to donate their art, collections such as Reed's were more likely to be auctioned or sold piecemeal rather than donated to a museum. Not wanting to see Reed's discerning collection cast to the winds, Jonathan and Reed's son-in-law, Theodore Allen, gathered like-minded artists and patrons and set out to buy and preserve the collection intact.[50] The lofty goal was to purchase the lot and establish a public art gallery, supported by yearly subscription and daily admission. The *Evening Post* heralded the gallery initiative as important to proliferate public art education and declared, "We hope it will be prosecuted with zeal...and that it will meet with success."[51]

On March 11, 1844, the New York Gallery of Fine Arts Association held its first meeting. There were fifty gentlemen named to the initial board of directors. The officers included Jonathan Sturges (President), Francis W. Edmonds, William H. Johnson and Thomas H. Faile. The Reed family wanted $15,000 for the collection, which comprised two hundred and fifty paintings, engravings, sculptures, and an array of shells and minerals. Jonathan negotiated a price of $13,000, and Reed's precious assemblage of art items was secured.

To minimize startup costs, the association received permission for rent-free use of the City Hall Rotunda when it was not in use by the city. They installed the exhibit and sold subscriptions for a dollar a year, or twenty-five cents per visit. The board sought the support of the press to endorse and promote their cause. They met with James Bennett, the editor of the respected *New York Herald*, and after seeing the names of the officers he said: "Why, these people know more about pork and molasses than they do about art!"[52] Although he endorsed the idea, it was a prophetic observation, as the board's enthusiasm outweighed their ability to make it a viable enterprise. They had counted on ten thousand low-cost life memberships but struggled to sell and give away even one thousand under this model. The interest of the trustees waned as subscriptions and attendance failed to finance the operation. In 1848, they were forced out of the rotunda by the city and the National Academy of Design took custody of the collection—Jonathan's initiative for a stand-alone public art museum at an end, for now. However, his energies and leadership in promoting fine arts were turned to the creation of an important fine arts association.

In 1847, Jonathan became a founding member of The Century Association, along with forty-five friends and associates, including Asher B. Durand, Charles Leupp, William Cullen Bryant, A.M. Cozzens, and Rev. Henry Bellows.[53] Unlike most of the other fine arts associations, it was as much about the social interaction between patrons, enthusiasts, artists, and authors as it was about the promotion of arts and letters. It evolved from the old Sketch Club, and then merged with the Column Club, a Columbia College Alumni Association. Today the club describes its founding:

> One hundred gentlemen engaged or interested in letters and the fine arts had been invited to join in forming the Association. Forty-two accepted the invitation and became founders; forty-six others joined during the first year…Membership has always been made up of writers, artists, and amateurs of the fine arts. The Century Association has been prominent in the community of creative artists in New York since its inception.[54]

Jonathan was a lifelong member, and the respect accorded him was highlighted by Joseph Choate, a club president:

From the beginning, moreover, the Club struck the right mean between dignity and jollity; it was an association of gentlemen who knew how to unbend ...Youngsters like William M. Evarts, Donald Grant Mitchell and Bayard Taylor sat at the feet of such talkative sages as Bryant, Verplank, John H. Gourlie and Jonathan Sturges. It was the beginning of a liberal education to be thrown among such men.[55]

Over its existence, The Century Association has claimed as members eight U.S. Presidents, eight unsuccessful candidates for president, ten Supreme Court Justices, forty-eight cabinet members, and a host of wealthy businessmen and other distinguished citizens. The club's emphasis on promoting and studying the arts was a core value of the entire Sturges family, and Jonathan and his children were champions and aficionados of the arts throughout their lives.

SIX

Building the Infrastructure and
Reaping the Resources of America

The stock is all taken for the railroad and now Father will be obliged to build it.

—*Virginia Sturges*

Jonathan's star was on the rise. He was becoming a national household name, foremost a man of commerce, philanthropy and unquestioned integrity. Jonathan and Luman Reed had weathered the cholera epidemic of 1832, the Great Fire of 1835, and then after Reed's death, the hard times brought on by disruptive monetary policies in the late 1830s and early 1840s. As a nationally prominent businessman, and one well-known to Daniel Webster, in 1842 he was one of a distinguished group of men invited to attend a dinner hosted by Secretary of State Daniel Webster, in honor of Lord Ashburton, the British negotiator of the Webster-Ashburton Treaty. This treaty resolved lingering border issues with Great Britain, formalizing Oregon and Washington as U.S. territories, and was one of the few accomplishments of the Tyler administration.

Continuing to prosper, Jonathan's estimated wealth in 1842 was $150,000.[1a] By 1846, that number had grown to over $200,000 and he was well-positioned to invest his growing capital in an emerging business opportunity.[2] Having established himself in the banking business, the next industry which he embraced was coal mining. The Big Vein coal deposit was discovered in Western Maryland in the early 1800s but had remained relatively untapped, as there was no efficient means to bring it to market. That changed when the B&O Railroad built a line to service the area in 1842, and several companies formed to mine the coal. New York businessmen had their fingerprints all over these ventures. Jonathan, with

---

a About $4.5 million in 2018 dollars.

fellow incorporators Robert B. Minturn,[b] Barrett Ames, Charles Denison, and Oroondates Mauran, took this opportunity to profit from the nation's natural resources.

Jonathan and his partners retained Samuel Semmes,[c] a well-connected Baltimore lawyer, as their corporation counsel—a man who had significant experience in drafting mining company charters. Semmes filed the papers in 1844, and the Maryland Legislature authorized the charter the same year.[d] Up to $1,000,000 in stock could be sold "for the purpose of purchasing, opening and working mines of coal and iron, and for the manufacture of iron, and of all articles of which iron is a component part, and for the vending of the products of the same."[3]

The New York Mining Company owned mines in Jennings Run, near Frostburg, Maryland. Their main mine was Union Mine #2 and they were affiliated with the large Union Mining Company, which was working the sister mine, Union Mine #1.[4] The company remained in existence until at least the early 1900s. It is unclear how long Jonathan remained on the board, but he still owned 678 shares of stock in 1874.

Next, Jonathan turned his attention to an emerging and capital intensive industry. As a young merchant, he had experienced firsthand the impact that the Erie Canal transportation network had on the commerce of New York and the Western region of the United States. The railroad was the next big evolution in national commerce and the growing infrastructure of the country, and certain projects in greater New York City led to his direct involvement.

"Railroads" in New York City at this time primarily referred to horse drawn conveyances.[5] In 1830, only twenty-seven miles of railroad track were laid in the United States. Steam engine powered railroad companies opened on short stretches of track to support parochial transportation needs. The New York and Harlem Railroad formed in 1831 with the authorization to construct and operate on single or double railroad tracks from any point on the northern boundaries of Twenty-Third Street [considered the northern point of New York City], to any point on the Harlem River by horse and/or mechanical power.[6]

---

[b] Robert Minturn was the first President of the Union League in 1863.

[c] Semmes was a Maryland State Senator from 1855-1866 and was the brother of Raphael Semmes, a future Confederate Naval Admiral who commanded the infamous raider ship ship C.S.S. Alabama.

[d] An Act to Incorporate the New York Mining Company passed at December Session, 1844, Chapter 220.

Much of the land in Manhattan was rural above Twenty-Third Street. The original limited vision of the thirteen incorporators of the New York and Harlem Railroad (NY&H) was to install powered rail transportation from Manhattan to the upper part of the city and the suburbs in Harlem, where the population was spreading. By 1837, the NY&H had built north to Harlem, and by 1839, south along the Bowery, Broome, and Centre Streets to City Hall. In a history of the NY&H, they noted, "[by] 1841 the railroad had six wood-burning locomotives and 240 horses to pull passenger trains."[7] Between 1840 and 1841, the legislature granted them the right to extend their tracks first to the Williamsburg Bridge, then to White Plains in 1844. Only sixty horses were still in use pulling NY&H cars by 1844. The NY&H's chartered right to bring trains into New York from the north or to connect to the city from Connecticut put them in the position to be a critical partner for any railroad company wanting to connect to New York City.

New York and Harlem Railroad Streetcar 1850s[8]

Credited with the early vision and drive for a New York to New Haven Railroad were Joseph E. Sheffield, Judge Samuel Hitchcock, Henry Farnum and Alfred D. Bishop. Sheffield was the early financial backer and fundraiser, Hitchcock spearheaded the charter, Farnum led the engineering, and Bishop, construction. One of the first public meetings held to attract investors for the railroad was in Boston, at the United States Hotel on April 10, 1844. The *Boston Evening Gazette* trumpeted the vision of a ten-hour train trip from New York to Boston, and a new artery of commerce not vulnerable to the maritime attacks and disruption of trade suffered during the War of 1812.

Civil engineer Alexander Twining completed the original survey for the line between 1835-1837, a survey funded by Sheffield. It confirmed the feasibility of the projected route, but Commodore Cornelius Vanderbilt, who was providing much of the maritime transportation needs, including having mail con-

tracts in the area, lobbied against it. However, the compelling vision and undeniable benefits of such a line prevailed, and in May 1844, the Connecticut
Legislature approved the charter. It required the nine incorporators[c] to raise
the required capital, spend $100,000 within two years, and complete the rail-
road within four years. Jonathan was not an original incorporator, however
Jonathan and Morris Ketchum became investors when Sheffield sold 12,000
of his shares in 1845.[d] Then one of the original directors, F.R. Griffin, resigned soon after his election and the board appointed Jonathan to his position.[9]

Those with country homes along the Connecticut coast eagerly anticipated the convenience of the proposed rail connection, such as the families
of Jonathan Sturges and Morris Ketchum of Westport. On January 3, 1846,
Virginia Sturges wrote to her Aunt Lucretia in Fairfield, happily looking
forward to more frequent visits:

> The stock is all taken for the railroad and now Father will be obliged to
> build it. Father says it will be done by a year from the coming spring, and
> then you will not have a chance to be lonely, we shall come up so often I
> expect the post office will not receive quite as many letters as it does
> now, for we shall come up once a week and say all we have to say![10]

The entire stock allotment sold by January 1846 but to connect with
New York City, the railroad still needed permission from the New York Legislature to enter the state. In May 1846, the legislature granted the New York
and New Haven Railroad (NY&NH) the all-important authorization to build
through the New York border and connect with the New York and Harlem
Railroad at the Williamsburg Bridge, the west end of the line.[11] Early in the
enterprise they had sought the independent right to build their own tracks
into the city, but the NY&H lobbied hard against it and was successful in
blocking that initiative. Jonathan and other key shareholders recruited Robert
Schuyler to be the railroad's first president in 1846. He was an engineer and
financier whose reputation and integrity were in high regard, qualities
considered critical to raising the required capital. Construction began later
that year, contracting with Alfred Bishop, G.L. Schuyler, and Sydney Miller of
New Haven. Early in the process, G. L. Schuyler transferred his interest to Bish-

---

[c] The original board of Directors were Robert Schuyler, Anson Phelps, Elihu Townsend, Morris
  Ketchum Henry J. Sanford, William P. Burrall, Stephen Tomlinson, Joseph Sheffield, F.R. Griffin
[d] The incorporators were Joseph Sheffield, Samuel Hitchcock, William A. Reynolds, Nathan
  Smith, P.P.F. DeGrand, S.S. Littlehall, Elihu Townsend, and Anson G. Phelps.

op. Bishop died soon after construction began, but progress continued without delay under Sydney Miller's direction.[e]

Although not on plan to complete by spring 1847, the railroad was making impressive headway and by March 1847, they were contracting to build the last forty miles of track. Progress was not without its challenges, however. In August 1847, a labor shortage threatened progress and the railroad was advertising to hire one thousand laborers at 87½ cents per day, a top wage for unskilled laborers.[12] In June 1848, an accidental explosion in a quarry of rocks along the construction line near Norwalk occurred, killing a laborer—"literally tearing him to pieces"—and seriously injuring two others.[13] Then, a major contractor walked off the job without paying his creditors. Their luck finally took a fortuitous turn in 1848, when they hired Roswell Mason of Bridgeport, Connecticut, as the railroad's Chief Engineer, and the railroad marched to completion.

When the Harlem's president Charles Parshall resigned in April 1848, the board elected Schuyler president, Jonathan vice president, and Morris Ketchum treasurer.[f] This change in the Harlem Railroad board of directors created the synergy to coordinate and smooth the way, both politically and operationally, between the two railroads. As a result, in 1848 the two railroads agreed on fees to enable the New Haven line to connect to the NY&H tracks that approached the border at Dover Plains, NY, leading to its Grand Central Depot in the City. It was a financially advantageous arrangement for the NY&H. The *New York Spectator* applauded the agreement in July 1848 and proclaimed: "It is estimated that the New York and New Haven road will bring to the city from 2,000 to 2,500 passengers daily, the first three months after it opens, and that it will increase before the expiration of the year to nearly double that number."[14]

It is hard for us to comprehend the trail that had to be blazed to construct a new railroad in the 1840s, within the primitive infrastructure of the day. Understanding and incorporating the latest technology, maneuvering through the political waters, obtaining the land and rights of way, building numerous bridges, getting the labor, much less securing the significant capital required, was a gauntlet through which only the most capable businessmen could navigate. Jonathan and his fellow board members

---

[e] Alfred's son William Darius Bishop was prominent in the railroad's success as its president in the 1860s.
[f] Other Directors elected in April 1848 were Richard M. Blatchford, Samuel Jauden and George Barker; elected to the board in May 1849 were William S. Wetmore, Philip Dater, Edward Bement Bement, Gov. Morris, T.W. Ludlow, Charles Denison and Isaac Haviland.

were some of those visionaries who prevailed, surmounting the adversarial conditions, and providing a coastal railroad route through Connecticut.

On December 29, 1848, the New York and New Haven Railroad opened on one track. It suffered low ridership for several months in 1849, due to a cholera epidemic in New York City—even worse than the one in 1832. However, ridership picked up, the needs outgrew its single track, and construction began on a second track by 1851. They started with five locomotives in 1848, grew to eleven in 1849, twenty-five by 1853 and fifty-four by 1856.[15] In eastern Connecticut, in May 1848, the New Haven and New London Railroad had received their charter from the legislature as anticipated, which allowed for the fulfillment of the vision of a rail connection between New York City and Boston.

After Jonathan's involvement and success in establishing the New York and New Haven Railroad, his reputation was solidified as a proven railroad executive. As a result, he was in demand to take part in other railroad ventures. In 1847, Jonathan was an early promoter of a railroad to parallel the Hudson River, but he did not become an active manager or board member of the enterprise.[16] He also discontinued his directorship with the Harlem Railroad in 1850, probably to concentrate on another major railroad startup in Illinois in 1851. He jumped into that undertaking along with an impressive board of incorporators and company executives, including the corporate attorney they had on retainer, an up-and-coming lawyer from Springfield, Illinois—by the name of Abraham Lincoln.

SEVEN

Be Charitable

[I must] Identify myself with all the interests of the community

—*Rules for the Christian Merchant*

In 1850, the Northeast was the regional hub for finance, with 26% of all national bank deposits in the State of New York, 18% in Massachusetts, and another 5% in Connecticut. In 1843, Jonathan resigned from the board of directors of the Bank of Commerce but re-entered the banking business in 1847, when he joined with some of his trusted colleagues to create the mid-size Citizen's Bank, where he served as a director.[1]

The explosion of wealth and capital in New York City created many jobs in and out of the city and drew thousands of job seekers to the area. As a result, the population of New York more than tripled from 166,000, when the Erie Canal opened in 1825, to 515,000 in 1850. These job-seeking immigrants, primarily from Europe and of African descent, many of whom had escaped enslavement, became crowded into dense, impoverished living conditions. In the antebellum period of America, there were no government safety nets or national charities and few, if any, locally established charitable organizations. Men of means and connections filled this void by leading and supporting occasional ad hoc efforts to assist with the basic needs for food, shelter, and healthcare for the burgeoning low-income populace.

One of the twenty-nine "rules" for the Christian merchant was to "identify myself with all the interests of the community."[2] In Jonathan's life he became involved with many benevolent groups and organizations. The genesis of each one of them had a similar path, which would start with a few individuals agreeing on a worthy object of their attentions, then these men recruited others, held a public meeting, and soon they had active support, financing, and an organizational structure for the endeavor.

An early avenue where he focused his benevolence was in establishing an enduring charitable body called the New York Association for Improving the Condition of the Poor. Organized in 1843, its goal was the "...elevation of the physical and moral condition of the indigent, and, so far as is compatible with these objects, the relief of their necessities."[3] This was one of the first large-scale social welfare organizations and Jonathan was an original board member and a primary financial manager. Fellow board members were his iconic merchant colleagues George Griswold, James Brown, John C. Green, and Robert Minturn,[4] of whom a nineteenth century New York historian commented, "all men of responsibility and high position, who commanded the confidence of the entire community."[5] In an era where government aid to the poor was virtually non-existent and unexpected, these organizations were key in establishing the premise that such safety nets were critical humanitarian efforts.

The Association divided up the city in towards, and there were four delegates assigned to each district who visited homes where aid was recommended or requested. The approach was to help the "deserving poor," not those who they deemed impoverished due to their own laziness, drunkenness, or other morality issues or bad choices. Although the charter of the organization assumed that each client was needy until proven otherwise, this could be a subjective judgment. With some delegates, a house that was too clean could give the impression that the family had the ability to work. A household that was unkempt, dirty, or had an inebriated parent could produce a verdict of "undeserving." The Association grew in its reach, and tens of thousands of people in New York City received aid each year. Jonathan was a financial member of the board for thirty years, and the organization set a high standard for efficacy of charitable endeavors.[a]

Jonathan's outreach also extended to international humanitarian crises— examples of how ad hoc charitable bodies formed and disbanded to address an emerging need. In 1847, it was the Great Irish Famine—a widespread starvation due to the failure of potato crops in Ireland. The Irish made up about half of all immigrants to the United States in the 1840s. A Central Relief Committee for the Aid to Ireland formed, both in Dublin and in New York City, backed by the merchants of New York. In February 1847, Jonathan and the standing committee, which included August Belmont (the legendary

---

a The Association continued its good work until 1939, when it merged with the Charity Organization Society to become the Community Services Society of New York that still exists today, to help low-income families to get back on their feet."

Rothschild banker), William Backhouse Astor, Sr. (son of John Jacob Astor), William Havemeyer (former NYC mayor), and merchants Moses Grinnell and Robert Minturn, met and facilitated a large offering for those suffering, including significant foodstuffs and monetary donations.[6]

Also, responding to the plight of the oppressed people in Hungary, Jonathan and Mary were active in their support of Lajos Kossuth, leader of the revolution that took place between 1848 and 1849. When no help emanated from the West, Russia came in on the side of Austria and the rebellion collapsed. Kossuth fled first to England and then to the United States. Queen Victoria was opposed to Kossuth's presence in Great Britain, however, America embraced him. He met with President Fillmore twice and addressed a joint session of Congress—only the second foreign dignitary ever to do so.[b]

Kossuth came to New York's Tripler Hall in December 1851 with great fanfare and gave a speech highlighting the Hungarian struggle for liberty and self-determination. The "elite ladies of New York" and their husbands, including Mary and Jonathan Sturges, hosted the meeting, and Jonathan's office served as the ticket location—"$5 for the parqueted and first circle and $2 each for the upper gallery."[7] These old New York merchants and their wives perceived Hungary's fight to break from the Austrian Empire to be akin to the American Revolution fought by their grandfathers and were particularly sympathetic.

Domestically, Jonathan turned his compassion to helping Mexican War veterans. In 1844, President Tyler, trying to bolster his chances for re-election and add a slave state to the Union, secretly negotiated an annexation treaty with Texas. It did not help him get re-elected; however, the legislation adding Texas as a state passed both houses and Tyler signed it on March 1, 1845, just days before he left office. Texas ratified the agreement, and President Polk signed it, annexing it in December 1845. However, Texas southern border disputes with Mexico simmered. Mexico claimed land to the Nuances river about 150 miles north of the Rio Grande River. In April 1846, Polk sent troops to the territory to enforce and maintain the border at the Rio Grande and Congress declared war in May.

To bolster military readiness efforts, the state of New York began enforcing the existing compulsory militia service requirements a few years prior to the start of the war, by either ensuring attendance at the annual required mus-

---

b The first was the Marquis de Lafayette.

ter or collecting fines. Jonathan was fined in years 1843, 1844, and 1845 for not reporting for muster with his assigned unit, the Second Regiment New York Artillery Unit.[8] In 1846, the state abolished compulsory service, although war with Mexico continued until the fall of 1847.

The Treaty of Hidalgo, in February 1848, brought an official close to the war. However, the soldiers returned after their long absence with little to no funds, no means of support, and many having suffered physical and mental maladies during their service. Observing their plight, Jonathan was raised into action. The *Spectator* (New York) highlighted his appointment to a committee to relieve the suffering of returning veterans, "The committee appointed under this resolution was, Ex-Mayor Mickle, Mayor Havemeyer, Jonathan Sturges, Esq. and the Hon. J. Phillips Phoenix."[9] Donations were generous, and many men received aid to begin a new life. Jonathan's participation in the cause for veterans' relief and the Irish famine were some of the earliest associations which seeded a lifelong friendship between Mayor Havemeyer and Jonathan—a friendship which would be on Havemeyer's mind at his death in 1874.

About a week after the end of the war, Jonathan's close friend and noted artist Thomas Cole passed away, just after his 47th birthday, with his son, Thomas Cole, Jr., still in his wife's womb. At Cole's memorial service, William Cullen Bryant delivered a moving eulogy that illuminated their mutual admiration and close friendship. Cole and Bryant were in that intimate circle of artists, fine arts aficionados, and promoters in New York City that created and fueled the early advancements in American art. The associations that they and their colleagues created such as the Sketch Club and National Academy of Design were the engines that drove the advancement of a generation of native artists, particularly the Hudson River School. Bryant and Cole also shared a love of the Catskills area of New York, and Bryant's eulogy so moved Jonathan, he commissioned Asher B. Durand to create a painting to memorialize their close relationship and as a gift to Bryant. As the Metropolitan Museum of Art says: "Invoking a phrase from John Keats's seventh sonnet,'O Solitude,' Jonathan asked Durand to portray the two men as 'kindred spirits' in the landscape."[10] The result was the masterpiece painting *Kindred Spirits*. Mrs. Bryant described the delivery of the painting:

> On the first of March, as William and myself were sitting by the fire reading, two young men came tugging in a large picture which was covered with cloth. William turned his head over his shoulder and said,

"You have made a mistake." They still advanced and he raised his voice saying, "You are mistaken, I have ordered no picture." One says, "This is Wm. Bryant's?" Yes, then I started, and raised the cloth, and what should I find but a beautiful landscape…In short, it is a beautiful picture, and I do not know how to describe it. The canvas, is about four feet wide and five long, set in a magnificent frame.[11]

Jonathan included this note to Bryant with the painting:

My Dear Sir,

Soon after you delivered your oration on our lamented friend Cole, I requested Mr. Durand paint a picture in which he should associate our departed friend and you as kindred spirits. I think the design as well as the execution will meet your approbation and I hope you will accept the picture from me as a token of gratitude of a labor of love performed on that occasion.

Very Truly Yours, Jon. Sturges[12]

Bryant replied to Jonathan with heartfelt thanks: "I was quite overcome this morning at the appearance of the beautiful picture you sent me as a present. You have had the skill to heighten the value tenfold by the occasion and manner of making it. The artist it seems to me has produced one of his best things and this is saying everything. I should be most proud to possess it."[13] *Kindred Spirits* was arguably Durand's most acclaimed work and one of the most renowned paintings of the Hudson River School. The painting represented the great strides made to develop American artistry, especially American landscape painting—truly a New York treasure. When Bryant passed away, ownership of *Kindred Spirits* fell to Bryant's daughter Julia, who in 1905 donated the painting to the New York Public Library, where his papers were archived.

One hundred years later in 2005, on the anniversary of its acceptance, the library Board of Directors decided that *Kindred Spirits* was not core to their mission and planned to sell it to make other acquisitions. Sotheby's scheduled an auction, but soon after the announcement the sale abruptly changed to a sealed bid to be submitted in one month's time. Initially, the New York Public Library indicated they would give a non-profit organization preferential staggered payment terms, but then switched course and declared that full payment would be due in one year. The Boards of the Metropolitan Museum of Art and the National Gallery of Art, both natural homes for this national treasure, tried to put together a joint offer to buy the painting but could not produce the required minimum bid of $25,000,000 within the short time allotted.

A.B. Durand, *Kindred Spirits*, c. 1849[14] (left); Henry K. Brown, *Thomas Cole*, c. 1848[15]

Unfortunately for New York, the Met, and the National Gallery, the Walmart heiress, Alice B. Walton reportedly bid $35,000,000 for the painting and went on display at the Crystal Bridges Museum in Bentonville, Arkansas. The museum editorializes that, "The friendship between Cole, Bryant, Durand, and the merchant Jonathan Sturges, who commissioned the painting, suggests the shared interest in nature among artists, writers, and businessmen in antebellum New York—the *Kindred Spirits* of the title."[16] Having also felt the loss of Cole in his life, Jonathan commissioned a bust of Cole with Henry Kirke Brown for his own collection, which he displayed proudly in his parlor.

In 1849, Jonathan was prevailed upon by the artist community to intervene on behalf of the financially troubled National Academy of Design. The lease on their clubhouse was ending, and to establish more permanency they had purchased a lot and begun construction on a building for their own unique use. However, the project was poorly managed and construction funds were depleted before the structure was finished. The committee resigned, and honorary members Jonathan Sturges and Charles Leupp were brought in as trustees to raise the required funds and complete the building. Their careful management put the Academy on a good financial footing and ushered the building to completion. However, the membership revenue they had budgeted did not materialize, as they were competing with the Art Union for members and attention, an organization also suffering from a lack of membership. Jonathan and Leupp began leasing out their exhibition space, and within a few years rental fees were paying the expenses.

Active in the promotion of the painting genre of fine arts he also valued the literary arts per Rule for the Christian Merchant #18 which says, "I must feel the necessity of constantly improving in knowledge and piety." In 1848-1849 Jonathan was a trustee of the New York Society Library which dated to 1754, one of the first library associations in the United States.[17] Then, in 1850, Jonathan launched the New York Athenaeum, an education initiative, promoting a public gathering place to peruse classic literature, educational publications and to become enlightened on the technological advancements and societal issues of the day. The *Evening Post* endorsed the undertaking: "A great want that has for so long felt to exist, of some institution to which merchants, citizens and foreign residents might have access for the purpose of reading scientific, literary and political journals of Europe, as well as those of the United States..."[18]

An earlier effort, twenty-six years before, had lasted about fourteen years, but with the recent success of the London Athenaeum, Jonathan felt it might have a better chance of succeeding. To avoid the incorporation process, they assumed the uncancelled charter of the original organization.[c] In April 1850, subscriptions were solicited at $12 per year to revive the institution. Modeled after the popular London club, it operated in the same building as the National Academy of Design and the New York Gallery of Fine Arts, both of which Jonathan managed. His vision included the cross-purpose of bringing in more traffic for gallery exhibitions. They published the *Athenaeum: Journal of Literature, Science, the Fine Arts and Drama* and the Athenaeum operated until 1869.

By mid-century, Jonathan was a merchant with more than a quarter century standing. He had led his firm since 1836 and was continuing to rise in affluence and in reputation on many business and philanthropic fronts. He now had the luxury to enjoy the fruits of his labor, experience the marvels of the era, travel, and once again move uptown.

---

[c] Washington Irving, J. Fenimore Cooper, and William Gracie, among others, established the earlier New York Athenaeum in 1824. It operated until 1838, when its assets were transferred to the New York Society Library, together with its real estate on the corner of Broadway and Leonard Street for the consideration of 318 shares of the library for its members.

EIGHT

Travel and Family Life Mid-Century— Jenny Lind and Tom Thumb

I shall always feel that the singing of Jenny Lind was one of the great treats
of my life.

—*Mary Cady Sturges*

In 1846, Mary was pregnant and staying in Fairfield for her confinement
while building an addition to the Cottage. Henry Cady was born May
31. She wrote in her *Reminiscences*: "I had my same old nurse, and all
went well. It seemed a little strange to take up the routine of a baby
again, and we found we needed more room. It was at this time that the
old nursery and bedroom adjoining were added," the first addition to the
Cottage.[1] Lucretia Sturges and Elizabeth Cady were there to help. In
December 1846, Elizabeth, who had been living at the New York City
home, married Hamilton Murray and left to embark on her new life.

In 1850, the Sturges family had six children: Virginia Reed (b.1830),
Frederick (b.1833), Amelia (b.1835), Edward (b.1837), Arthur Pemberton
(b.1841) and Henry Cady (b.1846). The Sturges family had an established
family routine; they lived nine months of the year in New York and sum-
mered in Fairfield. Virginia was a young lady in society and Frederick was
just getting involved in his father's business. Amelia, Edward, and Arthur
were all in boarding school, and Henry was a small child at home. Jonathan's brother Lothrop had made a great success of his shipping business
Sturges and Clearman, and he owned a shipyard in the Black Rock
section of Bridgeport, Connecticut. Lothrop also maintained a summer
home in Fairfield and Mrs. Lothrop (Jane) Sturges and her sister Mrs.
George Clearman were often seen at church in Fairfield when they were
in town.[2] Jonathan had jointly invested with Lothrop, George Clearman,

and two others, to build a ship in Swansea, Massachusetts, called *Reform* which was sold immediately after its launching in 1840.[3]

During the early winter of 1850, Jonathan lost his sister Mary Ann Lockwood. She left behind three adult boys between the ages of 25 and 31. In 1827, her husband, William, had preceded her in death from consumption. Within four years of Mary Ann's death, two of her three sons died from the same malady. The Sturges and Lockwood families had been close throughout their lives. One of Mary Ann's sons George, worked in Jonathan's firm, and George's wife Kate was a frequent correspondent with Virginia.

Over the winter of 1849-1850, Jonathan contracted a bad cough and had not improved by the spring. The doctor recommended a sea voyage South. Due to the changing demographic of their neighborhood to multi-family units, they put their Murray Street house up for sale and, becoming one of the early snowbirds, boarded a ship to Charleston. Mary wrote, "I think his cough left him when we were two days out. We left New York on Saturday, April 12th, leaving freezing weather behind us, and having rather a rough passage of three days. We came into Charleston on Tuesday morning to find the trees showing their tender green, the early shrubs and flowers in bloom, and the birds singing their joyous spring songs."[4]

In a historical coincidence, Jonathan and Mary arrived in Charleston as it was engrossed in the funeral arrangements for the fiery southern orator, Senator John C. Calhoun, who had died of tuberculosis, on March 31, 1850, in Washington, D.C. After three terms in the House of Representatives, Calhoun became Secretary of War in 1817. He further served two terms as vice president under both John Q. Adams and Andrew Jackson before becoming Secretary of State in 1844 and then returning to the Senate for South Carolina. While vice president, he penned the manifesto that spurred the "nullification crisis" in 1828.[a] Calhoun had seen the increasing population of the North and the following imbalance in the House of Representatives as a threat to the South's commerce and way of life. A staunch defender of slavery, he fought for years to ensure its continued existence, and to his last breath, pushed passage of the Fugitive Slave Law,[b] which was adopted after his death.

---

a The nullification crisis occurred when South Carolina threatened to nullify the Tariff Laws 1828 and to further secede from the Union if the federal government attempted to enforce it.

b The Fugitive Slave Law required all states and territories to allow the recovery and return of runaway slaves to their owners and empowered federal marshals to aid in the effort.

Calhoun's body arrived in Charleston on the steamer *Nina*, accompanied by several distinguished men from Washington including six U.S. Senators, among them Jefferson Davis of Mississippi, and several congressmen. His funeral procession to City Hall was extravagant, resembling that of a head of state. The mayor declared a day of mourning in Charleston on April 25 and hosted Jonathan and Mary at a lavish reception he held for visiting congressmen and luminaries. The next morning Calhoun's body was again accompanied by a procession of dignitaries and citizens and laid to rest at St. Philip's Church cemetery.

From Charleston, Mary and Jonathan departed for Augusta, Georgia, by railroad. They visited with their friends, the Gould and Adams families. The Adams and Gould daughters were friends of Virginia and Amelia and had visited the Sturges home when they attended school in New York. Now married, they had become Mrs. George MacWhorter (Ms.Adams) and Mrs. Bulkley (Ms. Gould). Later there would be a more intimate connection of the Sturges, Adams and MacWhorter family by marriage.[c] They departed Augusta via steamboat on the Savannah River, and Mary remembered the journey nostalgically:

> Travelers, who go by rail these days, have little idea of the romance of a sail down the Savannah River at that period, the beautiful winding river, bordered by trees, mingling their greenness with the long, gray moss; no one ever hurried in the South. The stops were made at the plantations, where bales of cotton were put on board by the slaves, having one or two overseers. This was done at night in some cases, the woods lighted by the glare of pine knots, and the black slaves running to and fro shouting, gave a most weird aspect to the whole thing.[5]

In Savannah, they visited with Jonathan's cousins, the Sturges and Hunter families. Jonathan's Uncle Oliver Sturges, Barnabas's brother, had moved to Savannah the same year Jonathan was born. Uncle Oliver was an alderman in Savannah in 1806 and again in 1822-1823.[6] He joined the firm of Harris Burroughs, which later became the firm of Burroughs and Sturges which was engaged in insurance and shipping. He lost everything in a downturn in the economy around 1819, about the time his brother Barnabas also

---

[c] The daughter Sarah Adams MacWhorter would marry Jonathan and Mary's son Henry in 1883.

failed in business. Oliver passed away in 1824, but he left two daughters, Elizabeth, who married William Hunter, and Lucretia who never married but kept in touch with Mary and Jonathan throughout her life.[d] Mary always remembered fondly the beautiful gardens in Savannah and would later lament what the war did to the area and the fortunes of the people.[7]

When Jonathan and Mary returned from the South in late spring 1850, they had a buyer for their home and sold it at the price of $25,000. It became a boarding house as soon as they moved out. They found a home uptown at No. 5 East 14th Street and contracted with architect Joseph Wells to oversee certain alterations to the house. Until their new home was ready, they stored their furniture at Jonathan's nephew Josiah Bennet's home and he provided them with a place to stay when they were in town.[8]

Having only a bedroom to occupy in New York, they spent much of their summer and fall in Fairfield. However, they made sure to be in the city for a historic event. P.T. Barnum, the master showman and promoter, brought the "Swedish Nightingale," Jenny Lind, to the United States. Ms. Lind had been performing all over Europe, and Barnum had secured a contract to manage a U.S. tour. He masterfully set the stage for her arrival, sending dispatches to America trumpeting her popular concerts and her favorite charities that benefited from her performances, making her every bit a phenomenon and an angelic figure when she arrived in New York. The *Commercial Advertiser* described Lind's arrival at Castle Garden, on the steamer *Atlantis* on September 1, 1850:

> Arrival of the Swedish Songstress at about one-o'clock yesterday, the piers, boats, houses and almost every place that men, women and children could stand upon were occupied....temporary gates had been erected for the crowd...When Miss Lind appeared at the gangway, upon the arm of Capt. West, the rush of the crowd became fearful...the temporary gates gave way...Many people were trampled upon, but none we believed were seriously hurt...Her vehicle reached the Irving House...five thousand persons were assembled and it took at least twenty minutes for her carriage to reach the door.[9]

Everyone was eager to see the famed songstress, and her concerts sold out quickly. The Sturges family was caught up in the hysteria and Jonathan and

---

[d] Today there is a commemorative plaque installed in front of the still standing Oliver Sturges House, albeit altered by renovations, on the site of the old John Wesley Methodist Church at 27 Abercorn Street in Savannah.

Frederick attended the first concert on Wednesday, September 11, 1850. Jonathan was so impressed that he secured tickets for friends and family for the next night. Mary and Virginia returned to New York to attend. Lind's concert left a lifelong impression on Mary, and her descendants inherited Lind's promotional daguerreotype which she saved all her life as a remembrance. Mary described the event:

> I will not attempt to describe the brilliant array of New York society which greeted her on this second night, or the overwhelming enthusiasm of the great audience which filled every part of Castle Garden... Barnum regulated everything in the most admirable manner as to the sale of tickets and the entrance and egress of the company... I shall always feel that the singing of Jenny Lind was one of the great treats of my life, and although I have heard most of the good talent in this and other countries, nothing ever quite equaled her in my estimation. There was a pouring out of joyousness, of volume, of flexibility of voice, seeming as if nothing was too much for her to do, which I have never heard equaled.[10]

Madame Jenny Lind Goldschmidt[11]

In September 1851, Virginia attended another of her concerts with 8,000 other appreciative fans. "When she appeared, there was an instant stillness, then as she came gracefully forward, such applause of which I never dreamed of.... it was exciting beyond description."[12] She heard her for the sixth time in November

1851 and noted the effect Lind had on the audience: "I saw men, proud and strong-looking, sobbing like little children."

The next year, Jenny visited Northampton, Massachusetts as she was winding down her tour in the United States.[e] A family friend and an occasional music night participant at the Sturges household, violinist Joseph Burke, accompanied Jenny Lind at the concert there. She had recently married her piano accompanist, Otto Goldschmidt, and was addressed as Mrs. or Madame Goldschmidt. Virginia related Burke's anecdote to her aunt:

> She gave one concert in Northampton and Mr. Burke was sent for to play at it...He arrived at Northampton at ten in the morning and found Mr. Goldschmidt waiting for him with a carriage... after dinner, as he knew Jenny was accustomed to taking a nap when she sang in the evening, he asked for a book to amuse himself. "Oh!" said Jenny, "Did you ever read Uncle Tom's Cabin?[f] You must read it; it is so interesting." So off she ran and brought it and said, "You can go in the dining room, I must practice a little, but don't mind that." He said he had read three pages when she began, and from that time he could not see one word. It was trills from the highest to the lowest notes, roulades and exquisite cadenzas, all with beautifully modulated improvised accompaniment, enough to make anyone wild I should think, and she is as happy as a bird and in better voice than ever.[13]

In January 1851, not long after Lind's first concert, Jonathan and Mary's family moved into No. 5 East 14th Street, very near today's Union Square. Interestingly, the Sturges home was built on leased land. Twice a year Jonathan wrote a rent check for $170—for a home they would occupy for twenty years.

In 1851, the Sturges family was vacationing at the fashionable Cozzens Hotel at West Point, New York. Two young West Point officers conducted a personal tour of the campus although neither was in the Adonis mold that Virginia and Amelia had romantically envisioned. William Cozzens, the owner of the hotel, hosted a dinner party in honor of Charles Leupp and William C. Bryant who had returned from a trip abroad, where General Winfield Scott and the Sturges family were among the attendees. Scott regaled the party with stories of his Mexican War and War of 1812 adventures, as journaled by Virginia Sturges:

---

e Lind returned to New York in May 1851 and May 1852. She parted ways with Barnum in June 1851, returning to England in May 1852.

f *Uncle Tom's Cabin*, published in March 1852, was the best-selling novel of the nineteenth century.

General Scott who ever fought his battles, for the benefit of intelligent listeners gathered round the table...At one time, he was a prisoner of war during the War of 1812. While in Cape Breton, Canada, (his prisoner ship blew to safe-haven there during a gale) he saw a man (Mr. Pain) who had lived on the island of Cape Breton entirely alone for eight years. He went there a year before the American Revolution...the only books he had were the Bible, Paradise Lost and Pilgrims Progress...When his clothes were worn out he made garments of the skins of such animals as could be found on the island...his amusement was committing his three books to memory.[14][g]

Mary Sturges and Virginia boarded a train in December 1851, likely traveling between New York and Fairfield, meeting another of Barnum's protégés. When seated, they found themselves directly across the car from General Tom Thumb,[h] a P. T. Barnum creation. Virginia recorded the incident in her journal:

He stood on one of the seats at the side of his tutor, reaching about to his shoulder. Mother took a seat directly in front of him, and I joined her soon afterward and commenced a little conversation with him. I was much amused with his shrewd remarks, like those of a smart child. There was a man in the corner with white hair that was acting quite strangely. Tom Thumb remarked to me, "that man is crazy." Mother said to him, "I don't think he is crazy, but very old." We soon afterwards found he was a veteran of the revolution 102 years old. He had fought against Napoleon and all the wars of our country. His face was marked in all directions with wounds long healed and one eye was gone. His name was Alexander MacDonald. He had been at Damascus, Cairo, Jerusalem, Constantinople and many other cities of scriptural celebrity...When the tutor of Tom Thumb heard who the old man was, he carried him up, saying, "the General wishes an introduction as he is a warlike man himself." The old man was delighted and said, "I'd rather see you my dear than Jenny Lind." It was curious to see the attention with which Tom Thumb heard the veteran fight his battles. He asked him if he still had his gun...and told him to come to the museum

---

g Scott's prisoner of war ship pulled into farmer Pain's location at Cape Breton in November 1812, where he purchased food for his soldiers. In January 1813, Scott was returned to active service in a prisoner of war exchange.

h Tom Thumb was born in Bridgeport as Charles Stratton in 1838. He grew to a height of only forty inches. P.T. Barnum, who was a distant relative, discovered him and made him internationally famous.

and leave his name at the door and ask for General Tom Thumb and he would have the pleasure of showing him some remarkable guns. It was quite an incident taken all together and one I was glad to witness.[15]

Jonathan, Mary and all the Sturges family were witnesses to many iconic events in American history during their lives. Calhoun's funeral, Jenny Lind's performance and their chance encounter with Tom Thumb were a few of those extraordinary experiences. Jonathan was next fated to further establish his own place in history while building the infrastructure of the country—as a founder of the Illinois Central Railroad.

NINE

The Illinois Central Railroad

The proposition comes from the heaviest railroad men in the United States—men known to the country, and whose promptness and the honorable fulfillment of their engagements, the utmost confidence may be reported.

—*New York Tribune*, 1850

The Illinois Central Railroad was as much tied to political support as the determination and abilities of the men who incorporated this new enterprise and made it a reality. First originated about 1835, the concept of a railroad for central Illinois had been the subject of many aborted attempts, and for much of the fifteen years the project was embroiled in an Illinois political fight between Judge/Senator Sidney Breese and Congressman/Senator Stephen Douglas. Breese was in the forefront of the early discussions and envisioned an east-west route through the state. Douglas, a State Attorney, Illinois State Representative and then U.S. Senator, encouraged a north-south route from Chicago and Lake Michigan to the southern-most point of Illinois (for further connection to New Orleans). Breese accused Douglas of promoting a north-south route to increase the value of his property holdings, however, Breese had similar business interests in advocating an east-west route.

Between 1835 and 1846, there were multiple failed efforts to construct a railroad in Illinois, wasting millions of dollars in investor and taxpayer money. The final state effort that started in 1843 was the The Great Western Railway, led by Darius Holbrook, and it was to run from west of Chicago, around LaSalle, and south to Cairo. This enterprise spent significant funds to develop the route but failed also, and the state repealed their charter in 1846.

In 1849, the state revived the Great Western charter. Breese, now a U.S. Senator and Chairman of the Senate Land Grant committee, and U.S. Senator Stephen Douglas, secured additional federal land grants of 2,500,000 acres within Illinois. More land grants for railroad construction through Southern states were added to the bill and this provided the requisite political support for passage in Congress. This was the first of the land grant railroads—an investment by the government to turn worthless land into a thriving path of commerce.

On Sept. 20, 1850, the act passed by the Thirty-First Congress, on the 17th of that month, was approved, "granting the right of way and making a grant of lands to the states of Illinois, Mississippi, and Alabama, in aid of the construction of a railroad from the southern terminus of the Illinois-and-Michigan Canal to a point at or near the junction of the Ohio and Mississippi Rivers, Cairo, with a branch of the same to Chicago, and another via the town of Galena to Dubuque in...Iowa.[1]

Route of Illinois (gray) and Chicago Central (black) Railroads[2]

Multiple enterprises were vying for the right to build the railroad, including a faction that favored a state-run operation. Prominent among these competing interests was the group led by Robert Schuyler, Robert Rantoul of Boston and Jonathan Sturges. The experience, unimpeachable reputations, recent success with the New York and New Haven railroad, and the sheer confidence that this Eastern association possessed and conveyed, made this group the overwhelming choice of the state to build their railroad.

Jonathan's fellow founders included experienced and successful railroad executives, bankers, and merchants—many with current success in the business. The *New York Tribune* in commenting on their proposal said: "The proposition comes from the heaviest railroad men in the United States—men known to the country and whose promptness and the honorable fulfillment of their engagements the utmost confidence may be reported."[3] William Ackerman, a one-time ICR officer and historian, described their character:

> In a small and dimly-lighted room at No. 1 Hanover Street, a little narrow street leading out of Wall Street, in the city of New York in the early spring of the year 1851, there met a number of gentlemen who were known in law as the incorporators of the Illinois-Central Railroad Company... Probably no body of incorporators, or directors as they afterward became, was ever imbued with more earnest determination, confident reliance, pride of undertaking, and honesty of purpose. And it may be added that no corporate body was ever formed that was composed of men of more indomitable energy, integrity of character, business capacity, sagacity, and foresight.[4]

These distinguished original incorporators were:

Robert Schuyler (president of multiple railroads; dubbed America's First Railroad King)

Jonathan Sturges (Merchant, banker; board member of NY&H and NY&NH railroads)

George Griswold (eminent New York South Street Merchant; Director, Bank of America)

Leroy Wiley (prominent southern merchant)

Robert Rantoul (lawyer; drafted charter of Illinois Central Railroad)

John F. A. Sanford (fur trader who bought out John Jacob Astor's fur trading business; great friend, peace broker and fur trader with the Native Americans)

Thomas W. Ludlow (First President, Panama Railroad Company; Director, New York Life Insurance Co.; related to Roger Ludlow, founder of Fairfield, CT)

Governeur Morris (NY&H director; chief contractor of NY&H Albany extension; among other railroad construction projects)

Franklin Haven (President, Bank of Boston)

Joseph Alsop (New York Merchant; Ohio & Mississippi Railroad incorporator)

David Augustus Neal (President, Eastern Railroad of Massachusetts and Reading Railroad)

William Aspinwall (New York merchant; organized & constructed Panama Railroad line)

Henry Grinnell (New York merchant, Grinnell, Minturn & Co.; First President–American Geographical Society).

These ambitious men had won the right to build the railroad, but they had taken on a daunting task as the many previous failures had proven, and it still had its skeptics, including Jonathan's own family. Virginia Sturges, an unmarried twenty-one-year-old, wrote in her journal on April 16, 1851 about one of those early meetings when the success of the operation was still a glimmer in the eye of the incorporators: "Father was out late, half-past twelve, last evening consulting over a railroad in Illinois, 700 miles long, which twelve gentlemen are to build. Mother sighs over it sometimes, and I almost long to look into the future and see if this great enterprise will succeed."[5]

The incorporators provided the initial $200,000 good faith deposit and elected Robert Schuyler president. Aspinwall, Grinnell, Morris and Ludlow either left the board in a short time or were passive contributors, but the rest of the board was engaged and invaluable to the operation.[6] Jonathan is widely credited with being one of the driving forces behind the success of the Illinois Central Railroad. With Schuyler running as many as five railroads during these start-up years, Jonathan, Ketchum, Alsop, Neal and Sanford stepped in to fill the void of leadership where needed.

Incorporated in 1851, a critical component of the Illinois Central Railroad Act of Incorporation was that it was assessed a state tax of 7%, but it was exempted from federal and local taxes—a key proviso for future profitability. They required that the corporation build a single-track operational railroad between Cairo and Chicago by July 4, 1854.[7]

Having the daunting task of installing seven hundred miles of track in three years, they set out by hiring as Chief Engineer Roswell B. Mason, well known to Jonathan and Schuyler as the former chief engineer on the New York and New Haven Railroad. They then secured rights-of-way and started the business of building a railroad. Ackerman noted, "In May 1853, the first portion of the road from La Salle to Bloomington, 61 miles, was put in operation, a temporary bridge was erected over the Illinois River, and cars were hauled to the top of the bluff—with ropes and chains by means of a stationary engine."[8] By July 1854, the railroad had constructed 128 miles of track from Chicago to Urbana, and trains were running. By the end of 1854, passengers were traveling from Chicago to Cairo. They still had much track to lay but impressive progress had been made and the legislature extended their charter for three years.

The path of the railroad and the locations of the stations were literally defining where the population spread, and those owning land along the route stood to gain. To finance the construction, the railroad's charter gave them title to a wide swath of land to sell. In some instances, entire towns were planned and laid out to take advantage of the train route. Dunleith, Illinois, now a township of East Dubuque, Illinois, was such a town, across the river from Dubuque, Iowa. It was on the Chicago Central Line and Jonathan was a primary investor in the enterprise. In Kett's *History of Jo Daviess County* he described the endeavor:

> In 1853, a town company composed of George W. Sanford, Jonathan Sturges, Morris Ketchum, George W. Jones [Iowa state senator], George Griswold, Charles Gregoire was formed, who were known as the Proprietors of the Town of Dunleith,...which was laid off in to lots, blocks, streets, avenues and alleys, and named...Dunleith, in honor of Dunleith, Scotland...The first public sale of lots was in the Summer of 1855... Frederick Jessup and Charles Gregoire were general managers for the proprietors...In making sales of lots, Jessup imposed the condition that...no spirituous liquors should ever be sold.[9]

"David Neal, George Griswold, Jonathan Sturges, and Morris Ketchum, together with R. B. Mason, the chief engineer, formed a company called 'Land Associates' to purchase key sections of land from the federal government. Because the men had advance knowledge of the final route through Illinois, and influence over the location of depots and stations, they stood to make a great deal of money from the sale of parcels in the new towns."[10]

The Illinois Central Railroad began Jonathan's lifelong involvement in not only the railroad but also the business interests of the "Western" part of the country. He increased his travels to the area, became a household name in Chicago and enhanced his reputation and personal fortune. However, it was now his daughter's romantic fortunes that would not only affect her future but would directly impact the fortunes of the railroad.

TEN

Virginia's Courtship—Daniel Webster—
Family Education Initiatives

If ever I should marry it may be someone who is my superior in every
respect, whom I can esteem and admire as well as love.

—*Virginia Sturges*

Mary Cady Sturges, c. unk[1] and John Luther Cady, c. unk[2]

Mary Sturges's brother John Luther Cady died December 2, 1851 from apo-
plexy.[a] Although he was fourteen years her junior, John and Mary were close,
and he was a partner in Jonathan's firm when he died. At Thanksgiving, Virginia noted that her uncle had not come down to dinner as "he said he was not

---

[a] A stroke in modern terms.

fit for company." After his death, she wrote, "Mother and Father mourned as for a dear child…The voice that sweetly sounded in our songs is hushed and the smile that was looked for with joy has faded."[3] His portrait, still owned by descendants, is thought to be the work of A.B. Durand, from the early 1840s when he painted other family members.

A trait that personified the close-knit Sturges family was a passion for reading and education for all, and for Mary, vocational training for the masses. Jonathan and Mary both supported groups or movements that promoted a Christian public education, such as the Board of Popular Education, and its sister organization in Hartford, Connecticut, the Committee for Selecting Teachers, which focused on placing teachers in the less populated areas of the West.[4]

Reading to each other was a favored Sturges family tradition. In 1852, Virginia wrote to her aunt about reading the novel *Queechy* by Susan Warner to her father:[5][b]

> Have you read *Queechy* yet? If not, you have a treat in store. I won't tell you anything about it, but if you don't think it one of the most beautiful books you ever read, I do not know your taste. I am reading it to Father now. We set up half the night, and one evening sent word to the door that we were engaged, so we might not have any interruption. The two girls [Susan and Ann, sisters] and Mr. Warner took tea with us a fortnight ago and we enjoyed the visit much…I think in *Queechy* there is a great deal of their own experience.[6]

Mary Sturges became a dedicated champion of multiple organizations promoting practical education for young girls, vocational education to enable unmarried women to support themselves, and young mothers to supplement the family income. In 1853, as Mary noted, "The School of Design for Women, located at the corner of Broome and Broadway, was organized by Miss Mary Hamilton as president, and myself as vice president" and established for girls of character.[7] *The New York Daily News* described its mission: "The object of this School is to give instruction to women, either gratuitously, or at very low rates, which will qualify them to earn a living by the practice of some of the branches

---

[b] The Warners were family friends, and both Susan and Anna Warner became noted religiously-themed authors. Susan Warner also wrote *The Wide, Wide World* in 1850, one of the most widely circulated stories of American authorship. *Queechy* was the story of an 11-year old whose parents die, leaving her to live with her aunt in Paris. They also wrote the children's song "Jesus Loves Me" and taught Bible studies to West Point cadets. Being so loved, Susan was buried in the West Point cemetery.

taught in it, or to become teachers in other schools. Pupils are taught elementary drawing, with reference to furnishing original design for manufacture and other purposes where ornamental designs are required."[8]

The managers and advisors were the major financial backers for the school, augmented by various fundraisers. Tuition was low but waived for students of promise and character who could not afford it. The School of Design for Women later merged with the Cooper Union and the name changed to the Women's Art School of the Cooper Union, where engraving, designing, and decorating were taught.

Mary was also a founding director of the Wilson Industrial School for Women,[c] an organization that focused their student recruitment on young girls dwelling in the tenements of the Five Points area in lower Manhattan, around Park, Centre, Broome, Bowery, Pearl, Baxter and Canal Streets:

> The objects of this Association are to gather into the School vagrant girls of different ages, who, from the poverty or vice of their parents, are unable to attend the public schools, and who gain a precarious livelihood by begging or pilfering; to give them ideas of moral and religious duty, to instruct them in the elements of learning, and in different branches of industry, and thus enable them to become useful members of society.[9]

The school fed, clothed and educated a countless number of girls living in challenging conditions but the real goal was perhaps not entirely altruistic, as the *New York Times* pointed out: "It was designed by the Society to introduce various trades into the school, and particularly to give instruction in all that relates to domestic service, cooking, baking bread, washing, ironing, &c., and thus to meet a want long felt in the community, of a school where servants may be well trained and instructed in their duties."[10]

The directors faced challenges working with these children and their families, but the initiative was very effective and efficient at removing some of them from sad circumstances, at least for the day, as one of their annual reports points out:

> In the management of the school, as before, the morning hours are devoted to instruction in reading, writing, etc.; the dinner is served at 12 o'clock, and in the afternoon the children are instructed in the trade or house work classes, or in plain sewing.... The average expense of each pupil for clothing during the year, is five dollars; the cost of dinner six days in the week

---

[c] The namesake and founder, Mrs. Wilson, resigned in the first year for unknown reasons.

week is about two cents daily, or a little more than six dollars for the year...a member of the Visiting Committee called on the family of a little girl attending the school, and found them in great distress, literally starving. A child of two years old had died the night before, and lay on the floor partly dressed; the father was out looking for work, that he might obtain the means of burying his child...the visitor, on entering one of these miserable abodes, found the mother intoxicated on the floor, but comfortably covered, and the two little girls, lately taken to the school from the street, cleaning the table and floor, and making everything as comfortable as possible for the expected return of their father.[1]

The Wilson School soon purchased a building on Avenue A for use as a Sunday school, which about one hundred of their day students attended, and Amelia Sturges was an instructor in school's early years. Later, Mary Sturges led a successful Christian outreach program added for parents called the Wilson Mission.[12] This Industrial School model received national attention, and chapters were established in many locations throughout the country, including Jonathan's hometown of Fairfield, Connecticut.

While Mary found a lifelong avocation in educating young ladies, Jonathan was engaged in trying to influence the 1852 national election. Although General Winfield Scott was a family friend, Jonathan was a supporter of his opponent for the Whig Presidential nomination. Massachusetts Senator Daniel Webster had been a land investor and an enthusiastic promoter of the Illinois Central Railroad land grant legislation in 1850. A letter of endorsement for Webster's candidacy, signed by Jonathan, Robert Minturn, Moses Grinnell and eight others, was sent to papers around the country, including the deep South Mississippi *Natchez Free Trader*. In part, the letter declared, "For the last thirty years he has been almost constantly before the public eye—what he has done is well known—he has given immortality to Whig principles and contributed largely to the renown of his country."[13] Less than receptive, the *Free Trader* replied:

CONFIDENTIAL DOCUMENT

We never knew until day before yesterday how high the Free Trader stood in the confidence of the leading Webster Whigs of the North. On Monday, we received the following autographed letter, addressed to "The Free Trader, Natchez, Mississippi," signed, as will be seen, by eleven of the leading Webster Whigs of New York City; and as we feel quite indisposed and utterly unable to extend that "co-operation," which is so "respectfully but earnestly" solicited, in forwarding the election of Daniel Webster to the Presidency...We have the same objections to Daniel Webster for the Presidency that we have for Millard Fillmore. Both are...avowed free-soilers. Webster, only a year since, in his Buffalo and Rochester speeches, declared that he never could admit any more slave territory into the union—"NO, NEVER!" So, we say he can never be a President for the South, with our co-operation and consent, "NO, NEVER![14]

Webster's most objectionable stance within his own Whig party was his endorsement of the 1850 Fugitive Slave Act, highly unpopular in key Northeastern states where he needed strong support, and as a result the nomination went to Gen. Winfield Scott.[d] As it happened, just weeks before the election, Webster fell from a horse and died of a cerebral hemorrhage.[e] Much of New York City closed at noon on November 16, 1852, to accommodate his funeral procession.

Hiram Powers, *Solomon Sturges*, c. 1862[15] and Harriett Bennet Buckingham, c. 1850s[16]

---

d "Old Fuss and Feathers"—the Senior General in the Army, commanding the army that assaulted Mexico City. In 1861, age 74 he retired. Scott lost in the general election to Franklin Pierce due to his anti-slavery stances.

e Jonathan and some of Webster's "personal friends" threw a sort of wake in 1854, on his would-be 72nd birthday.

In July 1852, Frederick and Virginia sojourned out West, while Jonathan took their son Edward on a trip to Chicago to attend to his Illinois Central interests. While there, he visited his first cousin, Solomon Sturges,[f] and his wife Lucy (also a Connecticut native), who had homes in Chicago and Ohio, where Solomon had significant business interests. After seasickness ended Solomon's training for a life at sea with his brother Eben, he worked for some years in a counting house[g] in Georgetown, Washington, D.C.[17] One of his fellow clerks there was George Peabody, who later formed a banking house in London and enticed Junius Morgan, father of J.P. Morgan, to become his partner.[18] Moving to the Western Reserve after the War of 1812, he had made a great success of himself. This included a lucrative ten-year contract between Solomon's company and the Illinois Central to set up grain elevators in Chicago and collect and manage all grain shipments on the railroad, likely due to the family connection.[19]

Virginia and Fred both kept in touch with their parents while traveling. They reported on a Sturges family reunion in Ohio with Solomon's other siblings, children, nephews and nieces, including the Guthries, Buckinghams, and Potwins, all families which Solomon's daughters had married into. Virginia wrote an amusing anecdote of their trip during a forced stay in Newark, Ohio, where they awaited a train for further travel to Zanesville, Ohio. She wrote, [Uncle] "Edward Sturges[h] accompanied us to Mansfield [from Putman, Ohio], and we found the advantage of it, for the landlord at Newark gave us his own parlor as he told Edward we were pretty good-looking. However, he added, the last stylish people he gave up his parlor to, used his toothbrush!"[20] Solomon's children, William, Sarah and Lucy, met Frederick and Virginia at the station in Zanesville. Their first cousin, Harriett Bennet, married John Buckingham in 1847 and settled in Fairfield. John was Ebenezer Buckingham's (Solomon Sturges' partner) son.

Virginia Sturges used her journal in the 1850s to record poems, biblical passages, random thoughts and many interesting events in her life, including an ill-fated love match to an unnamed man.[i] She had been out in society in her late teens and became engaged at eighteen:

---

f Jonathan's Uncle Dimon's son.
g An accounting firm or bank might have been called a counting house in that time.
h Solomon's brother, of E.P.& E Sturges store.
i Possibly Morris Ketchum, Jr., referred to as "companion of last summer" in a later entry.

I was tired of quiet, retired life. I wished to take my part on the great stage, no doubts of my capacity troubled me and as for him who was to be my companion through life it was sufficient that he love me. I required nothing else. Weeks and months passed away. I received congratulations and heard of numerous compliments directly and indirectly, well calculated to please my vanity (I once thought I had none) …It was one of the pleasant things about my new situation that I found myself more than ever before in my eighteen years of experience…Congratulations were over, and we settled down into one of a usual quiet nuance of life. I again began to enjoy reading more, pictures, and above all, conversations. I had pleasant thoughts on many subjects, and I often communicated them to my dear friend. They were listened to with a quiet smile, and some phrase of endearment was the only answer. This was pleasant at first, then as a matter of course, at last annoying. …I began to feel restless and sad, every time any marriage was alluded to by parents, friends, or by him from whose lips and allusions might have been welcome, a strange shudder chilled me to the heart… It was all ended…If ever again I am tempted to be governed by impulse I trust this page of my experience will be a warning and if ever I should marry it may be someone who is my superior in every respect, whom I can esteem and admire as well as love.[21]

As Virginia wrote later, referring to her Aunt Elizabeth's happy marriage, "the marriage state is either paradise or purgatory on earth." Avoiding her own purgatory, Virginia would soon enough find her admired and esteemed life partner.

After Jonathan's return from Chicago, the family traveled to visit with their good friends, the Dudley Fuller family. The Fullers' country home was at Hyde Park, New York, but they were spending this summer of 1852 farther north in Saratoga, where Jonathan and Mary joined them in August. They introduced the Sturges family to young William Osborn and his friend John Griswold. Osborn was from Boston and Griswold was the son of the well-known New York shipping merchant George Griswold. Both men were just back from Manila, Philippines, where they conducted a trading business.

Born in 1821, on his father's farm in Salem, Massachusetts, William Osborn had been a clerk with the S.C. Phillips trading house in Boston as a young man. He worked for them eight years before leaving to set up business in the West

Indies and then the Philippines. In 1852, he returned to the United States to establish his base of operations in New York City. Mary described the chemistry felt between Jonathan and William Osborn:

William Osborn, c. unk[22] and Virginia Reed Sturges Osborn c. unk[23]

Mr. Sturges and Mr. Osborn seemed to be mutually attracted. Having occasion to go down to the city during the week in a night steamer, they took a stateroom together, and as my husband afterwards told me, talked half the night—Mr. Osborn telling Mr. Sturges the whole story of his business life, leaving his native place into the employ of the Phillips' of Salem, Massachusetts, going to Manila, rising in reputation and business position by steady effort; failing in health, and ordered home by his physicians, still retaining his business position in Manila, carrying it on in New York for his partners.[24]

A couple months after this encounter with Osborn, Virginia, Fred and Amelia Sturges traveled together down the Eastern seaboard to Baltimore and Washington, then inland to Fredericksburg, Richmond and Staunton, to tour and visit family friends. In Fredericksburg, they stopped in to see Mary's good friend, Jane Howison Beale, who became an important and oft-quoted Civil War diarist. Born in 1815, Jane had been a pupil of Mary's, and they had become friends, and then faithful correspondents after Mary moved to New York. Fred wrote:

> We also went to the falls opposite Falmouth Saturday morning and paid Mrs. Beale a long visit afterwards. She is charming now, just such a person as one would like to have a daughter educated with, if they had to send her from home. She was as lovely as a girl! She says she gets many of her ideas from you, one of which was strict justice and impartiality...Once when you had a medal to bestow on the most attentive and industrious, she says you looked all around the class and your eyes rested on her (she had taken advantage of her knowledge that she was a favorite, not to be as studious and attentive as she ought), but it passed her and you gave the medal to another. She felt the justice of it in the midst of her mortification and anger and has never forgotten it.[25]

William Osborn kept in contact with the family over the fall and winter after the Sturges children returned from their journey, spending a lot of time with Virginia and Amelia. In January 1853, a European trip was planned for twenty-two-year-old Virginia and nineteen-year-old Frederick. It was common for people of wealth, especially young men, to go on a European tour before starting their business careers. The Grand Tour was regarded as an invaluable device to further their education through exposure to art, geography, architecture, foreign languages, and cultures. A bon voyage reception was hosted at the Sturges home on January 21, 1853. Virginia described the event to her aunt:

> Mother wished to give us a farewell party, as she had had no general company since we moved to 14th Street and obligations had accumulated. We fixed on last Friday evening the 21st and made our arrangements accordingly. Mother said she did not know till our list was made that she had so many acquaintances. After cutting it down, leaving out all Amelia's young friends and boys (Mother did not wish it to be considered her coming out party), the number stood over 250. I do not think Mother lost any of her old reputation for entertaining on that occasion. We had Dodworth's Band[j] but no dancing, and the greatest profusion of flowers I ever saw... Everyone

---

j Dodworth's Band was a popular and legendary band from New York City.

said it was the very pleasantest party they had been to in a long time and it was remarked that there was not one ugly or ill-dressed person in the rooms. That is saying a good deal among 200 people, don't you think so?[26]

Osborn was away on business when the reception was held. As an attractive daughter of Jonathan Sturges, Virginia had no shortage of prospective suitors, and this party was no exception. Many gentlemen attended to say their farewells. As Mary Sturges observed:

Osborn was much taken by surprise on his return and felt that he had no time to lose. He frankly made his wishes known to my husband, and in a few days, he and Virginia were engaged, without the slightest suspicion of such a thing on the part of our friends, except Mr. and Mrs. Fuller and Mary [daughter]…The friendship between my husband and Mr. Osborn became very deep and lasting.[27]

It was a somewhat unsettled engagement as Virginia departed for Europe within two weeks of them establishing an understanding of their future together. Virginia wrote in April that her first correspondence from Liverpool to William Osborn was awkward. Virginia lamented to her mother, "I wrote as I felt, miserably constrained and ill at ease. He seemed once more like a stranger, for the last two weeks we were at home were so surreal…that it seemed to me that it must be one of those ship dreams…I think I am quite recovered from that feeling."[28]

They had agreed that Osborn would join them toward the latter part of their European journey. Until he arrived, Virginia often mentioned her affectionate thoughts about his well-being. She was delighted he was a frequent visitor to their home and encouraged him to experience her beloved summer retreat. "I hope Mr. Osborn will go to Fairfield before he leaves America. I think he will find it charming."[29]

Virginia and Frederick traveled to Europe with Professor Tappan (Virginia's former teacher), Mrs. Tappan, and daughter Rebecca. Their travels included England, France, Italy, Switzerland, Germany and Belgium, before they returned to Paris for their last stop. Along the way, they visited historic sites, art galleries and working studios of acclaimed artists. They also ran across many acquaintances from home and artists well-known to the family, who were traveling and studying abroad, and they wrote many letters home during their voyage. Interestingly, the mail service was such that a letter Virginia sent to Jonathan and Mary in April, from London to New York, was delivered in error to a distant relative, merchant Russell Sturgis, in Canton, China, and then returned to sender, ending up in Paris in August.

In Paris, Frederick described how artists trained at the Académie des Beaux-Arts and Louis Napoleon III's support of the Catholic Church. Every year the school chose two students (one painter and one architect) to travel to Rome to study. The selection for the artist was based on their performance in drawing three sketches. "At the time of decision each of the pupils is obliged to paint three pictures; one in 18 hours, one in 36 hours and one in 54 hours, and on these sketches the decisions are made...."[30] He also noted men hard at work restoring Paris parks and landmarks and soldiers marching about Paris and "sentinels everywhere." "It is the influence of Louis Napoleon who is straining every nerve (as we are told here) to advance the Catholic Church in order to secure his power."[31] Both are telling observations of the political climate in France in the winter of 1853, a year after Napoleon III's coup in December 1851.[k]

Also in Paris, Virginia told of a visit they had in March 1853 with the distinguished Vicomte Alexis de Tocqueville and his English wife.[l] The Vicomte and his wife called on Professor Tappan and their traveling party and they "passed a very pleasant evening, where the gentleman talked politics." Mrs. de Tocqueville related an anecdote about the Paris custom of an arranged marriage to Virginia, Rebecca, and Mrs. Tappan:

> She said a niece of hers, all within the last fortnight, had inquiries made respecting her fortune by some unknown person. She supposed the dowry was satisfactory, for about 12 days later a request was made that some gentleman (still unknown) might see the young lady at some party. Her parents will take her there, the unknown lover will look at her and if her personal appearance is satisfactory some place will be appointed where she can see him. She looks at him for one evening (without speaking) and decides

---

[k] Louis-Napoleon Bonaparte went to war in March 1854 allied with Britain, the Ottoman Empire and Sardinia, against Russia. Napoleon joined the alliance to protect the Catholics in the Holy Land (controlled by Ottoman Empire), gaining favor with Catholics at home, solidifying his power and authority there.

[l] Author of the classic *Democracy in America*, the Vicomte was the French Minister of Foreign Affairs on the French Chamber of Deputies in 1851. The Chamber resisted Louis Napoleon's coup, accusing him of high treason but Napoleon prevailed, and the Vicomte was forced to retire from French politics. He died in 1859 of tuberculosis.

the next morning whether she shall take him for a companion for life. In six weeks, they are married. It is strange that French society should be so vicious.[32]

In Rome, they visited the studio of the renowned Irish-American sculptor Thomas Crawford, seeing many of his significant works, including the early form of the large statue of *George Washington on Horseback* destined for Capitol Hill in Richmond, Virginia. He had just accepted an important commission from the federal Capitol engineer, on recommendation from Massachusetts Senator Edward Everett, to sculpt eighty-foot pediments for the Capitol's east front—now known as the *Progress of Civilization*. Virginia noted, "We went to Mr. Crawford's studio on Wednesday where we saw a beautiful statue of *Flora* destined for Mr. Haight's[m] conservatory, and the figures of the *Babes in the Wood*[n] ordered by Mr. Lennox."[33]

T. Crawford, *G. Washington on Horseback* c.1852[34] (left), *The Babes in the Wood* c. 1851[35]

Virginia and Frederick connected with Asher B. Durand and William Cullen Bryant in Rome while visiting the studio of the German painter Johann Overbeck:

> After church, we visited Overbeck's studio…only open on Sundays from 12-2, it was our last opportunity. He himself is a strict Catholic and designs only scripture subjects. Mr. Overbeck was exceedingly kind and polite in explaining his sketches which are wonderfully elaborate, and pleased me to my surprise, exceedingly.[36]

---

[m] Presumed to be Richard K. Haight. of New York City.

[n] Babes in the Wood was owned by Hamilton Fish when it was donated to the Metropolitan Museum of Art in 1893.

In Florence, they visited the studios of the sculptor Hiram Powers. He was in the middle of modeling busts for Mr. Tappan's cousins, the Rays. Virginia's opinion was that "he certainly wasn't producing designs equal to Crawford's."[37] However, his scandalous statue the *Greek Slave* (c. 1845), a naked woman in chains, toured the United States for several years starting in 1847, making him famous, and the sculpture became one of the most acclaimed of the nineteenth century. Abolitionists embraced it as a commentary on slavery in the U.S. In Munich, they twice visited the studio of the artist and director of the Munich Academy, Wilhelm Von Kaulbach,° and observed his latest masterpiece-in-progress.

In Antwerp, Virginia lamented about not having such great pictures as Reuben's *The Crucifixion* in America:

> We entered the large room of the museum, I did not know that this picture was there, and it stood immediately before us. We all sat before it for ten minutes. I determined not to give way to the sick feeling of distress that was coming over me, but I had to walk away, and the rest of the time in the gallery was spent trying to recover from an emotion that would not allow one to speak one word or to look at another picture that expressed suffering…the Crucifixion has a divinity about it, but such intense quiet agony you would not think paint capable of expressing.[38]

Letters home were generally a happy travelogue of their many excursions and sights seen. However, later in the journey, tension developed between Frederick and Professor Tappan and it culminated in the two strong personalities clashing over a discussion Frederick initiated with the Professor, regarding Fred and Virginia's desire to return to Paris at the end of the tour. Tappan had firm plans to leave on a September sailing with his wife and daughter Rebecca. He thought his charges should return with him and Fred was just as determined to go back to Paris. Virginia became so stressed that she appealed to Jonathan to moderate the situation:

> Be sure of one thing, we will be quite ready to return with them if it is decided in that way…Fred has talked to Mr. "T" about it and I'm afraid has caused hard feelings on both sides. I think, and tell Fred, that he ought to make up his mind to bear patiently little things, to yield his opinion (which you know is a set one), and when he finds he cannot help a thing, make the

---

° Probably Wilhelm Von Kaulbach, who was painting murals in Berlin at the time.

best of it. Mr. "T" is always as you have seen him, kind-hearted…It is an episode of Fred's character and neither one of them quite understand the other. Please write to him about it, you know how to do it, and one word from you will have the weight of a hundred from me.[39]

Jonathan responded to Professor Tappan, endorsing their plan to stay, and the letter was so well worded that Mrs. Tappan declared it "exquisite in its delicacy" and all was resolved. Much relieved, Virginia expressed her appreciation to her father for his respect for them as adults:

> I only want to tell you that I don't believe out of a thousand fathers there is one like you bringing your children up to be your companions and friends, and I do believe we love you differently from most children. I think of this so much, now I am away it strikes me more from seeing other fathers and other children. They pet them and scold them but never think of making them their equals.[40]

Virginia wrote of Fred's growing fondness for Osborn. "Every letter brings him nearer, and with his usual kindheartedness…Fred and I talk of him often and I think Fred is truly attached to him. I read parts of Mr. O's letters to him sometimes and we have hearty laughs over these. They are exceedingly spicy…"[41] Virginia also was anxious about maintaining appearances in her delicate situation of traveling with a single gentleman:

> I have tried, and I will try with that divine assistance, which I so much need to do right. I feel the delicacy of my position more than anyone, and also the responsibility I am assuming, which requires from me double watchfulness, and it will be too pleasant and advantageous for me to have once more those long fireside conversations and counsels which I can now look forward to as really near.[42]

Virginia's correspondence home expressed concern about Osborn's safe arrival and her anxiousness he would get along with Professor Tappan, given the latest friction between the Professor and Frederick. To her relief, all went well, as Osborn joined the traveling party at the end of June in Heidelberg, Germany, and his relationship with Tappan became an easy one. She remarked, "His real, unaffected respect and deference to Mr. 'T' and consultation with his wishes in the arrangement of our plans, and his appreciation of the difficulties of the situation have made me quite at ease and happy."[43]

The party of six then traveled to Switzerland. Virginia was happy and excited to have her intended with her. In late August, the Tappans left them, and Frederick, Virginia, and William Osborn proceeded to Paris to do their shopping, to include purchasing her wedding trousseau and bridesmaid gowns. Confusing and disconcerting for other interested suitors, there were no official announcements of engagements. However, it was clear the word was out. Mr. Talmadge, a friend from the social circles in Newport, Rhode Island, wrote to Virginia reporting the gossip about them.[44] Mary Sturges noted later, "In Paris, Virginia bought her bridal trousseau...John Griswold had met them traveling together in Europe, saw how matters stood, wrote to his friends in this country, and it was no longer a secret."[45] Virginia confirmed the chatter to her parents,"...we are merely bubbles floating on the sea of gossip...We are both delighted that the gossip will be over before we return."[46] While in Paris, Virginia had Mary and Amelia's dresses made for the wedding. She teased her mother, "I will not tell you anything about your dress or Memie's[P], but they are in progress."[47] Gideon F.T. Reed of Tiffany, Reed, & Co. in Paris, assisted Virginia with her shopping. After Reed's retirement, the company name changed to Tiffany & Co.[48]

A Mr. Sanford called on them during this second visit to Paris. He was likely Henry S. Sanford who represented the United States in France, first as Secretary of the American Legation in Paris, then chargé d'affaires in Paris in 1853. Frederick and Virginia received not only firsthand exposure to world class art at elite galleries and studios, but an invaluable education in world affairs. The party returned to New York in October, now with a well-known engagement and a wedding to finish planning. Even for this family of high social standing, the Sturges invitations were simple handwritten notes such as the one Mary's sister, Elizabeth Cady received. Enclosed were calling cards for "Miss Sturges" and "Mr. Wm. Henry Osborn."[49]

> Mr. & Mrs. Sturges will be happy to see
> Miss Elizabeth Cady at the marriage of
> Their daughter on Wednesday evening
> Dec. 14th at half past eight.
>
> 5 East 14th St.

P Memie was a nickname that family and friends routinely used for Amelia.

William and Virginia married on December 14, 1853, with a reception of about seventy. Afterwards they took a two-week wedding trip to Fairfield and Boston to visit family, a larger celebration was held in New York. The newly-weds stayed with Jonathan and Mary for the winter before moving into their own home. William Osborn needed this relaxation and stability, as his talents would soon be required to deal the ramifications of a historic fraud at the New York and New Haven Railroad that weakened the railroad industry for many years.

ELEVEN

Mr. Schuyler's Great Fraud

[The fraud] was greater in amount than any similar case of crime ever recorded.

—New York Times

The first order of business for Jonathan and the Illinois Central board was to raise sufficient capital to begin the project. The London bond markets were a crucial source of railroad investment funds, but lack of confidence in the valuation of the bonds weighed on sales. Fortunately, in 1852 and 1853, European investors came back in the market, and the Illinois Central were able to attain a financially stable position.

Sketch of Norwalk Railroad Bridge Disaster, May 6, 1853[1]

However, in 1853, disaster struck the New York and New Haven (NY&NH) Railroad, shaking the confidence of railroad investors. A NY&NH engineer had failed to see the track signal that was indicating an open drawbridge ahead at the Norwalk River, causing a passenger train to plunge into the river— crushing or drowning forty-six passengers and injuring thirty others. There had been many Connecticut doctors on the train attending a medical conference, some of whom lost their lives in a setback for the state medical community.[2] This accident resulted in claims on the railroad approaching $300,000. NY& NH dividends were suspended until the damage could be determined and claims settled.

After this disaster, the Connecticut Legislature passed two pieces of legislation. First, feeling that an over-committed railroad president (Schuyler) was a contributing factor, it passed a law that barred Connecticut-chartered railroad presidents from holding the presidency of more than one railroad simultaneously, prompting Schuyler to resign as president of the ICR in 1853, among other railroads. However, he remained as president of the NY&NH railroad. Secondly, the new law required trains to come to a complete stop before crossing any bridge.

In the fall of 1853, Jonathan again traveled to Chicago and beyond, to survey Illinois Central construction. The gold rush in California began in 1848, and the westward movement of people was significant. He wrote Mary from Dubuque and further observed the following, "We are utterly astonished at the number of people in the cars, stages, and wagons, and more so at the immense amount of produce that must seek a market by rail."[3] Jonathan prophetically declared, "This [Chicago] is destined to be the largest city in the Western states."[4] The Chicago area held not only natural beauty but was attracting people and investments, including his own, and the railroad he was building was planned as a main artery that would feed further growth. Chicago's population would almost quadruple in the decade.

Hundreds of miles of tracks were laid, but connections and continuous sections of ICR track over long distances were still elusive. Heartened by the progress, state politicians trumpeted the great strides that had been made by the latest group of Illinois Central directors. However, due to soft credit markets, widespread crop failures reducing freight traffic, a legal challenge to the railroad's exemption from local taxes and competition for labor and cholera outbreaks within their labor force, the railroad was threatened with insolvency and bankruptcy. They had to cut costs and they immediately lowered wages, resulting in a bloody riot at LaSalle, Illinois, in December 1853, where a contractor and his foreman were attacked, and their offices pillaged. Several laborers were shot, and chaos ensued until the local sheriff arrived to quell the rioting and arrest the offenders. Furthermore, while trying to recover from these challenges, an unprecedented fraud in 1854 on the New York and New Haven Railroad struck a frightening blow to the entire railroad industry.

In early July 1854, there was unusual trading activity and a precipitous drop in the price of the NY&NH railroad's stock from 93 on June 14, to 83 on June 28, and 73 ½ on Jul 3.[5] Someone knew something. However, the directors apparently remained clueless.[a] Jonathan Sturges, Morris Ketchum and William Worthen, were finally prompted to review the stock transfer books. Jonathan's brother Lothrop had gotten wind of unusual stock sales involving Cornelius Vanderbilt and he asked Jonathan if it might be a good time to buy. Although Jonathan was confident it was, this prompted him to review trading activities. He visited the New York railroad office to inspect the transfer books before he departed to Connecticut for the holiday. Jonathan Sturges, in a later court testimony, described his visit:

> I went up and saw the transfer clerk [Abraham] Vandeventer. Mr. Schuyler was not in the office. I requested he hand me the transfer books for the last two months. I looked through the transfer books and saw various transfers, nothing that excited suspicion. I then went to the transfer clerk and said I would look at the stock ledger, my object to see what amount Vanderbilt held, as I thought this might govern my brother in his purchases; the transfer clerk did not feel authorized to show the stock ledger without Mr. Schuyler's consent. I said I was a director and presumed I had a right to see any of the company's books and would come in and see Mr. Schuyler about it. I went over to the Illinois Central Railroad offices to transact some business there and came back again between two and three o'clock for the purpose of telling Mr. Schuyler that I had been refused the ledger. The same clerk, Mr. Vandeventer, informed me that Mr. Schuyler had been there but was unwell and had gone home and would not be back that day....[6]

It was July 3 and although he was suspicious, due to the holiday closing Jonathan could not pursue it further, and he left for Fairfield. Fellow director William Bement visited Jonathan later that evening, who informed him of irregularities found in the railroad stock ledger, and that a director's meeting was set for the next day at Ketchum's home, in the neighboring town of Westport, Connecticut. Jonathan and William Osborn traveled there by the morning train on July 4 to meet with the other available directors.[7]

---

[a] In July 1854, the Board of Directors of the NY&NH Railroad were; R. Schuyler (President), W. Bement (Treasurer), W. Burrall (Secretary), M. Ketchum, J. Sturges, J. C. Sanford, J.E. Thayer (Boston Transfer Agent) and W. E. Worthen (Vice President), W. Boardman, W. Blackstone and J.E. Sheffield (New Haven Transfer Agent).

Ketchum had crossed paths with a lawyer working for Schuyler who informed him that Schuyler had sent a letter to Jonathan that day that addressed an overissuance of stock. This news, combined with the stock's low price that day, prompted him to visit the office. Ketchum later testified:

> I was led to examine the transfer books with a view of ascertaining who was selling their stock at those prices; in examining the stock ledger...
> with the clerk Vandeventer looking over me, I discovered at that moment, or suspected upon catching his eye, that he knew that something was wrong; whereupon I took the stock ledger, passed into an adjoining room, asking him to go with me, where I explained to him my suspicion, whereupon he placed his finger on a large transfer of stock from the Boston books to the New York books; I immediately, being on the point of leaving town, took the ledger with me, sent for several of the directors, when we made a thorough examination and discovered the fraud.[8]

Mary remembered how upset her husband was. He had only $10,000 invested, but it was clear what the overall effect would be on the enterprise, on which he had staked his reputation.[9]

Everything pointed to Schuyler, and the cavalcade of bad loans, debts, fraud and embezzlement were exposed. After a personal check bounced and a sixty-day loan came due without repayment, the bank put a hold on his account. On Saturday, July 1, the newspapers reported the failure of the R & G.L. Schuyler Company. On July 3, R & G.L. Schuyler failed to repay a loan to Cornelius Vanderbilt of $600,000, which Schuyler had secured with unbacked fraudulent NY&NH railroad securities. Vanderbilt met with Schuyler after reports of his business failure and offered him $150,000 and funds of up to $3,000,000 to shore up the railroad if he could assure him that "all was right." Schuyler could only shake his head. With the unusual stock sales causing inquiries, his failure to repay loans to the bank, Vanderbilt, and others, and now Jonathan, Ketchum, and the board making inquiries, the situation imploded around Schuyler.

An extraordinary resignation letter, delivered to Jonathan upon his return to the city from Schuyler's attorney and cousin, Alexander Hamilton, Jr., read in part: "I beg to resign my seat in the Board of Directors of the New-York and New-Haven Railroad Company and of the office of President and appointment of Transfer Agent of the stock of the company. Your attention to the stock ledger of your company is essential as you will find there much that is wrong. The details can be furnished you with precision, though I cannot do so."[10] Robert Schuyler was president and New York transfer agent for the railroad, authorized to issue company stock. Besides New York, there were also transfer books and agents based in New Haven and Boston. Today, stock issuances must be signed by at least two agents, due to the shocking breach of trust that was soon revealed. Jonathan testified later:

> ...up to this time I had no suspicion that anything was wrong with the affairs of the company. I suppose he [Schuyler] took the alarm from [my] examination of the stock accounts. I have reason to suppose so as the next day he sent a letter to me enclosed to the directors, stating that we should find there much that was wrong with the stock ledger...I went over there the next morning and met Mr. Ketchum, Mr. Burrill and Mr. Bement. We commenced the examination and found two fraudulent entries of $5,000 each to R & G. L. Schuyler to which they were not entitled; after making this discovery I left for the city to stop other transactions in the stock.[11]

It was worse than they could have imagined. The *New York Post* reported the shocking revelation: "Shares representing $1,900,000 had been transferred by the transfer agent, who is Mr. Robert Schuyler, into the hands of Messrs. Robert and G.L. Schuyler...The legal capital of the company is $3,000,000 in 30,000 shares, the stock now on the market is 49,000 shares representing $5,000,000."[12] They soon found that the funds of the NY&NH railroad had, almost from the beginning, been commingled into the accounts of the R. & G.L. Schuyler company, dating back to 1848, the Schuyler company benefiting from the use of the railroad's capital. The same accountants were working for both companies, using the Schuyler bank accounts to pay railroad expenses. As a result, it was hard to ascertain over the six years of commingled cash how much railroad funds went to pay the expenses of Schuyler's company.[13]

Schuyler's actions were inconceivable, so unprecedented that there were no regulations or securities law governing such a situation. The *New York Times* stated the fraud was greater in amount than any similar case of crime ever recorded. Robert Schuyler was the grandson of General Phillip

Schuyler of the Revolutionary War, a nephew of Alexander Hamilton, and his grandmother a Van Rensselaer, all the most distinguished of American families. Many lamented, "if you can't trust Robert Schuyler, who can you trust?"

Schuyler was at one time the president of five railroads, and although by then he held only the presidency of the New York and New Haven Railroad, he remained the transfer agent for five other railroads. One of his lines was facing forfeiture due to lack of funds and progress, and it is thought he diverted funds to shore up that line.[14] Schuyler and his brother had also suffered a great financial loss in February 1853, when their uninsured steamer *Independence* (leased to Commodore Vanderbilt), on a route supporting the gold rush transport needs from Nicaragua to San Francisco, sank off the coast of California, with the loss of life of 150 passengers.[15]

Robert Schuyler and the Schuyler company had clearly been in distress for some time, and the extent of Robert Schuyler's tangled web of fraudulent activity was just beginning to be unveiled. Overissued stock in the amount of 4000 stocks at $50 per stock was also subsequently discovered at the Harlem Railroad. Schuyler did not remain to answer for his actions. He slipped out of town traveling under a false name, last seen boarding a train for Burlington, Vermont, for onward travel to Quebec, where he took a steamer to Liverpool.

In a curious twist of this story, it was revealed that Schuyler had been living a double life as Mr. Spicer. He maintained two homes, coming in late to the Spicer home and leaving early, his wife Lucinda and four children assuming he was an exceedingly busy business person who traveled extensively. This was all revealed shortly before the fraud was uncovered and this revelation stunned his colleagues, including Jonathan, who assumed he was a bachelor.

The railroad board had been duped by one of their own, and all would suffer the consequences both personally and professionally. In trial records, Jonathan Sturges was among those defrauded (50 shares).[16] Thus, Jonathan was both a defendant and a plaintiff in railroad litigation. In September 1854, a judge issued a formal warrant for Schuyler's arrest for the sale of forged stock certificates. Six months after his departure from the country, the New York Grand Jury indicted Schuyler on two counts; embezzlement and grand larceny. At least two major firms failed because of the fraudulent issue of these securities. The term "Schuylerizing" became synonymous with dishonest and fraudulent behavior and was made a felony.[17] Schuyler was living in Nice, Italy,[b] when he died after a period of failing health on November 15, 1855, penniless and disgraced, returning in a box and buried by his family in a lonely grave at Greenridge Cemetery, Saratoga Springs, NY.

Upon Schuyler's resignation from the New York and New Haven Railroad, William Boardman became acting president. In October 1854, Jonathan and the other directors were forced to resign, per the call from the stockholders. This regrettably ended Jonathan's involvement in the New York and New Haven Railroad. He and his fellow directors had built a railroad and achieved a great triumph through hard work and perseverance, but it had all ended with an appalling betrayal by a man they trusted implicitly. This should have served as a wake-up call, but he and many of his contemporaries appeared to remain incredulous and naïve regarding the long-term implications—less prepared to navigate an industrial age that increasingly featured business tactics such as securities manipulation, insider trading, and monopolies—still not installing the safeguards even in their own businesses to deal with such actions in the future, which would soon haunt his friend Morris Ketchum. Litigation dealing with the legitimacy of the spurious stocks continued for the next twelve years.

Having had to resign from the NY&NH board, Jonathan turned his efforts to the business of the Illinois Central Railroad. The ICR and the entire railroad industry suffered the backlash of the fraud and the stock plummeted, losing $1.5 million in value. The fraudulent stock took almost $2,000,000 of railroad investment funds out of circulation and the capital markets dried up. The ICR was also being weighed down by more crop failures, and its north-south track route that was not positioned to take advantage of the pervasive east-west movement of people and freight. Jonathan felt personally threatened from the railroad industry's financial woes. In his conservative way, he removed his son Edward from his classical studies and placed him in a merchant house to apprentice for a career in business. Mary commented, "Our grown children all showed the greatest consideration for their father, willing to work, economize or assist in any way they could."[18]

---

[b] Nice, Italy, is on Schuyler's gravestone as his place of death. Nice was part of the Kingdom of Sardinia from 1814 (after Treaty of Paris) to 1860. King Victor-Emmanuel II of Sardinia began to unify Italy under his control in 1859. He and Louis Napoleon of France negotiated a secret deal to transfer Nice back to France for Napoleon's cooperation in fending off the Austrians. A popular vote in 1860 endorsed the change of sovereignty.

The fallout of the Schuyler fraud reverberated across the economy and even into Jonathan's philanthropic involvements. In 1852, the artist-led National Academy of Design purchased investment property and an office building behind the offices where they were renting. In January 1853, a new trustee group led by Jonathan Sturges, and including Charles Leupp, Thomas Cummings, Francis Edmonds, and A.B. Durand, took the lead in selling the investment property, purchasing a new location, and erecting Academy facilities. The investment building sold at auction in May 1853 for $80,000. The buyers had begun to alter the property for their new purpose and rent out the building. However, by the terms of the sale, they had paid only the $10,000 down payment—the balance was not due until July 1, 1854. Unfortunately, the final payment date coincided with the Schuyler fraud and the ensuing panic in the market. The new owners were given time to regroup their finances, but in early 1855, the trustees were forced to foreclose, evict tenants, and restore the building to a rentable state. Thereafter it became a profitable rental property.[19]

Jonathan had many interests that divided his attention during this trying time. He had steadied his own business and sorted out financial issues for the National Academy. However, the crisis at the ICR required a younger man's energy to spearhead the massive effort that would be needed to stabilize the company. Jonathan recruited his son-in-law William Osborn to take on the challenge. The ICR board endorsed Osborn's involvement. Mary Sturges later remarked:

> Mr. Osborn has proved himself a friend beyond all price, his fresh, clever business head, his matchless skill as an accountant and his active, thorough insight into men and things, has made him such a helper as my husband has never had since Mr. Reed died. Virginia says, "What is work to some is play to him, his own business not being half enough to employ him." She says, "it is only right that Father, who has been taking care of people all his life should have somebody to take care of him now."[20]

Osborn's selection to shepherd the next phase of the railroad was a critical and fortuitous move by the board, and likely saved the railroad from the same fate as the previous groups that tried and failed, but he had a daunting task ahead of him.

TWELVE

William and Virginia Osborn and the Illinois Central

When the dark-days of the panic of 1857 overshadowed them, they might have abandoned their trust and sold their respective interests for what they would bring...but their names had been identified with it, and they felt that they were resting under a moral obligation to save it from pecuniary loss if possible.

—William Ackerman

Per Jonathan's recommendation in August 1854, William Henry Osborn and his friend, John N.A. Griswold, an original incorporator's son, became directors of the Illinois Central Railroad. The next year Griswold was named president, but his tenure was planned to be a short one, and six months later, Osborn, at the young age of thirty-four, was elected president of the railroad. Osborn was reputed to be a gruff and demanding boss. One historian described him: "Often dressed in a white suit and a straw hat, he was an oddity in the black-suited, beaver-hatted 1850s. However comical or eccentric he may have appeared to others, those who knew him well were aware that Osborn was a stern, no-nonsense employer who could not be beaten when it came to business."[1]

Chicago's population was exploding, growing from less than 30,000 residents in 1850 to over 80,000 by 1855. However, the infrastructure, shopping, and services lagged far behind the needs of the growing populace. In these early years of the company, the officers of the ICR became close, even living together as a matter of necessity in a town that lacked adequate housing, and the organization was skeletal, where managers wore many hats. The original gamble and the hard work paid off when he railroad was completed per the charter on September 26, 1856."...on the day following, Col. Mason, the engineer-in-chief, telegraphed the Board of Directors in New York that the completion of the 705.5 miles of the Illinois Central Railroad had been accomplished."[2]

William Henry Osborn[3]

Virginia and William Osborn were in Chicago for the winter of 1856-1857, due to the death of Mr. Doan, a key man with the railroad. Osborn was struggling to adequately finance railroad operations and was frequently away from Chicago selling bonds. Also, from time to time, he rode the rails to survey the line in wilderness areas. On one trip to the prairie, he described his traveling party as "three gentlemen, and a motley crew of indigent trappers, negroes, mulattos, and one woman. the squaw wife of a trapper."[4]

In her husband's absence, Virginia occupied herself with raising her namesake daughter (Virginia). However, she had never suffered through such harsh winters as were typical in Chicago where socializing was at a minimum. She particularly missed her family and those "Sturges talks," and used her entertaining and provocative letters as a substitute. Virginia vividly described to Jonathan a friend's visit to her home:

> Mr. Kirkland came over and brought a wild Indian. Mrs. Austin and I were reading together and were a little startled by this apparition. His head was shaved close except the scalp lock and painted brick-red, his ears were bored in three or four places, and filled with rings that rattled when he walked. We treated him to cake & wine... and to reward us for our hospitality he got up to go and said in good English, "give me money" (which was all he knew). What a request for the chief of a tribe![5]

Sick of the winters in Chicago, missing their family and friends, the Osborns were eager to return to New York, planning to do so by the fall of 1857.

By early winter, Virginia was pregnant with their second child. She wrote to her aunt of her anxiousness to get home:

> I shall go back to New York the first of June, not to return. Mr. Osborn counts the days till next fall, which is his limit and is twice as homesick as I am, because poor fellow he is overworked all the time. I might not believe he would be able to leave it did I not see the army of men of honesty and capacity he is drawing from all parts of the country to fill every department, even those who will be capable of taking the head of the company...don't imagine for a moment we are going to settle here for life, we have such delightful friends and resources in our own home.[6]

In 1857, Osborn added former Army Captain and War Department railroad advisor George McClellan to replace the original Chief Engineer Roswell Mason. McClellan graduated second in his class at West Point, considered one of the strongest engineering schools in the country. McClellan received a three-year contract at $3000 a year, a significant increase over his army salary, and was assured he would be named vice president in the near term, with executive authority over the railroad during Osborn's absences from Chicago. He was also directed to refrain from local politics. Virginia routinely hosted the officers of the company for dinner and wrote of McClellan's business promise: "Judge Lane is perfectly delighted with Capt. McClellan, as are Mr. Clark and Mr. Jacobs, and Mr. Osborn says he is quick as a flash to understand anything, so there is a reasonable prospect he will be capable of taking the head of affairs here next fall and releasing Mr. Osborn."[7]

In 1857, the railroad was again in dire straits for cash due to tightened credit markets and was forced to cut costs and defer maintenance. These cost-cutting measures created friction between Osborn and George McClellan, who, although on the job less than a year, thought he knew better how to allocate resources. McClellan even attempted unsuccessfully to re-enter the Army because of this friction in late 1857. The railroad went into assignment and was threatened with liquidation—Osborn stopped taking a salary. Within a few years, through Osborn's close management of the enterprise, the financial issues were resolved, and it became a profitable enterprise. As ICR historian Ackerman states, "When the dark-days of the panic of 1857 overshadowed them, they might have abandoned their trust and sold their respective interests for what they would bring...but their names had been identified with it, and they felt that they were resting under a moral obligation to save it from pecuniary loss if possible."[8]

Many accomplished men worked on the Illinois Central Railroad in those early years of William Osborn's leadership and Jonathan Sturges' service on the board, including:

> Abraham Lincoln–Attorney for the Illinois Central Railroad 1853-1860; Jonathan Sturges came to possess a table from Lincoln's practice in Illinois where Jonathan and Lincoln worked together on Illinois Central business, which now is at the Union League Club in New York City.[9]

Lincoln Table[10] [a]

General George McClellan–West Point Class of 1846; a favorite of Secretary of War Jefferson Davis, who sent him on a survey of railroads to determine logistical capabilities for military use; resigned his Army commission in   January 1857; Hired as ICR Chief Engineer January 1857; became President of the Ohio and Mississippi Railroad in 1860; Major General in the Civil War in command of the Ohio militia; promoted to General-in-Chief of the Army of the Potomac, relieved of command in November 1862; An outspoken critic of Lincoln and ran for president against Lincoln in 1864.

General Ambrose Burnside–(West Point 1847)–Resigned his Army commis-sion in 1853; invented the Burnside carbine; unsuccessfully ran for Congress.

---

[a] The table was donated to the Union League by Jonathan's granddaughter, Mary Fuller Sturges Wilson

on the Democratic ticket in Rhode Island; Treasurer of the Illinois Central Railroad 1858-1861; Brigadier General for Rhode Island Militia and Major General, Army of the Potomac in Civil War; first President of the National Rifle Association (NRA).

General Nathaniel Banks–Governor of Massachusetts; Speaker, U.S. House Representative; replaced McClellan at the ICR as resident director in Chicago in January 1861; appointed Major General by Lincoln May 1861.

Roswell Mason–Chief Engineer of the ICR; Engineer in charge of cleaning up the Chicago River in the 1860s; Mayor of Chicago during the great fire of 1871 when Mrs. O'Leary's cow was said to have knocked over a lantern, starting the fire.

These men were intimate friends of the Sturges family, as Mary said: "These were all active officers in the Illinois Central Railroad, much attached to Mr. Osborn personally, and at one time very well-known to us all."[11] They worked side-by-side on the business of the railroad, and in prosecuting the Civil War for the Union, with the Illinois Central Railroad attorney, Abraham Lincoln, leading the nation.

While Osborn was away seeking railroad financing in New York and London, McClellan led operations. Lincoln, the railroad's attorney, would have received guidance and direction from McClellan as the Resident Director and Vice President of the ICR, including the years before the 1860 election. However, McClellan was not a fan of Lincoln as a politician, and he failed to refrain from politics as directed. McClellan supported Stephen Douglas in the 1858 Illinois Senate election, even giving Douglas the use of the railroad's office car as needed, while Lincoln had to travel on a pass like any other employee or passenger.[12] However, Lincoln and McClellan would soon have their roles reversed, which probably didn't sit well with McClellan. As he had clashed with Osborn in managing the railroad, so would he clash with Lincoln in prosecuting the Civil War when Lincoln was president and McClellan was leading the Army of the Potomac.

Using the vehicle of the ICR, Jonathan and Mary found an opportunity to evangelize by funding a traveling colporteur, a salesman of religious publications. Mary excitedly outlined these efforts to her mother in March 1856:

I must not close this letter without telling you of a plan we have in view for our railroad, the Illinois Central. It is to control all the literature, books, papers which circulate along the whole line of the Road, and in the first place we are to have two more colporteurs (Mr. S- has kept one at his own expense on the branch for two years or more), to preach and circulate the publications of the Tract Society, and we hope to get them to take charge of the boys who sell books and papers of a secular character.... We hope to have libraries at all stations...you might want to support a colporteur yourself.... the expense of a colporteur is $150.00 per year...[13]

Jonathan sponsored Rev. J. W. Osborne between 1856 and 1857, in conjunction with the American Tract Society. Osborne reported "leaving precious seeds, both day and night, passing through all the lights and shades of railroad life," and ministering to many souls in desolate areas where no organized religious services or publications were readily available.[14]

While traveling the railroad on business, Jonathan and Mary found an additional evangelizing opportunity in the prairie town Amboy, Illinois:

...we got decent accommodations, a room in the second story of a store, which was used as a church, Presbyterian in the morning, Baptist in the evening... After the service was over, the children were gathered for Sunday school, which seemed to be starting without much plan, or means in the way of books. After the lessons were over, Mr. Ferguson made a pleasant address to the children, and we promised to send suitable catechisms and other books, which we did on arrival in Chicago.[15]

Jonathan Sturges was one of those who were key to the success of the Illinois Central Railroad. He was a founder, long-time director, and had a stint as acting president (president pro tem) around April 1854, during William Burrall's term as president.[b] He was commended in Illinois Governor William Bissell's 1857 inaugural address:

It is reasonable perhaps that I should avail myself of the opportunity of distinguishing certain individuals who were prominent in the inception of this great enterprise. To Morris Ketchum, George Griswold, David Neal and Jonathan Sturges are we mainly indebted for the successful carrying out of this great project...these gentlemen risked their own private means to an extent which had the enterprise failed, would have involved, some of them at least, in irretrievable ruin.[16]

---

[b] It is not entirely clear why he filled in for a time as President, but there is evidence that Burrall was on an extended visit to the construction activities in the remote southern area of the line.

Due to these extraordinary efforts, the ICR line was completed, financially supported, and became a good investment. Jonathan was presented with a ceremonial plate upon his short-lived resignation as a director in 1862. As the board wrote, his "name and fame (is identified) with the creation and success of one of the grandest and most beneficent public works of modern times, whereby a vast wilderness has been converted into a granary for the world and peopled with happy Christian homes."[17]

THIRTEEN

Contented Family Life

I desire to add to the price of the woods picture; the trees have grown more
than the worth of that sum since 1855.

—Jonathan Sturges to Asher B. Durand

Reed and Sturges Warehouse, c. 1855[1]

With the Illinois Central Railroad being shepherded by William Osborn in the
late 1850s, Jonathan could reduce his travel to Chicago and spend more time
with his family and in philanthropic pursuits. Frederick started his business
career at Jonathan's firm full-time in 1855. Mary Sturges wrote in March 1856 of
Frederick's first year at the firm: "Fred is just as settled and sedate as if he were
an old man, indeed almost too much so for his years. He is a very safe businessman and his judgment is much respected. His first year's business has been a
good one and given him a good start in the way of capital."[2]

In 1856, Amelia was out in society, and sons Edward and Arthur were in school, with Edward back studying full-time again and being tutored by a Mr. Goodhue. Henry, about the age of ten, attended the college preparatory school Flushing Institute on Long Island. There he became conspicuous for his studious habits and for a school library he started which became well known.[3]

Virginia was from all accounts happily married and growing her family. She and William Osborn took a cottage at Niagara Falls during the summer of 1856. Amelia visited Virginia for lengthy periods of time in the summer, and these visits were repeated for the next few years. Memie described the inspirational efforts of their friend, artist Frederic Church. "Our cottage is now decorated by a charming sketch of Niagara from Mr. Church's brush. He is intoxicated with Niagara. He rises at sunrise and we only see him at meal times. He is so restless away from the Falls that he cannot keep still, always feeling as if he were losing some new effect of light."[4] Church, the next year, created the painting *Niagara*, three and a half feet tall by seven and a half feet wide, from the study sketches mentioned by Memie.

After four weeks at Cozzens, Virginia lamented to her mother: "We miss the vegetables and fruits from Fairfield but console ourselves by thinking we eat so much there that we are lazy half the time!"[5] Back in New York in December, Amelia wrote to her Aunt Lucretia:

> Father has been sick in bed for a day or two with one of his attacks of pain in his side. He was taken on Tuesday night very severely but was able to sit at the table on Friday when we had a gentlemen's dinner—ten guests. Among whom were Gen. Scott and his son-in-law Colonel Scott, Mr. Henry Sanford, Mr. Grinnell, Mr. Leupp, Cozzens, Bryant, etc. The dinner went off delightfully...it was twelve o'clock when the gentlemen left the dining room, but father was asleep in his bed long before that and has felt no worse for it since.[6]

Jonathan's malady was a repeat occurrence of that which was treated in the past by the cupping procedure. Virginia embraced her parent's belief in homeopathic medicine. Before her marriage, and while traveling in Europe, she described the introduction that Mr. Osborn had to the family's devotion to homeopathic treatments: "He means to pay us off for having had to listen in silence to your enthusiastic descriptions of Dr. Reisig's wonderful cures, which he has not much faith in."[7] Reisig was a family friend and Jonathan endorsed his practice in newspaper advertisements.[8]

Virginia Sturges Osborn c. unk[9]

In June 1857, Virginia left Chicago for the summer and returned to New York—seven months pregnant. While vacationing at Fairfield in August, Virginia went into labor two weeks early and delivered her second child, a son. Mary Sturges had to hurry back to Fairfield from Plainfield, where she was visiting family. Virginia so loved her time and memories of life at the Cottage she named this newborn son Henry Fairfield Osborn.

Jonathan hoped that Virginia and her husband would build their own country home in Fairfield and he was scouting for property when William Osborn became enamored with certain land in Garrison, New York. An Osborn family story passed down through the generations reads:

> In 1857, William Henry Osborn and his wife, Virginia, occupied on the high bluff across the Hudson, a little hotel cottage adjoining Cozzens Hotel, then the most fashionable hotel in the East. One Sunday they crossed the river in a small rowboat, landed at the little dock from which Arnold had taken his flight in 1780, and walked by the brook and across the Beverley Lane. Here near the gate they found a spring, from which flowed a cold and delicious stream. Every traveler, every wayfarer, every tramp, every bird, every dog, knew of the spring and stopped to drink there. William Henry Osborn drank freely of the water and liked it so much that he went back the following Sunday.... After this visit he told his wife, "Virginia, I like that spring. The water agrees with me"...seeming to affect a complete cure of a trouble from which he had been suffering since his residence in the Philippine Islands..."I am going to buy the bit of land in order to come into possession of that spring."[10]

In 1858, Osborn bought the land that he was so smitten with from the owner Mr. Dutilh, which also contained a small, four-room house known as Wing-and-Wing. Virginia had to inform her father they were establishing their country home elsewhere, and Jonathan and Mary lost Virginia's frequent summer visits. Virginia spent much of that summer with her growing family again in the West Point, New York, area in a cottage attached to the Cozzens Hotel, while alterations were being done to their Wing-and-Wing house across the river. Amelia spent several weeks there while William Osborn spent most of his time in Chicago. Mary Sturges also visited Virginia there in July 1858 with her mother Elizabeth and her sister Olivia. Family friend and noted painter Frederic Church was also staying at Cozzens, busily engaged capturing the beauty of the area on paper and canvas. One day he accompanied the party of Sturges ladies on an excursion and coincidentally that evening they all encountered a society celebrity:

> In the afternoon, we went up to Fort Putnam right to the foot of the peak when the driver informed us that he could go no further. To my surprise, Mother said she would walk up, and with the help of a stick and Mr. Church's arm she climbed to the top of the old fort...(we) passed the evening in the parlor listening to old Madame Jerome Bonaparte![a]—whom she remembered seeing in Plainfield when on her bridal trip, alas a young girl.[11]

Frederic Church, Asher Durand and many other native artists were close friends and associates of the Osborn and Sturges families, and they were generous art patrons for these gentlemen. In 1851, Jonathan commissioned William Sydney Mount to paint *Who'll Turn the Grindstone,* which sought to illustrate the axe to grind colloquialism, referring to a person who holds an ulterior motive. The painting depicts a Tom Sawyer-like story where a passing man coaxes and flatters a young boy to sharpen his axe, then dismisses him while admonishing him for being late for school. In 1852, Jonathan commissioned A.B. Durand to paint *God's Judgment Upon Gog.* It was a biblical scene depicting Ezekiel commanding the birds and beasts to

---

a Madame Bonaparte (née Elizabeth Patterson), a title she insisted on being used, had created an international scandal, when she married Jerome Bonaparte, Napoleon I's brother. Even though they had a son, Napoleon ordered Jerome home to France where he facilitated a divorce and a more advantageous marriage to Princess Catharina of Wüttenberg, making him King of Westphalia.

feed on Gog's defeated troops—a theme suggested by Jonathan. It met with mixed reviews, some not very complimentary, although today it is considered a classic Old Testament themed painting.

After this attempt at a biblical subject, Durand turned his attention to painting landscapes. In 1855, Jonathan commissioned Durand to paint the landscape *In the Woods*, which became one of his most critically acclaimed works. Jonathan so treasured this painting that two years after receiving it, he sent an additional $200 check saying, "I desire to add to the price of the woods picture, the trees have grown more than the worth of that sum since 1855."[12]

(top) *Who'll Turn the Grindstone*, c. 1851[13]
(left) *God's Judgment Upon Gog*, c. 1852[14], (right) *In the Woods*, c. 1855[15]

In 1858, Jonathan had to set aside his dream of a public art gallery. Theodore Allen, the New York Gallery of Fine Arts co-founder and Reed's son-in-law, died in 1850, and it had become clear that the public art gallery vision would not be a financially sustainable operation. Several opinions were voiced as to why it failed including the fact that many of the paintings were copies of originals of debatable quality and that the original paintings were already dated. Also, with no government support or significant endowment, the organization could not purchase additions to its holdings, and it was a constant struggle to pay basic administrative expenses. The two main financial supporters had been Jonathan and Thomas Faile, who concluded, along with those board members still interested, that it was time to transfer the paintings to a more permanent institution.

In 1858, the executive board transferred the assets to the New York Historical Society and the American Art-Union did the same with their holdings. Merging these two art gallery collections gave the Historical Society the start of a public art gallery of distinction, which the organization had determined was a goal of the institution. Jonathan continued his stewardship of the collection, and Reed's legacy, as a member of the New York Historical Society's Art Committee until his death.

FOURTEEN

The Courtship of Amelia Sturges and J. Pierpont Morgan

As Amelia said, Father was afraid to take her anywhere, as he lost Virginia at Saratoga; and it was in Newport she was introduced to J. Pierpont Morgan.

—*Mary Cady Sturges*

As Mary said: "Amelia was regularly in society, though never very gay, always occupied, studying German with Edward, attending Bible class, teaching at the Wilson School, and practicing her music, as she always had a master (voice teacher) during the winter season."[1] A devoted Christian, Amelia often wrote to family about sermons that touched her, such as one in 1857 delivered by Dr. McLain in Fairfield:

> I feel as if we could not be too thankful that we shall be under such a pastor this summer... One thing struck me very much in his long prayer: when he prayed for the poor he prayed also for the rich, that they might be enabled to lay up treasure in Heaven where moth and rust doth not corrupt and where thieves do not break through steel [sic]. It was the first time in my recollection that I ever heard a minister pray for the rich. They seem to forget that they, as a class, need and wish the prayers of good people as much as the poor.[2]

Amelia was busy and content, pursuing her many interests and enjoying Virginia's young family. However, it was now time for her life to take a heartwarming development. Mary Sturges related the story of where Amelia and J. Pierpont Morgan met. "I think it was during the summer of 1857, in July, that my husband took Amelia and myself to Newport for the first time. As

Amelia said, Father was afraid to take her anywhere, as he lost Virginia at Saratoga; and it was in Newport she was introduced to J. Pierpont Morgan."[3]

Newport was becoming a favored social scene for the wealthy of New York and Morgan was visiting with the William Wetmore family the week they were there.[4] He was under the close tutelage of his father Junius, a banker and bond trader in London. In Newport, Morgan had his head turned, and he began spending a lot of time with Amelia. Mary remembered the growing attachment, "It was here that our acquaintance with Mr. Morgan became quite intimate, as he made Cozzens his Sabbath boarding place for the summer, and he enjoyed nothing more than spending his afternoons in Virginia's cottage, playing with the children," and of course staying close to Amelia.[5] In a small newspaper column in 1952, reminiscing about old times, it mentioned Morgan's visits to the Sturges home where they hosted their musical evenings. The columnist noted that Jonathan owned the first grand piano in New York City with which they would host frequent musical evenings on Sunday afternoons, which J.P. Morgan would often attend.[6] However, his primary interest wasn't the music.

Mary Sturges reminisced about their friendship with the senior Morgan. "It was in the winter of '58 and '59, that we first became acquainted with Mr. Junius Morgan of London. He had gone out several years previous, as partner to George Peabody from Hartford, which was his native place. Early in life he had married the beautiful Juliet Pierpont, daughter of the Reverend John Pierpont of Boston."[7] Coincidentally, Mary Sturges was in a small boarding school across from Reverend Pierpont's church when she was a young girl and met him when he happened to visit the home one day.

Jonathan and Junius Morgan originally became acquainted through Morgan's previous employment in New York with Jonathan's colleague Morris Ketchum (sometime before 1854). Jonathan and Junius were also engaged with William Osborn, in selling Illinois Central Railroad bonds in London.

By 1859, it was apparent that Morgan had a deepening affection for Amelia. Junius Morgan invited Amelia to visit them in London. This invitation appeared to have been a surprise even to young Morgan, perhaps issued to assess her as a future member of the family. Jonathan and Mary were taken aback by the proposal but acquiesced to the plan with the caveat that she return in the spring unless they joined her.

Amelia left for London in the middle of February. Junius Morgan and his family were leasing a townhouse at No. 13 Princes Gate, overlooking Hyde Park on Kensington Road. Mary reminisced about Amelia's activities there. "Mr. Morgan was very kind in arranging for the young people to see the sights of London. Amelia had a riding dress made, and Mr. Morgan took her riding with him whenever the weather would permit."[8] The "young people" probably included Sarah Goodwin, a niece of Junius Morgan, two years younger than Amelia, who became a close friend. The Morgans were so enjoying Amelia's company that Junius wrote to Jonathan and Mary facetiously suggesting they could delay their trip to join them, due to icebergs and unfavorable sailing winds.[9] The elder Morgan was surely enjoying Amelia's youth and vigor in contrast to his wife's constant health issues, real and imagined.

In London, in March 1859, Amelia noted in her diary that among the many letters she received, at least one was from Captain George McClellan.[10] Until 1859, McClellan and A.P. Hill (future Confederate General) had both been pursuing Mary Ellen (Nellie) Marcy, the daughter of George's former Commanding Officer Randolph Marcy. Nellie accepted Hill's proposal, but he had to withdraw from the engagement, as Nellie's parents did not approve. After Hill's withdrawal, McClellan restarted his courtship of this lady, but not until late in 1859, marrying her thereafter.[11] It is possible George McClellan had an attraction to Amelia. An interest toward the daughter of a prominent New York businessman, in a family he knew well, would not have been unusual. In any case, soon it was clear that the lovely Amelia was all but spoken for.

Mary and Jonathan made plans to join Amelia in England and travel to the continent, as the Illinois Central Board had a need for him to meet with investors in London. Jonathan's passport described him as seemingly diminutive: "five feet seven and one-half inch tall with a dark complexion, long face, and hazel eyes." However, his height was above the era's average of five foot six inches. J. P. Morgan contributed to their preparations by writing a now famous grand tour travelogue to Jonathan in April 1859:

Dear Sir,

In the accompanying memorandum, I have endeavored to furnish you with a foundation stone upon which you may build during your proposed visit to Europe. Having been carefully over most of the ground myself, several times, I am convinced that you will find the order in which I've arranged your visit to the various cities, best conducive to the pleasure of the present trip & to the satisfaction of future retrospection. As you will see I have not attempted to give you any details which you will easily find in Murray's Guide or any other…Trusting Mrs. Sturges and yourself will have a speedy safe voyage.

Yours Sincerely,
J. Pierpont Morgan[12]

The Grand Tour in the 18th Century[13]

An accomplished traveler already at twenty-two, Morgan provided ten handwritten pages of travel recommendations, starting from the train at London Bridge Station, to Calais, Antwerp, Brussels, Holland, Berlin, Potsdam, Dresden, Vienna, Wiesbaden, Frankfurt, Strasbourg, Munich, Paris, Marseille, Milan, Venice, Bologna, Florence, Pisa, Rome, Naples (with many excursions), Madrid, back to Marseille, Paris, London, and steamer back to the United States.[14] He expertly pointed out specific hotels at each stop, sights to see, and what transportation to take between destinations.

Amelia was thoroughly enjoying herself in London, especially the museums and rides through nearby parks. She wrote to Virginia about how comfortable she felt with the Morgan family. Virginia replied, "I am so glad you are so happy at Mr. Morgan's and it is very kind of them to treat you as if you were a relative and make you feel so much at home."[15] The warm feeling soon became mutual between the families.

Jonathan, Mary, Edward, Arthur and Henry Sturges joined Amelia to commence the Grand Tour. The family sailed for England in April 1859, experiencing a ten-day voyage:

> I think we sailed on Wednesday and reached Liverpool a week from the next Saturday, which was considered a good voyage for that time. We were met at Liverpool by Mr. Sherlock, an agent, who took the entire charge of our luggage, getting it through the custom house and sending it to our rooms, which were engaged for us at the Adelphi Hotel…and went up to London on Monday. Amelia and the Misses Morgan were waiting to greet us in our boarding house which was Edwards Family Hotel, George Street, Hanover Square, opposite St. George's church, in which, at that time, all the fashionable weddings took place… The house in former years had been the residence of Lord Palmerston.[16]

Jonathan emphasized to his children the fine points of a good letter. They had to be full of content, informative, cheerful, grammatically correct, and answered promptly. Both Amelia and her sister Virginia were adept at it. Memie's many letters from Europe were very descriptive and entertaining. One of them described a social event they attended in London:

> I am sitting now all dressed to go to a Ball with Father. The first one I have been to in England. It is called the Goldsmith's Ball and is given by a very rich association of gentlemen. We received an invitation through one of them, Mr. Trotter[a], who has been in America and knew Virginia, so Father thought we had better go & see how they do these things in England.[17]

In Brighton, they visited the Pavilion of George the Fourth from which, Memie noted that P.T. Barnum took inspiration for his own home Iranistan in Bridgeport, Connecticut. Before leaving England, the family took a trip to Aldershot, an army town in the county of Hampshire, where the Queen was to review the troops. Memie described the scene:

> Monday morning, we left Brighton, taking a train for the camp at Aldershot where the Queen was to review 13,000 troops. This review I will not

---

a Alexander Trotter was a stockbroker for Coutt's Bank in London and had become personally acquainted with William and Virginia Osborn in 1858, while traveling in the U.S. The Osborns hosted them in their rented cottage at the Cozzens Hotel due to the sold-out status of the hotel. The ball was likely at the Goldsmiths Hall in London.

attempt to describe to you, but it was something worth going a long, long way to see. The camp ground was a perfectly barren heath many miles in extent…At the close of the fight the Queen moved down into the valley and then I told the carriage driver to get as close to the Queen as possible, which he soon succeeded in doing. The Royal cavalcade finally stopped at the bottom of a hill…We got to within one of the mounted guards around Her Majesty and you would have laughed I guess to see Father jumping up on the top of a cab to get a better view of Royalty. Mother and I jumped up on the driver's box where we could get a better look at the motion of the Queen. She stood up in the carriage with the Princess Anne at her side and how do you think she was dressed? She had on a drab cloth cloak, a waterproof I should think, a green silk bonnet, trimmed with a plain red ribbon. Many a lady who goes to Fairfield Church would feel herself very shabby if she were to dress like either the Queen or the Princess, but if the story is true that the Queen economizes in order to pay her father's debts, it is praiseworthy and a most uncommon instance as sovereigns are only too ready to lavish all the money they have on useless extravagances.[18]

Leaving England, they departed for Paris, following much of the itinerary outlined by Pierpont, taking Miss Goodwin as a traveling companion for Amelia until Paris, when she went her own way. After travels to Vienna, Lucerne, and Switzerland in August, the family was off to Italy. In Rome, Amelia observed:

The people are poor as poverty itself, and filthy to the last degree. Beggars crippled and deformed swarm about you wherever you go. It seemed like nothing but the fear of God was needed to make this country an earthly paradise, while now it is a land of beggars and thieves. The people all live in the streets. I think the children are allowed to take care of themselves and play in the dirt all day, a thing I believe children always will do if allowed.[19]

Back in New York, Virginia was pregnant again and Pierpont spent many Sundays with Virginia during her confinement. After one of his visits Virginia wrote Amelia:

Pierpont Morgan came in and has cut my letter short. He does not think your excuse for not writing valid and still expects his letter. We had a pleasant hour talk together. Mr. Osborn when he wishes to take me to task does so on account of Pierpont, but I do enjoy the overflow of life and energy he has in him and was amused with Aunt E., who thought him gauche the first evening, being entirely won by his honest downrightness.[20]

After the birth of her son, Virginia wrote to Memie in July 1859: "We propose to call him Frederick Sturges. My husband says there is no one we think more of than the dear old fellow himself, and he is utterly opposed to fancy names. He [Osborn] says it is a good English fashion to preserve the name of a mother to her children."[21]

In October, the Sturges family was in Italy, including Florence and Naples, and then back in London by November. There, Jonathan found himself very engaged with the Illinois Central Railroad investors, many of whom had traveled from other parts of England to meet with him. Shareholders had just been assessed $10 a share to shore up the financial condition of the company. *The Economist* reported on this meeting: "The London agents of the Illinois Central Railway Company at the request of the London committee of shareholders...concur with the Board in New York (a member of which, Jonathan Sturges, is now in London) that he interests of the company require that these temporary measures (delaying calls or assessments on stockholders) should be discontinued."[22]

Morgan joined the Sturges family in London in November. It had been nine months since he had seen Amelia, and he made the most of his time with her for the next few weeks, accompanying her each day to visit galleries and other London attractions. The family returned to the United States by early December 1859.

From Charleston in January 1860, Morgan wrote to his cousin Jim Goodwin mentioning the Sturges family. After denying an engagement rumor ("No truth in the report" he declared), he encouraged Goodwin to get to know the family better, saying, "Now that you have become acquainted with the Sturges', I would advise you to nourish the acquaintance...there are few if any more desirable families to be on intimate terms with in the city of NY. This between us and the post."[23] At the same time in January, Pierpont's sister Sarah was spending the week with the Sturges family in New York.

Pierpont had developed a deep affection for Amelia and great respect for her family, although he was still seeing other lady friends from time to time. Morgan was not necessarily a natural or the most appropriate match for Amelia, as claimed years later by a newspaper article emphasizing the "human side" of the titan Morgan:

> He [Morgan] was not regarded as a proper suitor for the lovely Amelia Sturges. There was in particular one young man, since prominent in the business world, who had distinct aspirations himself for Miss Sturges's hand and whose contempt for "that brute Morgan" was intense. (Except for the difference of years, Mr. Morgan's personal appearance was much the same then as it is now.) But Mr. Morgan paid such skillful suit to Miss Sturges that he won her, and there was no pretext under which the other young man could interfere. Morgan never had a victory that seemed as great to him as this.[24]

Amelia Sturges, c. 1859[25] and J. Pierpont Morgan, Paris, c. 1859[26]

When the Sturges family arrived back from Europe, Morgan was a frequent and attentive visitor and as Mary Sturges said: "His acquaintance with my daughter, Amelia, soon ripened into a warm attachment."[27] Morgan was about to sail to London to meet with his father in July 1860. Before his departure he paid a visit to Virginia, again summering at Cozzens Hotel at West Point. Virginia tells how she first heard of their new understanding:

Mr. Osborn went to Saratoga this morning with Col. Foster to remain till Saturday night and while I was sitting quietly at dinner with Mr. Whitredge and the children, in walked Pierpont unexpectedly, though you had said he would come to see me before he sailed. I think it flashed across instantly <u>why</u> he had come and when he showed me a letter from Mother and said he would not give it to me until after dinner …And now my darling sister as I consider the possession of a perfectly true straight forward manly heart precious beyond everything, I congratulate you. You will prize it more with every year that rolls over your head, for I can assure you the tie straightens, and much as has been written about young love, it's not half so deep or tender as the love of years standing. I have always liked Pierpont for his own sake and you may be quite sure I shall now love him for yours, and I am very thankful he is not a stranger whom I have to learn to like.[28]

Virginia's greatest fear was that Junius would order Pierpont to faraway lands to do his bidding, but Morgan assured her that a distant posting was not in the plans. So, Amelia Sturges and J. Pierpont Morgan were engaged. As was the custom, engagements did not become public for a time, although there was always talk when two young people spent a significant time together. Amelia informed her brother Henry in September 1860 of the news:

I don't know whether anyone has told you my dear Henry that something has happened…I hope one of these days that you will have for a brother Mr. Morgan and a good, kind one I am sure you will find him, so you see I have engaged a courier[b] for life, but perhaps after all you will take a European tour with us for you know he is a great traveler. I don't wish of you to speak of this outside our own family as it is not known at present…now I want you to write to me and tell me if you are pleased with the choice I have made. Mr. Morgan has always liked you very much.[29]

During their courtship, he romantically carved their initials, JPM + AS inside a heart, on a large beach tree outside the Cottage during one of his many visits. They planned for an October 1861 marriage, but the country's fortunes and Amelia's health would complicate their happy plans.

---

[b] A "courier" was engaged by the wealthy to facilitate their travel, set up lodgings and transportation abroad.

FIFTEEN

The 1860 Election and Run-Up to War

We saw Abraham Lincoln as he rode through this street...he is a bright, pleasant looking man, rather young looking, he has a hard lot before him.

—*Mary Cady Sturges*

Jonathan Sturges, 1860s[1]

The 1860s were a remarkable time for the nation and for Jonathan and Mary Sturges. The growing divide between the North and the South, primarily over slavery, made the 1860 election both pivotal and chaotic. Jonathan had been a Whig for over twenty years, and as such, wasn't always an abolitionist nor an avid Lincoln supporter. His membership in the Colonization Society pro-vides key insight to his view on slavery.[a] Connecticut had a rather tempered view of the institution and it was a Colonization Society stronghold—sometimes referred to as the "Georgia of the North." The Society advocated a repatriation of the slave population back to Africa, where they could live and govern themselves under a banner of equal rights, believing that equality with whites was not realistically achievable. Lincoln, even early in his presidency, held the same opinion. Most Black leaders were outspoken in their opposition to the Colonization Society, preferring former slaves to stay and work for a better life. However, the Society continued undaunted in its mission, later evolving to emphasize missionary goals. Liberia was founded in 1821 as a direct result of this movement. As a long-time public subscriber to this repatriation viewpoint, it affected his political choices.

The winds of impending internal conflict were building as the decade of the 1850s ended. John Brown's actions in Missouri and at Harper's Ferry fanned the Southern torches of outrage, which needed little to be ignited. Jonathan, his close business associates, and thousands of other leading citizens endeavored to moderate the situation by calling a grand meeting in December 1859 in New York City. They denounced John Brown's insurrectionist activities and sought to assure their Southern brethren they desired to maintain the Union per its constitutional principles, and not interfere in its institutions.[2]

On Monday evening, February 25, 1860, Lincoln spoke at New York City's Cooper Union, sponsored by the National Union Executive Committee, a newly formed pro-Union organization. William Cullen Bryant was a board member of the group and he chaired the meeting and introduced the speaker. Lincoln set out his case that the Constitution was clear that the Federal government had the power to prohibit the extension of slavery but not where it [already] existed. Said Lincoln, "...in their understanding, no line dividing local from federal authority, nor anything in the Constitution, properly forbade Congress to prohibit slavery in the federal territory..." The speech was a turning point in his campaign. His simplicity in delivery, powerful reasoning, and absence of fluffy rhetoric impressed the crowd and gained him financial backing from many of these businessmen.

Considering his close association with Bryant and others endorsing Lin-coln, it is curious that Jonathan wasn't in the forefront promoting this gathering.

---

[a] Mary's Colonization Society membership certificate is archived at the Fairfield Museum and History Center.

The explanation was in his ardent desire to preserve the Union and flow of commerce with the South, and the emotionally charged and fractured political scene. In April 1860, the divided Democratic Party met in Charleston, South Carolina, to construct its platform and nominate its candidate, but it was slavery that was the dominant issue for most delegates. Leading candidate Stephen Douglas, a moderate, advocated state's choice as to the extension of slavery. The Southern contingent promoted Mississippi Senator Jefferson Davis and demanded that slavery extend to any new states or territories added to the Union—Davis declined any nomination. The *New York Times* reported:

> The Democratic Convention at Charleston is unable to frame a platform sound enough to sustain a united party. The difficulty lies in finding a safe man between the Douglas extreme on the one hand, and the Alabama fire-eaters on the other; and if the multitudinous attempts thus far made ineffectually are indications of the future, there is little hope of a platform, and less of a candidate.[3]

Adjourning without a nominee, they reconvened in Baltimore. Northern Democrats nominated Douglas, but Southerners could not endorse Douglas and walked out. Southern Democrats then met in Richmond, Virginia, and nominated Vice President John C. Breckinridge of Kentucky and Joseph Lane of Oregon, a ticket endorsed by President James Buchanan.

The Whig Party had collapsed in the mid-1850s after the deaths of Clay and Webster. The void was filled by the Republican Party, which nominated Abraham Lincoln, and the Constitution Union Party, a group formed by compromise-minded Democrats, "Know Nothings"[b] and some former Whigs trying to find middle ground that would preserve the Union—which included Jonathan Sturges. The *New York Times* declared: "The unmixed Whig character of the ticket does not escape remark. An occasional Democrat suspects that this is little less than a Whig Convention."[4] At their convention in Baltimore, they nominated Senator John Bell of Tennessee and former Governor and Senator Edward Everett of Massachusetts.

With the Democratic party divided between Douglas and Breckinridge, and Republican support split between Lincoln and Bell, Jonathan and his colleagues envisioned that the election would likely go to the House of

---

b Former "American Party"—semi-secret, anti-Catholic, anti-immigrant, nativist political group. When members were asked about the activities of the party, they were to answer that they "know nothing."

Representatives and Bell would be the compromise candidate. On the eve of the election it was clear that support for Bell was weak and a run-off was not likely. Wealthy capitalists, including Jonathan, pragmatically threw their support behind Lincoln as the most acceptable and electable candidate:

> The *New York Evening Post* gives a list of leading capitalists in that city, Bell-fusionists before, who have now answered…to vote direct for Lincoln. The list includes Wm. A. Booth, late president of the American Exchange bank; J. Q. Jones, President, Chemical Bank…Jonathan Sturges, A.A. Low, Morris Ketchum, John Jacob Astor, Charles H. Marshall, C.V.S. Roosevelt[c] (brother of Judge Roosevelt), etc.[5]

The *New York Herald* published a Memorial petition signed by Jonathan Sturges and other well-known merchants, inviting the public to a rally in support of their belief that "the election of Lincoln is the only means of preventing the transference of the present contest for the Presidency to the halls of Congress."[6]

On the same day, anticipating a Lincoln victory, Southern secessionists began discussions with France as to their willingness to support a separate government in the South. Armed conflict was now all but assured. On November 6, Lincoln won the election with 39% of the vote, without being on the ballot in ten southern states and getting no more than 2.5% in three others. South Carolina seceded on December 20. Preparations for war began in both the North and the South. New York City was generally sympathetic to the Confederate cause. The cotton trade was over one third of New York's shipping activity and Mayor Fernando Wood advocated for New York to become a free and independent city.[7]

In January 1861, still trying to seek a compromise short of division and war, Jonathan and several other prominent citizens sent a Memorial to Congress suggesting modifications to the Fugitive Slave Act. It emphasized the United States justice system's lawful control of the process in protecting the rights of the slave owner, former slaves, and protection against free African-Americans being kidnapped and enslaved by southern vigilantes.[8] However, it was too little and too late—a Southern confederation was a fait accompli.

On his way to his inauguration in Washington, Lincoln paraded through New York in an open barouche carriage as the Sturges family looked on near

---

[c] Paternal grandfather of President Theodore Roosevelt.

their E. 14th Street home. Mary Sturges told her mother: "We saw Abraham Lincoln as he rode through this street...he is a bright, pleasant looking man, rather young looking, he has a hard lot before him."[9] By the time of his inauguration on March 4, seven states had already seceded from the Union, and the Confederate States of America became a reality. Buchanan, the outgoing president reportedly said to him, "If you are as happy entering the presidency as I am leaving it, then you are a very happy man."

Lincoln now had to walk a fine line to prevent further secessions, especially in Virginia. The Union commander at Fort Sumter in Charleston Harbor was directed to evacuate by the Confederate military contingent there. All local supplies were cutoff, and rations were running low. Lincoln wanted to avoid becoming the aggressor and sought a middle ground. He notified the South Carolina governor he was sending ships to resupply Fort Sumter with provisions only, which prompted the Confederacy to push for the immediate evacuation of Union troops. Major Anderson, the fort commander, although knowing it was futile, declined to evacuate. Confederate troops fired upon Fort Sumter on April 12, 1861. They conducted an artillery bombardment for thirty-three hours. The Confederates had fired the first shot and become the aggressor. Major Anderson surrendered the fort on April 13 to his former West Point artillery student, Confederate Brigadier General Beauregard. Anderson and his men were permitted to evacuate and return North. No casualties were suffered during the shelling; however, the nation was now at war. On April 15, Lincoln called for 75,000 ninety-day volunteers to restore the Union. On April 17, Virginia approved an Ordinance of Secession, and Arkansas, North Carolina, and Tennessee followed suit by June 8.

Jonathan and his colleagues from the New York's Chamber of Commerce took the early lead in shoring up patriotism and the public morale. On April 20, they sponsored a public meeting, "regardless of political party or affiliation," to endorse the Union cause.

Jonathan and the organizing committee asked that no other banner but the American flag fly that day and that businesses close at two o'clock to allow for attendance.[10] Major Anderson and his men from Fort Sumter were honored attendees at the gathering. As Virginia Sturges wrote: "The day Major Anderson was fired upon, every man in the city of New York was roused from his lethargy and in one week these people were willing to sacrifice their property and their lives."[11]

Mass Union Meeting, April 20, 1861[12]

Declarations supporting the Union cause went forward from the Chamber of Commerce to President Lincoln, who "read the resolutions with the highest appreciation of the loyalty, patriotism and liberality of that body; and to the end they might find a just place in the history of this most important crisis."[13] Many Chamber members lent substantial sums of money to the government and further opened their purses to raise and equip troops. Jonathan and other Chamber members subscribed more than $115,000 toward outfitting volunteers.[14]

Jonathan, even though a latecomer to Lincoln's candidacy, was conspicuous for his pro-Union activities. More personal and concerning to him and Mary, was that both of his sons, Frederick and Edward, were in uniform during the war, albeit briefly. When the Civil War began, enlistments were for a ninety-day period, and many of those early enlistees served their entire time in training encampments and returned home, having seen no action. In both Frederick's and Edward's cases, their regiments were state militias, and mainly used as emergency surge units, for the defense of the home front. These militias typically performed active duty for thirty to ninety days and then returned and mustered out. Edward Sturges was a Private for his entire military service and affiliated with the famed 7th New York State Militia Volunteers, Company B—the pride of New York City. Historians Coates and Kochan described the regiment:

> The 7th New York State Militia was one of the finest military regiments in the entire country prior to the war. Finely outfitted and armed with the best weapons, they were the ideal to which every other military regiment could be judged. The 7th was organized and headquartered in New York City and its ranks were filled with young men from some of the city's finest

families. They frequently paraded in the city, where their expertise at drill was evident to all who saw them.[15]

7th Regiment New York Militia, Marching Down Broadway[16]

On April 19, New York's finest were marching off to protect the Capitol. The Seventh Regiment's march down Broadway was an exciting and historic event. Businesses closed, and enthusiastic citizens were hanging from every vantage point to view the celebrated regiment depart for war. Troops formed a line between Fourth and Eighth Streets around Lafayette Place, down Great Jones Street, and on to Broadway. Although the Mayor and most of the city populace were anti-war, now their sons', brothers', fathers', friends' and cousins' lives were on the line, and on this day the crowded streets were brimming with patriotic spirit. Henry Sturges journaled the stirring atmosphere as the family watched their friends and neighbors march away. A military historian noted, "It was less a march than a triumphal procession. Many thousands joined the moving column preceding the march in escort or following in rear. Streets, sidewalks, open areas, fences, stoops, balconies, windows, roofs, trees, lampposts, awnings, every foot of available space, held spectators, and for long distances on the side streets the compact throngs struggled for a glance."[17] As each company passed by, they paused in front of Major Anderson's review position to honor him. Virginia described the pervading national feeling:

Actions of the North are inspired by God himself. No one can understand it that hasn't been in our midst from the commencement of these troubles. Four weeks ago, people did not hesitate to say, "New York is governed by its pocket and will never fight against the South if so by doing it endangers the commercial prosperity." Our form of government has proved itself a failure and we no longer have any country or any laws which govern the people...it would be very hard to find anyone anywhere who has confidence either in Mr. Lincoln or Mr. Seward...The very fact that the Seventh Regiment took with them one of almost every family of standing made the struggle that night one of life or death.[18]

The 7th Regiment served thirty days, fortifying Washington, D.C., then returned to New York to great accolades, credited with saving the Capitol from Southern aggression. Twenty-four-year-old Private Edward Sturges followed with the next detachment of the 7th Regiment for thirty days in May.

However, all too quickly it became clear that both sides were in the fight for the long haul. Virginia, writing to her mother on December 12, 1861, lamented: "We don't expect to have very merry holidays; everyone here is so anxious as what may be the fate of our country."[19] Edward was called up for duty a second time. Mary's niece, Lizzie Babcock, daughter of Mary's sister Olivia, noted Edward's departure while visiting Fairfield on May 20, 1862:

> Cousin Eddie was reading the paper this morning, saw a notice to the Seventh Regiment to be ready to start for Washington. Aunt Mary was coming down on the evening train...Uncle S. telegraphed her, and she got down about an hour and a half before he went away. She did not feel half as bad as she did last year when he went away. Cousin Eddie came down with his nice grey uniform on and his knapsack, and other accoutrements strapped to his back. He looked very nice and his eyes sparkled. He was glad to go.[20]

Ed served ninety days. He wrote home on August 21, 1862, from Federal Hill, Baltimore, just before returning home:

> I have made many pleasant acquaintances here and I flatter myself I am now a pretty good soldier, still our life here is at best a roving one and I long to settle down to a regular life again. I come in sometimes from our drills which have been very severe with both mind and body exhausted with no desire to read or write, this will account somewhat for me being such a poor correspondent...[21]

In 1858, as the threat of war rose, Frederick Sturges and his associates founded the 22nd New York State Militia, known as the Union Grays, a militia unit to protect the city. Starting out as an elite social club, it had many sons of wealthy families, consisting mainly of businessmen and clerks, as was the case with the Seventh Regiment:

> There were in New York a number of unattached military companies (that were) no part of the regular National Guard, which had been previously organized under the growing apprehension of trouble that had existed in the public mind for some time. A number of these availed themselves of the organization of the Union Grays to enroll themselves as members. Among these were the City Cadets, which joined as Companies G and H. This had its origin in "The White Ball Club" which was formed in 1858 and named after Charles Trumbull White. Among the leading spirits of this club were George DeForest Lord, Walter Edwards, Fred Sturges, A. G. Agnew and Thomas Denny. The club was remarkable for nothing more than the social standing of its members.[22]

Frederick was ordered to muster into Company G of the 22nd Regiment on May 28, 1862. Fred felt it was his duty to serve, and he proceeded with preparations to leave. Jonathan objected to Fred's plans, believing he did not have the constitution for army life. Jonathan had arranged for Fred to go overseas. Lizzie Babcock wrote on May 27, 1862: "The plans are changed again, he (Fred) has given up his company and goes to Europe next week."[23] However, s Frederick's letters attest, he asserted his will and served with his regiment for a ninety-day posting. They spent their time in the Baltimore area through early June and then at Camp Hill, Harper's Ferry, Virginia. He wrote Mary from there on July 6:

> I was truly in the spirit of the day...I went to the river and took a bath... put on clean clothes throughout, blacked my boots, put on my new [illegible], trimmed my mustache...and ate my breakfast...and sat down with my little prayer book...it was one of the most beautiful days you ever saw. I could not help thinking it was quieter than usual and that it was indeed the Lord's day...There are strong reasons for believing that we must go to [illegible] to look after the bushwhackers, this would be a great business for us I think, however, we will remain here for the present. I find that I am obliged to live a great deal of time on crackers and jelly, not be able to eat pork yet and I wish if you can and if you have any left, if you would send me about a [illegible] of black jelly and red jelly.[24]

Harper's Ferry (left), Camp Hill, c. unk [25], 22nd New York State Militia, c. 1862 [26]

Both Union and Confederate troops occupied Camp Hill at different junctures in the war. Probably the most well-known regiment to camp there was Frederick's 22nd New York State Militia. Their notoriety came not from fighting but from the many photographs they left as a record of their time in Harper's Ferry during their encampment in the summer of 1862.

Frederick's regiment mustered out in New York on September 6 under the command of Lieutenant Colonel Lloyd Aspinwall.[d] The only casualty was an officer who died of disease.[27] However, after an uncomfortable camp experience, Frederick relented and followed his father's advice, moving to Paris to represent the firm there. He was in place by December 1862 and wrote to his father advising Edward to "give up his connection with the 7th Regiment and give his whole attention to his business. I shall resign in my own company."[28]

While both Edward and Frederick were on active duty in mid-1862 in Maryland and Northern Virginia, the fighting was mainly in Southern Virginia, Kentucky and North Carolina. The most noteworthy conflict was the Seven Days Battle near Richmond that ended July 1. This period of the War was characterized by indecisive and timid battle tactics by General McClellan (former Illinois Central Chief Engineer), where in lieu of retreating or regrouping, an immediate counter-offensive might have struck a decisive blow to the Confederate forces. Union prospects were discouraging, and the country was $500,000 in debt and counting. Lincoln was forced to enact an income tax to finance the war. He also had to call up an additional 300,000 men for three-year enlistments, bringing the army to a strength of 500,000.

---

[d] Founder and first president of the historic Jekyll Island Club—founded in 1886 as a vacation retreat for wealthy northerners. He died before it opened, but as the ghost story goes he still pays an occasional visit to the grounds.

With the war not going well for the Union, Jonathan and his colleagues sought to help the government more effectively prosecute the war. He played key roles in founding and managing multiple support organizations that significantly aided the Union, all of which had lasting legacies. One of these organizations was the United States Sanitary Commission.

Dr. Henry Bellows was the inspiration and leader for the Sanitary Commission. His idea was to establish an auxiliary association to aid the overwhelmed army medical corps in attending to wounded and ill Union soldiers. He began by petitioning the government and obtained tacit approval from the interim Surgeon General Dr. Lawson. However, the next appointed Surgeon General, Dr. Clement A. Finley, resisted the whole idea. To him and other Army "regulars," it was an uncomfortable admission that they could not handle their own medical requirements. Bellows reached a frustrating compromise with the Army that underscored the military's priority in allocating resources to treat professional army soldiers.

> After much explanation and negotiation, it was agreed that the operations of the Commission should be confined to the volunteers, and in that shape the project received at last the reluctant approval of the Surgeon-General...That volunteers could ever make good soldiers, and especially that their officers could ever be fitted for high commands, or learn how to take care of their men, was long esteemed rank heresy according to the creed of professional soldiers.[29]

On June 9, 1861, the Secretary of War issued an authorization for "A Commission of Inquiry and Advice in Respect of the Sanitary interests of the United States Forces." There was an office provided for their use in Washington D.C., and they served without compensation from the government. "They were to direct their inquiries to the principles and practice connected with the inspection of recruits and enlisted men, the sanitary condition of volunteers, to the means of preserving and restoring the health and of securing the general comfort and efficiency of the troops, to the proper provision of cooks, nurses, and hospitals and to other subjects of a like nature."[30] Undaunted by the restrictions imposed, they went into action organizing and appointing directors and officers, which included Bellows as President and Frederick Law Olmsted (Central Park architect) as General Manager.

Next, they formed a finance committee to fund and manage expenditures for the organization. Sanitary Commission historian Stillé describes Jonathan's role:

Certain prominent gentlemen in New York were invited to act as a Central Auxiliary Finance Committee... The following named gentlemen composed this Committee: Hon. Samuel B. Ruggles, Christopher R. Roberta, Robert B. Minturn, George Opdyke, Jonathan Sturges, Morris Ketchum, David Hoadley, J. P. Giraud Forster, and Charles E. Strong... Through the exertions of these gentlemen large sums were contributed by public institutions and private individuals throughout the country.[31]

For the war's duration Jonathan served on a crucial sub-committee with Morris Ketchum, A.A. Low, and later John Jacob Astor III, to solicit larger donations from banks and other moneyed institutions of the city.[32] In a time of increasing debt for the country, trade with the South cut off, and a significant number of men serving in the military, discretionary funds might be expected to be scarce. However, for those supplying the war machine, many of whom lived in New York, it was a boom time for business, and they gave generously to these causes. Its efforts spared countless lives and made better the conditions for the wounded and ill. At the 1863 Battle of Antietam alone, it was estimated that their field operations saved the lives of at least 1,000 soldiers.[33] The mission was continued after the war by Dr. Bellows in the form of the American Association for the Relief of the Misery of Battlefields (1866-1872) —the direct predecessor of the American Red Cross.

Wagons and Workers of U.S. Sanitary Commission, c. 1865[34]

Jonathan and his colleagues were invested in the war effort in many ways, and this was one of the first of many endeavors initiated by this remarkable group of patriotic gentlemen. For Jonathan personally, these efforts would help occupy his mind during a sorrowful turn of events within his own beloved family.

SIXTEEN

Civil War and the Marriage of Amelia and J. Pierpont Morgan

I wish you could see his loving devoted care of me, he spares nothing for
my comfort and improvement.

—Amelia Sturges Morgan

In January 1861, Virginia wrote of the quiet life being led by the family, of
how her husband was "too tired and preoccupied to enjoy society," and that
they play "Darby and Joan" by their fireside.[1a] Meanwhile, the betrothed
couple had also become quite domesticated, with Pierpont visiting on
almost a daily basis and Amelia preferring to do nothing with Morgan in her
comfortable home to doing the same thing in a crowd, although, as Amelia
noted to her aunt, she appreciated having a willing attendant when she went
out.

Amelia had been enjoying remarkable health and in February 1861 she
sympathized with her Aunt Elizabeth, who had been suffering with some
lingering affliction. "I know so little of sickness that I cannot realize what
you are going through, but you have my very warm sympathy."[2] Sadly, she
already carried the deadly germ that would manifest itself a month later. On
March 2, 1861, Mary Sturges wrote to her mother: "Amelia has had another
bad cold and still coughs," and it was not relenting.[3] The doctors did not yet
know it was more than a stubborn cough. However, by August, she was so
severely sick she thought it best to call off the marriage, but Pierpont would
not relent in his resolve. Mary late recalled: "She was advised to go abroad to
a milder climate. Algiers had a good reputation for such cases, and the question was, who was to accompany her? Mr. Morgan insisted they be married
and go together."[4]

---

a *Darby and Joan* is a one act play depicting an older couple who fall asleep next to the fire dream-
ing about their own courtship (dreams acted out while they slept).

The two families agreed on the plan for them to marry and seek treatment in Europe and Algiers. The nuptials took place in the Sturges family home on East Fourteenth Street in October 1861. Amelia was so weak that Pierpont carried her from her bedroom to the wedding ceremony. Jean Strouse, the J.P. Morgan biographer, noted, "She was so frail, he had to hold her up at the altar. She kept her veil over her face during the ceremony because she felt herself so thin that she wasn't pretty anymore."[5] The newspaper announcement was simple: "In New York, Oct 7th, at the residence of the bride's father, by the Rev. Thomas DeWitt, D.D., J. Pierpont Morgan and Amelia, daughter of Jonathan Sturges, Esq., all of the city."[6]

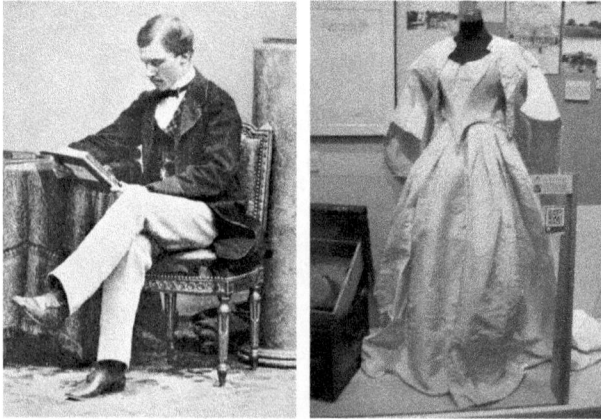

Pierpont Before Marriage[7] and Amelia's Wedding Dress[8]

On October 9, Mr. and Mrs. J.P. Morgan, and a maid named Anna, sailed away on the steamship Persia. The couple's first stop was London where they consulted a doctor, then to Paris where they consulted lung specialists. It was confirmed there that she was afflicted with consumption, now known as tuberculosis. In November, they departed for Algiers. However, "there a new danger met her. An epidemic of the bowels was prevailing, and she took it; this much reduced her strength and increased her cough."[9] In stark contrast to the intimidating and imposing capitalist and financier which the world later came to know, Amelia wrote to her mother describing Pierpont's attentiveness: "I wish you could see his loving devoted care of me, he spares nothing for my comfort and improvement."[10] Morgan was on a mission to save his dear Memie. Unfortunately, on December 28 in Algiers, he had to write a difficult letter to Jonathan:

… But my dear Mr. Sturges, I cannot hide from myself that Memie is very, very sick. The trouble with the left lung which had commenced when we arrived has progressed with rapidity since we have been here, and Dr. Feuillet acknowledged to me yesterday that the lower part of both the left and right lungs were affected. I cannot tell you what a blow it is to me. We can only trust and hope, although it may be against hope, that our heavenly father may yet pour without our drinking yet. In the very reduced state in which Memie lies, you will readily understand how anxious I am for Mrs. Sturges to be with us and I trust she is already on the way.[11]

In mid-January, Morgan again urged Mary to join them in Paris, that Memie's health was further deteriorating. Mary and Edward had already left on January 15. They received news en route that the Morgans had left for Nice and had settled in at the Villa St. George.

After Mary and Edward arrived in Nice, Pierpont left for London at the request of his father to discuss business matters. He returned ten days later, but Memie's condition had only worsened in his absence. Jonathan wrote to Memie on March 3 attempting to spiritually prepare her for the next life, "We had hoped to hear better accounts of your health… If our prayers for your restoration to us are not answered as we desire, I shall always feel that it is the blessed savior that desires to have you with him."[12] Memie never received her father's letter. On the Sabbath, February 16, 1862, Memie sat up and had dinner with the family. She told her mother, "I was always very happy, I have not a care about myself," and as she looked lovingly at Mary and Pierpont next to her she said, "I believe in ministering angels." After a bad night, she passed away the next evening. The family in New York received the news two weeks later. Besides Arthur, it was Memie who Henry felt closest to. Darkening the border around the pages in his diary on March 5, 1862, Henry wrote, "I received the news from Fred that dearest Memie died at Nice on the 17th. Oh God, give me and mother and father strength to bear this."[b]

Pierpont, Mary and Edward did some sightseeing in France and Italy after Memie's death, a much-needed respite after the sad events of the prior three months. They were back home by the end of April. Services were scheduled for May 1 but then rescheduled to May 3 due to the weather.[13] Henry commented in his diary on May 1, "It was a good thing we're not able to hold the funeral

---

[b] During the Victorian era, it was common for those in mourning to have correspondence bordered in black.

today, for if they had had it, it would have been doubly dismal, such a rainy disagreeable day. I feel very tired and with God's blessing hope to sleep safely and soundly."

Train schedules governed the timing and plans for such events that included New York residents and Amelia's services were no exception. Henry wrote, "Virginia, Mr. Morgan, Mr. and Mrs. Goodwin came over on the 8 oc [sic] train.ᶜ All the rest of the friends came up with the body on the 11:24. The funeral service was beautiful. It almost killed me to see dear Memie…It was all over in time for the 5:21 train." Memie was buried in the family plot of the East Cemetery on the Old Post Road, in the town where some of her happiest memories were forged. The inscription on Amelia Sturges Morgan's gravestone carries a spiritual message, Not Lost But Gone Before—foretelling of a reuniting in heaven.

Pierpont and the Sturges family leaned heavily on divine guidance as they grieved. Jonathan referred to Pierpont's reliance on his faith in his last letter to Amelia. "It is a great comfort for us to know that your dear husband is able to apply the beautiful services in the prayer book to his own comfort. There is nothing but child-like submission to the will of his heavenly father that can give him comfort…"[14]

Virginia wrote of her grief from Chicago to her brother Frederick: "Some of my sweetest earthly dreams have been connected with Memie….thoughts of our families growing up together seemed the greatest happiness I could know… but those dreams faded away and instead have been replaced with thoughts of the happy meeting when I too shall be called."[15]

An outpouring of sympathy came to the Sturges family from London to Savannah, and Fredericksburg to Illinois, with messages of sympathy, faith and prayer. Jonathan, writing to Mary in July 1862, stated: "Everybody sympathizes so with me. I never knew I had so many friends. I have to put an extra [illegible] in the tithe to make up for deficiencies."[16] Jonathan's pastor wrote of a reunion in heaven to come. "It was for her Christian character that we loved her most… He has said to her, 'child come up higher'…Yours is the sorrow of parting but soon it will be the joy of reunion in a world where there are no more partings."[17] A friend in London, William Evans, wrote, "I assure you of my deep sympathy for your terrible bereavement. …Trusting you will arrive safely (from Europe),

---

ᶜ Jim Goodwin was a pallbearer.

find Mr. Sturges and your family well and the unhappy troubles of your glorious country approaching a proper solution."[18]

Morgan took Amelia's loss hard. He felt responsible for taking her on a journey that may have worsened her condition, even though it was clear that her case had been hopeless. In January 1862, his Aunt Goodwin lamented: "I realized when she went away that she would never come back."[19] However, like Morgan, Aunt Goodwin had not yet reconciled herself to the irreversible path of Memie's disease. The Sturges family embraced Morgan as a loved family member and they leaned on each other in their shared grief. In the fall, Morgan became very sick with a variant of small-pox and Mrs. Sturges nursed him until family could arrive to take over. Morgan remained in close contact with the Sturges family all his life.

Expedition to the White Mountains—Edward Ketchum, J.P. Morgan, Miss Cornelia Ketchum, Arthur Sturges, Mrs. Edward Ketchum, Miss Saltonstall and Colonel Pride[20]

Morgan was a widower at twenty-four. After burying Memie, he threw himself into his work but remained a close companion to the Sturges boys. Jean Strouse in *Morgan: American Financier*, related an outing Morgan had with Arthur and Henry Sturges in 1863:

> Eighteen months after Memie's death Pierpont was returning to a fuller engagement with life. At the end of July 1863, he arranged an expedition with several friends including Arthur and Henry Sturges, and

Edward Ketchum, Morris's son. The party started at West Point, proceeded by train and stagecoach to Lake George, in the Adirondacks and continued mostly by sailboat to Lake Champlain. From Burlington, Vermont they drove across the state to New Hampshire's White Mountains. Pierpont swam, sailed and rode, and one day climbed both Cannon Mountain and Mount Lafayette. Another day he won a race up Mount Washington, beating Henry Sturges by a neck.[21]

As Amelia's health deteriorated, Jonathan immersed himself in various patriotic endeavors. With deep family and personal ties to Connecticut, Jonathan had been a member of New York City's New England Society since 1850, and an original member and on the standing committee of a New York wartime organization called the Sons of Connecticut.[22] This organization formed in September 1861 to act as a hospitality committee for Connecticut soldiers traveling through New York on their way to and from the front. "The Eighth Regiment was the first to receive the courtesy and attention of the Sons of Connecticut with a breakfast served-up on the morning of October 18; and on October 25 they visited the Eighth's temporary camp at Jamaica, L.I., to present the regiment with a superb stand of colors."[23]

In 1861, as Memie and Pierpont were sailing away, Jonathan, the Sons of Connecticut and Massachusetts, and the Chamber of Commerce were hosting soldiers from Massachusetts. On their way to the front, one thousand men came through New York to an enthusiastic welcome, with banners and citizens lining their route through the city. They held a grand breakfast for Colonel Wilson, the 22nd Massachusetts Infantry Regimental Commander and his staff, at the Fifth Avenue Hotel. Among their distinguished hosts were Jonathan Sturges, Gov. Morgan (NY), Hon. George Bancroft, William Cullen Bryant, Gen. Sherman, A.T. Stewart, Thurlow Weed, Rev. Dr. Bellows, et al.[24] Although he tolerated only two weeks of travel and camp life, the seventy-six-year-old Rev. Dr. John Pierpont,[d] J.P. Morgan's maternal grandfather (guest at the wedding of Amelia and Pierpont the day before), was the regiment's chaplain.

Jonathan was financially ensuring the medical requirements of soldiers were being met but he was equally concerned with their spiritual needs Sometimes confused with the Sanitary Commission, the Christian Commission

---

d Rev. Pierpont's son James Lord Pierpont, a Confederate soldier from Savannah, was the composer of *Jingle Bells.*

provided pastoral guidance and creature comforts for the troops. Vincent Colyer of New York City was a Quaker, an artist, and on the Army Committee of the Young Men's Christian Association (YMCA) governing body. Colyer and a few associates took it on themselves to minister to the soldiers. These men were afraid soldiers in the field would forget their Christian teachings and fall into evil ways, without "shepherds" to encourage and guide them. They began the work when the first soldiers came through New York on their way to Baltimore.

Maimed Soldiers at Office of U.S. Christian Commission, Washington, D.C.[25]

After seeing the great need of such ministry at such horrific battles as Bull Run, Colyer wrote to the YMCA national leaders and urged them to establish a national network to continue the work on a larger scale.[26] His proposal was accepted and in November 1861, the YMCA founded the United States Christian Commission (USCC) in New York, later moving to Philadelphia. Jonathan was appointed to the General Board of Management and the Standing Committee on Finance for the national organization of the USCC.[27] As the *San Francisco Bulletin* editorialized:

> They are to do for the brave men on the battlefield, or when borne to the hospital, or mewed up in tents, what their fathers and brothers would do for them...be the medium of communication between the homes of soldiers and their wounded, sick or dying sons...the distribution of religious and moral publications...[and] personal items.[28]

The Christian Commission's members, consisting of merchants, businessmen and clergymen, felt it was their duty to use their means to further the efforts to spread moral and religious teaching and guidance. The Commission was a hybrid of a mobile church and the United Services Organizations (USO) of recent years, providing social services, religious publications and ministerial needs. During the war, five thousand delegates helped distribute over $6,000,000 worth of goods and supplies to the soldiers at the battlefields, camps, prisons and hospitals. [29]

In March 1862, the Union received encouraging news from Norfolk, Virginia, regarding a battle between the *USS Monitor* and the *CSS Merrimac.* Young Henry Sturges wrote in his diary: "Norfolk is over, and the *Merrimac* blown up. A great naval engagement between the north's gunboats and the rebel's flotilla."[30] However, good news regarding the war was scarce.

By mid-1862, the Union's poor prosecution of the war, decreasing public support and skeptical world opinion of the Union's prospects, formed a dark cloud around Lincoln, the Army, and the administration. Lincoln called for 300,000 more men and a serious possibility of international intervention developed. The war's significant economic impact on England helped spur a decidedly pro-Confederate opinion by the English government and business leaders there. They were delighted to see their former colony divided and were quietly supplying armaments to the South through blockade running ships. British leadership would have liked nothing better than to ally themselves with a Confederate South and obtain the cotton, tobacco, and other foodstuffs to feed their factories and people and enable tariff free trade. Conversely, it would have provided the Confederacy with an industrial infrastructure—thus establishing a partnership that would be a beneficial alliance for both sides. However, the South's dependency on slavery made such an alliance politically difficult with the English people, and they anxiously looked for trends on the battlefield that foreboded an inevitable military victory by Southern forces. They also tried to sway public opinion through certain London papers such as the *Illustrated London News,* which disseminated the Confederate perspective of the conflict.

This growing threat of military intervention by Great Britain, conceivably staged from the British province to the north, fueled a movement to establish a canal around the Niagara Falls, enabling gunboat access to the Great Lakes through U.S. territory. The Canadian owned Welland Canal took five years and a large investment to build and was regarded as a great military advantage for Great Britain, controlling the maritime passage between Lake Ontario and Lake Erie. Jonathan and other prominent New York Chamber of Commerce members and Western businessmen took an active interest in promoting this proposal for a United States controlled canal. However, it was one fraught with political and physical hurdles, not unlike the Illinois Central Railroad project, and had an even longer history of failure and entrenched opposition, dating back to before the Welland Canal was built in 1829.

There were many aborted efforts to build such a canal. In 1836, an official government survey laid out a route on the United States side of the isthmus. In 1853, and again in 1858, Niagara Ship Canal companies were formed and chartered but the projected high costs and lack of government funding stymied the effort. The event that re-energized interest came during the Civil War in November 1861. The Union had advance knowledge that Confederate representatives planned to travel to Britain to promote an alliance. They tracked them to Havana where they boarded a British vessel. A United States warship crew boarded the RMS *Trent* in the Bahamas channel on its way to London, capturing Confederate agents James Mason and John Slidell. This incident, known as the Trent Affair, and the fact that Britain had sent troops and some additional ships to Canada where gunboats could easily access Lake Erie, heightened tensions with Great Britain. This represented an alarming military threat, and a certain contingent declared it an unacceptable situation that the only maritime route to the Great Lakes was through a potential enemy's waterway. Jonathan Sturges was one of those actively promoting an American canal and it was gaining momentum—now with strategic military importance.

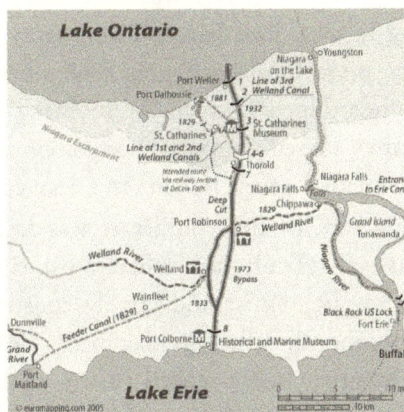

Canada's Welland Canal[31]

In 1862, Jonathan and the Chamber of Commerce declared that a U.S. canal around Niagara Falls was a pressing military necessity. Vice President Hannibal Hamlin presided at a National Ship Canal Convention held in Chicago, June 2-3, 1863. The grand vision of the conference included widening the Erie Canal to enable larger ships to traverse it and to connect the country via a steamboat route from the Great Lakes to the Gulf of Mexico. It was, "Resolved, the construction of a ship canal on American soil around the Falls of Niagara, thus completing the great chain of lakes, and giving them an outlet to the ocean, is preeminently a national enterprise that the National Government should execute at the earliest practicable day."[32]

In January 1864, Jonathan was an incorporator for the canal enterprise that planned for a capital stock authorization of $6,000,000, to build it from Lewiston, NY, for a length of eight miles south around the Falls, commence the project within two years, and complete it within ten years.[33] Unfortunately, by February 18, 1864, the Niagara Ship Canal Bill was "indefinitely postponed." The House of Representatives passed an authorization bill, but the Senate voted it down, with the two New York Senators voting "nay." It was the concerted opinion of the New York contingent that a new canal would divert traffic from Lake Erie through Lake Ontario to Canada, and that the loss of tolls and commerce through the full route of the Erie Canal would be unacceptable to New York. Last, the route to the ocean would be under the guns of the potential enemy on the St. Lawrence River, and so would be too vulnerable even for military use and unnavigable during winter months due to freezing conditions. Although the canal was again tabled, the Erie Canal widening initiative to increase capacity was successful, and it was widened multiple times starting in 1863. Jonathan and colleagues attempted to build an American canal one more time starting in 1868 when a $10,000,000 bill was debated in Congress, but after years of lobbying and legislative activity, Jonathan's initiative closed in 1874. Discussions and various schemes continued into the twentieth century, but an American canal was never built.

At this critical juncture in the conflict it was important to rally the morale of the citizens—a difficult task when most citizens in New York City were anti-war, anti-abolitionist and largely constituents of Tammany Hall. In July 1862, only months after his daughter's death and having seen Edward off to war, Jonathan was engaged to fire up the public's patriotic fervor, chairing the Committee of Arrangements for a mass meeting of the people. It was the largest public meeting ever held in the city. Attendance estimates varied from 30,000 to 100,000. Five speaking stands commanded the crowd's attention. The *Boston Post* reported:

> The great city seems to have given itself up to the demonstration. The stores in the business streets were all closed, and men of all classes congregated at the rendezvous to join in a demonstration for the Union. Bands of music, discharge of cannon, cheering and popular enthusiasm marked the event. Ladies were present in great numbers. Jonathan Sturges called the meeting to order, read the "call," and introduced Mayor Opdyke as Chairman.[34]

During this July mass meeting, the mayor announced the formation of a New York City National War Committee. This was to be a civilian group formed to identify the means and methods to aid in the "vigorous prosecution of the war and a speedy destruction of the rebellion." Jonathan and four other members had been selected in early July, by the New York Chamber of Commerce, to join with concerned New Yorkers and representatives of other "loyal" leagues to form a national union defense alliance. Jonathan was assigned as the financial manager, along with Mayor Opdyke, A.T. Stewart and Peter Cooper.[35] The crowd heard several letters of support sent from President Lincoln and other luminaries who could not attend, and many speeches, including an address from Jonathan Sturges. The Committee submitted a letter calling for the Governor to vigorously pursue raising state militias to capacity to defend the state, something which was not a priority for the anti-war governor.

Months later a public dispute broke out between Mayor Opdyke, Jonathan, the committee, and the ultra-wealthy Copperhead[e] August Belmont. Belmont had contributed $1000 to the committee, then later accused them of using the money to raise militia not backed by the state and requested his money be returned. An exchange of public letters occurred, the first from Belmont acknowledging the return of his donation and his intention to re-donate to the local federal Irish regiments (Tammany Hall constituents). The second letter in rebuttal from Mayor Opdyke announced he rejected Belmont's donation due to the insulting communication he had received inferring a misuse of funds.[36] This exchange was illustrative of the political divide among members of the city's elite and their divergent views of the conflict with the South.

Separately, the Chamber of Commerce, which Jonathan represented on the committee, proclaimed a series of resolutions supporting the Union war effort.

---

[e] Anti-war Union citizens not supportive of the emancipation of the slaves.

One of these was a call for President Lincoln to emancipate the slaves—with some curious timing:

> Resolved, That the time has come fully when we must strike for our national life, using every weapon God has given us, and calling to our aid every person who can be drawn from the rebels or added to our cause... we most respectfully and earnestly call upon the President to act in his capacity of Commander-in-Chief of the Army and Navy of the United States, and immediately issue the order that will take from the Rebels their great source of strength, while it will diminish their army while calling to the defense of their homes large numbers of Rebel officers and men, and we assure the President that in this, as in every act of his administration, the people of the free states will sustain the policy while the whole civilized world will applaud the Proclamation of Emancipation.[37]

This group of businessmen, among the most respected and successful in the country, issued one of the first, if not the first, public plea from such a body of conservative businessmen, for a presidential declaration to emancipate the slaves. The *New York Post* highlighted the conservative nature of the signatories:

> But let us first explain to our distant readers the composition of this Convention, which speaks so emphatically on the needs of the present crisis. It is no chance assembly of hot-heads and impracticables [sic]; it is no abolition conventicle; it is no conclave of politicians looking craftily to the spoils of office; but a grave and solemn selection of the wisest and worthiest persons among us.[38]

The resolutions also emphasized emancipation as a war measure to weaken the enemy, not the more controversial abolitionist or humanitarian approach, which would have had a larger backlash among the Copperheads and weakened support for the primary goal of preserving the Union. An example of the potential fallout and the fine line of emotions they were dealing with was illustrated at the July mass meeting, when Jonathan read Horace Greeley's name, a leading abolitionist, as a vice president of the gathering. His name was immediately met with extended groans, hisses, and angry calls to strike his name from the list.

The Chamber wrote this emancipation resolution a week after Congress passed the Confiscation Act of 1862, which allowed property, including slaves, to be confiscated from the areas in rebellion. Curiously, these resolutions were announced just a few days after Lincoln had privately presented his Emancipation Proclamation draft to Secretary of State Seward and Gideon Welles, Secretary of the Navy, on July 22. This proclamation resembled Lincoln's draft in its main ideas, and it is not inconceivable that Seward, a former New York governor and abolitionist, may have strategically leaked Lincoln's draft, and that this Chamber resolution was to add credence and urgency to such a proclamation. In any event, Jonathan's thoughts on slavery had evolved, and he was now eager to abolish it without delay.

The state and city also had ongoing quotas for recruiting soldiers. One approach to entice recruits to enlist was to provide increased bounties to prospective volunteers. In September 1862, Sturges, Bennet and Co. and other grocer firms called for a meeting to discuss sponsoring a regiment in this way. They appointed Jonathan as chairman of the committee with "full power to collect money and expend the same in procuring men to enlist as soldiers in the army."[39] By the end of the month, they had raised more than $21,000, which enabled them to offer an extra cash bounty of $10 for all 2100 recruits in addition to other bounties.[40] Jonathan also worked with Mayor George Opdyke as the Treasurer for a general bounty fund for all city recruits.[41]

When war broke out, Union blockades cut off cotton exports, forcing English and Irish mills and factories to close or cut production significantly. This caused devastating unemployment, starvation, and a lack of shelter and clothing for these mill workers. Lancashire, England, was particularly hard hit. In December 1862, Jonathan was on a Chamber committee formed to facilitate the gathering and shipping of goods to England to relieve their suffering: "A person well acquainted with the people of Illinois believes that they will furnish corn for almost any number of vessels, to supply the wants of the workingmen of England, if our merchants will pay the transportation and charter the ships."[42]

However, there was much speculation among merchants that the leadership of Great Britain would view the gesture as foreign interference in domestic politics and a rebuke of the ruling elite's Confederate sympathies. One person asserted these laborers would rather suffer and be out of work than further the cause of the South and the institution of slavery. However, others believed that any donations should first go to the country's own soldiers in the field. Jonathan then told of a $10,000 donation that the American Bible Society had received from the English Bible Society and although returned for lack of need, the sentiments were only based on Christian benevolence.[43] Jonathan's compassionate approach was adopted, and the group soon garnered donations totaling $108,000, with contributions ranging from the Griswold family's princely sum of $20,000, including the use of the ship the *George Griswold*, to the fifty-cents donated from a little girl in Connecticut, and the stevedores loaded the ship without charge.[44]

The nation's war debt was increasing, and many wealthy citizens lent significant funds to the government to help pay its debts. They also formed organizations to provide auxiliary support, such as the Sanitary Commission and the National War committee. These patriotic endeavors shored up morale, home defense, and war fighting abilities. A few visionary men had another idea on how to further focus these patriotic endeavors, and Jonathan became a founder of one of the most consequential of these organizations— The Union League Club of New York.

SEVENTEEN

Leading Support of the War Effort — The Draft Riots

You bound up our wounds and poured in the oil and wine of Christian kindness. We were hungry, and you fed us. We were naked, and you clothed us.

—Rev. Garnet

By late 1862, the Union finally experienced some success on the battlefield, beginning with the Battle of Antietam in September and followed by successful actions in Mississippi, Texas, Oklahoma, Louisiana and Kentucky. After the victory at Antietam, Lincoln issued his preliminary Emancipation Proclamation, to take effect January 1, 1863. Despite the successes, General McClellan was frustrating Lincoln by what he saw as a reluctance to prosecute the war with the Union's largest body of soldiers. Even sixteen-year-old Henry Sturges weighed in on McClellan's performance, commenting in May, "McClellan seems to be going it slow at Williamsburg. He is renewing his character of being inactive." In November, Lincoln's patience with McClellan had worn out and McClellan was relieved, replacing him with General Burnside (former Illinois Central Treasurer) in November. A string of bumbling defeats followed, including a terrible loss of life at Fredericksburg in early December. The Army and the country needed their morale bolstered.

The National War Committee, which began in July 1862, served the purpose of collaborating with other like-minded groups in supporting war efforts. In that vein, a movement was percolating to form a national network of social clubs to advocate for and support Union needs. Dr. Henry Bellows attributed the concept of a New York "Loyalist Club" to fellow Sanitary Commission member Professor Wolcott Gibbs, who asserted that such a club "should be devoted to a social organization of the sentiment of loyalty to the Union."[1] Gibbs chose Frederick Law Olmsted to consult with in this endeavor. Olmsted mused on membership:

> First, men of substance and established high position socially. I mentioned Minturn and Brown as first occurring to me last night. Men of good stock, or of notably high character, of legal reputation, would be desirable; Strong and Jay also, men of established repute in letters and science...especially those of old colonial names...A large proportion of this sort I consider essential...Second, clever men, especially of letters, wits and artists who have made their mark. Third, promising young men.[2]

The U.S. Sanitary Commission held a quarterly meeting in Washington, D.C. in late November 1862, with attendees from chapters throughout the Union. Members of the Philadelphia Commission had been part of organizing a loyalist club there and related their experience to the New York contingent on the train ride home. This discussion was the spark for the New York group to act on their ideas.[3] They felt their organization would be more comprehensive than the Philadelphia Club or others around the country and debated whether the name should be National Club or the Union League. They settled on the Union League Club, and within months, Jonathan Sturges and other like-minded men established a national network of loyalist clubs, with headquarters in Washington D.C.

Jonathan and the New York Union League organizing committee were the impetus behind a grand loyalist rally on March 6, 1863, at the Cooper Institute.[4] It was an enthusiastic, standing-room-only crowd that filled the amphitheater an hour before the rally was to begin, with over four thousand people attending. Inspiring speeches and resolutions went forth to energize the crowd's patriotism, and to promote an enthusiasm for the new loyalist club network. The New York clubs met later that month to organize in Utica, New York, under the name of the Loyal National League.

A month later, the second anniversary of the Sumter attack, the many "loyal" clubs throughout the state sponsored a mass public rally of the people in the city. The gathering served to officially open the New York City Union League Club. Robert B. Minturn called the meeting to order, where tens of thousands gathered to cheer the Union. The charter they established included the all-important pledge of unadulterated loyalty to the Union and support of its efforts to suppress the rebellion.[5]

Signing the New York charter at George T. Strong's[a] house on February 6, 1863, Jonathan became one of the sixty-six founders and original twelve vice presidents of the Club. Robert B. Minturn was their first president, and the club leased a space at 17th Street and Broadway. The headquarters fronted Union Square and was officially opened in May.[6] It was a social club based foremost on common political and patriotic ideals. However, the job of sustaining support for the war in a Copperhead dominated area of the country was tenuous, and pent-up, angry emotions were about to explode.

By May 1863, military intelligence indicated that the Confederate Army was moving to invade Pennsylvania and Maryland. President Lincoln ordered the militia to provide an initial surge force of 100,000 troops to protect Union territory and its citizens. Edward Sturges' old Seventh Regiment was called to duty for a three-month period of service to defend against this invasion. The regiment headed for Harrisburg, but as intelligence evolved, the thought was Lee might be headed for Baltimore, and the Seventh Regiment was sent to Frederick, Maryland. On June 28, they received word that a skirmish between forces had, as earlier predicted, occurred at Harrisburg, Pennsylvania. Just south of there on July 1, the two forces converged for the bloodiest battle of the Civil War—in a small crossroad town called Gettysburg.

The Battle of Gettysburg was both a triumph and a turning point for the Union. They won with superior numbers and battle positions, but the terrible loss of life and limb on both sides of the conflict was horrific, including 2000 casualties. It became necessary to obtain more soldiers. The National Conscription Act had been passed in March 1863, mandating compulsory military service for men, implemented through state quotas and conscription. A provision allowing payment of a $300 fee to avoid service made it a poor man's draft.

A Workingman's Congress had just concluded, which sought to organize workers against the government and employers. These laborers felt that they and all men of the lesser classes were being exploited both at work and in the draft. Additionally, they were angered that the war had become a conflict to free the slaves, who would then come in great numbers to take their jobs at lower wages. On June 3, the Peace Democracy, consisting mainly of artisans and

---

[a] A well-known New York City Civil War diarist featured in the Ken Burns Civil War documentary.

longshoremen held a large peace demonstration and they planned an anti-conscription rally for the 4th of July. Tensions were high, and violence was threatened if their Copperhead legislators could not stop the draft.

The drawing began at the draft office at Third Avenue and Forty-Seventh Street as planned on Saturday, July 11, with no disturbances noted. It was to continue Monday, July 13, but a mob gathered there early in the morning, driving out the officers, killing one person, and burning the building. Once the draft office was destroyed, the violence and chaos spread across a large section of the city, and those with looting, destruction, and cruelty on their mind saw their chance.

This reign of terror lasted for three days. "The mid-July violence wrecked stores, shops and homes, which included Mayor George Opdyke's home."[7] Samuel Morehouse, a Fairfield, Connecticut native working near the Colored Orphan Asylum, wrote to his wife: "I have on several occasions been told by the mob to fall in. They march in lines through the streets and force people to join them."[8] Rioters seeking scapegoats targeted persons of color, the wealthy, abolitionists, police and military. Those caught were mercilessly beaten, and their property stolen or destroyed. Some were left in the street to die and others hung from lampposts—the mob daring others to come to their aid or claim the body.

Burning of the Provost Marshall's Office[9] and Riot Mob Dragging Col. O'Brien[10]

Landlords ordered their Black tenants to leave their property to prevent its destruction and thousands fled the city, never to return, refugees from the violence. The rioting was of the largest scale the nation had ever experienced. The small police force was overwhelmed, and federal troops were requested to restore order. New York veteran troops including the Seventh Regiment and war-weary Gettysburg veteran regiments were ordered to New York. Their impending arrival was well known and eagerly anticipated by the citizenry. Entering the city on July 16, regiments were garrisoned around the city and order was restored within days. The draft was rescheduled, albeit with a lower quota, and donations provided to pay for substitutes for many of those who could not pay.

The Union League leadership regarded these 1863 Draft Riots as a Confederate-planned "Northern insurrection against liberty, nationality, and the law...to accomplish a revolution, converting New York into a rebel city," and providing an international showcase of public dissension and anger over the war.[11] A Confederate officer in Europe publicly announced that New York City was by that time in the hands of the Confederacy. Conspiracy or not, the deaths, physical assaults, destruction and the blow to morale was significant. Left in the riot's aftermath were hundreds of fatalities (120 officially documented) thousands of injuries and two million dollars in property damage. The major target of the violence had been free African-American residents. This beleaguered populace had lost what little they had, and a determined Jonathan Sturges set out to lead the effort to provide relief and begin the healing.

Jonathan and Henry J. Raymond, editor of the *New York Times,* formed the Committee of Merchants for the Relief of Colored People.[12] Jonathan presided at the organizational meeting on July 20. There was a rumor that rioters planned to break up the meeting and physical harm was feared. Despite this serious threat, Jonathan decided to carry on with the gathering and took his place on the dais. Just as Jonathan was set to begin, a large burly man "tore like a whirlwind up the aisle and took a front seat facing Mr. Sturges, who felt sure the enemy had now come."[13] Undaunted, Jonathan continued, but the man, unknown to the organizers, soon stood up and addressed the audi-ence, not as a man to be feared, but as a friend and supporter. It was Jackson Shultz, a young man who would become a force behind the success of the effort and a future President of the Union League Club. Jonathan delivered these inspiring words to kick off this charitable undertaking, reported by journalists nationwide, which read in part:[b]

I have been for forty-nine years a merchant in my present location. During this period, I have seen a noble race of merchants pass away. I cannot help

---

[b] In November 1865, his speech was reprinted again nationally to support the Constitutional amendment for African-American suffrage, highlighting Jonathan's assertion of their solid character.

calling to mind the many acts of charity which they performed during their lives. I hardly need to name them; you all know them. You all know how they sent relief to Southern cities when they were desolated by fire or pestilence; how they sent shiploads of food to the starving people of Ireland. This last act of brotherly love we had the privilege of imitating during the past winter; and as often as occasion requires. I trust we shall be quick to continue these acts of humanity, thus showing that the race of New York merchants is not deteriorating.

We are now called upon to sympathize with a different class of our fellow men. Those who know the colored people of this city can testify to their being a peaceable, industrious people, having their own churches, Sunday schools and charitable societies; and that as a class they seldom depend upon charity; they not only labor to support themselves, but to aid those who need aid. This is their general character, and it is our duty to see that they are protected in their lawful labors, to save themselves from becoming dependent on the charity of the city. We have not come together to devise means for their relief because they are colored people, but because they are, as a class, persecuted and in distress at the present moment.

It is not necessary for our present purposes to inquire who the men are who have persecuted, robbed and murdered them. We know they are bad men, who have not done as they would be done by. Let us not follow their example, let us be quick to relieve those who are now in trouble, and should we ever find those who have persecuted the Negro in like trouble, let us be quick to relieve them also, and thus obey the injunction of our Divine Master, "Bless those who persecute you."[14]

The committee received over thirty thousand dollars in contributions by the next week including $500 from Sturges, Bennet and Co.[c] A central relief depot was established at 350 Fourth Street. General John Dix assured the colored population they would be protected as they returned to their lives and work. Jonathan (Treasurer) and the committee, chaired by John McKenzie, adopted four extraordinary resolutions:

Whereas; The condition of the colored people of this city, who have recently been deprived of their kindred by murderers, of their homes by fire, and of their accustomed means of support; having been forcibly driven

---

[c] About $10,000 in 2018.

by an infuriated mob, without cause or provocation…should receive prompt pecuniary assistance and aid. That this may be effectually accomplished, we do hereby (resolve to):

…have full power to receive, collect and disburse funds in the purchase of necessary food and clothing, and in relieving the wants of the suffering colored population.…

…obtain redress from the County, under the Statute Laws of the State of New York, and that have authority to collect funds and employ Counsel for that purpose.

…protect the colored people of this city, in their rights to pursue, unmolested, their lawful occupations, and we do hereby call upon the proper authorities to take immediate steps to afford them such protection…

…we will not recognize or sanction any distinction of persons, of whatever nation, religion or color, in their natural rights, to labor peaceably in their vocations, for the support of themselves and those dependent upon them; That what we now propose doing for the colored man, we shall ever be ready to do for any class of our fellow men, under like circumstances.[15]

These resolutions called for the end of discrimination regarding nationality, religion or color in pursuing their "natural rights,"—remarkably progressive words in this era. This was an early recognition, by the most prominent of businessmen in the financial capital of the United States, that these residents of African descent were citizens of the nation, who deserved the same rights in their pursuit of happiness as those of any other national origin, religion, or color. Jonathan had now come full circle in his views, from a pragmatic businessman's peace seeking view of placating the South and ending slavery through legislation, to an ideological and moral stand—equal rights for all citizens under the law, an evolution that may have had its seeds in his grandfather's actions to advocate for the freedom of slaves in Connecticut.

Due to Jonathan's leadership, a diverse array of people joined with the group to aid the sufferers. Hand-selected committee members worked with Black religious leaders in the community to identify victims and their needs and to distribute aid. Delegates from the Association for Improving the Condition of the Poor, an organization of which Jonathan was a long-time board member, were also used as conduits to the victims. The relief depot was open from 9:00 to 4:00 every day for over a month. A committee report described the scene:

Thursday, July 23rd, 38 applicants received aid. On Friday, July 24th, the wants of 318 were attended to, and on Saturday, July 25th, the streets in the neighborhood were literally filled with applicants.... At ten o'clock, Fourth Street, near Broadway, was filled with colored people of both sexes, and all ages. They presented an aspect of abject poverty; and many of them bore evidence of the assaults made on them during the riots. The building where relief was given to the applicants at No. 350 Fourth Street was soon surrounded by nearly three thousand Negroes. Some of them had come into the city from woods and fields in different parts of the state where they took refuge.[16]

Within one week, they had distributed $7,000 to thousands of sufferers. Committee members, especially Jonathan, were careful to ensure there was documentation for each claim and any suspicious cases were investigated, although those were few. Interestingly, one case came up where the victim had claimed her house had been ransacked in the riots and had suffered the loss of five unmade silk dresses. Jonathan immediately jumped on this claim to uncover suspected fraud. Jackson S. Shultz (a member of the relief committee and a Union League President), speaking at a banquet in 1886 about the incident, said:

> "Now," said Mr. Sturges, "this confirms my suspicion that we are being imposed upon. I mean to go to the bottom of this imposition, and if I find that this woman has presented a false claim, I shall insist upon punishing her." He took the papers in that case home with him, and the next morning, on coming before the Committee, he said, "Dinah is right. She did have all these unmade dresses, at her rooms, that she always kept aside and apart from my house, where she did on occasion meet with her children and grandchildren, and the rioters broke open her rooms and did destroy all her furniture and did steal all these dresses. These dresses were presents to her from my own family." We had no further trouble with Mr. Sturges. From being a doubting Thomas, he became a radical and prompt giver.[17]

Each day, beginning one hour before, and for one hour after normal hours, lawyers were on hand to provide pro-bono legal support for victims. Through the help of these lawyers, claims for damages against the city totaled more than $145,000. However, in January 1864, Jonathan was forced to arrange a meeting at City Hall to expedite payments which had not been forthcoming. A telling newspaper entry (erroneously making Jonathan a general) describes how payments suddenly began. "The Colored Relief Committee, of which General Jonathan Sturges is treasurer, were to have held a meeting yesterday, for the purpose of raising sufficient funds to pay each colored sufferer by the July riots fifty percent on his claim: but as the Comptroller had commenced to pay these claims in the morning, no meeting was held."[18] Reportedly more than $120,000 was eventually paid out by the city to the victims.

By the end of the effort, they had assisted an astounding 13,000 people, clergymen had made over 8,000 visits, about 2,000 pieces of clothing were distributed, and many victims received help in finding jobs. On August 22, the committee concluded their work. Treasurer Jonathan Sturges reported they had raised over $41,000 in aid funds and disbursed all but about $12,000.

At a gathering to celebrate and conclude the relief efforts, Rev. Henry Highland Garnet, a leading Black clergyman in New York City and friend of Jonathan's, thanked the committee. He said in part:

> You bound up our wounds and poured in the oil and wine of Christian kindness…We were hungry, and you fed us. We were thirsty, and you gave us water. We were naked and you clothed us…Gentlemen, this generation of our people will not, cannot forget the scenes to which we allude, nor will they forget the noble and spontaneous exhibition of charity…You did not hesitate to come forward for our relief amid threatened destruction of your life and property…This ever memorable and magnanimous exhibition of heroism has had the effect to enlarge our bosoms the sentiment of undying regard and esteem for you and yours.[19]

The Black community started returning to work, and life was nominally back to normal, until the transit companies suddenly denied them access to public transportation in the city.[d] Rioters had threatened them with violence and destruction if service was not denied to the Black population. This threat and limited transportation options crippled the ability of persons of color to work and compete for jobs. Led by Jonathan, the committee quietly went about rem-

---

[d] The right for Blacks to ride desegregated public transit had been legally won in New York City in 1855. A young lawyer, Chester A. Arthur (future President) was one of the lawyers representing Elizabeth Jennings who successfully challenged a transit company's right to segregate trolleys after she was thrown off a "white" trolley on her way to church in 1854.

edying the situation without seeking fanfare, publicity, or personal political gain. Jackson S. Schultz explained:[e]

> This "Relief Committee" performed a service for the colored people of this city with which they were not charged by their appointment, and I venture to say had the conservative members of it been made acquainted at the outset with the services they so heartily performed at the end, they would have hesitated or refused. We saved $5,000 from the merchants' contribution to test the right of the city railroads to exclude colored people from their cars. The management of this delicate matter was entrusted to Mr. Sturges. He summoned all the [transit] presidents to our rooms by a note, and when assembled he told them our purpose. He said in substance; "You can have legal contests and agitation, or you can have peace with honor. But we mean, before we complete our duties, to have colored people ride in your cars like white people." A brief consultation on behalf of the presidents resulted in assent to the proposal and there has been no exclusion since.[20]

Black men in places like Boston clamored to join the army when the first call for recruits went out after the attack on Fort Sumter. However, they were turned away due to a federal law from 1792 that specifically limited conscription and bearing arms in the militia to white, male citizens. In July 1862, the Militia War Act authorized the use of freed slaves in any capacity in the Union army, but in practice it was mainly in Southern locations and they were used as laborers to free up white soldiers to fight.

The first regiment of color from the North was recruited from Massachusetts in February 1863, but the rest of the country was less than enthusiastic at the prospect, including New York State, led by Copperhead Governor Seymour. Due to war necessity and the many Blacks who were eager to enlist, Lincoln issued his order in May 1863 creating the Bureau of Colored Troops which authorized men of color to fight and authorized the recruitment of such regiments as a pressing military need. New York still dragged its feet. Colonel Bliss, at an 1886 banquet, related how the Union League Club first set out to recruit colored troops, and how Jonathan, then a vice president of the Union League, put a damper on it but provided astute counsel.

> About five or six days after that time we made up our minds that we would... go in for the colored regiments, but we didn't dare to avow it. Good old

---

[e] At a banquet to commemorate the anniversary of the formation of the 20th Colored Regiment.

Jonathan Sturges who was, I think, then the president of the club, and who was also certainly an active member, if not the chairman of the Merchants' Committee appointed to relieve the colored men who had suffered during the riot and had shown in that way his sympathy with the colored men, came around to the members of the committee and took each one of us aside. "I want to assure you, sir," said he, "that you have no right to go into this business of raising colored regiments. You are exceeding your authority; you are committing the club to a thing which it never agreed to and you must not do it." Well, we didn't dare at once to say anything about it. We set to work and the first thing we did we wrote a letter to Governor Seymour.[21]

Gov. Seymour's response, not surprisingly, included the same assertion as Jonathan and referred them to the War Department for authorization. The Union League next appealed to Secretary of War Edwin Stanton asking him for permission to recruit troops of color, but he was dragging his feet on this initiative. It was pointed out to the recalcitrant War Department "that here was the Union League Club asking his authority to raise a colored regiment and that if he refused that authority he would discourage five hundred of the leading and active citizens of New York!"[22] They received approval on December 5, 1863, to raise the first troop regiments of color in the State of New York and they set about recruiting.[23]

Robert Minturn submitted his resignation as president of the Union League Club in November 1863 because of a planned absence abroad. A vice president of the Union League from its founding, Jonathan was named the second president of the organization in January 1864 and he proceeded to oversee the recruitment of colored troops. The committee had difficulty finding a headquarters as most landlords were not supportive of recruiting Blacks to fight. They found a familiar location at 350 Fourth Street (same as used for the draft riot relief depot) and began work The committee, headed by Vincent Colyer, met with local Black leaders and clergymen, such as Jonathan's friend Reverend Garnet, to solicit their support in encouraging Blacks to enlist. This strategy proved key to their success.

Since early 1863, Frederick Douglass had been prolifically recruiting men of color all over New York for the 54th Massachusetts, the first colored regiment. As Douglass had asserted, this was their call to arms to end slavery and earn full rights as citizens, as it had been in 1776 for colonists in America who took up arms seeking liberty from a distant autocrat. There had been a stream of Black men volunteering for units in other states while, as noted, New York had sat on its hands. Eager to stop the flow of these recruits out of state, by Christmas they had recruited over 1,000 troops for the 20th Regiment, re-designated the 91st U.S. Colored Troops in April 1864. In early January, it was estimated that there yet remained only 1500 male Black citizens of age that were eligible for recruitment in the city.[24] [f] Despite the numbers, they filled a second Regiment by January 27 (26th Regiment, re-designated as the 94th U.S. Colored Troops in April 1864) and supplied 400 more recruits for a third regiment, who joined recruits from Connecticut to become the 31st U.S. Colored Troops. Sadly, the 31st Regiment sustained large losses at the ill-fated July 1864 Battle of the Crater at Petersburg, VA, a horrific engagement where there was no quarter given to Black troops, being mercilessly gunned down by Confederate forces.

Jonathan's Union League had raised a total of 2,400 troops, remarkable results where in 1860 only 9,000 colored men of all ages were documented as living in New York City, more than a 25% volunteer rate. These enthusiastic volunteers and the admirable service performed by them were key to the country justifying the final abolishment of slavery and in securing their rights as citizens.

After his rise to the presidency of the Union League in 1864, Jonathan undertook an ambitious initiative—to establish an art gallery of distinction at the club. It established "...the Club's policy of acquiring American art and admitting artist members by accepting paintings in lieu of dues."[25] Expanding on this idea, he and Mary were key players in what became a large focus for Union League Club members and their wives. This effort in New York, to benefit the U.S. Sanitary Commission, became known as the Metropolitan Sanitary Fair—an arts and crafts bazaar of the most elaborate kind.

Sanitary Fairs became the largest source of funding for the U.S. Sanitary Commission. These fairs became major social events and spread around the country. Chicago held the first Sanitary Fair, raising $60,000; Boston followed, with an impressive $140,000; and Cincinnati with $250,000. It was a way

---

f The government did not have arms for the recruits until March, so the regiments weren't formally designated until April 1864 at Ryker's Island. They served admirably and all were discharged between August and November 1865.

g This ugly battle began with the digging of a tunnel to a position under Confederate troop entrenchments. The explosion and ensuing confusion, lack of effective Union leadership and the laser focus by Confederate troops on punishing Black troops, resulted in three times higher casualties for the Union than the Confederacy.

to earn a large amount of cash at one time, to augment the smaller donations they previously relied on to sustain operations.

One of the biggest and grandest of these fairs was the Sanitary Fair in New York City in 1864. The President of the Fair was Major General John Dix, and Jonathan Sturges was his right-hand man and First Vice President to Dix for the "Gentleman's Association;" however, it was to be a fair run by the ladies of New York.[26] Mrs. Mary Sturges was on the Executive Committee of the Ladies Association and co-chairman of the Art Committee with the artist John F. Kensett and his wife. Their mission was to obtain paintings for exhibit and sale. In November 1863, the vision for a national scale Metropolitan Fair was, "In short, it must be inspired from the higher classes, but animate, include, and win the sympathies and interest of all classes."[27]

A distinguished group of ladies from New York met on December 11, 1863 to begin the planning. They created an Executive Board of twenty-five ladies to act in concert with an Advisory Committee of twenty-five men, appointed by the Sanitary Commission.[28] This was a huge undertaking, with hundreds of people on dozens of committees.

The fair was first scheduled for late February 1864, but rescheduled to April 4, to allow enough time to develop the extensive exhibitions. In 1865, a historian described the undertaking: "The fair was primarily held over a two-block section in New York City on 14th Street at the site of the 22nd Regiment Armory. Fundraising events connected with the fair were held all over the city, in both public and private venues, with a myriad of organizations contributing to its success. A.T. Stewart personally gave $10,000, Sturges Bennet & Co., $2500, and the New York Fire Department by itself raised $30,250!"[29]

West Wing-Metropolitan Fair 1864[30] and Metropolitan Fair-The Art Gallery[31]

Mrs. Sturges's art committee sent out a flyer to "Americans Abroad," appealing to their patriotism and seeking donations, with a specific outreach to American artists and collectors for items to exhibit. This appeal worked through the various consulate offices and other designees around the world. The response was heartwarming as it became a truly international affair—expatriates all over the world sent donations. These contributions included paintings, engravings, photographs and even autographs from European Royalty.

About 200 paintings were loaned from collectors and artists and covered the gallery walls and over 350 were donated for sale. The painting *Washington Crossing the Delaware* by Leutze took up most of one wall, and Church's *Niagara,* sketched while traveling with the Osborn family, was exhibited along with two of Jonathan's paintings, *Newsboy* by Henry Inman and *Forest Scene* by A.B. Durand.[32] Coincidentally, J.P. Morgan made his first art purchase at this event. "It was the portrait of a young and delicate-looking young woman, the work of an artist named Baker, and he paid $1500."[33] In the end, the Art Committee realized sales and donations of $83,668.62.[h] Results were similar throughout the departments of the Fair, making it a great success. Total profit reached an astounding $1,176,672.[34][i]

Jonathan Sturges and his family were deeply invested in supporting the Union war effort, and fortunately they did not live in a location in immediate danger of being in the middle of the conflict. This was not so true of family and friends in the South on the other side of the war, who were just as committed to their own cause.

---

[h] About $1,300,000 in 2018
[i] About $18,000,000 in 2018

Eighteen

Friends and Family in a Country Divided

Must their precious young lives be sacrificed, their homes made desolate, our cause be lost, and all our rights be trampled under the foot of a vindictive foe, Gracious God avert from us these terrible calamities!

—Jane Howison Beale, Fredericksburg, VA

Virginia and William Osborn were in Chicago for most of the war, but also about 1859, they began using their country home at Garrison, New York, across the river from the Cozzens Hotel. By this time, their family had grown to include four children; Virginia Sturges (1855), Henry Fairfield (1857), Frederick Sturges (1860) and William Church (1862).

Virginia Osborn[1] (left) and William and Frederick Osborn, c. 1867[2]

William Osborn was engrossed in moving soldiers and war supplies during the war as president of the Illinois Central Railroad, but in September 1862, he contemplated serving the country in a higher profile way. Virginia wrote to her mother: "Mr. Osborn yesterday asked me what I would think of him running for Congress in Illinois. I told him I believed the time would come when our men of uprightness and integrity have got to take part in our government, and we should yet have to educate our boys to be statesmen, and I do think that the upper-classes in this country will have to view politics differently from what we do now, for we cannot expect Providence to help us if we do not help ourself."[3]

Osborn did not make a run for Congress although he was active behind the scenes in politics in 1860 in Massachusetts. Governor Nathaniel Banks from Massachusetts was lobbying to be the Republican presidential candidate in 1860. Bank's moderate views weakened his support in Massachusetts, and he was having difficulty building support for a Republican Party candidacy, even in his own state. William Osborn and Robert Rantoul (founding director of ICR), both with strong ties to Massachusetts, and both Lincoln supporters, intervened to head off this potential Lincoln opposition, offering Banks a lucrative position with the Illinois Central Railroad. This appeal worked and at the state convention Banks informed the party he would not run for re-election as Governor or for the Presidency. He moved to Chicago in early January 1861, charged with selling railroad owned land to reduce the ICR's debt.

The elections of 1862 were a bleak time for Republicans. The draft, the war taxes imposed, and the Emancipation Proclamation, combined to weigh down Republican prospects at the polls. Above all, as the casualties piled up the people grew impatient and weary of the fighting. Virginia, along with many Americans, felt that lives were being wasted through poor leadership. "How thankful we should be that our boys are both back safe, for those who go, seem only to go to be slaughtered. There must be some terrible want where our Generals are all quarreling and charging each other with inefficiency instead of checking the enemy's advances."[4]

After doing his stint in the army, Frederick Sturges moved to Paris to conduct business for Sturges, Bennet & Co. Living there was somewhat unwelcoming, as he said there was scant social intercourse, and little political support for the Union, as most people there were "secesh,"[5] (Confederates sympathizers) and "everything is colored to fit the cause of the

South."[6] He returned to New York later in 1863 to marry his sweetheart, Mary Reed Fuller, the daughter of the Sturges's good friends, Mr. and Mrs. Dudley B. Fuller, the granddaughter of Luman Reed, and a close friend of Virginia's. Frederick and Mary were blessed with their first child, Jonathan Sturges, in Paris in 1864. Edward Sturges also rejoined the firm.

Mary Reed Fuller Sturges[7]

Any discussion of the Fairfield Sturges family, the Civil War and support of the troops should also include the efforts of Jonathan's first cousin of Ohio and Chicago, Solomon Sturges. Solomon was from Fairfield, six years older than Jonathan, and the son of his mother's brother Dimon Sturges. He had become a wealthy man by the outbreak of the Civil War. Sturges, Buckingham and Co. owned two 120-foot grain elevators with a capacity of seven hundred bushels, next to the Illinois Central Railroad terminal in Chicago. These elevators made his company the largest grain warehousing firm in Chicago in the busiest city of the heartland.[8]

Solomon Sturges donated liberally and publicly promoted Union efforts. He was an associate of Lincoln's, and his intimacy with him was such that in April 1860, during the campaign for President, Solomon offered his house in Chicago to Lincoln for his use during the convention, although Lincoln did not take him up on his offer.[9] Solomon loaned $100,000 to the government to finance the war in September 1861. He also spent $20,000 outfitting a regiment of troops from Chicago at the outbreak of the war, authorized by Abraham Lincoln himself. Solomon's regiment became known as the Sturges Rifles and mustered into service May 1861. He purchased the latest technology rifles for their use from Hartford based Sharps Rifle Manufacturing Company. The 1859 model Sharps Rifle was "the single trigger...seldom seen .56 caliber percussion, single-shot breech loader issued to an early war contingent of some one hundred Illinois volunteers."[10] The Sturges Rifles served as General George McClellan's bodyguard regiment throughout his war campaigns.

Solomon became emotionally involved in the prosecution and progress of the war, to a fault. This obsession with the war reportedly affected his mind to where he became mentally unstable in 1862, writing odd, passionate letters to newspapers. *The Daily Illinois State Journal* wrote: "We see by the *Chicago Journal* that a commission of lunacy was issued against the well-known and wealthy Solomon Sturges, at the instance of his son, George Sturges. A jury declared Mr. Sturges to be insane."[11] Not being cognizant of the proceedings against him, and to get him near an appropriate facility, the family created a ruse to have him travel to Hartford, Connecticut. The *Hartford Courant* reported:

> Solomon Sturges, a well-known and wealthy banker of Chicago, was taken to the Insane Retreat in this city on Tuesday. He has manifested such a deep and intense interest in the rebellion and for the vigorous prosecution of the war, that his mind became diseased. A letter was written to him ordering him to proceed to Hartford to buy a large quantity of rifles, which he immediately started to do. Upon his arrival here, the officers of the Institution were waiting with a carriage, and he was hastened to the Asylum.[12]

In January 1863, his mental health restored, control of his business interests were returned to him.[13] However, six months later, he suffered another attack of "mental aberration" and was again admitted to the Asylum in Hartford. Solomon passed away at home in Zanesville, Ohio in October 1864.

The Civil War divided not only New York City but many localities throughout the nation. Jonathan was part of a merchant-led fundraiser that sent aid to the islands off the coast of North Carolina, a forty-five mile stretch between Hatteras and Oregon inlets, which had largely remained loyal to the Union.

Jonathan and Mary, like many Americans in the Civil War, had loved ones deep in the other side of the conflict, including his cousin Lucretia in Savannah, and a friend of Mary's from Fredericksburg, Virginia. They were as patriotic in their loyalty to the Confederacy as Jonathan and his family were to the Union. In 1861, Lucretia wrote Jonathan of Savannah's war preparations:

> The city is in constant excitement what with state troops going to and returning from the Fort[a] causing a sadness...that it should be necessary to take such a step for the preservation of our property...God forbid that we should have the horror of war thrust upon us...Our negroes are very much alarmed at the state of things and many hundreds of them are working at the Fort to get all in readiness for any emergency and I believe would fight for their owners.[14]

Jonathan's first cousin's son, Jonathan Sturges Beers, Jr., of Fairfield (a great-grandson of Judge Sturges), married Frances "Fannie" Dimon in 1852. Seventeen-year-old Amelia Sturges was an invited guest and danced the night away. She wrote: "It was quite a gay scene for Fairfield...the floors were covered with white linen...they had a very nice band of music and beautiful flowers... a party in the country is such an uncommon thing that everybody goes...I did not go to bed until a quarter to one...I enjoyed myself very much indeed."[15]

The Beers moved to Louisiana in the late 1850s. At the outbreak of the war, Jonathan Beers joined a Confederate Louisiana Artillery company. Just as the war had begun, Fannie Beers was pregnant and returned to her hometown of Fairfield to be with family for her confinement. It became known she was a Confederate sympathizer, and that she had in her possession a small Confederate flag. A mob formed outside her home to confiscate the flag but a kindly doctor from Fannie's childhood interceded and dispersed the crowd, assuring them he would take care of the matter. When he asked her if she had a flag she assured him, "only the one close to my heart."[16] The doctor departed, satisfied, but did not know that she had pasted a flag on her chest to conceal it. Soon after this mob incident, she was forced to sneak out of town and was eventually spirited back to Confederate territory by her brother, a Union officer stationed near enemy lines in Virginia. Fairfield's Fannie Dimon Beers became a legendary nurse for the Confederacy and was deemed the "Florence Nightingale of the South" by historians.

While in Fredericksburg, Mary Sturges had formed a close friendship with Jane Howison Beale, from a prominent Presbyterian family.[17] Prior to her move to New York, Mary had been both a Sunday school and academic school

---

a Probably old Fort Jackson on the Savannah River.

teacher at the Union Academy in Fredericksburg. Jane Griggs Howison was one of her students there. She was one of twelve children, and her family's home was downtown, where Mary visited the winter of 1832-1833, just before Jane married William Churchill Beale in 1834, at nineteen. Mr. Beale was a widower and twenty-four years her senior when they married, and they lived at 307 Lewis Street, at the corner of Lewis and Charles Street,[b] about one block from where she grew up, and three blocks from the Rappahannock River in downtown Fredericksburg.

After the birth of their ninth child, William Beale had a heart attack and died, just after her mother passed away. Jane was left with nine children, no husband, parents, or means of support, and her husband's mill was sold to pay his debts, which enabled her to stay in her home. She was in despair, but she had her children to think of and couldn't allow herself the luxury of wallowing in pity. Jane augmented her finances by taking in boarders and starting a school in a small building behind her house, inspired by one of her favorite teachers, Mary Cady Sturges.

Jane also started a diary, ostensibly as therapy to get through desperate times. Her first entry in 1850 documented the departure of two of her sons to live with relatives and sought support from the Almighty to bear the separation. Like Mary Sturges, Jane leaned heavily on her Christian faith. They corresponded little during the war due to their divergent loyalties, but when they did, they did it stealthily, as illustrated by one diary entry from 1862:

> I commenced the morning by writing a letter to a "lady" in New York who was once my teacher and has proved herself my warm friend by many acts of kindness since, we have as a matter of course had no communication since this war commenced she married a wealthy man, but he belongs to the Black Republican Party. I only wrote to her now to bespoke her kind offices in favor of two English ladies who are about to leave here with a view of returning to England by one of the New York steamers and will probably need the aid of a gentleman in their embarkation.[18]

Jane also refers in her diary to a letter being received from Mrs. Smith, that was from Mary and Jonathan and included welcome monetary support.

---

b Mary Ball Washington, the mother of George Washington, had coincidentally lived in the house across the street, at the same intersection of Lewis Street and Charles Street before her death in 1789.

Bombardment of Fredericksburg from Stafford Heights, December 1862[19]

Jane was a staunch supporter of slavery and the Southern cause. Union forces first established a presence in the Fredericksburg area in April 1862, when Union troops led by the newly appointed Military Governor, General Patrick, took a position across the Rappahannock River in Stafford. On April 12 Jane wrote:

...it is painfully humiliating to feel one's self a captive, but all sorrow for self is now lost in the deeper feeling of anxiety for our army, for our cause, we have lost everything, regained nothing, our army has fallen back before the superior forces of the enemy until but a small strip of our dear Old Dominion is left to us, our sons are all in the field and we who are now in the hands of the enemy cannot even hear from them, must their precious young lives be sacrificed, their homes made desolate, our cause be lost and all our rights be trampled under the foot of a vindictive foe, Gracious God avert from us these terrible calamities! Rise in thy Majesty and strength and rebuke our enemies.[20]

On May 14, 1862 Jane illustrated her view on slavery:

The enemy has interfered with our labour by inducing our servants to leave us...or demand wages...but it strikes at the root of those principles and rights for which our southern people are contending and cannot be submitted to, it fixes upon us our incubus of supporting a race, who were ordained of high heaven to serve the white man and it is only in that capacity that they can be useful and respected.[21]

During the first Battle of Fredericksburg in December 1862, Jane and her children sheltered in the basement of their home, until her brother arrived and evacuated them as the shells were starting to fall.

Drawn into the aftermath of the Battle of Spotsylvania in May 1864, Jane's house was commandeered as a hospital for the Union wounded. She nursed soldiers for three weeks, and there were about one hundred of them in her house, with many officers among the ranks. There was a continual "interchange of kindness" between them, and Jane "never heard a disrespectful word" from any of them.[22] However, she had to breakup her school due to the war and condition of the house. Following the return from her second evacuation in December 1864 she was distraught and wanting for all the basic needs. "I cooked, washed and ironed for my family for months and at that we had nothing to eat but cornbread without butter, and rye coffee without sugar, and very glad when we could get that."[23] After the war, in 1867, she expressed to Mary Sturges her concern about the "col'd" population:

> [Due to] circumstances to which they have previously been placed, most often are tempted to supply their wants by aggression upon others and thus although we have the most orderly and well-behaved col'd people here that can be found in the whole country, there is not a meat-house in the whole town that has not been robbed, and we cannot keep chickens in our coops or even vegetables in our gardens. This is a bad state of things for which there seems to be no remedy at present, we can but hope that as they advance in education and enlightened morality, our condition will improve with theirs and I'm sure we ought to do everything we can to improve them.[24]

By the late 1860s, letters to Mary from Jane included her significant, sad financial problems. She had been behind in her mortgage since early in the war and was having trouble making ends meet. Jane pleaded with Mary and Jonathan: "If Mr. Sturges could help me a little now, my heart will bless him for it and I believe he will have a better blessing than any poor mortal can give him but tell him it is not worthwhile for him to relieve all my difficulties; that would be far more than I expect or would be reasonable."[25] Mary and Jonathan remained steadfast friends and continued to send stipends and other gifts such as clothing to meet the necessities and to keep Jane in her home.

Discovered about 1971, Jane Beale's journal, published by the Fredericksburg Historical Foundation in 1979, is acclaimed as one of the best descriptions that historians have of a civilian's experience during the Battle of Fredericksburg in December 1862 and life after the war. Jane's enlightening letters to Mary Sturges further illuminate the deep feelings that were invoked in her during the war and the economic consequences in the aftermath. Jane Beale is now the most quoted diarist of the battle—the Mary Chesnut of Fredericksburg.[c] Her story is regarded as so important and descriptive that the 2003 movie *Gods and Generals*, the sequel to the 1993 movie *Gettysburg*, featured Mary's friend Jane Beale, portrayed as a Fredericksburg socialite, played by Mia Dillon.

---

[c] At this writing, the introductory film, describing the battle shown to visitors at the U.S National Parks Service Fredericksburg Battlefield Visitor Center, features Jane Howison Beale's description of the activity in the town while the battle raged.

Nineteen

Art Promotion and Wartime Charity

To Messrs. John Green and Jonathan Sturges that great credit is due.
For them the prayers of thousands of innocent little children and
happy fathers and mothers daily ascend to the throne of the Almighty.

—*New York Times, 1869*

Thomas P. Rossiter, *Representative Merchants of America* c. 1857[1][a]

Still highly engaged in the New York art community, in 1862 Jonathan
took on a project on behalf of the New York Chamber of Commerce that
sought to purchase and complete a historically significant painting. Thomas
Prichard Rossiter, a noted portrait artist of the time, received a commission

---

[a] Gentlemen depicted, in alphabetical order: John Jacob Astor, W.H. Aspinwall; Wm. Appleton
(Boston), Joshua Bates (London), James Brown, James Boorman, P.C. Brooks (Boston), Peter
Cooper, Thomas Cope (Philadelphia), Erastus Corning (Albany), Alexander Duncan, Albert
Gallatin, Wm. Gray (Boston), Stephen Girard (Philadelphia), Jonathan Goodhue, Robert Gilmore
(Baltimore), Henry Grinnell, George Griswold, Philip Hone, Jas. G. King, Abbott Lawrence
(Boston), N. Longworth (Cincinnati), A.A. Low, Charles H. Marshall, Robert B. Minturn, W.
Bogden (Chicago), George Opdyke, Pelatiah Perit, George Peabody (London), Thos. H. Perkins
(Boston), A.T. Stewart, Jonathan Sturges, and Moses Taylor. Note: Thirty-one men of the thirty-
three designated are depicted in this portrait. It is unknown which two were not included.

from William Wright to execute a large mural-size painting (measuring II feet by I6 feet) to depict a representation of the leading merchants in America. Rossiter's original study depicted forty-three merchants with an upper tier balcony of merchants on the left. He was still painting individual portraits for his thirty-three subjects when Wright died. The painter never received Wright's $1000 commission.[2] Although records do not identify each person by position in the painting, Jonathan can be found the second from right in the back row which is a close facsimile of one of his known portraits.

In the end, it appears that the Chamber did obtain the painting, but the final product was still not complete as it depicted only thirty-one men and contained no balcony. The painting was later obtained by the YMCA of New York City in 1873, an organization of which Jonathan was a founder, and eventually came to the New York Historical Society. It is now in a deteriorated state and in storage.

In 1860, the National Academy of Design decided to build a new home. To accomplish this, their existing clubhouse eventually sold for $120,000, realizing a profit of $69,000, leaving the Academy with net funds after debt of $60,000. Charles Leupp and Jonathan Sturges had advanced the money to purchase the existing clubhouse and had remained as trustees in the deed until the sale. However, Leupp, owner of a successful tanning business, ended his own life in 1859 after twenty-one-year-old Jay Gould took advantage of Leupp's old-merchant-trust in the integrity of fellow businessmen. Gould went into business with Leupp but early in the partnership, and unbeknownst to Leupp, Gould used Leupp's credit to corner the market on the tanning industry. Caught short before he achieved his goal, Gould bankrupted the company and Leupp was ruined, driving him to commit suicide.[3] After Leupp's death, Jonathan became the only non-artist entrusted with Academy management.

To effect the funding, find and purchase a site and construct a new NAD building, Jonathan was again a trustee, along with artists Thomas Cummings, Asher Durand, and Francis Edmonds.[4] They found a site at 23rd Street and 4th Avenue for $50,000 but struggled for three years to raise the funds to construct a building.[5] Finally, the means were achieved and under Jonathan's vigilant oversight the building was begun in 1863 and opened in 1865. In recognition of his critical contributions, the Academy commissioned a portrait of him in 1863 to display at the Academy.[b]

---

[b] As of this writing the painting was in long-term storage.

National Academy of Design, c. 1865[6]

Jonathan always made charitable efforts a priority in his life, including during wartime in New York. Not unlike his start in railroads, Jonathan's involvement and reputation as a philanthropist was enabled by his associations and financial means, but it was a deeply-held belief that drove him, as stated in his retirement speech: "I have never believed that any man could be happy who lived entirely for himself."

Jonathan and Mary Sturges supported multiple organizations providing charitable medical care, with a special affinity for homeopathic medicine and non-surgical treatments. Their life experiences drew them to this philosophy, and they worked hard to facilitate the success of two pioneering holistic medical institutions in the city. As Samuel Hahnemann, the father of homeopathic medicine, espoused: "The current therapies of bloodletting, purging, puking and the administration of heroic doses of harsh drugs are barbaric and inhumane."[7] In this vein, in 1858 Jonathan became a founder and lifetime board member of the Homeopathic Medical College of the State of New York, near Union Square in Manhattan, at the corner of 3rd Avenue and E. 20th Street.[8] It was second only to the Hahnemann Homeopathic Hospital of Philadelphia[c] for its longevity in the United States, helping tens of thousands of needy patients.[9d] It was the first of three hospitals Jonathan incorporated.

---

c Second Homeopathic Hospital in the world, established 1848

d In the 1930s the College moved away from the Homeopathic mission, merged, moved and changed its name to the New York Medical College, which exists today about fifteen miles north of New York City in Valhalla, New York.

New York Homeopathic Medical College and Hospital c. 1868[10]
and Dr. James Knight Home & Hospital c. 1860s[11]

Jonathan's Association for Improving the Condition of the Poor sponsored many home visits by its delegates, exposing deplorable living conditions. To a certain visiting doctor, it also revealed many cases of deformed or crippled children and adults, who had no access to the medical care or devices that could provide them a better quality of life.

Dr. James Knight was the enlightened doctor who observed these wanting medical conditions, and in March 1862, he called on Robert Hartley, the Secretary of the Association for Improving the Condition of the Poor, to ask for his help. Knight asserted that "a large percentage of our population was suffering from hernia or rupture; that many are also afflicted with varicose or enlarged veins, and various deformities of body and limb, especially among the laboring poor."[12] He saw the need for a specialty institution to treat this class of maladies. Hartley fortuitously decided it was a worthy extension of the work of the Association, and a meeting of philanthropically minded citizens was convened in April, to solicit their cooperation and financial support. The *New York Post* reported, "Twenty large-hearted men came forward and pledged themselves to maintain the institution for a term of three years, and thus it began."[13] The New York Society for the Relief of the Ruptured and Crippled was born and Jonathan was an incorporator and fixture on the Board of Managers as the long-time treasurer.

The hospital began with twenty-eight beds in Dr. James Knight's house on Second Avenue, who leased it to the Society for $1,200 annually. Dr. Knight's treatments did not involve surgery, very much in keeping with Jonathan's own preference for non-invasive medical treatments. He was in fact not a surgeon by training, but a general practitioner who had specialized in treatments involving mechanical devices, medicine and external therapy for musculoskeletal diseases or spinal disorders. In the original 1863-1864 journal of care, the first recorded "out-door" patient was a young William Haggerty:

> A white, native, four-year-old, from New Brunswick, New Jersey...Good bodily health, until a slight ailment at about eighteen months being then seized with complete paralysis of the left leg...Treatment: steel support from the hips to the foot, the front supported at the right angle to the leg... apparatus to be taken off night and morning, after which the surface to be cleansed with warm water having a small portion of soda or potash in it... and apply a small portion of strychnine ointment to the front of the leg.[14]

The first "In-door" patient (resident) was Maggie Fliednar (or Fliedner):

> White, native, 10 years of age; residence Broadway, between 68th and 69th St. Ailment: feeble and extremely scrofulous.[e] Treatment: an extension apparatus, applied to the leg...cod liver oil taken internally, one tablespoon night and morning... Sweet oil applied night and morning to the con-tracted muscles, bathing the limb daily with warm water containing a small amount of potash.[15]

In-door patients were children undergoing long-term rehabilitation, and the average stay was two years. In the 1860s, one half of patients were under the age of fourteen. In November 1864, the Society reported that in the six months prior they had received 507 patients, and 1335 since its opening eighteen months before, of which 1214 had been relieved.[16]

Their work was universally lauded. One visiting *New York Times* journal-ist in 1869 noted, while walking through the patient living areas, the happy and well-cared-for appearance of the children, their contented countenances, and their warm greetings for Dr. Knight, as they would greet a kindly grand-father. There were countless stories of children who arrived as hopeless cripples but were being transformed into mobile and functioning people. The journalist remarked that "it is to Messrs. John Green and Jonathan Sturges that great credit is due. For them the prayers of thousands of innocent little children and happy fathers and mothers daily ascend to the throne of the Almighty...so [they] may be rewarded afterward."[17]

---

[e] Scrofulous – having a diseased run-down appearance or morally contaminated.

In the late 1860s, they had outgrown Dr. Knight's house and required a larger facility to expand their operations and educate the young patients while in-residence. In 1866, they purchased No. 97 2nd Avenue to provide storage and administrative space but no further proper facilities could be found for operations. A building fund was inaugurated with Jonathan chairing the efforts with a goal of raising $200,000. The fundraising was slow, but they were able to purchase land in the country on 42nd Street, where livestock was grazing in the surrounding areas. In April 1869, they had begun construction of a two-hundred bed facility. and completed the basement and second story of the new building and started work on the third floor, but still required $100,000 to complete the hospital. At a board meeting in April 1870, Jonathan reported that they were still short $50,000 minimum to build the hospital.

The Board voted to take out a mortgage, but the president of the association, John Green, was absent, and he possessed the sole authority to obligate the organization financially. Green, who had made his fortune in the China trade, refused to mortgage the property. Instead, he declared that he would donate $50,000 if Jonathan and the board of managers would raise a matching amount within thirty days. "Their solution to mortgage was rescinded, and it was voted to endeavor to raise $50,000 within thirty days."[18]

Hospital of the Ruptured and Crippled, 42nd & Lexington, c. 1870[19]

The funds were raised, and the hospital opened in May 1870, becoming a model for orthopedic treatment and medical instruction. Hospital historian Dr. David Levine commented, "The emergence of such a specialized facility in the middle of the nineteenth century during a time of medicine in its infancy, our country at war and the city of New York racked in poverty, disease, civil riots, and political corruption is a story not necessarily appreciated in our day."[20] In his next report to the board, Jonathan declared, "We have a hospital capable of housing 200-250 children. We have assets amounting to $100,000. We owe no one anything but love."[21]

Cornelius Vanderbilt opened his Grand Central Depot next door to the hospital the year after it opened. This hospital building at the corner of 42nd and Lexington was sold forty-two years later to Alfred Vanderbilt, extending the Vanderbilt real estate footprint.[f] After the sale of the property, the hospital bought land a few blocks down on 42nd street between 1st and 2nd Avenue for $307,125, their third location.[22] Today the Hospital for the Ruptured and Crippled has become the world-renowned Hospital for Special Surgery and is on East 70th Street.[g]

---

[f] Alfred Gwynne Vanderbilt, a grandson of Cornelius Vanderbilt, purchased the site for $1.35M about 1912 and built a hotel, now the Grand Hyatt, above the Grand Central Terminal.

[g] Jonathan's Hospital for the Ruptured and Crippled has been the Hospital for Special Surgery since 1940. It relocated to its current location at 535 East 70th Street on the east side of Manhattan in 1955 when it became affiliated with the New York Hospital-Cornell Medical Center. Virginia and William Osborn, William Church Osborn, and their heirs further ensured that the Sturges/Osborn families were involved in the work of the New York Society for the Ruptured and Crippled Hospital, and its successor organizations, for seven generations.

TWENTY

Banking—1864 Election—
War Refugees—Lincoln's Death

Fenton's action gave the opponents of the scheme time to organize and
ultimately to defeat it. He thereby deferred underground transit in New
York City for almost half a century.

—*James Walker, Rapid Transit Historian, 1918*

The City of New York pressed Jonathan into service to address several key
economic and governance issues of the day for the rest of his life. Forefront
among them was the management of the nation's banking system. The
country had been struggling with a fragile banking system since the Jackson
administration dismantled the Bank of the United States and dispersed
federal currency reserves thirty years before. The National Banking Act of
1863 sought to reestablish federal regulation and put in place a charter
system for national banks and a national currency backed by the federal
government. This was to counter the state-issued charter system, and bank
notes prone to counterfeiting and value fluctuation.

Jonathan chaired a meeting on October 21, 1863, at a Fifth Avenue
hotel to discuss the initiative. Hugh McCullough, appointed by Secretary
Chase as Comptroller of the Currency, was tasked with managing the
national banking system, and was promoting the establishment of a flagship
bank in New York. McCullough addressed the assemblage and shared the
goals of the administration.[1] The group adjourned with resolutions to establish the Fourth National Bank with a starting capital of $5,000,000, go-
ing upwards to $50,000,000 if needed. Although a lead promoter, Jonathan
did not become one of the early directors, but his friends Morris Ketchum,
Peter Cooper, and former son-in-law J.P. Morgan became directors in
April 1864. The national banking system was on its way to stability again;

however, they were in the infancy of establishing a credible national currency, and gold remained king in commercial transactions.

Gold was subject to manipulation during the Civil War. Most businessmen relied on metal currency to trade, and gold prices fluctuated in the aftermath of significant battles or other news that affected the public's perspective of the war. Speculators were overjoyed when a Confederate victory occurred, spiking the price of gold. Sturges, Bennet & Co. traded primarily in tea, coffee and spices. However, for a short time the firm also traded in gold. In just seventeen days during March-April 1864, the company profited an astounding $164,650.[2a] There were dozens of merchant houses trading gold, but his firm's participation is curious, considering his steadfast commitment to non-speculative business practices. In fact, the firm does not appear as a gold trader before or after these seventeen days, and it may have been the initiative of his partner, Benjamin Arnold, whose tendency to speculate would infamously surface later.

A proponent of the free trade of gold, the *New York Times* reported: "It is of course well that speculation should be made difficult and dangerous, because it is a form of gambling, and as such demoralizing; but the notion that making it a penalty will materially help the national finances, is simply folly and very childish folly to boot."[3] To stabilize gold prices the government passed An Act to Prohibit Certain Sales of Gold and Foreign Exchange on June 17, 1864, barring futures trading in gold. Unfortunately, the act had the opposite effect, and gold spiked to $300 an ounce, hoarding became rampant, and the value of non-metallic currency plummeted. Jonathan and his colleagues took determined action to turn the tide.

The New York City Chamber of Commerce gathered on June 22 and reached an agreement to press for the repeal of the Gold Bill. Five representatives were appointed to consult with Secretary Chase and Congress on its negative effect on commerce. The *New York Times* editorialized, "The [Chamber] Committee represent that passage of the Gold Bill has completely unsettled affairs in New York, and if not repealed or modified, it will seriously embarrass business interests there."[4] The Committee on the Gold Bill, Messrs. Jonathan Sturges, S.D. Babcock, E.S. Jeffray, Charles Hoffman and James Brown left for Washington, D.C. the next day.[5] Their visit was a

---

a About $2,600,000 in 2018 dollars.

success, and on July 1, 1864 the bill was repealed; thus it was passed and repealed within two weeks. Speculation continued to occur, and bad news of the war still sent gold higher, but the wild price fluctuations were averted.

Although this was a tumultuous and divisive time for the country it was a boom time for business. Simultaneously, there was significant population growth in New York City, creating an increasingly dense housing situation in southern Manhattan—and it was pushing northward. The streets were chaotic and dangerous to travel, as described by a subway historian:

> The city rested mostly below Twenty-Third Street…Most citizens lived south of Forty-Second Street. Many streets were not yet paved, and citizens had to walk through dust or mud in order to reach the horse cars or omnibuses….Conditions became intolerable in 1864. Broadway was a dangerous place for pedestrians because the intense rivalry between omnibus companies increased as drivers drove over people in their haste to beat their competitors for waiting passengers.[6]

The city was ripe for mass transit, and but for some unfavorable politics, history might have regarded Jonathan Sturges as a father of the city's subway system.

The vision was to build an underground railroad from the Battery at the south end of Manhattan to Central Park, the first subway to be built in the United States. In March 1864, Jonathan and fifty other incorporators of the Metropolitan Railway Company appealed to the legislature for a charter. The London underground opened in January 1863, and Hugh B. Wilson, a director of the New York company, had experienced it and was foremost of those pushing strongly to construct such a system in New York. The *New York Times* editorialized on the initiative:

> The bill of which we spoke the other day, authorizing the construction of an Underground Railroad from Central Park to the Battery has been introduced into the Legislature. In addition to the main line, it is proposed also to construct branches, connecting it with the Harlem, New Haven and Hudson River Railroads. There are to be stations at convenient points, say at the City Hall, Canal-street, Astor-place, Union Square, Madison Square, etc. The corporators, fifty in number, embrace some of our most substantial and respectable citizens, among whom we may name Jonathan Sturges, John J. Astor, Jr., Moses Taylor…It proposes to adopt what has proved to be a complete success in London where an underground railway has been in operation for more than a year past…For this purpose no less than \$40,000,000 has been raised.[7]

There were twenty schemes being promoted at the time for rapid transit, but the Metropolitan Railway Company was the only one backed by the city government. Jonathan's son-in-law, William Osborn, was also an initial investor and director of the corporation.[8] The plan was to dig up the areas where the underground was to be built, construct the tunnels with brick and stone and then cover up the tunnels as they went. Steam locomotives would pull the cars. This group had the money, a well-engineered plan, and public support. The underground transit legislation passed, but Governor Fenton vetoed it. His official reasoning was that he foresaw endless delays and significant upheaval to the commerce of the city due to disruptive construction, and too much public area taken up by depots. However, the real, underlying reason seemed to have been heavy lobbying by the horse-drawn railroad operators, such as William Tweed, and those backing elevated railways. Rapid transit historian James Walker asserted: "Fenton's action gave the opponents of the scheme time to organize rival projects and ultimately to defeat it. He thereby deferred underground transit in New York City for almost half a century."[9]

Don Matias Romero[10]

While business was thriving in New York City, by mid-1864 the American Civil War, though still being fought on many fronts, was marching to its conclusion. However, it was not the only war being fought in North America. It's neighbor Mexico had just been invaded by French forces led by the Archduke Maximilian of Austria who was crowned Emperor of Mexico. He was the younger brother of the Emperor Franz Joseph who had imperialistic ambitions.

Senior Don Matias Romero, Mexican Envoy to the United States, was working to build American support for their struggle against the invader. Jonathan was invited to attend a state department dinner in his honor at the fashionable Delmonico's. As Seward became more confident in the Union's probable victory, he warmed to their cause, and orchestrated the evening to honor Romero and Mexican sovereignty. Seward introduced each participant and highlighted their high achievements.

Jonathan was introduced as an "American Maecenas," a term in honor of the Roman literary patron Maecenas Gaius, a trusted advisor of Augustus Caesar and a patron of Homer and Virgil—a moniker used to describe recognized patrons of the arts. Jonathan curiously declined to speak for the arts and instead spoke forcefully of the country's support for the Mexican government and offered that it wouldn't have been "sixty days before our own troops would have entered to help, if our own affairs were settled."[11]

Although Jonathan was civic minded, he was never an active politician although early in his career he was a Whig Party supporter. With the demise of the Whigs, he threw his support to the Republican Party. In the 1850s, and more so in the 1860s, he endorsed candidates who espoused transparency in government, including Robert T. Haws for city comptroller in 1858[b] and State Senator William Lembeer in 1863.[c] However, Jonathan's involvement in influencing politics and government took on more urgency late in the war and much of this activity flowed through the Union League.

The powerful New York City Tammany Hall political machine had been formed in 1786 as the Society of St. Tammany. By 1850, it had gained clout representing a growing immigrant population, dominated by Irish Catholics and Copperheads, and was a primary force in city politics starting with the 1854 election of Mayor Fernando Wood. This pervading sentiment was demonstrated in 1860, when New York defeated a voting rights bill for Blacks by a 60% vote, and when war was imminent, Wood proposed to make the city independent and neutral, on neither side of the war.

Partially in response to this development, there was a proliferation of organizations and clubs formed by wealthy men for both political influence and social interaction. Although the Union League's premise was that it was an apolitical body to support the Union cause, by its mission and dismissiveness of any opposition, it was inherently political and staunchly Republican, and was one of the first of those clubs. Jonathan and most of his Union League colleagues threw their support behind the re-election of Lincoln in 1864. However, the unquestioning support of the government was becoming problematic even for many Union League members. The election caused heated exchanges between some members of the club and highlighted the growing divergence in political views.[d]

---

[b] Nominated and elected from Republican Party in November 1858 on the third ballot.

[c] Not elected until 1866 and served one term.

[d] Democrats formed The Manhattan Club after the war in 1865. John Van Buren was the club's first president

The Republican Party was fractured over whom to nominate and Lincoln's re-election was more doubtful than assured. Secretary of the Treasury Chase believed early in 1864 that Lincoln was not electable and opposed his candidacy. Even President Lincoln, as late as August 1864, was convinced he would not be elected again. No longer the party of Lincoln, a faction of the party known as the Radical Republican Party nominated John Fremont for president due to the perceived weakness of Lincoln's candidacy. A consortium of Republicans and Democrats still pressing to preserve the Union united their support under the National Union Party, which nominated Lincoln for re-election.

Lincoln's primary opponent in 1864 was George McClellan, whom he fired for a reluctance to prosecute the war. McClellan was popular among soldiers, Copperheads and peace Democrats. Jonathan and his family were professionally and personally acquainted with McClellan, but McClellan's sympathies were with the Confederacy. He had many West Point classmates and friends in the South and preferred an end to the war with an armistice, and a tolerant policy toward slavery. However, by September 1864, two months before the election, at a Union League gathering, Jonathan quoted a now pragmatic McClellan: "We agree with General McClellan where he expresses his opinion, 'After a calm, impartial, patient consideration of the subject, that a necessary preliminary to the re-establishment of the Union is the entire defeat or the virtual destruction of the organized military of the Confederacy, and such a result would be followed by conciliatory measures.'"[12]

Lincoln won the 1864 election with 55% of the popular vote and electoral votes from twenty-two of the twenty-five remaining union states including New York. Only Delaware, New Jersey, and Kentucky went to McClellan. Lincoln's turn around in popularity was propelled by multiplying successes on the battlefield by Grant and Sherman's capture of Atlanta. Republicans had successfully asserted that a vote for McClellan was nothing less than a retreat, traitorous to the country, and disrespectful to those who had fought and died for the cause. However, in New York City, Lincoln took only about one-third of the popular vote. The Union League persevered but with the formidable task of bolstering support for the government where 66% of the city and 45% of the national vote supported a different direction for the country.

In mid-1864, a workingman's rally was held in England to oppose government assistance to the Confederacy. Coupled with increasing Union victories, Prime Minister Palmerston's government, with vocal leadership by William Gladstone, Exchequer, and Lord Russell, Foreign Minister, discontinued their active, albeit veiled, support of the Confederacy. The threat of foreign intervention was now one less thing for the Union to worry about.

As the war's outcome was turning in favor of a Union victory in late 1864, the nation was ready to give thanks at its second official Thanksgiving approached. Jonathan, as President of the Union League Club, and Theodore Roosevelt, Sr., treasurer of the initiative, set out to ensure "that no soldier in the Army of the Potomac, the James or the Shenandoah, and no sailor in the North Atlantic Squadron does not receive tangible evidence that those for whom he is periling his life, remember him."[13] One historian noted, "The reaction of the Northern public to this plan was overwhelming…over $56,000 in cash was raised, an enormous sum at the time, 250,000 pounds of fowl, and large contributions of foodstuffs of every kind. The Union soldiers and sailors loved their feast and the reminder that they had not been forgotten by the people back home."[14]

Unfortunately, the logistics of getting an offering to General Sherman's troops deep in Georgia was too tough for the committee to overcome. Union League President Jonathan Sturges wrote an apologetic letter to Sherman for not including his troops in the Thanksgiving food distribution. Sherman, in the middle of leading 60,000 soldiers from Atlanta to Savannah on his March to the Sea campaign, replied tongue-in-cheek to President Sturges, in a now famous anecdote from the war, telling him not to worry: "But if you've run short of turkeys, we've a lot that we can let you have!"[15]

As the war dragged on, returning disabled and indigent soldiers became a common sight. Though the government provided support for returning regular members of the army, most of the soldiers in the Civil War, who were volunteers, could not receive such support. A compassionate vision arose to assert that the country owed them an equal helping hand. In December 1864, Jonathan joined with General Ulysses S. Grant, William C. Bryant, Horace Greeley, Henry W. Longfellow, William E. Dodge, P.T. Barnum, George Bancroft, John Jay, Richard Morris Hunt, and Peter Cooper, among others, in lobbying to establish a national home for the disabled soldiers and sailors of the Army and Navy of the United States. They petitioned and pressed the issue with Congress, and Senate bill 479 passed both the Senate and House in March 1865, "to incorporate a National Military and Naval Asylum for the relief of the totally disabled officers and men of the volunteer forces of the United States."[16] The first Asylum opened in November 1866, in Togus, Maine and other branches around the country soon followed.[17] Thus, the tradition of taking care of the country's veterans was established and the organization is a recognized predecessor agency of the modern Veteran's Administration.[18]

Lincoln called once more for recruits in early 1864, and New York City executed an unannounced draft that was completed March 15 to fulfill its quota. Fortunately, that was the last that the city would see of conscription as the war's outcome was now inevitable.

As President of the Union League in 1864, Jonathan presided over the recruitment of pioneering Colored Troops and many others to fill Union troop needs. He and fellow Union League members aroused Congress to authorize a home for war veterans and oversaw club efforts to re-elect Lincoln. His initiative also established the beginnings of an art gallery of note. As Colonel Ethan Allen wrote, "Many times he [Jonathan] addressed his fellow-citizens from the steps of the Club in Union Square, advocating strength of purpose, firmness, and immediate action at the great crises in the affairs of the country."[19] However, in late 1864, having missed multiple meetings over the year, Jonathan resigned the presidency due to declining health. His resignation letter to the Executive Committee on November 7, 1864, read:

> I desire to tender to the club my resignation as its President, to take effect as of the annual meeting. Having fully intended not to be a candidate for re-election. I send my resignation now, in order to give the club ample time to select my successor. I beg to assure the club that I take this step with regret and solely on account of my physical inability to perform the duties of the office to my own satisfaction. Thanking the members for their uniform kindness and courtesy to me and asking them to excuse any failure on my part in the performance of my duties. I am, most sincerely yours, Jon. Sturges.[20]

Although the war was not over in January 1865, their Southern brethren were staring down a hopeless cause and a broken economy. What little production infrastructure existed before the War had been destroyed and

and crops had not been planted. Trade was at a standstill and Confederate currency was worthless. There were countless widows and orphans and many families were truly desperate.

A charitable group met to address the plight of the destitute population of Savannah, which had surrendered. Jonathan's family connection to the city through his cousins Lucretia and Elizabeth made it personal for him. Representatives of bankers, brokers, insurance companies, shipping, dry goods, grocers, and the Corn Exchange gathered to raise funds to send necessities to the suffering populace. Jonathan represented the grocers. As there was still a state of war, many worried the food would come into the custody of Rebel soldiers, and their good intentions would end up helping the Rebel cause. After discussion, it was agreed if they were sending aid to Lancashire and Ireland, they could extend compassion to the people in Savannah, who were fellow countrymen once again. Two steamships were provided gratis to convey the collected items. Foodstuffs were gathered and loaded within one week, and the *New York Times* reported, "The steamship *Rebecca Clyde* sailed last evening, deeply laden with provisions, etc., for the relief of the citizens of Savannah, and, as she went down the bay, gaily dressed in colors, she was greeted with cheers and salutes from all sides."[21] This was the first of several Southern relief committees that Jonathan would take part in to aid the beleaguered populace, be they former planter or former slave.

Henry Sturges wrote in his diary on April 12, "Grand News, Capture of Lee's Army" which had occurred on April 9. On April 15, he sorrowfully wrote: "Frightful News, Assassination of the President by Booth the Actor," which occurred the day before. On April 16, Henry lamented: "The city in mourning, all amusements closed for the day." The city turned its attentions to grieving for their fallen president.

In a memorial to Lincoln, the Union League Club came together again in one of its last major wartime efforts. A devastated Jonathan traveled to Washington, D.C., as a representative of the club and the merchants of New York, to pay his respects to the late president and to the new president. An excerpt of their official letter to President Johnson read in part:

Washington, D.C., April 19, 1865. To the President of the United States:

Sir, Delegates from the Union League Club of New York, not a party organization, but united by a common principle of loyalty, we have come to pay our last tribute of love and honor to the memory of Abraham Lincoln. We have come also to assure you, as you enter upon your unprecedented task, that amid every difficulty and danger, you may rely upon the same unwavering support that the loyal citizens whom we represent so cordially gave to your lamented predecessor... respectfully, your fellow country-men—John Jay, Jonathan Sturges, Charles Butler, James W. Beckman, Theodore Roosevelt, [Sr.].[22]

Lincoln Funeral East Room White House[23]

Johnson responded to the Union League thanking them for their support. At the official funeral proceedings, Jonathan was afforded an honored place with other men of national stature:

When the funeral exercises took place, the floor of the East Room had been transformed into something like an amphitheater by the erection of an inclined platform...This platform was covered with a black cloth, and upon it stood the various persons designated as participants in the ceremonies. No seats being provided. In the northwest corner were the pallbearers —Senators Lafayette S. Foster of Connecticut, E.D. Morgan of New York...Lieutenant General Grant, Major General Halleck...Vice-Admiral Farragut...The New York Chamber of Commerce was represented by its officers, and the New York Merchants by Simeon Draper, Moses Grinnell, John Jacob Astor, Jonathan Sturges...[24]

Jonathan was on the stage and witness to one of the most sobering events in our nation's history, alongside the most senior military officers and statesmen. Family oral history has it that Arthur Sturges obtained a relic from the death bed of Lincoln, a piece of a pillow slip Lincoln laid his head on, which the family still has in its possession. Arthur may have accompanied his father to the funeral proceedings and obtained it while there, as bits of bedding and anything else in the room where Lincoln died were being sold as souvenirs, but the specific details are lost.

Lincoln's body passed through several major cities on its way to Illinois, where large gatherings were staged to honor the slain President. Henry Sturges wrote on April 24: "Arrival of the body. The President's body arrived at 10 p.m. Went down with the girls to Wall Street." In New York, Jonathan, and a group of twenty-four other gentlemen, were tasked with coordinating the events associated with the arrival and procession of Lincoln's coffin.[25] More than 100,000 New Yorkers lined the streets. Henry wrote on April 25: "Funeral Procession...great sorrow." The next day Henry was back to school and playing billiards. Life went on for all.

With the end of the war and the death of Lincoln, a chapter closed for the nation. It also ushered in a new era for the Union League, an organization that had been entirely focused on defeating the rebellion and preserving the Union. In the immediate aftermath of the war, the Union League Club membership evolved their purpose to promote civil rights, fight city corruption, and support other civic and philanthropic projects.

In June 1865, the club adopted a strong policy of supporting and promoting civil rights and suffrage for African-Americans. Jonathan was part of a club group that raised funds for the New York Branch of the American Freedman's Union Commission, believing no means more effectual towards securing equal rights to Blacks than education.[26] The Commission funded one hundred-fifty teachers in 1866.[27] The Freedman's Commission joined forces with the American Union Commission in 1866 to provide relief to war refugees in areas such as Nashville, Louisville, Vicksburg, and Cairo where many large encampments had formed.

After the war ended, returning generals became national heroes and were celebrated wherever they traveled. General Grant was foremost among them as the man given credit for leading the Union to victory on the battlefield. In June 1865, Grant visited New York City and was cheered and followed by a mob of citizens wherever he went. During this visit Jonathan personally hosted him at the Union League for about an hour, where he viewed a club exhibition celebrating the victory in the recent rebellion.[28] On November 20, 1865, the "Solid Men of the Metropolis" (as dubbed by the

New York Herald), honored General Grant at an exclusive reception at the Fifth Avenue Hotel. It was officially limited to one hundred and fifty selected individuals, paying $150 each to attend the reception. The tickets were so coveted that they could have been sold for ten times that amount. However, two to three hundred more people obtained access without tickets, physically overwhelming the gathering, making it a chaotic affair.[29]

Thousands had gathered at the front of the hotel, some sleeping overnight to get a good position to see their hero General Grant, as he arrived. The anxious crowd waited for Grant's arrival through a heavy rain, but he slipped in through a side entrance. Later, he appeared on the hotel balcony and was met with deafening cheers and a display of fireworks. Just after eleven o'clock, General Grant left the reception and proceeded to an even more select banquet at Delmonico's. It was not unusual as the Gilded Age approached for these exclusive dinners to start at eleven or twelve midnight and end in the wee hours of the morning. Jonathan and Mary were among the select group of forty invited to the private dinner.[30] An unremarkable speaker, Grant said only two sentences of thanks to the gathering. Henry Ward Beecher, the famous religious leader from Brooklyn, Rev. Dr. Thompson, and John Van Buren[e] delivered addresses in tribute to the general. New York's Seventh Regiment escorted Grant down Broadway the next day as he left town. Jonathan's intimacy with the general would be a factor in his effectiveness at addressing several financial and economic issues affecting the nation during Grant's term.

When most men his age would be pulling back from demanding activities and looking at retirement, Jonathan became even more involved in civic activities and charitable pursuits. Although his wartime endeavors were arguably his high-water mark for civic and philanthropic efforts, it could also be said he was just getting started.

---

[e] Lawyer, noted speaker, and son of President Martin Van Buren.

Twenty-one

Death of a Son—Ketchum Defalcation—Colonization

Just before he died he said, "I believe in Jesus".

—*Virginia Sturges Osborn*

Henry Sturges was fifteen when the Civil War broke out, the youngest of the six children, five years younger than Arthur, and was attending the Flushing Institute on Long Island. His father lectured him on many fronts:

I'm glad to see the tone of your letter is more cheerful than that to your mother. I trust you will not write any more of those doleful letters to anyone…you must be careful about your writing and spelling…I wish you to improve in all these things…. you must take exercise out of doors. You will not have any muscles, of course, if you do not exercise…Good Angels watch over those who think to do right.[1]

Henry's daughter later recalled a story her father told her about his youth. Henry formed a private police force, then a volunteer fire brigade as he got older:

They were armed with picks and axes, as well as the hose. The boys raced to the firehouse at the first alarm. The first one to arrive had the honor of going in with the hose. One day, Father was well in the lead when his shoe became untied, and he had to stop and tie it. Another boy beat him in and went in bravely. A wall collapsed on him and he was killed.[2]

Although of military age, Arthur entered Columbia College in 1861. He was a fierce student, being tutored in and out of college settings on various subjects. The predominant theme of his 1863 journal is a record and discussion of his academic pursuits and the books he was reading. He was particularly gifted as an orator. Virginia wrote to Arthur in December 1861 encouraging him in this vein: "What new piece of poetry are you learning? Don't give up the study of elocution. I think there is no gift for a man like that of moving multitudes with true eloquence. It is as rare as the gift of song in a woman, for you seldom hear a woman sing whose voice really touches the heart."[3]

At Columbia College, Arthur was a member of the Philolexian Society, a college literary club, and he was taking lessons in drama and elocution from an instructor who he admired by the name of Mr. Vanderhoff. The Society held frequent elocution contests, much of which were of original composition. In December 1862, Jonathan was a featured speaker at the sixtieth anniversary exercises for the Philolexian Society of Columbia College. There were over 2,500 attendees as Arthur read the poem "Shamus O'Brien."

Arthur Sturges, 1860s[4]

The *New York Times* had special praise for Arthur after the event. "The most successful effort of the evening was the exquisite rendering by Mr. A.P. STURGES of "Shamus O'Brien, ... gave full scope to his power of oratorical interpretation."[5] "Shamus O'Brien—A Ballad," written by J.S. Le Fanu, was popular for public recitations, although many who heard Arthur's reading thought it to be original.[6] After reading the *Times* article, Virginia Sturges wrote to her mother: "I really cried for joy when I read the notice of Arthur's speech in the *Times*. It is such a great gift for a man to be able to move the masses with the tone of his voice."[7] After his encore reading of "Donald Lorn" at the Philolexian Society meeting in December, the *New York Times* dubbed it a "masterly rendering" that was "well delivered and reflected great credit upon its author."[8] In a 1902 history of the Philolexian Society at Columbia, he was memorialized as one of the most brilliant speakers and debaters of the 1860s.

Arthur Pemberton Sturges entered college in the fall of 1861 and graduated June 1864. From the first he was a very active member of Philolexian; and the minutes of the society and the testimony of his contemporaries, all bear witness to his zeal and talent. He was editor of The Philolexian Observer and was elected time after time to represent the society as their star speaker. He first obtained public recognition at the anniversary at Irving Hall, December 19, 1862, in his masterly rendering of "Shamus O'Brien," and at subsequent anniversaries he wrote for and delivered before the societies the two poems of "Johnnie McKay" and "Donald Low" [sic]. Many now living will gladly bear witness to the delight with which they were received.[9]

In February 1862, Jonathan noted to Mary that Arthur was particularly interested in his Sabbath School lessons and Arthur later journaled of his enjoyment filling in as an instructor of the young men's Sabbath classes.[10] In furtherance of this interest, he decided to apply his extraordinary oratory talents and deep religious faith to become a minister. After his graduation from Columbia College in June 1864, he was set to enter the Theological School at Princeton. However, the War Department had other plans, and in July, when New York County was assigned the quota of providing 23,140 recruits, Arthur was drafted. In contrast to his older brothers who had served in New York Militia units, Jonathan paid for a substitute, Alexander Clapperton, a three-year-man enlistee to serve in his place, and he entered Princeton University in the fall.[11]

While at Princeton, Arthur wrote to Henry imploring him to put off his life of self-indulgence and sin and come to his Savior. He further asserted that "one goes through life either in the service of God or in the service of Satan," that there was no middle ground. He lamented to Henry of his deep concern for Henry's lack of spirituality and hypothesized to himself, "You are preparing to save the souls of your fellow man, what if before your preparation is complete and God should see fit to take from the world your own brother."[12] Interestingly, Memie delivered the same sermon to Arthur in October 1860: "Let me implore you not to trust in your own strength. No one is sufficient for these things and if you ask your Heavenly Father for his Holy Spirit to guide you, He will hear your prayer, this is a time in your life when you particularly need Divine Assistance."[13] Although Arthur accepted God's grace early in life, he never served God in the way he planned. Increasingly ill and weak over a six-month period, he tragically passed away in his twenty-fifth year, on Sunday, July 1, 1866, at the Cottage.[a]

Jonathan, Mary, all the children and Ellen Woodhouse, Arthur's nanny since he was a baby, and his girlfriend Sarah, were all present in his final hours. Virginia wrote letters to extended family informing them of the sad news, including this one to Grandmother Cady:

> He breathed his last at half-past one after seeming to suffer a great deal for several hours. We think he was scarcely conscious for much of the time though once or twice when several of us were in the room he said, "please, all go downstairs." He failed very rapidly for two days past, losing something each day which he never regained. The physicians think that he had overtaxed his brain for a long time. Dr. Grey said if he had been taken from his studies two years ago it might have saved his life. Ellen was with him constantly and he called for her if she left his side for a moment, long after he had ceased to know anyone else. Just before he died he said, "I believe in Jesus" and "how long will it take for the life to leave my body?" I think he suffered so much he longed to go. All Father's children were together, including Fred's wife and Sarah Davison, who seems like one of ourselves.[14]

In a second note to her Aunt she lamented:

> …you cannot conceive of how emaciated he became during his illness. The food has furnished no nourishment to the brain for some time past, but his will was so strong that he dragged his poor limbs around and up and down stairs until he had to be carried up the last time and laid in his bed until Wednesday night…. Poor Sarah Davison is heartbroken. She has gone through it all with so much self-control and now she feels as if life for her is over…. Mother and Father were as lovely and patient as they were when Memie died, but it is a terrible blow to them.[15]

Services for Arthur were held at the Cottage on Tuesday, July 3, after the arrival of the eleven o'clock train.[16] He was buried in Fairfield with Amelia in the East Cemetery.

---

[a] A family journal written by Henry Sturges' daughter Mary in 1980 wrote that Arthur died of a vitamin B12 deficiency.

Jonathan and Mary had now lost a second child, and they once again had to lean on their faith as they grieved. One of the many letters of sympathy Jonathan received after Arthur's death was from his friend Reverend Garnet, an African-American Presbyterian minister, abolitionist, and an orator of some note. He had worked with Jonathan to aid the victims after the July 1863 draft riots and to raise Black regiments. Mr. Garnet had just sent his condolences to Jonathan regarding his sister who had passed away three months prior. Lucretia had never married but had been an integral part of their family since the death of her mother. The East Cemetery in Fairfield became her perpetual resting place, where she was born and had spent the better part of her life.

In 1865, J. Pierpont Morgan married Frances Louise Tracy, known as Fanny, a daughter of a prominent lawyer. Frederick, Virginia and their spouses often socialized and traveled with the Morgans. Fred's children addressed Morgan as Uncle Pierpont, and Fred and Virginia were Uncle Fred and Aunt Virginia to Morgan's children. During the Morgan's honeymoon, Virginia and William Osborn joined them in Paris, and Fanny was not feeling well—already pregnant with their first child. The Morgans had four children, including J.P. Morgan, Jr. (Jack), Louisa, Anne and Juliet, all of whom addressed Jonathan and Mary as Grandpa and Grandma. Fanny developed a warm relationship with the Sturges family, and they corresponded often. In one instance, she returned a book to Mary, presented to Amelia as Queen of the Century Ball, which Amelia had taken on her honeymoon. Poignantly, there was a dried flower pressed inside the book, a treasured memento of Amelia that Mary Sturges kept for the rest of her life.

Jonathan turned sixty-three in 1865, and in May he was re-elected for the third time as the Second Vice President of the Chamber of Commerce, along with A.A. Low, President, and William Dodge, First Vice President—an impressive triumvirate of leading merchants.[17] Jonathan, Dodge, John Green and A.T. Stewart were further tasked with financing and building a new Chamber of Commerce building, and its opening was celebrated seventeen months later.[18] However, Jonathan's friend and fellow Chamber member Morris Ketchum was probably not one of those celebrating.

The era of rising greed ambushed Ketchum, one of Jonathan's closest friends. He stunningly found his firm bankrupt due to a speculative business dealing orchestrated by his son Edward. Well known to the Sturges family, Edward was on the adventure with J.P. Morgan and the Sturges boys in the White Mountains in 1863 and his brother was briefly engaged to Virginia.

Unfortunately for his father, Edward fraudulently pledged securities belonging to the firm to secure his purchases. These speculations failed, and his losses were staggering. This was still a time when the merchant class's success was built not only on their business acumen, but on the reputed character of the partners. Blindsided, stunned, and ashamed, Morris Ketchum asked Jonathan and four other business associates to arbitrate the situation.[19]

Creditors were gathered, about one hundred and fifty interested parties, on September 1, 1865. Jonathan and his fellow arbitrators determined that Edward had lost $2,500,000, and the total liability for the company was $4,000,000, an amount that threatened to liquidate the company. This was an astounding loss for the time, on the scale of the Schuyler fraud of 1854. Jonathan and his committee ruled that about $2,400,000 in assets could be paid out or liquidated to pay back creditors 60% of the $4,000,000 owed. This settlement allowed Ketchum's firm to stay in business.

In 1866, Edward received a sentence of four years and six months for forgery of securities and was incarcerated in Sing-Sing Prison in New York. His irresponsible behavior was considered so inconceivable that he had to have been mentally deranged. About halfway through his sentence, Jonathan and other friends and associates appealed to the governor for a pardon, on the grounds of temporary insanity. The newspapers of New York had also supported the pardon of Edward, given his age, generally respected character, and the low chance of his repeating such a crime. Those petitioning Governor Fenton included Jonathan, J. Pierpont Morgan, George Opdyke, Horace Greeley, Peter Cooper and over fifty other gentlemen, all attesting to Edward's good character before his inexplicable actions.[20] Jonathan testified at the pardon hearing: "I can only attribute the transactions which came to light in August 1865, to a stupefaction of his mind, which amounted to a species of insanity or monomania." Morgan had a similar refrain in his testimony: "Large stock speculations of the kind and amount he was led into bring on a very great excitement of the brain, and people are often wild and irregular in their judgment and actions. They do not know what they say or do."[21] Interestingly, Edward had engaged Morgan in late 1863 in such a speculation when they successfully made a bold and successful play in the gold market with the knowledge and backing of his father Morris Ketchum —an experience that likely served as encouragement for Edward.

With such overwhelming support by the most influential of New York City's capitalists, it seemed a foregone conclusion that the governor would pardon him. However, Democratic Governor Fenton responded in part: "...if I were to grant the pardon it would tend to impair the confidence of the public in the administration of criminal law."[22] He was released in November 1869, eight months early, due to exemplary conduct, a privilege rarely earned, his repentance now complete.

In Jonathan's own business, the firm's name Sturges, Bennet and Co. had remained the same for twenty years, which included Frederick Sturges's promotion to partner. They had added storage space with the construction of a cellar under the firm's buildings at 125 and 127 Front Street in 1858, and they officially changed the firm's mission from a grocery house, as the firm was identified in its earlier days, to focus on the tea, coffee and spices trade. In January 1866, the firm's name changed to Sturges, Arnold and Co. when Josiah Bennet retired, and Edward Sturges became a partner.[23]

Arthur and Lucretia's deaths took their emotional toll on the Sturges family and they decided to take Henry and go on a therapeutic trip to Europe in 1867. Arthur's death had been particularly hard on Henry. He had been closest to Arthur and Amelia, now both gone. His closest sibling in age was Edward, who was nine years older and had been working in Jonathan's firm for many years. He became very isolated from his remaining siblings. Mary recalled this family therapeutic trip:

> My son Arthur, after a decline of nearly six months, had died during the summer of '66, and his death had afflicted us so much, and especially my husband, that my children all said, "We must go abroad again." My husband at first said, "No;" but after considering it during the winter, we were absent between four and five months, returning in the fall. Our trip on the Continent was short, and the time was spent largely in England, Scotland, and Ireland....I ought to say that we had a charming visit with Sir James Caird[b] at their country place on the Firth of Forth, and in London we visited the family of Mr. Richard Cobden.[24][c]

Meanwhile in the American South, the assimilation of former slaves was a dark cloud hanging over its recovery. Many, even in the North,

---

b James Caird was an agricultural expert in the United Kingdom and member of parliament
c Richard Cobden was a manufacturer, statesman and Union supporter during the Civil War.

had little faith in their prospects for a full life. Jonathan and Mary had been active in the American Colonization Society, an organization focused on the resettlement of former slaves to Liberia since the 1850s, and Jonathan was a founder of the New York American Colonization Society branch in the late 1860s. Before emancipation, the Colonization movement received support from both abolitionist groups, and proponents of slavery. Proponents embraced it because it removed some of the discontented element from the United States and aided in avoiding insurrections coming from the non-enslaved Black population. Supporting abolitionists maintained that colonization freed them from the undeniable prejudice and social chains that would prevent them from living a quality life.

The New York organization emphasized that relocation was voluntary, for the benefit of the African race, and would serve as an invaluable tool for Protestant missionary activities in Africa. Rev. Kellogg, pastor of Grace Church, described this vision well: "Sending one or two missionaries to Armenia, India or Africa was like sending out picket guards who were easily swept away...In sending a colony, you send a consolidated regiment and can never be put back."[25] Although most African-Americans preferred to remain, due to the continuing marginalization of citizenship status for this group, colonization movements continued with some small successes into the twentieth century, not only to Liberia[d] but the Caribbean, Europe, and particularly England.

As all these important issues took more of his time—the plight of African-Americans, city corruption and the devastated Southern economy—he was spending less time at his own business, an enterprise he had now been leading for over thirty years. It was time to call an end to his active involvement in his firm.

---

d Today more than 80% of the Liberian population is of the Christian faith.

Twenty-Two

Retirement—Gen. Grant—Native Indians

Jonathan Sturges calls himself successful and the merchants honor him as such, not because in long life he has built up a colossal fortune, but because he has reached that fortune without a stain upon his character.

—*Sound Doctrine, 1868*

At the end of 1867, Jonathan's income and wealth was in the top tier of New York residents and was included in a newspaper's list of "Heavy Taxpayers" in New York City. Financially secure and ready to turn the page, Jonathan retired from his firm. The reaction from his colleagues was immediate and heartfelt. They invited him to a dinner at Delmonico's restaurant to commemorate his career:

New York, December 30th, 1867

Jonathan Sturges, Esq.,

Dear Sir,

The intelligence which comes to us, that, with the closing hours of this year, it is your intention to retire from the active pursuit of business, makes us feel sensibly the loss which the merchants of New York are about to realize.

Your life among us of nearly half a century, in the same locality in Front Street, we can truly say has been such as commends itself to everyone, both old and young, who regard that which is true, just and noble in mercantile character.

We regret that the relations which have so long existed between us must cease; but we rejoice far more that Jonathan Sturges's name, character and memory will be treasured by the merchants of New York when we all shall have passed away.

In conclusion, may we request that you will name an early day on which it will be your pleasure to meet with your friends at a dinner to be given by us as a slight testimonial of our regard for you as a man and a merchant.

Respectfully, your obedient servants,[1]

The thirty-two signatories to the letter represented an auspicious group of men with whom he had served with on many boards and causes. Jonathan replied:

New York, January 14, 1868

Messrs. John Caswell, Thomas F. Young and Benj. B. Sherman:

Gentlemen—I am in receipt of your communication, requesting me, in behalf of yourselves and "a number of my old friends and fellow merchants," to name a day when I will "join you at a dinner to be given by you to me as a token of respect and esteem, upon my withdrawal from mercantile affair."

I recognize in the list of signers to the invitation the names of those with whom I have had pleasant business and social intercourse for nearly half a century, and it would be mere affectation on my part not to acknowledge the pleasure it will give me to accept such an invitation from the merchants who have done me the honor to send it.

Any day next week will be agreeable to me; or any day the week after, if more agreeable or convenient to those you represent. With warm regards for each of you personally, and for those you represent, I am,

Your obedient servant,
Jonathan Sturges

The dinner took place on January 27, 1868. His longstanding friend and colleague, A.A. Low, presided at the celebration and said of Jonathan:

He seeks at least partial retirement from the activities of a business life, as he certainly remained engaged at a high level… industry, frugality and rectitude have, in the person of our friend, met their just reward, giving him the highest claim to our regard; because our distinguished guest, standing at the head of one of the first commercial houses of this city, guiding and directing its large and extended affairs, has gained a name for probity and honor which, like the aroma from flowers, has gone forth a fragrance and a blessing to all within the sphere of its influence…. in the days of adversity, those who have needed advice have found in our guest a judicious counselor and true friend…he leaves the pursuit of business without an enemy.[2]

Low's speech was frequently interrupted by applause. Jonathan was much affected by the heartfelt demonstration of respect and had to gather himself for his speech. The *Evening Post* covered the dinner and commented:

The response of Mr. Sturges to the first toast and to the address of Mr. Low will long be remembered by those who heard it. It was natural, simple, unaffected, and as interesting in its details as it could be. Mr. Sturges held a paper before him, on which he had minuted what he had to say, but he seemed all the while to be talking as one would talk to his intimate friends, and at times with no little emotion.[3]

The attendees thought the speech and proceedings so profound it was recorded and archived for posterity at the Library of Congress. Jonathan's address made a significant impression on the assembled group, and many toasts were offered to his life and character. Excerpts of Jonathan's speech were printed nationally—from Nevada to South Carolina, Ohio to New Orleans, Pennsylvania to Maine and Illinois to Tennessee—and often reprinted under the title "Lessons from an Old Merchant" (Appendix IV). Multiple magazines highlighted his speech as sage wisdom for success in life. The *Christian Advocate* labeled it "Golden Words from a Merchant," and long after his death, an 1881 "Boys and Girls Treasury" section of *Arthur's Home Magazine*, titled it "Words from a Wise Man." As a prologue to the reprinted speech, *Arthur's* wrote, "[The speech] contains lessons of the highest value to young men, and teaches those old-fashioned doctrines of faithfulness, integrity and patience, which have been the basis of true success in commercial life."[4] *Sound Doctrine* said:

Young men starting in life, in any department of business, may be assured of the truest success if they will take heart of these simple lessons: Do faithfully the work before you; Make the interest of your employers your own; Shun all evil or questionable companions. These rules may be disregarded, and wealth may be accumulated by fraud and chicane[ry]; but its possessor is generally heartily despised, if not cordially hated; and if his ill-gotten gain is not swept away by retributive justice, it becomes a curse to its owner. The rich man is not necessarily the successful man or the happy man. Jonathan Sturges calls himself successful and the merchants honor him as such, not because in long life he has built up a colossal fortune, but because he has reached that fortune without a stain upon his character.[5]

The *Evening Post* wrote later in a "Front Street Reminisces" article that "Jonathan Sturges has long lent the dignity and weight of a very high character to his branch of business. He is a strong pillar in the metropolitan temple of finance."[6] Jonathan had led his firm for almost thirty-two years, and it was reputed to be the oldest grocery house in the United States. He was one of the last of his era—merchants who went through incredible struggles in an unpredictable business environment and earned their wealth through hard work and conservative business principles. These men built up New York City as both the trade and financial capital of the country and established banking as a reliable and honorable avocation. They possessed the vision and capital to build the infrastructure of a young nation, provided the resources for the Industrial Age to occur and created the financial engine that powered a new nation to world business supremacy. However, those principles of business which Jonathan held sacrosanct for so long, were becoming more window dressing than committed practice for many businessmen rising to prominence as Jonathan retired—to seem rather than to be.

With Jonathan's retirement, the firm became Arnold, Sturges & Co. Frederick Sturges retired at the same time. Edward Sturges stayed on as a partner and Benjamin Arnold became the lead partner. Jonathan kept an office at 125 Front Street and the next seven years of his life was characterized by philanthropic activism and ensuring transparent and effective governance at the local and national level, starting with the election of Grant in 1868.

Former Confederate states were finally being accepted back into the Union, which officially kicked-off the Reconstruction era in the South. Tennessee had quickly been reinstated in 1866 but the rest did not become official states again until 1868 (Arkansas, Florida, Alabama, Louisiana, North and South Carolina) and some not until 1870 (Georgia, Virginia, Texas and Mississippi). This precluded the last four states' participation in the 1868 election. For the rest of the country that had been observing the political chaos in Washington, there was an increasing weariness with politicians. Conflict on legislative priorities between President Johnson and Congress had been ongoing almost since he became President after Lincoln's death, culminating with his impeachment by Congress in February 1868. Even the Union League did not defend President

Johnson, and Republicans ejected him from their ranks. Johnson was not convicted by the Senate, but by the time of the 1868 election, the electorate was ready for someone perceived as an apolitical leader.

In 1868, General Ulysses S. Grant was still very popular, the people's hero. In December 1867, Jonathan became part of an influential New York group formed to elect Grant for president. They held an apolitical rally at the Cooper Union to promote Grant's" nomination by acclimation" regardless of party affiliation. Grant was nominated by the Republican Party and ran on a platform that supported full citizenship rights for Blacks. At the time of this election, all states except Florida granted presidential electors according to the popular vote—a significant change on the political landscape. As a result, Grant benefited from the electoral support of some 500,000 of the newly enfranchised Black voters. The Democratic opponent was Copperhead New York Governor Horatio Seymour. Grant won the election by a large margin in electoral votes, although the popular vote was much closer—53% to 47%, about 300,000 votes, with Seymour winning New York.

In December 1868, after Grant's election, there were major "testimonial" donations given by New York businessmen to both President-elect Grant and General Sherman. It had become generally known to New York merchants that General Sherman was moving to Washington, D.C., but could afford only the humblest of quarters. A fund was created for both generals to allow them to live more comfortably. Jonathan gave $500 to General Grant and $1,000 to General Sherman. The total of Grant's donations was $105,000, and Sherman's total was $102,750. A.T. Stewart presented the "subscriptions" to the generals and said: "I assure you that this may be accepted without any feeling of obligation, as it is contributed with the sincere belief that your noble and effective services in behalf of our country in her hour of peril can never be compensated."[7] However, certain newspaper editorials expressed dismay that Grant accepted these personal "donations"and that already there were contributors who had received appointed federal offices from President Grant, which unfortunately characterized his administration—but that list did not include Jonathan Sturges.[a]

As the war ended, Jonathan had gone into the insurance business as a director of the National Life and Travelers Insurance Company, which had just changed its name from the National Life and Limb Insurance Company.[8] Its

---

[a] Federal officials receiving such gifts was not specifically illegal (except bribery) until the 1960s.

mission at its founding in 1863 was to insure soldiers against death and casualty. However, with Jonathan's arrival, the company split into a casualty company and a life insurance company that focused on civilian life insurance. The life insurance entity evolved to become the modern Metropolitan Life Insurance Company.[9] In 1868, Jonathan additionally founded a company called the Amicable Mutual Life Insurance.[10] [b]

Like the banking industry, the insurance business in the 1860s had little regulation. States were filling the void with spotty but growing oversight. In 1851, the first state insurance commissioner was appointed in New Hampshire. New York was next in 1860 and other states began to follow their lead. In the late 1860s, the State of Virginia advocated for the federal government to regulate the insurance industry. However, in a key decision in 1869, the U.S. Supreme Court in *Paul v. Virginia* ruled that insurance was not an act of commerce—thus the regulation of insurance remained at the state level.[c] Having no federal regulating body but a need to standardize insurance regulations, discuss common concerns and best practices, the first national insurance convention was convened (later to become the National Association of Insurance Commissioners) in New York in May 1871.

The New York Chamber of Commerce was asked to present their recommendations for regulation of the industry to this inaugural national gathering. Jonathan Sturges, A.A. Low, and three others were appointed to represent the Chamber and address the most compelling issues. Jonathan and the committee quickly put their focus on addressing the high-risk fire insurance companies that were much more susceptible to becoming insolvent with one major fire. Their primary recommendation asserted that states should not pass regulations that require fire insurance companies to have minimum funds deposited in each state in which they conducted business (which New York and other states were considering). They asserted that it would have the effect of rendering such a company unable to have unfettered access to its funds to pay claims in the case of a widespread fire or other catastrophic loss. They also recommended the creation of an insurance bureau in each state (only fourteen states had them at the time), requiring auditable annual reports and legislation to govern arson and fraud crimes.[11] Jonathan's personal experience with the

---

[b] Other notable founders of this company were W.H. Aspinwall, W.M. "Boss" Tweed, Sr., and William Tweed Jr. (company counsel), James Stuart, George Opdyke and his former partner B.G. Arnold. The Company was sold and merged into Guardian Mutual Life in 1872 and Universal Life in 1873. In 1879 Universal was liquidated.

[c] Although this case was later overturned in 1944, in 1945 Congress legislated regulation back to the states.

calamitous Great Fire of 1835 would have influenced his thoughts on fire risk, and his personal preference for investing only in life insurance companies, rather than fire and casualty. Later that year, in the aftermath of the Great Chicago Fire, one third of the two hundred fire insurance companies operating in Chicago became insolvent, illustrating the urgency of further oversight in this area.

As Jonathan had predicted, Chicago had become a major hub for western commerce. The horse-drawn coaches and mail carts of his early career gave way to railroads like the Illinois Central, which were proliferating across the country. In 1869, the country became connected by the Intercontinental Railroad when the Golden Spike was driven in place in Promontory, Utah, constructing rail lines from Omaha to San Francisco. This rail connection facilitated an even larger movement of settlers to Western territories. These settlers were spreading out everywhere including those areas that had just been deeded to Native Indians as reservations. This made the Army's task to protect Native Indian land rights increasingly difficult.

Not unlike Jonathan's view of the suffering of the African-American population in the wake of the 1863 draft riots, he was similarly appalled by the treatment of Native Americans. By the late 1860s, their removal from the Eastern seaboard was long since completed. However, conflicts continued to flare up in the West between Native Americans, U.S. troops, and settlers encroaching on Native American lands. Much of the Native American population was on reservations and had become virtually wards of the federal government—starving and unable to support themselves. Although a major goal of Indian Affairs administrators was the assimilation of this population, they were afforded few resources to do their job, and their supervision was largely ineffective, and even punitive for their wards.

Jonathan was one of a small group of twenty men who set out to intervene and bring public and government attention to the unjust treatment of Native Americans. It was the concerted opinion of this group that broken treaties, failure to protect reservation rights and an unequal citizenship status versus whites were the main causes of conflict between the government and Native Americans. The organizational meeting in May 1868, was attended by religious leaders and businessmen and presided over by his friend Peter Cooper. The group, which dubbed themselves the United States Indian Commission, attracted former abolitionists and those concerned with humane treatment and spiritual guidance for all of God's children.

They were fighting an uphill battle against prejudice and a lack of national concern for the "barbarians." Not surprisingly, the *Helena Weekly Herald* dismissed the meeting as the work of naïve meddlers, saying: "These Reverend gentlemen who are so prone to dabble in a matter that they know nothing about...Men may theorize until their brains and tongues fail them, but Indians will be Indians, and the only way to reduce them to obedience, prevent bloodshed, great swindles and corruption, is to do away with all Commissions and put the whole business in to the hands of the War Department."[12]

The public's Native Indian perspective mirrored their view of African-Americans—an inferior race that foremost needed to be controlled and disciplined into obedience. Even within the commission that was seeking to ensure humane and fair treatment, they were not unusually enlightened. At a Commission meeting in June 1868, Rev. Howard Crosby, D.D. spoke rather condescendingly of Native Indians, stating: "He did not desire to make the Indian out to be better than he is. He is a barbarian; but that is no reason why he should be cheated and treated cruelly."[13] At the end of 1868, they issued a four-page Memorial to Congress to bring attention to their plight, highlighting broken treaties, land swindles, white settlers encroaching on Indian lands, unwarranted murders and assaults on Indians, non-citizen status denying them justice in court, and shameful misdirection of funds appropriated for Native Indians.

The government approach focused on containing the native populace in a restricted area that required minimal oversight, with the primary mission of protecting white citizens from hostile Native Indian actions. It was estimated that it was costing the federal government between $1,000,000 and $2,000,000 a week to protect the Plains population alone.[14] Due to their ward-of-the-state existence, lack of legal standing and strained government resources, there was no compelling reason for the government to hold up the bargains made.

One example of the work of the committee involved an exploitive situation surrounding the implementation of the 1865 Drum Creek Treaty with the Osage tribe. This agreement outlined a plan to move the tribe from their granted lands in Kansas to land in Oklahoma. Settlers had been encroaching on Osage owned land and the military could not enforce their sovereignty, so they sought to move them to less contested land. The 1868 proposed plan to sell the land in Kansas was referred to as the "Osage Treaty Swindle" or the "Sturges Osage Treaty."[15] It was to be a direct sale to the Leavenworth, Lawrence and Galveston Railroad, headed by William Sturges, son of Solomon Sturges, Jonathan's first cousin. The railroad was to pay nineteen cents per acre for just under eight million acres, one-quarter or less of its market value, with favorable delayed payment terms. New York's *Commercial Advertiser* stated that it was clearly a "pretended treaty, improperly obtained...[Indians] being cheated out of the full value of their lands."[16] Jonathan and the Commission signed a petition in July 1868, urging the U.S. Senate not to approve the treaty before them.[17] Due to the pressure and lobbying by the Commission and the general desire to open the Kansas land for settlement rather than deed the land to the railroad, the Sturges treaty was not approved. The tribe was moved to Oklahoma per the terms of an 1865 treaty, with payment of more than $1 an acre for their Kansas land.

The Commission achieved its goal of bringing to light the poor treatment of the Indian population. From this publicity and the constant attention brought to the situation, a federal commission was grudgingly created by President Grant.[18] On June 7, 1869, this took the form of the presidentially-appointed Board of Indian Commissioners, placed under the purview of the Secretary of the Interior, and tasked with overseeing the management of the Native Indians. One of the appointees, William E. Dodge, was drawn from the U.S. Indian Commission, bringing the Commission's viewpoint to the federal administration of the population.

However, with the creation of the presidential commission, the work of the independent U.S. Indian Commission trailed off in the early 1870s, eventually disbanding as an active organization. In 1871, the Indian Appropriations Act prohibited additional treaties or recognizing further tribes as independent nations. The unfair treatment of the Native Indian population continued for some years, and skirmishes and battles recurred until the 1890s. Native Indians were not granted official United States citizenship until the Indian Citizenship Act of 1924.

The United States had become a world melting-pot. However, a widespread socially-inferior classification had been placed not only on the Native Americans and African-Americans, but also the under-educated of any race and those ethnic groups that were not white Protestant, native English-language speakers. This created an increasingly large, economically disadvantaged, and exploited labor populace, particularly in New York City, whose population was almost one million by 1870. These citizens could not afford to pay for private medical treatment, and about two dozen charitable hospitals emerged to serve this populace. Jonathan became a founding board member of one of them.

James Lennox was from an old merchant family whose father, Robert Lennox (the same man who hosted Jonathan in his church pew upon his arrival in New York), had bought significant parcels of land in Manhattan. In 1868, he sold $3,000,000 of his extensive holdings. Prompted by his African-American servant being refused service at several hospitals, James Lennox sought to establish a hospital that would take patients of all creeds and colors.

To this end, in January 1868, Lennox sent a letter inviting thirty-two Presbyterian gentlemen to discuss moving the initiative forward. The assemblage agreed to support the venture and the Presbyterian Hospital of New York was incorporated the next month.[19] Flush with cash and land, in June, Lennox donated property at Fourth and Madison between 70th and 71st Streets and added $100,000 in cash. Jonathan was one of the founding thirty-two Board of Managers.

They hired famed architect Richard M. Hunt and started work on a three-story building. In 1870, they formed the Society of the Presbyterian Hospital which required $1000 donation from all managers or a yearly $100 membership —raising an additional $180,000. Also, Lennox increased his donations to a total of $500,000. This enabled the hospital to start operations in a state-of-the-art building in October 1872, "for the poor of New York without regard to race, creed or color."[20] Jonathan remained on the Board of Managers for the rest of his life.[d]

Also concerned about the moral development of young clerks, in 1869, Jonathan and his fellow trustees shepherded the establishment of a new class of YMCA.[e] Not just a place to sleep, it was a place for both physical and spiritual wellness, continuing education, and artistic endeavors for young men. It provided a base for young professionals who came to the city to start their careers—a Christian familial support system, away from immoral influences at cheap boarding houses. It included a gym, a great hall with a fifteen-hundred-person capacity a library with twenty thousand volumes, and smaller rooms for instruction in classes such as foreign languages, writing, bookkeeping, and drawing. Designed by architect James Renwick (St. Patrick's Cathedral architect), it featured a French Renaissance edifice and was the first purpose-built YMCA building.

---

d The Presbyterian Hospital eventually merged with other hospitals and it is now known as the New York Presbyterian/Weill-Cornell Medical Center. Thus, a circle was completed between the two hospitals that Jonathan helped found after the former Hospital for the Ruptured and Crippled became affiliated with the Weill-Cornell Medical Center. Fred was a board member and/or President of Presbyterian Hospital for four decades.

e The other trustees of the inaugural YMCA building were Stewart Brown, Frederick Marquand, Robert L. Stuart, James Stokes, Robert Lennox Kennedy, Percy R. Pyne, Charles C. Colgate and W.E. Dodge, Jr.

The new building contained a gymnasium to encourage "physical work" and was the first YMCA to hold evening high school classes.[21] The Great Hall had a magnificent organ installed and it hosted many concerts. Shops were rented out on the basement and first floors to pay the operating expenses, and it included upwards of forty artist studios and an exhibition gallery modeled on the one in the Tenth Street Studio. All studios were rented prior to its opening, due to the artist connections of the YMCA's trustees. Louis Comfort Tiffany was an early tenant, renting his first studio in the building. It was referred to as "the Association building," at Fourth Avenue and East Twenty-Third Street, across from the National Academy of Design.

YMCA Building, c. 1869[22]

TWENTY-THREE

Anti-Income Tax—The Tweed Ring—Committee of Seventy

During all the later years of his life he took a most studious interest in state and national affairs.

—Boston Daily Advertiser, 1874[1]

Charitably motivated and fair-minded, Jonathan believed that government should be responsive and of high integrity and those blessed with means were obligated to help those less fortunate. However, he was also a businessman who promoted minimal intrusiveness and responsible expenditures by the government, and a redistribution of the wealth, to be put in the hands of corrupt politicians, was abhorrent to him.

After he retired, Jonathan served as chairman of the Chamber of Commerce's Foreign Commerce, Commercial and Revenue Laws Committee. With this committee as his pulpit, Jonathan was embroiled in the movement to repeal the national income tax. The income tax had remained a thorn in the side of the wealthy since its inception in 1861. This law was enacted to pay the debts of the war and was set to expire in 1870. It started at a 3% rate and rose as the war progressed. As an example, in 1864, Jonathan paid $1500 on a valuation of $30,000, a rate of 5%.[2] In 1870 the tax was renewed as law, albeit at half of the war rate.

In 1871, Jonathan became a vice president of the Anti-Income Tax Association long with other iconic New York business men such as Astor, Belmont, Dodge, and Brown. This formidable group opposed the continuance of the national income tax, asserting the assessment efforts to collect the tax cost more than what was collected, and furthermore, that the assessing of a tax based on individual income was unconstitutional. Their compelling argument was based on three sections in the Constitution:

(1) Article 1. Section 2, paragraph 3. Representative and direct taxes shall be apportioned among the several States which may be included within this Union according to their respective numbers;

(2) Article 1. Section 9, paragraph 4. No Capitation or other direct tax shall be laid, unless in proportion to the census or enumeration herein before directed to be taken;

(3) Article 8. Section 1. Paragraph 1. All duties, imposts and excises shall be uniform throughout the United States.[3]

Therefore, the Constitution directed that states were to be taxed per the number of people residing in the state and uniform throughout the country. Given these guidelines, and the fact that the income of states was not apportioned by population and was not uniform between the states, it was infeasible to apply an income tax per the law; therefore the income tax was unconstitutional. Jonathan's anti-tax group urged citizens to pay the tax but provided a form to enclose with payment to protest the tax and reserve the right to appeal payment in court.[4]

The Anti-Tax Association and Jonathan were correct about the constitutionality of the income tax. The tax was repealed in 1872, except for a brief stint in 1894, when a flat tax was levied but declared unconstitutional by the Supreme Court the next year. It did not reappear until the Sixteenth Amendment to the Constitution was ratified in 1913 and reads: "The Congress shall have power to lay and collect taxes on incomes, from whatever source derived, without apportionment among the several States, and without regard to any census or enumeration." Forty-two states ratified the amendment by 1912. The legislatures in Connecticut, Rhode Island, Utah and Virginia, all rejected the Amendment, and Florida and Pennsylvania never put the Amendment up for a vote.

Jonathan and his associates were successful in repealing the tax; however, in their own wheelhouse, reckless, ill-considered domestic business pursuits and a lack of recognition of developing international financial difficulties brought on the financial Panic of 1873. The main contributing factors were considered to be the failure of the major Philadelphia banking house Jay Cooke and Co. (whose overcommitment to the struggling Northern Pacific Railway bankrupted the firm), overproduction in a declining trade market, and a developing depression in Europe originating in Vienna (causing loans to American businesses to be called in)—all a classic recipe for an economic crash. A currency bill to increase the circulation of unbacked currency (Greenbacks) by $40,000,000 to strengthen the credit markets was passed by Congress in response to the crisis.

Run on 4th National Bank, 1873[5]

However, as Jonathan viewed the bill, it was an action that would effectively decrease the value of the currency that was already in circulation and create objectionable inflationary conditions for business. He and about twenty-five hundred businessmen signed a petition to President Grant urging him to veto the bill. Jonathan Sturges, James Brown, Cyrus Field and four other selected members of the New York Chamber of Commerce went to the White House and presented the petition to the President. This direct appeal was successful, and Grant vetoed the "Inflation Bill" on April 22, 1874. Although it helped these businessmen in the short term to avoid inflationary conditions, it was highly unpopular with Western commercial interests that were starving for capital funds. As a result of the bill's repeal, the West's anger over its rejection and the dozens of seats in the House newly allotted to growing Western states, the Democrats crushed Republicans in the mid-term elections, taking control of the House, and the general economic downturn lasted until about 1879.

Jonathan was also in the forefront of establishing an infamous U.S. Post Office building during this time in New York City. Congress passed a resolution to fund a post office, and the mayor, postmaster, and Chamber of Commerce were to select and purchase a site in New York.[6] Jonathan, as Acting President of the New York Chamber of Commerce, endorsed a site chosen in City Hall Park on the triangular south end near City Hall, the Customs House and other public buildings.[7] Designed by architect Alfred E. Mullet, it was built between 1869 and 1880, was $5,000,000 over budget and its design obsolete by the time it was finished. The resulting structure deemed "Mullet's Monstrosity", was an architectural eyesore on the New York land-scape, with an internal design deemed not adequate for the purpose for which it was built. The architect took his own life in 1890 and it was finally demolished in 1939.

The construction of this building was started during Boss William Tweed's reign and at the same time as the infamous Tweed Courthouse. This experi-ence with the Tweed machine probably became an up-close-and-personal exposure for Jonathan to the atrocious government corruption in the city. Jonathan and his civically-minded colleagues had clearly had enough.

New York City Post Office at City Hall Park, c. 1887 [8]

In the 1860s, the United States business community had taken a dubious and irreversible turn to means and methods designed to make a quick profit, increasingly more speculative and opportunistic. In tandem with the growing audacity in business dealings, there materialized in city government a faction that systematically hijacked control of city contracts, unmatched in its time for its reach and abuse of taxpayers' trust. Jonathan and sixty-nine other impas-sioned colleagues united to form a historic organization of which Jonathan took a leading role. It was originally dubbed the Citizen's Reform Association, founded in 1864 in answer to the increasing corruption in city government. Jonathan Sturges and Peter Cooper were elected vice presidents of the 18th

Ward. Jonathan could have written its creed, which read in part, "we as citizens of New York, deeply deplore the evils under which we have for many years suffered, our public resources having been squandered, justice corrupted, and life and property made insecure; and these evils have reached a crisis which demands the intervention of all honest men, as our city government is yearly growing worse and worse...'Rings' of corrupt politicians combine for the avowed purpose of public plunder."[9]

In March 1864, Jonathan, A.T. Stewart, Peter Cooper, and other select members of the committee urged a bill that would empower the mayor or any high taxpayer (over $500 a year) to prosecute complaints against city officials and to appoint a commission to investigate complaints.[10] However, it was akin to using a fly-swatter to combat a hornet's nest. The malfeasance had become systemic and its tentacles controlled the flow of city money at every turn. Those in its circle of influence either got on board with Tammany or were pushed out of the way.

At the lead of the corruption ring was William "Boss" Tweed. He got his start in a volunteer fire department that he organized, Americus No. 6, or the "Big Six." It became ground zero for gang violence between fire stations vying for the right to fight the fire, sometimes while buildings burned. He developed a reputation as an intimidating axe wielder and formidable firehouse leader and eventually became an alderman. Tweed was elected to an unremarkable two-year term in Congress in 1852. However, he was more interested in city politics and did not run for a second term. Tweed returned to run the Seventh Ward for Tammany Hall and was elected to the city's Board of Supervisors in 1858, where his infamous kickback system began.

By 1860, Tweed was Deputy Streets Commissioner, controlled Democratic nominations for city offices and was forcing city contracts through his so-called law office. He bought the city's preferred printing company, giving him first exposure to all city documents and contracts. Tweed ensured that his allies were elected to the comptroller and district attorney positions, among others, and his corruption and kickbacks scheme became entrenched. Contracts with the city soon required at least a 15% "Tweed overhead" added to the bid. The classic project was the New York County Courthouse that began construction in 1861, budgeted to cost well under one million dollars. However, with the Tweed overhead, it cost upwards of $13,000,000.

Tweed became chairman of the Democratic General Committee and Grand Sachem of Tammany Hall in 1863, with full control over the politics and purse strings of New York. The brazen corruption was abhorrent to Jonathan. In November 1864, Jonathan chaired the organization's meeting to review their first nine months of operations. They had been vocal in their disdain for the rampant misdirection of public funds and distributed two million publications to highlight the fraudulent and wasteful expenditures by the city, mismanagement of operations, neglect of the public health, and high tax increases.[11]

By mid-1865, the Citizens Reform Association was spending hundreds of thousands of dollars to promote candidates who would champion transparency in government. The newspapers largely ignored their efforts due to Tweed's control over many of them. However, at least one editorial in the *New York Times* in June 1865 spoke of this rising voice: "Let it suffice that there is established a moral power among us, embodied in combined capital and intellect, comprising as its constituent parts our ablest and purest men, intelligent, earnest and financially equal to whatever work of reform they undertake or endorse."[12]

The reform movement backed John Hecker as an independent candidate for mayor in 1865, and Jonathan worked on the committee to promote his election. The *New York Times,* backing the Tweed candidate, characterized Jonathan and the reform movement as having "utter weakness and fatuity" for supporting Hecker.[13] In response, the *New York Tribune* accused the *Times* journalist of being in Tweed's pocket. The reform movement's backing of Hecker had no effect and Tweed's candidate, John T. Hoffman, was voted in by a wide margin.

Although its major focus was to ensure a transparent and responsive city government, in its first years the Reform Association additionally created and financially supported the Council of Hygiene and Public Health, who performed a full survey of tenement living in the city. This council produced a report in 1865, exposing deplorable living conditions in dense housing areas, and proved to be a "landmark in the history of public health for its systematic approach towards studying the urban environment, and its motivating principle that a city's moral and economic prosperity was intimately tied to its resident's physical well-being."[14] This established the importance of monitoring hygienic conditions and led to the founding of the New York Metropolitan Board of Health in February 1866, the first modern municipal health authority.

The Citizens Reform Association of New York officially evolved in 1871 to the more formal Executive Committee of Citizens and Taxpayers for the

Financial Reform of the City and County of New York. Jonathan was appointed to a committee of five members to permanently organize the association.[15] He was characteristically appointed to the finance committee. This was the beginning of the end for Tweed, and his hold on the city started to unravel. The anti-corruption, transparency-in-government movement was reinvigorated as described by the *Daily Graphic:*

> At a mass meeting of the citizens of New York on the 4th of September 1871, a committee of seventy gentlemen were appointed…to remove the cause of the present abuses, and to assist, sustain, and direct a united effort by the citizens of New York, without reference to party, to obtain a good government and honest officers to administer it.[16]

The group was famously known as the Committee of Seventy, which takes its name from the Bible, referring to the seventy elders who were appointed to assist and advise Moses on governing the people. Members of the ring saw the reformers closing in, as the extent of the corruption was exposed, and popular support of their operations waned. Some of the members of the ring began testifying to the details of the operations for clemency or fled the country to escape prosecution. The account books of the Tweed ring were found, and William Tweed finally met justice for his crimes, which included jail time and a fine. He was sued for many millions of dollars that had been taken from the taxpayers, and he went to jail for his actions but escaped to Spain. He was found, returned to jail, and died there in 1878.

With the Tweed Ring busted, the organization turned to electing upright and reform-minded candidates to municipal office and accomplishing the removal of remaining corrupt officials. Regrettably, some of the reformers sought to gain personally from their involvement. Samuel Tilden was one of the more famous Committee of Seventy members. Tilden built a political career on his actions with the Committee, becoming Governor of New York in 1871 and a presidential candidate in 1876. In addition to Tilden's leap to higher office, many of the original Committee of Seventy began, one by one, to take government jobs, including William Havemeyer, who became mayor (again) in 1874 and John Dix, who became governor. No less than twenty-two of the members had state, county, or city jobs by May 1873, and another six more had partners or family appointed to city positions. This developing cronyism and self-interest were appalling to Jonathan Sturges.

On June 4, 1873, the Committee gathered to discuss whether it had outlived its purpose and had in effect compromised its integrity through the personal gain realized by its members. The situation was deliberated by a sub-committee who voted to table the question until September. Jonathan stridently asserted that they had compromised themselves and he submitted his resignation letter on that day as reported by the *New York Times:*

> We publish this morning a letter from Mr. Jonathan Sturges, in which he withdraws from the Committee [of Seventy] and gives his late colleagues some very sensible advice. When a gentleman of the high character and social standing of Mr. Sturges puts on record his opinion that he "can be of more service to the Reform movement out of the committee than in it," it is exceedingly probable that the process of resignation will not stop here. The fact is, for all practical purposes the Committee of Seventy is dead already...[17]

No.40 East Thirty-Sixth Street

June 4, 1873

James M. Brown, Esq. Chairman of the Committee of Seventy:

> Dear Sir: Recognizing fully the importance of a proper committee to perform the duty originally assigned to the Committee of Seventy, it would give me great pleasure to continue to act with the committee did I feel that its present organization was such as to promise the desired results. In my judgment, the committee needs immediate and careful reorganization to be of much service to the reform movement.
>
> I voted, last evening, for a committee charged with this duty. By a very strong vote a subsequent resolution was passed, postponing the report of this committee until September. Under these circumstances, I believe I can be of more service to the reform movement out of the committee than in it. I therefore beg leave to resign my position as a member of the Committee of Seventy.

Very Truly Yours,

Jonathan Sturges[18]

Despite Mayor Havemeyer's pleas for them to remain on the job, the Committee had its last meeting in October and the group was dissolved. The vote had been taken at a previous meeting, with a 15-14 vote for dissolution—there was to be no appeal.[19]

Twenty-four

Life in the 1870s—Art and The Met— Bryant 80th Birthday

It has sometimes been questioned whether a lover of fine arts elevates a people, because art has flourished in the most corrupt ages. I think it would be more natural to ask what the people of those times would have been without the softening influence of art.

—*Jonathan Sturges*

Henry Cady Sturges, c. 1860s[1]

Unlike Arthur, Henry rarely mentioned his studies in his diary, although he followed in Arthur's footsteps and became a member of the Philolexian Society at Columbia College, where he cultivated many friendships. His congenial nature was recognized as the recipient of the Columbia College Goodwood Cup, awarded to the "best fellow" or the most "uniformly amiable" member of the junior class.[2] Of black walnut and handsomely chased with silver, the

Cup was given to him at an evening celebration. It was inscribed "Presented to Henry C. Sturges, June 12, 1868," on one side, and on the other, "Class of 1869, Goodwood Cup, Columbia College.[3] Henry was the Chairman of Arrangements for his 1869 class's graduation, where he received a Bachelor of Arts. Jonathan had an honored position on the speaker's platform with Secretary of State Hamilton Fish, whose son was also graduating.

The Sturges family moved north one more time. In 1869, Jonathan and Mary decided to move from 14th Street to uptown Manhattan, where affluent neighborhoods were developing. An auction map from the 1860s depicts the lots he purchased on 36th Street and 4th (Park Ave) in the Murray Hill neighborhood. Construction plans were submitted in August 1869 for two adjoining townhouses, one for Jonathan and Mary and one for their son Frederick and his family. Gambrill and Richardson were the architects for the townhouses, and the Sturges families moved in after completion in November 1870. A Henry Hobson Richardson historian noted:

> Among Gambrill and Richardson's limited work in New York City were two adjoining townhouses on Park Avenue, built for father and son Jonathan and Frederick Sturges in 1869-70. These brick and brownstone mansions displayed a highly restrained classical design with contrasting quoins, a single entrance bay and a mansard roof with pedimented dormers.[4]

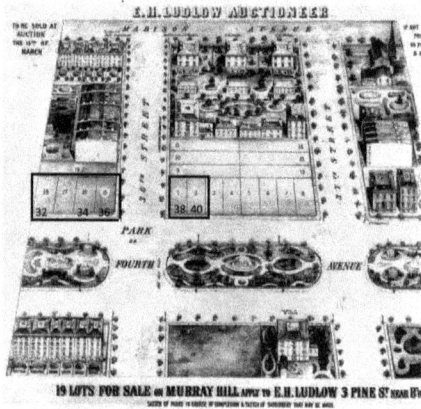

Murray Hill Auction Map 36th, 37th and Park Streets[5]

Both townhouses were built at a cost of $60,000 in 1869.[6] Jonathan and Mary's townhouse was at 40 E. 36th Street, on the southwest corner of the block, a 28 ft. by 108 ft. lot. William and Virginia Osborn built a house at 32 Park Avenue, just a few houses down. A photograph of the Sturges parlor shows some of the famous paintings on the walls that Jonathan collected. *Flower Girl*, on the back right corner of the photograph below (subject thought to be Mary Perkins of New Orleans) was painted by Charles Ingham in 1846, a man he worked with in various art associations. *Sunrise on the Cordilleras*, by Frederic Church, is on the wall left of the mirror and fireplace.

Sturges Parlor[7]

As an art patron and a philanthropic stalwart, Jonathan had few equals. An interviewer arrived at Jonathan's house one day in the 1870s, only to find eight to ten men waiting outside ready to present their pleas for his charitable support:

> [The writer] met Mr. Sturges in his library one morning, by previous appointment, when the clock was upon the stroke of nine. "I don't know, Mr. Sturges," observed the visitor, "whether you intended me to be literally so prompt; but having learned something of your habits, I concluded you might be busy with something else after this time." He smiled pleasantly and observed: "You are almost the only person outside my own family to whom it has occurred that I was not a man of entire leisure. I don't think I was ever more busy in my life, and you did right to come at the time named as nearly as possible."[8]

One of those commitments was his service on a national advisory committee[a] to select those American paintings to exhibit at the 1867 Paris World's Fair.[9] Due to limited display space, the United States could submit only a few.

[a] Others on the committee were J. Taylor Johnston, M.O. Roberts, Robert L. Stuart, W.T. Blodgett, H.T. Tuckerman, Wm. P. Wright, A. M. Cozzens, Sheppard Gandy, R.M. Olyphant, M. Koedler, C.L. Tiffany, S.P. Avery, J. Harrison, Jr., and George Whitney.

paintings of modest size and the selection process was controversial. Most of these men were from New York and members or associates of The Century Association and National Academy of Design. These men favored the landscape artists of the Hudson River School and paintings done since 1855. Jonathan's painting *In the Woods* by Asher B. Durand was one of those exhibited in Paris.

The reviews of the American art exhibition were mainly critical. An American art critic, James Jackson Jarves, collector of early Italian paintings, said that the American paintings were "emotionless and soulless." Critics also noted the absence of typical American scenes, such as a Western prairie, pioneers, or New England home life.[10] Many established artists paid little attention to the critics, but some took heed and sought training in Europe, many at the Ecole des Beaux-Arts in Paris, with European masters and/or establishing studios there.[11]

One of the art promotion endeavors that had not yet come to fruition for Jonathan was his vision of a public art gallery. The success of the Sanitary Fair's art exhibit and sale further made the case for the need of a quality public art museum, and before the decade ended, the vision was resurrected.

In November 1869, John Jay, a lawyer, collector, and president of the Union League, called a meeting at the clubhouse to rally civic leaders, businessmen, artists, art collectors, and philanthropists to establish a city art gallery.[12] Jay cited New York's prominence in the world and the inexcusable absence of an art museum in the mold of the Louvre in Paris and the National Gallery in London. Opportunities to advance New York as a world cultural center, and to further the cause of art appreciation for the residents of the city, were being missed every time a wealthy art collector passed on and sold or donated their treasures elsewhere. Jonathan was appointed to the provisional committee organizing the endeavor.

The Century Association served as the hub for organizing the proposed Metropolitan Museum of Art. John Taylor Johnston, one of Jonathan's fellow Paris Exhibition art committee members, hosted a gathering in his New York home for the Board of Trustees in December 1870, to view his gallery and meet the officers. Johnston, Jonathan Sturges, William Cullen Bryant, Richard M. Hunt, Samuel F.B. Morse, Frederic Church, John Kensett, Samuel J. Tilden, Theodore Roosevelt, Sr., Alexander Van Rensselaer, and about 100 other trustees pledged to raise $250,000 to begin operation of the museum. At this meeting, they seeded the organization $45,000, and never looked back.[13] The "Met" was on its way.

William Cullen Bryant, Jr. credited members of the Sketch Club and Century Club as the driving force, singling out Jonathan, Johnston and his father (W.C. Bryant, Sr.) as being those individuals to whom the Met owes the largest debt of gratitude for its origin.[14] Other than early encouragement and monetary support, Jonathan's advanced age probably prevented him from getting more involved in the operations of the Metropolitan Museum of Art. However, he had to be very gratified to see this public museum coming together—a dream he envisioned when he and a small group bought and preserved the collection of Luman Reed, creating the earliest of public art museums in the city.

However, Jonathan maintained stewardship of the Reed legacy in his role as the long-time Chairman of the Committee on Fine Arts of the New York Historical Society.[15] His extensive art collection, art patronage, many dear friendships with noted artists of the time and his work in managing several art associations, formed a major legacy of his life. Jonathan later poignantly reminisced about the impact of art on a people's culture, saying, "It has sometimes been questioned whether a lover of fine arts elevates a people, because art has flourished in the most corrupt ages. I think it would be more natural to ask what the people of those times would have been without the softening influence of art."[16]

His passion for the arts in New York was exceeded only by his ardent devotion to his family. Over their life, he and Mary had lost two children but had gained two sons-in-law, two daughters-in-law, and many grandchildren. Mary's mother, Elizabeth Cady, died in Plainfield, Connecticut, in April 1868, and their nephew, Lothrop's son, Charles Sturges at the young age of 42, the same year.[17]

Frederick and Virginia lived next door to Jonathan and Mary on Park Avenue in New York with their families. Fred maintained a summer home in Fairfield, called the "White House," just a few hundred yards away from the Cottage. This closeness enabled many opportunities for Jonathan and Mary to spend time with their grandchildren. The following photograph taken in the early 1870s, captured Jonathan with Virginia and Fred's children, likely at the Cottage in Fairfield.

Jonathan Sturges and Grandchildren, c. 1872[18] [b]

The Sturgeses lost their nephew and niece, Hamilton and Martha Murray, on their way to a European tour for the winter. In late November 1873, their ship the *SS Ville du Havre* collided with the *Loch Earn* in the middle of the night on its way from New York to the continent. In this tragic accident, all but eighty-seven of the three hundred souls on board lost their lives. Jonathan's brother Lothrop also passed on in December 1873. Only his younger sister Abigail and older sister Deborah remained of his brothers and sisters. His former son-in-law, J.P. Morgan, and his wife Fanny were blessed with the birth of J. Pierpont Morgan, Jr. in September 1867. Virginia Osborn wrote Pierpont congratulating him on the birth of his son and looked forward to his big sister Louisa (born one year earlier) coming to see her "Auntie" Virginia soon.[19] In 1872, Frederick, his wife, and their son Jonathan (Jontie) traveled in Europe with Pierpont, Fanny and their family. Fanny wrote to Mary Sturges from Cologne, telling her of her daughter Juliet's fascination with Jontie and shared her thoughts on building their own country home at Highland Falls. She looked forward to the day when their children might enjoy it as much as Virginia's children enjoyed their home at Wing-and-Wing across the Hudson River and closed with: The Children...send much love to

---

[b] Standing (L-R): 1-Frederick Osborn; 2-Virginia Osborn; 3-Jonathan Sturges, Sitting (L-R) 4-Emily Main Sturges; 5-Jonathan Sturges; 6-William Church Osborn; 7-Arthur Pemberton Sturges; 8-Henry Fairfield Osborn; 9- Mary Fuller Sturges.

their Grandpa and Grandma Sturges. Mary, my sister, sends her love with mine, of which there is always a large supply for each and all of your family, whose kindness and affection for Pierpont and me, make one of the brightest places in our lives."[20] The Osborn and Morgan families remained close and, humorously, while at their respective country homes on the Hudson, their children flew homing pigeons across the river to exchange messages with each other.[21]

Osborn Wing-and-Wing, Garrison, New York, c. 2013[22] and Virginia Sturges Osborn[23]

Jonathan continued to cross paths with Morgan on many civic, business and philanthropic committees and boards, as when he served with Morgan to manage preparations for the visit of Russian royalty in May 1871. *The Monied Metropolis* highlighted the mixing of the business generations in a high society event of the day: "When preparations were made for the Grand Duke Alexis of Russia, such old-timers as Jonathan Sturges and John Jacob Astor served along with railroad entrepreneur William H. Vanderbilt, banker August Belmont... and financier J. Pierpont Morgan on the reception committee."[24]

Most of Jonathan's contemporaries were retiring and one by one disappearing from the scene. Each birthday was a reason for celebration. In 1874, William Cullen Bryant, his dear friend since the 1830s, celebrated his eightieth birthday and his many friends decided to present him a testimonial of best wishes. It was signed by thousands of his friends and acquaintances. Jonathan headed the testimonial committee that gathered together at noon on November 3, at The Century Association. At one o'clock the group walked to Mr. Bryant's house on Sixteenth Street and Jonathan presented the testimonial to him:

We have come, dear Bryant, to congratulate you upon reaching the ripe age of eighty years in such vigor of health and intellect; to thank you for all the good work that you have done for your country and for mankind and to give you our best wishes for your happiness…We thank you for ourselves, for our children, for our country, and for our race, and we commend you to the providence and grace of Him who has always been with you, and who will be with you to the end. We present to you this address of congratulation, with signatures from all parts of the country, and with the proposal of a work of commemorative art[c] that shall be sculptured with ideas and images from your poems and be full of the grateful remembrances and affections of the friends who love you as a friend, and the nation that honors you as the patriarch of our literature.[25]

Bryant accepted the Memorial with a short speech of his own, closing with: "Gentlemen, again I thank you for your kindness. I have little to be proud of, but when I look around upon those whom this occasion has brought together, I confess that I am proud of my friends."[26] An amusing anecdote describes an exchange between Jonathan and New York governor-elect and future presidential candidate, Samuel Tilden at this event. Tilden gave a picture of himself to Bryant, the honored guest. Seeing this exchange, Jonathan couldn't resist a bit of levity:

> "You might as well give me one," said Mr. Sturges, "I should like to have it." "I will," answered Mr. Tilden; "and if I find I have no time to attend to it at once, I'll send it to you from Albany." "Ah!" said Sturges, jocularly, "better send it to me before you go. After you get there you might do something I should not like, then I would not value the portrait as highly." "If this should even turn out," said Tilden, "I give you leave to forward the picture to me again, so that if I see it come even without note or comment, I shall know the meaning of it." "Very well," Sturges answered, "then we'll agree upon these terms." "And I shall keep my word to him," he afterward added to this writer, [I'll be] "returning the photograph if, in his capacity of Governor, he does anything that seems to me really wrong."[27]

A Greek vase by Tiffany & Company was commissioned at the time of his birthday for later presentation, which Jonathan did not live to see.

---

[c] The vase is in the collection of the Metropolitan Museum of Art and is inscribed "Truth crushed to earth shall rise again."-from Bryant's poem *The Battlefield*.

TWENTY-FIVE

Virginia Sturges Osborn's
Bellevue Nurse Training School

Wishing your association God-speed with all my heart and soul.

—*Florence Nightingale*

Jonathan was a leading advocate for providing medical treatment for those who could not afford it and had been among the founders of three hospitals in New York. His daughter picked up the torch in 1871. Virginia Sturges Osborn and another impressive woman, Louisa Schuyler, were the principle founders of the first Florence Nightingale inspired nurse training school in the United States. Schuyler was a refined young lady of blue bloodlines, descended from both Alexander Hamilton and General Phillip Schuyler. Encouraged by her family doctor, Louisa took an interest in the efficient medical care of the poor, elderly, crippled, and infirmed in the poorhouses and sick asylums of the city. Virginia, raised in a Christian household with a tradition of active benevolence, embraced the cause, and their joint efforts produced a historic advancement in the treatment of patients and for a professional nursing corps in the country.

After the American Civil War broke out, Schuyler answered the call for nurses from America's first female doctor, Emily Blackwell. Blackwell had studied Florence Nightingale's approach to nursing and was eager to extend her work to the United States. Despite being devoid of any nursing experience, Schuyler was appointed president of the Women's Central Association Relief (WCAR), an agency that recruited and trained nurses for the war effort. The WCAR was soon working in tandem with Jonathan's Sanitary Commission and they were a key part of the success of their operations.

Schuyler traveled to Europe after the war to recover from her strenuous nursing efforts. Urged by her family doctor, upon her return she visited a local poorhouse hospital where she observed there was no resident physician. Sixty children were being cared for by one woman—the only assistant was her own illegitimate child, a patient in the ward! She also observed there was no resident physician. To compare conditions between the poorhouse and an established hospital, Schuyler visited and observed operations at Bellevue Hospital. Similar standards prevailed at Bellevue, with former inmates and poorhouse residents providing patient care.[1]

Determined to improve conditions, Louisa Schuyler adopted the cause. She had wartime experience in organizing nurses but was not skilled in the critical area of fundraising and rallying others to the cause. The first woman she contacted for help was Virginia Sturges Osborn in January 1871. Virginia embraced the cause and recruited some of her lifelong friends to help, including Elizabeth Hobson. Virginia casually asked Elizabeth to accompany her to a gathering to discuss a charitable endeavor she might have interest in. Hobson reminisced about this first meeting in her memoir *Reminiscences of a Happy Life:*

> I entered the room a perfect stranger. Mrs. Osborn introduced me, and Miss Schuyler invited me to take a seat by her side. She stated the object of the meeting. Then, suddenly turning to me, she handed me a pencil and a piece of paper and asked me to "take the minutes." I had never attended a meeting of any kind in my life and knew no more about taking minutes than a baby!—thus commenced my education in philanthropy and…I found to my surprise and dismay that I was appointed Chairman of the Subcommittee to visit the Surgical Wards for Women.[2]

Elizabeth Hobson recalled her friend, Virginia Sturges Osborn:

> How can I describe her? She always seemed to me made of different clay from the rest of us. We had sat side by side at Mr. Tappan's School, and the very first association I had with her is hearing her recite Hood's "Song of the Shirt." Now that I recall the poem which so impressed me then, I feel that it may have been one of the memorable moments of her life, leading her heart in sympathy toward human sorrow which during her long life, it was her chief joy to alleviate. The child of wealthy parents and the wife of a man of importance and large fortune, Virginia Osborn cared for money only as a means of doing good, never spending it on herself but recognizing not only the wants of the poor but the tastes of the rich and taking pleasure in satisfying both. We were intimate and devoted friends until her death,

and I have often thought that there must be more good in me than I suspect because Virginia Osborn loved me.[3]

None of these women were prepared for what they saw but they were aided in the beginning by a physician sympathetic to their cause, Dr. Wylie, and Gen. Bowen, the Chairman of the Commissioners of the State Charities Aid Society. Wylie could not officially point out the great deficiencies in the nursing care of patients, as this would jeopardize his job, but he quietly guided them where to look. What they witnessed was appalling.

Relating in her memoir what she observed, Hobson noted that nurses were nothing more than the cheapest housekeepers they could find. Attendants did laundry in a pot of hot water but with no soap, when they could get to it, and served meals by dumping food on a table where patients could retrieve it. Those patients who were physically able brought food to the invalids. The one bathtub was used only as a bed for the attendant. Rats scampered through wards at night, and with only a night watchman assigned to work, patients would often die during the night, only discovered when ward attendants came in to work in the morning. There were no antiseptics in use, and attendants would go from one patient to another, giving prescribed doses of medicine and dressing wounds, without washing hands. This was the scene that Virginia Osborn and her associates met in that winter of 1871-1872.

Florence Nightingale had founded a successful and thriving training school in London in 1860. However, into the 1870s, training programs for nurses in America were rare. The Women's Hospital in Philadelphia had started a school in 1863 and then Boston's New England Hospital for Women in 1872. Neither of these pioneering schools in America had embraced the unique Nightingale approach to patient care. The organized on-the-job instruction provided for nuns at Catholic hospitals was the closest thing to a training program existing locally for nursing.

Elizabeth Hobson's illustrative exposé was given to the wider committee and unlike previous visiting committee reports, which only emphasized the positive things being done, it revealed widespread abhorrent conditions. Virginia, Schuyler and the other committee members endorsed Hobson's scathing report and took it to the State Commissioners of Charities and Corrections, who embraced their work to challenge the standards of the hospital. After three months of visitation and support, the women were convinced that they could make the most difference by establishing a professional nursing corps through a training school for nurses. In 1872, the State Charities Aid Association empowered the organizers to put together a plan for this new school and they appointed Virginia Osborn to chair the effort.

A defensive posture by hospital staff and doctors immediately surfaced. They maintained that Virginia Osborn and her committee were "ignorant women interfering with what was none of their business," and that they just needed nurses "that would do as they were told."[4] However, they persevered and documented their observations, with Virginia Osborn adding these notes:

> February 5th, 12th, and 19th, 1872: The number of patients, about eighteen to a ward. All Irish Roman Catholics, most of them of the most common class. We took books and papers to them all. The nurse, whose wages are sixteen dollars a month, seems kind, willing, and obliging, [and] having been six years in the City Hospital has the advantage of experience…The dinner is, one day corned beef and cabbage, another day soup, a third meat and potatoes and so on. The supper at six, which both nurse and patients pronounced nauseous, and bread with a little butter. We were greatly impressed by the deficiency of night nurses. The one who attends Ward 19 had charge of five wards from nine P.M. to seven A.M., two of the wards being on one floor, three on another…the doctor informed us that whenever he had a very sick patient he was obliged to force a convalescent to act as nurse… close proximity of small pox and fever patients to the lying-in wards… at present the feeding is spasmodic and cannot be relied on…took Mr. Whitely, the Boston Range Manufacturer, to see the kitchen. In answer to his inquiries as to where the utensils of the kitchen were washed, he was told, "On the floor. They are all put together in a heap and the water poured over them near the drain"… (workers) from Blackwell's Island find it a privilege to come to Bellevue, where they get such comfortable quarters and very little to do…clerks and lodgers staying in the wards of the hospital… one hundred women taken from the most degraded classes are employed at Bellevue…100 men hanging about Bellevue receiving no wages but no positive work assigned to them…found Annie Shay (patient) crying for opium…the night nurse, who had been employed to watch her after the operation, had given her large doses at her own discretion to keep her quiet and then had helped herself to Annie's brandy for her own gratification.[5]

The committee reported their findings to the executive committee and State Charities Aid Association. Concerned by these reports and desiring to effect improvements, the Charities Aid Association endorsed the training school as a solution. Persuaded by the prospect of improving conditions for their patients, the Bellevue Medical Board approved the initiative to begin operations in May 1873. They found a few experienced nurses of adequate experience to serve as supervisors but were struggling to find a qualified superintendent for the school. After an earnest search, Sister Helen of the All Saints Sisterhood (Protestant), late of the University College Hospital of London and on a leave of absence from her post in Baltimore, volunteered her services.

In 1872, they sought and received official guidance from Florence Nightingale. She provided an outline of her recommendations of how to organize a nurse training program as she had provided for certain other hospitals in Europe. It included a letter of instruction to Dr. Wylie (the doctor who gave early support), "wishing your association God-speed with all my heart and soul." She stressed that nurses are there to "carry out the orders of the medical and surgical staff, including the whole practice of cleanliness, fresh air, diet, etc."[6]

On May 1, 1873, the school opened and took charge of three wards at Bellevue Hospital. They put into practice the Nightingale principles that emphasized cleanliness and attentiveness to the patient. They also instituted a uniform, but the early designs intimidated the patients. One pupil, Miss Euphemia Van Rensselaer, from the blue-blood family of the same name, committed herself to nursing after the death of her father, Brigadier General Henry Van Rensselear, from typhoid during the Civil War. She designed a uniform that became a classic, "blue and white seersucker dress, white apron, collar and cuffs, and a very becoming cap."[7] This uniform was adopted and became a familiar sight as the nursing corps expanded to other hospitals. Miss Van Rensselaer later replaced Sister Helen as superintendent, becoming Sister Delores, dedicating her life to nursing and the Sisters of Charity.

The training school operations gradually spread to other wards. However, when school management proposed to extend their nurse trainees to the maternity ward, another group of obstinate doctors surfaced. Virginia, Mrs. Griffin and Elizabeth Hobson met with the obstetrical staff to discuss the proposed expansion but again were met with angry accusations of meddling and interference. It was such a hostile response that Mrs. Griffin abruptly stood up and stated, "Gentlemen, we will not prolong this interview; you will hear from us in a few days."[8] Virginia and her committee returned to the State Charities Aid Association, which sent three commissioners to meet with the hospital medical board. They cleared the way for establishing a professional nursing presence in the maternity wards and a nurse by the name of Mrs. Richards was charged with their supervision. She would later start a nursing school in Japan.

Nursing staff soon uncovered the possible cause of the resistance to the professional nurse's presence in the maternity wards. In a startling find, 40% of women delivering babies in the maternity ward were dying of ill health after delivery. After some independent research by Schuyler, it was determined that doctors moved from general surgery to the maternity ward to perform deliveries with the same instruments used in previous surgeries. This practice spread bacteria to the new mother's birth canal and infected the genital areas, which became fatal for many mothers. After this discovery, the maternity ward moved to another building.[9]

The Bellevue Training School for Nurses became independent of the State Aid Society with their own charter in 1874 and nursing diplomas were awarded to the first six graduates in 1875.[10] The first official building for the school, that included both classroom space and student rooms, opened in 1878 at 426 E. 26th Street.

In 1877, Virginia's brother Frederick was a manager and trustee of the Presbyterian Hospital, of which their father was a founding board member. They sent a request to Bellevue Hospital to provide trained nurses for their staff. Other hospitals followed, and some even started their own training schools. Frederick Sturges followed his sister's lead and established the Presbyterian Hospital School of Nursing, where he was at the lead from its founding in 1896 until 1912 and is credited with its success. Virginia remained involved with the Bellevue school for four decades. Virginia and Frederick were in the forefront of establishing nursing as a professional vocation in the country, attracting some of the best members of society to the calling. It can be easily asserted that their actions saved countless lives through facilitating skilled care of patients on a broad scale.

Both Frederick and Virginia followed the example of their parents in their dedication to charitable causes. This deep-rooted charitable disposition, coupled with the evangelical ways of the Sturges family, served as cornerstones for their lives.

Twenty-six

A Sturges Evangelical Life

The root of all his excellence lay in a simple, earnest Christian faith.[1]
—unnamed minister, 1874

The American Tract Society's Rule #11 for the Christian Merchant (Appendix III) states, "I must always begin the day with God, and worship God twice a day in my family, whatever the pressure of business." Likewise, a deep religious faith guided Jonathan and Mary Sturges in their own family's lives. In 1834, Mary exhorted to Jonathan: "Religion I have long felt should be the guiding principle in all (things)...that faith must be shown by works, for faith without work is dead."[2] She vowed to find more time in her schedule, outside her "wifely duties," to devote to acts of faith. Mary had been a Sunday school teacher at an early age, well-schooled in the scriptures, and their musical evenings were a repertoire of spiritual music. The family's correspondence was sprinkled with biblical references, including direct pleas to family members to seek divine guidance, and a concerted commitment to always honor the Sabbath.

Through studying his correspondence, it is apparent that from early in Jonathan's marriage his faith served as the foundation for his life. However, one of his acquaintances, Rev. Lyman Atwater, wrote of Jonathan's faith in a tribute to him and commented that he did not "venture upon a public profession of religion until middle life."[3] This may be why his sister-in-law Elizabeth didn't believe he had fully embraced the faith and felt the need to evangelize to him in 1846:

[I fear] what my feelings would be if called to watch upon your sick and dying bed and if I had not before that evil day said all that was in my heart to say to you...You the descendant of pious ancestors, having passed your boyhood in the moral atmosphere of New England...have gradually turned away from all these things and your example in making the holy day one of idle pleasure has appeared to countenance wickedness... I beg you to think much and seriously about the subject.[4]

This letter filled many pages, imploring Jonathan to save himself from an evil life and focus on God's ways. Coincidentally, ten years earlier, in 1836, Jonathan wrote to Mary with similar sentiments about properly observing the Sabbath and ensuring that the children were getting a proper Sabbath education at home.[5] Each of the children (except perhaps Henry) in their own time became endowed with a deep Christian faith and sought opportunities to evangelize where appropriate. Jonathan and Mary often promoted Christian education and were quick to provide Bibles and other Christian publications to those who might use them.

In an 1860 letter from Arthur Sturges (at Princeton's theological school) to his brother Henry, he urgently encouraged him to embrace God's ways, to turn away from sin. In 1871, Virginia also pleaded with Henry to look to God for spiritual guidance:

> I often look at you and wish I could take away that tired sorrowful look your face so often wears. I know as if you had told me that you look forward to the future with no particular pleasure and the year that is just closing has certainly not brought you many happy times ...Now there is only one thing that I or anyone who loves you can do to help you and that is to pray that God will show you the truth...Now I shall pray at the commencement of a New Year and day by day at its close will see you blessed with the unspeakable gift of God, the peace which passes all understanding.[6]

During the war at Harpers Ferry, Frederick proclaimed, "it's the Lord's day" and immersed himself in his little prayer book he kept with him. Amelia constantly referred to church services and scriptures that had touched her, and was spiritually prepared for the next life, as Jonathan and Mary had striven to accomplish for all their children. Edward, during military service in Baltimore, stargazed and spoke of the Heavenly Father and the immortality and everlasting peace that Amelia had surely achieved, assuring Pierpont at Memie's death, "all is well with her."[7] The last words of their son Arthur before his passing were: "I believe in Jesus."[8]

Jonathan supported Christian evangelical organizations such as the U.S. Christian Commission, American Union Commission, American Bible Society, the American Tract Society and various relief efforts for the starving and the destitute. In the 1850s he began to build a national profile as a leading evangelical supporter.[9] He was an organizer of a Union Missionary Convention in New York in 1854 and was designated to organize a follow-on national convention of churches involved in missionary work in 1855. In September 1865, he was a Dutch Reformed Church New York delegate to a national evangelical convention in Cleveland, Ohio. Their goal was to create an organization to spread the word of Jesus, a sort of Christian Commission for the world.[10] He became even more involved with these kinds of Christian causes as he transitioned to retirement.

In 1872, Jonathan led an effort to build and establish a Temperance Reading Room, combining both his belief in education and Christian living. His nineteen-year Athenaeum reading room initiative for the professional class had ended three years before. With few public libraries and modeled after an existing British establishment, it was a quiet place for workingmen to spend the Sabbath and what other leisure hours they may have after work. They could educate themselves with the latest journals and magazines, read newspapers, partake of conversation with like-minded Christian men, and enjoy non-alcoholic beverages and snacks at a nominal cost. They established the reading room next to the Wilson Industrial School for Girls, which Mary managed. The *New York Evangelist* described the cause:

> There is work of philanthropy going on in England which deserves the attention of practical Christians on this side of the Atlantic...for the improvement of working men, by means of what he calls public-houses without drink. His inns, as he describes them, contain two rooms, in one of which smoking is forbidden (and in both, if the guests will stand it), liberally supplied with the daily papers. These rooms are brightly lighted at night and in winter, and have bright, warm, open fires.[11]

In an excerpt from an article in the late 1800s, highlighting charitable work being done in New York, an epilogue of Jonathan's reading room effort is provided:

> The writer of this had the Reading-room on the brain for many years, when, at length, on talking over the subject with a gentleman in the eastern part of the city—one whose name has since been a tower of strength to this whole movement—he consented to further the enterprise and be the treasurer. The rooms were spacious and pleasant, furnished with plenty of

papers and pamphlets…We were right among a crowded working population, and everything promised success. At first there were considerable
numbers of laboring-men present every day and evening; but, to our dismay,
they began to fall off…The coffee did not suit him; the refreshments were
not to his taste. Finally, the attendance became so thin and the expenses
were accumulating to such a degree, that we closed the room.[12]

Soon after, Peter Cooper established reading rooms in his Cooper Union
Institute, thus providing such facilities for the public.

Continuing in this vein of educating the laboring classes, Jonathan was
an early, active and strong supporter of public schooling for all children. In
1874, he was a member of the Committee on Education for the New York
City Council of Political Reform. This progressive group advocated education as a cure for poverty and crime and promoted compulsory education
for children. They petitioned the state legislature: "To enact a law that
requires the attendance at some school, public or private, during the school
terms and the school hours of each day of the children between the ages of
eight and fifteen years."[13] Their efforts were successful, and that year New
York's first compulsory schooling law was passed for children between 8
and 14 years of age (at least 14 weeks of school annually).

In 1868, Jonathan was recognized for an act of international Christian
benevolence in support of financially stranded Japanese students studying in
the United States. Guido Verbeck, a missionary for the Dutch Reformed
Church in Japan, became a political advisor for the Japanese government.
One of his initiatives was to encourage and facilitate a Western education
for students at colleges in the United States. In 1868-1869, a revolution in
Japan, overthrowing the rule of what became the last Shogun ruler (Tycoon),
interrupted the flow of government aid to these students. Verbeck approached Jonathan and a few other philanthropically-minded citizens to
provide aid until the conflict could be concluded:

The following persons were the contributors; Jonathan Sturges, James
Schieffelein… General Robert H. Pyron and Mrs. Anna M. Ferris. When
the revolution of 1868 was decided, the advances, for which the students
had given due bills, were repaid. When the last company of commissioners from Japan, led by Mr. Iwakura, visited this country, they prepared a
paper recognizing the generous kindness and saying that it had had more

effect in confirming the friendly regard for the United States by the government of Japan than any event in their intercourse with this country.[14]

Jonathan and Mary's interest in supporting these students evolved later into the establishment of a long-standing missionary school in Japan named the Jonathan Sturges Seminary.

From 1853 to 1874, Jonathan was on the Board of Managers for the American Bible Society.[15] As an extension of this work, he was an active member of the New York Sabbath Committee for ten years, from 1864 to 1874, and a primary organizer for the first National Sabbath Convention in New York City, staged to draw attention to the sanctity of Sunday as a day of worship and quiet reflection.[16] In furtherance of protecting the Sabbath, in 1869, Jonathan petitioned the New York State legislature against passage of an excise law that would allow the sale of beer on Sunday. For most of the 19th century, laws were on the books excluding Sunday sales. Jonathan, along with several hundred leading citizens, signed the petition to the legislature, asserting: "Because it opens the way to the unlimited illegal sale of liquor under the cloak of lager beer; Because the proposed amendment defeats the efficiency and their right to a quiet and undisturbed Sabbath, and will open the way to its constant desecration, it shouldn't be supported."[17] However, in April 1870, the amendment making for the practical repeal of the Sunday liquor prohibition passed, and beer was once again legal to drink on Sundays.

Although very sick, Jonathan put his name to a public petition to protect the Sabbath, published on November 28, 1874. The *New York Times* editorialized:

[Mr. Sturges] earnestly sought to secure to all his fellow-men the opportunity of its enjoyment…his last public act was to put his name to a petition asking for the enforcement of a statute intended to guard the interests of all classes, the sacred rights of rest and worship.[18]

The *Jacksonville Gazette* reported that: "A protest against Sunday theatricals addressed to the police commissioners asking for the enforcement of the laws prohibiting such amusements, is published and signed by Edwin D. Morgan, John J. Cisco, Jonathan Sturges, Thurlow Weed, William E. Dodge, and several hundred other prominent citizens."[19] The proprietor at the Tivoli Theater said he would comply and have musical concerts instead, and that the offending event, *The Seven Dwarfs*, would then begin at midnight.[20] This ban against amusements on Sundays stayed in place for many years, with Sunday baseball for instance, only being allowed in 1919.

Mary and Jonathan were members of the Presbyterian Collegiate (Dutch) Reformed Church. This congregation was one of the oldest in the Colonies, forming in 1628 when the Dutch East India Company was prominent in New York. The church, built in 1854, became known as the Marble Church for its Tuckahoe marble exterior.[a] The Roosevelt family was a member there for many years, including future President Theodore Roosevelt's parents. Young Teddy and Virginia's son Frederick Osborn were close friends and fellow members of Teddy's Natural History Society that the boys formed in 1874 in New York City. "Fred's brother Henry told of the time the boys were on a walk and doffed their hats upon meeting the carriage of Hamilton Fish, United States Secretary of State, and his wife. A frog jumped from under Theodore's hat, stored there because his pockets were full."[21] In 1875, Fred wrote to Teddy inviting him to Garrison to visit and shoot worm-eating warblers—a letter the future President saved all his life, due to the tragedy that struck his friend soon after.

Jonathan was a national Elder of the Dutch Reformed Church for the last twelve years of his life. He was the Ruling Elder in 1874 and was a delegate to a national meeting in Philadelphia on November 18, 1874. There was an active discussion at the time to merge the Dutch Reformed Church and the German Reformed Church. Jonathan was on the Synod Committee of Conference on the subject and hosted delegates at his home, as chronicled by the New York *Evening Post*:

> It is only a few months ago that delegates from the southern Presbyterian Church were in this city to confer with representatives of the Dutch Reformed Church in reference to a union. In this movement, he (Jonathan) took a deep interest, entertaining the southern delegates, and many will remember the reception given to them at his house when the meeting was over.[22]

They took a vote at the end of the meeting but did not reach a majority vote for merging the two churches. Jonathan returned to New York feeling ill, and sadly this was the last trip in the earthly world that he would take.

---

[a] Norman Vincent Peale would later be a Pastor at this church for over 50 years, starting in 1932. It still stands today at 272 Fifth Avenue.

TWENTY-SEVEN

"This Season is Somewhat Lonely Because Jonathan Sturges is Not with Us"

Art mourns an appreciative student; charity is grieved at the loss of a
bright example and firm support; social and political reform misses the
stalwart form of their defender
— *Rev. Dr. Ludlow, 1874*

After returning from the church meeting in Philadelphia, which adjourned
November 19, 1874, Jonathan came down with a cold, which progressed to pneu-
monia on Tuesday, November 23. He succumbed to his illness only days
later, on Saturday, November 28, at his residence. As he laid in his deathbed,
he made his peace with God, quoted his favorite Bryant poems and, "The good
old man, loved, honored, passed to his rest, uttering, almost with his last breath
to his bereaved household gathered around him, the words which seemed the
keystone of his life—'be charitable.'"[1] The inscription on his gravestone
reads, "Mark the perfect *man*, and behold the upright: for the end of *that*
man *is* peace." Perhaps in tribute to Jonathan, the *New York Post* announced
above his obituary: "Superintendent Walling has today instructed the police
captains to enforce the law prohibiting theatrical and musical productions
on Sunday."[2]

A private memorial service was held in the morning at the Sturges home
for the family:

> The coffin was held in the center of the room, covered by beautiful offerings
> of rare flowers. A prayer was said by Rev. Dr. Adams, and a hymn was sung
> by a quartet from Dr. Ormiston's choir. The coffin was then opened, and a
> farewell look taken by the members of Mr. Sturges' family and reclosed, was
> covered with palm leaves and calla lilies, and taken to the church, which
> was full to the doors.[3]

The Dutch Reformed Church at Fifth Avenue and West Twenty-Ninth Street hosted the public service. The church was overflowing with family, friends, associates and admirers, where the prominent and poor alike took hat in hand to grieve. The Importer and Grocer's Board of Trade met at noon the day of the funeral to construct a fitting testimonial to Jonathan from its members. They closed their offices at 2:30 to allow members to attend. Jonathan's pallbearers were William Cullen Bryant, Daniel Huntington, T.B. Schieffelin, James Brown, John C. Green, Junius S. Morgan, Benjamin A. Arnold, William Hunt and William E. Dodge. Other notables who attended included J.S. Schultz, J.H. Choate, Peter Cooper, J.B. Cornell, A.A. Low, A.T. Stewart, Hon. Samuel B. Ruggles, and countless others of the old guard of merchants, as well as many of the poor whom he had touched with his generosity. Delegations from the Union League, National Academy of Design and The Century Association were also there in force. The respect for him within the religious community was so great that there were seven clergymen presiding at the service. Hymns "My Jesus, as Thou Wilt" and "Rock of Ages" were featured. Rev. Dr. Ludlow addressed the assemblage:

> Mr. Sturges' peculiar characteristics were deep practical wisdom, wonderful devotion to things noble and honest, remarkable clarity and devotion to the service of God…The name of Mr. Sturges is a household name, and the business of this city feels the shadow of his fall. Art mourns an appreciative student; charity is grieved at the loss of a bright example and firm support; social and political reform misses the stalwart form of their defender.[4]

Dr. Fields, another clergyman from New York City, offered this tribute:

> As a merchant, he commanded that perfect confidence which is gained only by strict integrity, maintained through a long business career. The wealth that came to him was all the fruit of honest industry… Though so public-spirited and active in all that concerned the public good, he never sought anything for himself. And yet under his simple exterior and quiet ways an observer soon recognized the elements of great strength of character.[5]

Jonathan's Christian faith, thoughtful counsel, charitable disposition and self-effacing character personified his life. The artist William S. Mount once said, "It is our duty to speak of men that adorn their walls with pictures rather than looking glasses. He [Jonathan] has apartments richly decorated with paintings and busts by native artists, and I believe he has only one mirror."[6] At his funeral, his dear friend William Cullen Bryant remarked: "He knew how to be munificent without ostentation." After services in New York, Jonathan's casket remained in the church overnight, and was sent to Fairfield the next day for interment in the East Cemetery.

Tribute articles ran nationwide. A Nevada newspaper editorialized, "Jonathan Sturges, the eminent New York merchant, recently deceased, worked his way up to wealth from the position of porter in an importing house. It is a noteworthy fact that throughout his long and active life, his walk was so ordered that he never made an enemy."[7] Secretary of State Hamilton Fish, a neighbor of his daughter Virginia Osborn, sent his condolences to Jonathan's son Henry, lamenting his inability to attend the funeral, saying: "How consoling it must be that he was so universally esteemed by his fellow citizens as the embodiment of the high-loved, liberal, generous-hearted, Christian merchant."[8] On December 19, *Frank Leslie's Illustrated Newspaper* ran a long tribute article to Jonathan, including a drawing of him devoid of the beard he had sported for many years before his death:

"Jonathan Sturges," *Frank Leslie's Illustrated Magazine*, c. 1874[9]

The Union League expressed profound sorrow at the death of their former president and founding member of the club. They said in part:

Identified with the city of New York and with its best interests for more than half a century…He sought no honors and shrank from public observation, but whenever called upon, he was sure to be in every public emergency... His advocacy of human freedom, his devotion to the cause of education, his many works of charity, his earnest promotion of the art, and his zeal for everything that went to the improvement and advancement of the city as a home for its citizens, will long be remembered by a grateful community.[10]

The New York Chamber of Commerce memorialized Jonathan's life:

The life of Mr. Sturges was of that well-rounded, symmetrical kind, and was in all that the phrase implies—good and true. It was a life worth living. It presented the highest sagacity of the merchant and the noblest virtues of the private citizen...Although conducting a large business, he nevertheless found time to devote to philanthropic and Christian work. Truly his long life was well spent... Rich as Mr. Sturges was in this world's goods, he was richer still in honor...[11]

Jonathan had become a wealthy man but not famously so. The *Cincinnati Daily Gazette* estimated his estate at more than $1,000,000 in December 1874.[12] *The Christian Intelligencer* (a Dutch Reformed Church newspaper) memorialized Jonathan's Christian life, but also acknowledged that such a faith-based business approach was considered a fool's path by modern businessmen:

It is worthwhile of young men who are shaken by the contempt in which modern infidelity holds religious faith to know that the cool head of one of the shrewdest practical men of our city has ever known, found commanding evidence on the side of the gospel... Mr. Sturges was preeminently a thinker.[13]

Jonathan's friend and fellow merchant, Charles Talbot, passed away the day after he did. The next day his close friend, Mayor William Havemeyer, returned from a trip to Rhode Island to visit a sick friend. He entered his office having difficulty breathing and sent for some brandy. "Then he drank the brandy, and he was soon seemingly relieved. He took his seat and his mind at once reverted to the recent sudden death of his long-time friend. 'Mr. Sturges had no physique, I have, Sturges was weak, I am strong', said he, straightening up his portly form."[14] Just then, Havemeyer suddenly fell on the floor, pale and lifeless, dead of an apparent stroke.

The city felt the loss of these stalwarts of civic activism and philanthropy. The *New York Evangelist* lamented: "Who of our young merchants will rise to fill their places and pursue the same course of usefulness and honor?"[15] Jonathan and his fellow Christian merchants of his generation lived by a code that valued integrity, diligence, public-spiritedness, and selflessness, all characteristics being increasingly devalued amid the rising robber barons, except as a facade for their public persona.

The contents of Jonathan's will was widely reported. Mary, Fred and William Osborn were named executors. First and foremost, he acknowledged his Christian faith and that his assets were a gift from God. Mary received the city residence, use of all furnishings there and at the Cottage during her life, and a yearly stipend went to Mary and his remaining two sisters. Fred received a property at Mill Place known as the "White House." The remainder of the estate was divided among his four remaining children.[16] About the importance of benevolence, Jonathan omitted specific donations, but he instructed his children:

> I desire to charge each of my children and descendants with the responsibility of administering the means placed in his or her hands. They know my views and practice in this respect, and the objects I cherish, and I confidently hope they will always realize the happiness of promoting, as they may be able, the best interests of our race, and of dispensing of their abundance to the relief of those who may be straitened [sic] under the visitations of adversity.[17]

Jonathan exemplified the American work ethic. Starting with nothing, he knocked on doors until someone gave him a chance. He became a partner and a leader among merchants, the most exalted of business professions of his time, his firm's credit was "gilt-edged" all his life. He led the oldest of grocery houses in the tea and coffee trade for over three decades, and had a hand in founding two railroads, two banks, three hospitals, an insurance company and the first of the modern YMCAs. Jonathan commissioned priceless works of art, and was a spark behind numerous philanthropic, patriotic, arts and literary societies that still endure. He was a patriot in every sense of the word. He applied both his industry and his wealth to support the Union war efforts, the Civil War soldier's medicinal and spiritual needs, veterans, the sufferers of the draft riots, and those in the war-ravaged South.

Jonathan was a ready advisor to multiple Presidential administrations and effectively worked to bring down historic corruption inside New York City. When others in the civic reform committee were benefiting personally from the reform work, he resigned and forced its dissolution. He was a household name across the country and kept company with men of the highest integrity. It was said that he probably never made an enemy, and his friends were many.

Jonathan had become the epitome of his family's crest and motto, Esse Quam Videri, meaning "to be, rather than to seem." He was what he appeared to be—a man who had lived his life by certain principles guided by a strong faith, unimpeachable integrity, remarkable ability and a charitable disposition. As Jane Beale, Mary's Fredericksburg friend, said: "All the grief must be for ourselves, and the sadness for this poor world, who has so few men like him."[18] At the end of his life he had become one of the last of the men of a proud but bygone business age—but all he and his contemporaries accomplished and represented had been a critical prerequisite to the business revolution that was then underway.

In June 1875, a letter to the *New York Evening Post* from "S.O." in Fairfield, who after attending the funeral of of his grandaughter, described the void left in the community with his death :

> … and by her side (daughter Amelia) her father's body rests, and how good it is to associate him (Jonathan) with all the noble charities and beautiful arts that crowned his honorable career! I rode by his house and farm after the funeral of the grandchild, and the hillside where he was often seen last year directing his men, was all luxuriant with the grass and grain that he then planted. Such cheering memorials of our good neighbor are greatly needed, for life here this season is somewhat lonely because Jonathan Sturges is not with us.[19]

TWENTY-EIGHT

Business and Family Epilogue

The law of mutation, however, is relentless even among the pillars of commerce.

Troy Daily Times, 1883

Jonathan's firm became Arnold, Sturges and Co. after his retirement, with Benjamin Arnold as the majority partner, and then changed again to Arnold & Co. after Edward Sturges left the firm at the end of 1871.[1] Arnold followed Jonathan's lead with his involvement in many business and civic associations and the firm continued as a leader in the coffee and tea trade. However, he did not follow Jonathan's conservative and risk-averse business approach and his first major misstep was described by a New York historian of the era:

> Arnold, our best-known coffee dealer…was daring enough to engineer with Bowie Dash, in 1875, the purchase of several hundred thousand bags of Java coffee, intending to corner the market. Being the only holder, he did command as much as 20 cents per pound for lots which were urgently needed. It looked as if the speculators would make money, until, in 1877, a competitor had the audacity to order 10,000 bags by steamer from London. Coffee declined faster than it had risen.[2]

The firm survived that event, albeit weaker in capital. However, in 1880, Arnold & Co. again invested in a significant volume of coffee and tea. The price of coffee and tea plunged, primarily due to the death of a prominent Boston trader by the name of O.G. Kimble—the loss was devastating. It was estimated that the company was in debt $750,000 to $1,000,000. It was forced to sell at a large loss and did not have the capital to cover the shortfall. Creditors considered allowing the firm to carry on and repay its debts over time, however, the deficit was too great, and Arnold & Co. became insolvent. In 1883, the *Troy Daily Times* observed:

When a powerful mind is severed from a firm, a marked difference will soon appear in its management. There will be a lack of efficiency, which, like a leak in a ship, will gradually lead to final and hopeless wreck. How little such men as...Jonathan Sturges...imagined the fate which (befell) their successors. The law of mutation, however, is relentless even among the pillars of commerce.[3]

For thirty-two years, Jonathan's conservative approach had ensured that his company survived and thrived. Within fifteen years of Jonathan's departure, his former firm, the oldest grocer and import house in the country failed, the gilt-edge eroded. It sent shock waves around the nation. Despite this, modern business leaders were not deterred in their ruthless pursuit of wealth—and his iconic former son-in-law J. Pierpont Morgan was leading the charge. Mentored by Jonathan in banks, railroads and art, he became involved in many of the businesses and philanthropic organizations that Jonathan either founded or was an active member. However, Morgan took finance to a higher art form. He famously sold a large block of public stock in Vanderbilt's New York Central Railroad and spearheaded the sale of $40,000,000 in Northern Pacific bonds in partnership with Anthony Drexel, at one time controlling about one sixth of America's railroad lines. Morgan and his syndicate of businessmen shored up the nation's gold reserve in 1895 when the government was within days of insolvency; bought U.S. Steel from Andrew Carnegie in 1907; and locked up leading financiers of the nation in his library to solve a national financial crisis in 1907, among other sensational deals. Today his name adorns the largest bank in the United States: J.P. Morgan Chase.

J. Pierpont Morgan's marriage to Fanny yielded four children. However, early in their relationship, it became evident that their interests and preferred lifestyles were not compatible. Pierpont developed a wandering eye and undertook much independent overseas travel. In 1882, Morgan was traveling without his wife in France, with his father and others, when he took a nostalgic trip to visit the Villa St. George, the site of Memie's last days. He picked pansies and sent them to Fanny to forward to Mary Sturges in loving remembrance.[4] A Morgan biographer asserted that, "Her memory was the most poignant of Morgan's life. She touched in him an emotional chord no one else had been able to touch."[5] Morgan carried on with less than private affairs throughout his life. With their similar travel and art interests, mutual family friends, and the relationship he had with the Sturges family, it is interesting to contemplate whether these affairs would have occurred had he remained married to his first love, Amelia Sturges.

Following Jonathan's lead in art and education, J.P. Morgan became one of the foremost rare book and art collectors in the world, adorning his walls and halls with numerous masterpieces. J. P. Morgan's house and library annex in New York City now houses the Morgan Library and Museum. It is about one block from where Jonathan and Mary lived on Park Avenue. In the Library are paintings of the zodiac signs on the ceiling, representing important things in his life. "With its zodiac signs, divinities and configuration of stars, the villa ceiling is, in effect, the banker's horoscope...Morgan's first marriage, to his childhood sweetheart, Amelia (Memie) Sturges, lasted only four months, and her death on Feb. 17, 1862, is symbolized by the sign of Aquarius, near the muse of tragedy."[6] A large cache of Sturges family papers and photographs are preserved in the library's archives, where Jonathan Sturges and family are embraced as Morgan family members.

When J. P. Morgan died in 1913 he had amassed a fortune estimated to be $200,000,000. In his will, he memorialized his lost love, his dear Memie, by designating $100,000 for the "Amelia Sturges Morgan Memorial Fund" to benefit the House of Rest for Consumptives. Morgan, also in his will, directed his executors "to make provisions for the perpetual care of the burial lot in Fairfield, Conn. in which his first wife is interred." Jonathan had deeded Amelia's burial plot in Fairfield to Morgan as part of his will. Before his death, he also donated a twenty-five hundred pound church bell in memory of Amelia Sturges Morgan to the First Church of Christ in Fairfield, later known as the First Church Congregational. Jonathan's son Frederick was instrumental in rebuilding the church after an arsonist destroyed it in 1890.[7] J.P. Morgan's children also remained close to the Sturges family. J.P. Morgan, Jr. named one of his sons Henry Sturges Morgan, after his Uncle Henry.

Jonathan had a significant influence on his other son-in-law's successes, especially in railroads. Without Jonathan, William Osborn would not have been asked in 1854 to take charge and turn around the struggling Illinois Central Railroad, which was laboring under a debt of $20,000,000. When he left the office of presidency in 1865, his careful management had reduced the debt significantly and it had been paying dividends since 1863.[8] Osborn resigned as president but stayed on the ICR board to focus on the financing needs of the railroad, finally retiring in 1881.

In 1877, he became president of the Chicago, St. Louis, and New Orleans Railroad. Both he and Virginia were champions of many charitable pursuits. William Osborn stayed closely involved with the Hospital for the Ruptured and Crippled and served as president later in his life. He also became an important collector and patron for native artists per the example of his father-in-law.

Jonathan's art collection consisted of over a 100 paintings, engravings, drawings and sculptures, much of which has been donated and sold over the years by the family. There was no comprehensive inventory kept of the pieces that he owned. Over time researchers have tried to identify the items he collected, and many of these art pieces reside in private art collections and distinguished museums around the country, including the National Gallery of Art, the Metropolitan Museum of Art and the Museum of Fine Arts in Boston.[a] A base listing of known items has been pieced together by this author from earlier research, exhibition records, artist biographies, newspaper articles and art journals, and is provided in Appendix V.

Jonathan's Union League Club transformed itself along with the evolving and diverging business, social and political trends of the affluent. It now describes itself simply as "a social club providing its members and guests with a quiet sanctuary and relief from the hustle of the city." Upon entering its doors at its current location on Thirty-Seventh Street, just a few blocks from Grand Central Terminal, one is faced with a classic, dark, wooden, two-sided staircase leading to a landing at the top adorned with a picture gallery. From this entrance gazing upward, Jonathan's portrait can be seen displayed on the wall at the left side of the landing, with his thoughtful gaze turned downward to the book he is reading. This portrait was commissioned in 1889 by the New York Chamber of Commerce to commemorate his time as a vice president from 1863-1867. Daniel Huntington, one of Jonathan's pallbearers and a Union League member, was the artist. His likeness was taken from a photograph of him late in life, that still hangs over the fireplace in the Cottage library. One additional portrait of Jonathan hangs in the dining room of the Union League Club, painted by the portrait artist Thomas Hicks.[b]

---

[a] A working list of his artworks, engravings, drawings, etc. is provided in Appendix V. It is considered a dynamic listing, which is updated continually by the author, as more information becomes available, primarily through the increasing digitization of sources. Notwithstanding, the list provided can be considered largely comprehensive.

[b] The painting was loaned from the Union League to the James A. Michener Art Museum in Doylestown, Pennsylvania in 1998 for a short time as part of a special exhibit of Thomas and Edward Hick's work, although there is some doubt by the club as to the identity of the artist.

Huntington, Daniel, *Jonathan Sturges,* Oil on canvas, c. 1889[9]

When Jonathan passed away, he tasked his children with the duty to "be charitable." Virginia made a significant donation not two years after his death. In 1876, she contracted to purchase the old Cozzens Hotel, on the Highland Bluffs at West Point on the Hudson River, for $65,000. This is where, in its heyday, she and Amelia had stayed in the early years of Virginia and William's marriage, where Pierpont had courted Amelia, and where so many famous generals and other dignitaries had dined and danced the night away. Virginia announced that she was donating it to the New York Hospital Society, for use as a convalescent hospital, with the stipulation that patients must be admitted without regard to national origin or religious affiliation. However, within a month, the sale was voided due to a deed issue, and the neighborhood leading citizens protested having such a hospital for the poor in their midst. Six months later it was purchased by a group which reestablished it as the Cozzens hotel.

Virginia Osborn stayed on the Board of Managers of the Bellevue Hospital nurse training school the rest of her life. The following tribute was written of Virginia by Elizabeth Hobson, her fellow founding board member:

> I wish I could give an idea of what she was to the School. Her devotion to it was absolute; ...No one could work with Mrs. Osborn without being affected by her deeply religious nature, without respecting and loving her.

Her generosity knew no bounds...she was always doing little kindnesses,and great kindnesses, too, for superintendents, nurses and patients, of which only they themselves could ever know...When Mrs. Osborn died, the whole School mourned her, the whole hospital mourned her, their most steadfast friend for all those thirty years.[10]

The Honorable Joseph Choate spoke in New Jersey in May 1910 on the 50th anniversary of Florence Nightingale's training school in England, and paid a touching tribute to Virginia: "That woman of sainted memory, Mrs. William H. Osborn, who led their activities in the creation of that great school, and who gave so much of her heart, her soul, her life and her treasure, to the building up of that school."[11] Virginia's sons, Henry Fairfield Osborn and William Church Osborn became benefactors of the school, as did her daughter-in-law, Mrs. William Church Osborn (Alice Dodge), who took a leading role in the school during her lifetime.

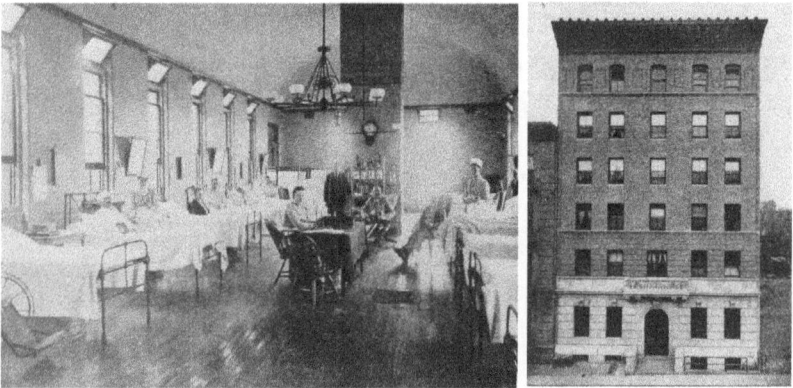

Bellevue Hospital, Sturges Pavilion (left) c. 1892[12] and Osborn Hall[13]

In 1878, the Osborns purchased a house next door to the Nurse Training School and leased it for use as a Nurse's dormitory. It was in use for more than thirty years and was known as Osborn Hall.[14] William and Virginia Osborn built the Sturges Pavilion at Bellevue Hospital in 1879, in honor of Jonathan Sturges. In 1911, in memory of Virginia and financed by the Osborn family, the hospital merged the Osborn Hall property with an adjoining lot and remodeled. It provided for a clubhouse for graduate nurses, an assembly room and housing for nurses and other self-supporting women. The Hunter-Bellevue School of Nursing took over operations in 1967.

Daughter Virginia Osborn c. 1860s & 1870s[15] and Memorial to Frederick & Virginia Osborn[16]

William and Virginia Osborn lost two of their children tragically within the same year—just five months after the death of Jonathan. Their oldest child, Virginia Sturges Osborn died in Paris on May 8, 1875, at age twenty, stricken with an illness referred to in the nineteenth century as brain fever.[c] Their son Fred drowned at the young age of sixteen while swimming with his brother Henry Fairfield on July 2, 1875, near their home at Garrison, NY. A Teddy Roosevelt historian captured the tragic moment:

> Friday, July 2, Henry and Fred went swimming in the Hudson River, south of the railroad station at a spot called Mine Point. A strong current swept them both under. Henry tried to save his brother but finding that they both were sinking said "goodbye" and released his hold. Henry escaped to shore by reaching out to an oar held by another boy. Two gentlemen dove in several times without success…Fred's body was finally discovered on July 4th.[17]

Both children were buried in Fairfield near Jonathan, Arthur and Amelia. The Osborns donated a stain glass window at St. Philip's Episcopal Church in Garrison, New York, in memory of young Virginia and Frederick. The church altar is dedicated to Virginia, inscribed, "To the Glory of God and in Sacred Memory of Virginia R. Sturgis [sic] Osborn 1830-1902."

---

[c] Any acute cerebral infection coupled with fever, such as meningitis, typhus and encephalitis.

Castle Rock, Garrison, New York[18] and View from Castle Rock overlooking Hudson River[19]

In 1881, William and Virginia built a small castle known as Castle Rock up the hill from their Wing-and-Wing home. William Osborn passed away in 1894, and Virginia Sturges Osborn followed in 1902. Their legacy lives on in their many charitable works and in those of their heirs. They are buried at St. Phillip's Church in Garrison, New York.

Henry Fairfield Osborn inherited Castle Rock upon Virginia's death. Castle Rock is no longer owned by the family and the surrounding 200 acre property was purchased by the state in 1979. It is in disrepair and gutted inside, after a failed attempt to make it an events space. At this writing, it awaits someone either to restore it to its former glory or modify it for other purposes. Wing-and-Wing is owned at this writing by a descendant of William and Virginia Osborn, after a one-owner possession outside the family. In 1919, their grandson Frederick Osborn built his mansion, Cat Rock, nearby in Phillipstown, NY. Cat Rock was sold to a non-family member in 2015, and at this writing is owned by a New York art dealer.

Their son, Henry Fairfield Osborn, was a renowned geologist and paleon-ologist, and was the President of the American Museum of Natural History for twenty-five years, credited with naming the predator dinosaurs Tyran-nosaurus Rex and Velociraptor, as well as unearthing dinosaurs Pentacer-atops and Ornitholestes. Henry was arguably the best-known scientist of his time outside of Einstein and was very active in the eugenics movement. He was an expert witness during the famous Scopes Monkey Trial in Dayton, Tennessee, in 1925. John Thomas Scopes, a high school teacher, was tried for teaching evolution. Osborn testified for the defense to prove evolution and religion could co-exist in teaching, asserting that evolution was part of God's plan—an approach conflicting with both sides of the argument. His son Henry Fairfield Osborn, Jr., followed in his father's scientific footsteps as an environmentalist and a board member of the New York Zoological Society.

Henry Fairfield Osborn, c. 1890[20]

William and Virginia's son, William Church Osborn, named after their close friend Frederic Church, was the heir of his wealthy parents' estate and occupied the 32 Park Avenue home until his death. William Church Osborn, or Will, as Virginia referred to him when he was growing up, married Alice Dodge (granddaughter of William Dodge), joining the families of two of the most respected and successful merchants of the nineteenth century. Virginia Osborn refers to their happy engagement in a letter she wrote to Fanny Morgan, J.P. Morgan's second wife:

> Your love and sympathy has been so precious to us in all our sorrows that I am glad when I can call upon you to share our joys. When I saw you last week, I was not at liberty to tell you of Will's engagement to Alice Dodge. It took place just before he left to join Charlie Murray in the Yellowstone Park, but he and Alice were very desirous not to have it known until his return which took place last Saturday night. We have all known Alice since she was fourteen years old and always for the same loving true-hearted Christian girl.[21]

William Church Osborn was a lawyer and an active philanthropist. He was the president of the Children's Aid Society from 1902 to 1947 and continued the Sturges tradition of leadership in the fine arts as president of the Metropolitan Museum of Art. He was also a chairman of the New York State Democratic Party (1914-1916) and ran for the Democratic nomination for governor in 1918, losing to Alfred E. Smith by a wide margin. He was a long-time president of the Hospital for the Ruptured and Crippled. His great-granddaughter was appointed a Life Trustee on the Board, by then renamed the Hospital for Special Surgery, the seventh generation to serve on the board. William Church Osborn's son, General Frederick Osborn, was the Chairman of the President's Advisory Council on the Selective Service during the Second World War and represented the United States on the United Nations Atomic Energy Commission.

Another legacy of the Sturges-Osborn family is the "Osborn Gates" at Central Park built in honor of William Church Osborn. These wrought-iron gates were vandalized over the years and put in storage until recently restored. The Osborn Gates now reign again at the restored Ancient Playground in Central Park, just north of the Metropolitan Museum of Art.[22]

Frederick Sturges, Sr. (Jonathan's son) retired in 1868 at the age of thirty-five, at the same time as his father. After Fred and Mary's first child Jonathan (Jontie) in 1864, they were blessed with Emily Main Sturges (1865), Arthur Pemberton Sturges (1867), Mary Fuller Sturges (1870), Virginia Reed Sturges (1872) and Frederick Sturges, Jr. (1874).

Frederick remained involved on several boards for both business and philanthropic organizations including, the Bank of Commerce, Illinois Central Railroad, New York Stock Exchange, The Century Association, as well as being a supporter of the Metropolitan Museum of Art and an officer with the American Bible Society, an organization which his father managed for many years. Frederick served as an original trustee of the New York Public Library along with Andrew Carnegie, J.P. Morgan, Mayor Greenbaum and Virginia's son, Henry Fairfield Osborn.

In 1894-1902, Frederick, Sr. was both treasurer and president of the New York Society for the Relief of the Ruptured and Crippled and William Church Osborn was for many years Recording Secretary. Arthur (Frederick's son) was on the Board of Managers for many years starting in 1894. Frederick, Sr., served on the Board of Managers of Presbyterian Hospital, and was Chairman of the Executive Committee, Vice President, President and Trustee between 1877–1917, forty years of service.[23] He knew most of the staff personally during his association and sent flowers from his gardens at Mt. David Farm in Fairfield to adorn the rooms at the hospital. The assembly hall in the nurses' residence at Presbyterian Hospital was named Sturges Hall in honor of Frederick Sturges, Sr.'s work in founding the nursing school.

In concert with Frederick Sr.'s involvement in hospital management, in 1879, he was a founder of a charitable cooperative called Hospital Saturday and Sunday Association.[24] This organization operated by soliciting funds from churchgoers on a designated weekend each month to raise money for benevolent hospitals in New York. It was the predecessor entity for the now well-known United Hospital Fund.[25] Frederick passed away on December 22, 1917, leaving an estate valued at $3,700,000. He and Mary are buried in the family plot in Fairfield.

Frederick Sturges c. late 1890s[26] and A. Sterner, *Jonathan Sturges,* c. 1912[27]

Frederick Sr.'s son Jonathan Sturges, a Princeton graduate, became a noted writer and talented translator of French works. He was a handsome man but crippled with polio since he was young. His short stories were published in national magazines and newspapers. This Jonathan Sturges (Jonathan's grandson) was an intimate friend of the famous writer Henry James and he associated widely with well-known artistic and literary figures such as James,

McNeill Whistler, John Singer Sargent, Oscar Wilde, William Dean Howells, and the wealthy George Washington Vanderbilt of Biltmore fame.

The intimacy of his relationship with Henry James may or may not have extended to the physical, but it was clear that James had a deep affection for Jonathan. In a letter to an associate, James offered this playful description of his dear friend: "Jonathan Sturges lives, year in, year out, at Long's Hotel, Bond Street, and promises to come down here and see me, but never does. He knows hordes of people, everyone extraordinarily likes him, and he has tea-parties for pretty ladies: one at a time. Alas, he is three quarters of the time ill; but his little spirit is colossal."[28] Whistler referred to him playfully as "the little dwarf", as well as "true and noble" and a "preux Chevalier" (a gallant knight). Jonathan spent a considerable part of his life in Paris where he was born, much of that with James until 1900, becoming an invalid in the 1890s, and dying there in 1911. Jonathan's sister Mary commissioned a pastel sketch of him, drawn by *Harpers* illustrator Albert Sterner, from a photo she owned. A copy hung over Henry James's desk at his death in 1916 and bears a striking resemblance to his grandfather Jonathan Sturges.[29] Today his translation of Guy de Maupassant's *The Odd Number: Thirteen Tales*, among other writings, is sold by most national booksellers.

Frederick, Jr. became a leading citizen in Fairfield. He sold the property northeast of the Cottage to Walter Lashar, a prominent wire manufacturer in Bridgeport, who in 1920 built Hearthstone Hall there. The mansion, now known as Bellarmine Hall, and property are now a part of Fairfield University.[30] Frederick, Jr., also gave twelve acres of land to the town of Fairfield in 1946, which was turned into Sturges Park. The deed signed over to the town embodies Jonathan's respect for the Sabbath, as it stipulated, "For a period of twenty-five years from this date the property shall not be used on the Sabbath for baseball, football, soccer games or similar athletic contests that might attract crowds of people and thus disturb the peace of the neighborhood."[31] Today Sturges Park is a town landmark and used as a multiple use sports field, and is the site of a winter sledding hill for the children of the town. Two years later, after the Sturges Park donation, Frederic Sturges, Jr. sold the town an additional nineteen acres of land. The original Mill Plain Elementary School was built there, and the building was later modified and expanded as part of the Roger Ludlowe High School project. Frederick, Jr. also endowed many nursing scholarships at Presbyterian Hospital.

The Fairfield Museum and History Center used the Sturges farm buildings as a model for the design of several out buildings. They were designed by project architect James Childress, a partner in Centerbrook Architects of Centerbrook, CT, [who] considered form and functionality in creating a structure that emulates the sprawling farm owned by Frederick Sturges in the nineteenth century Mt. David Farm.[32]

Edward maintained an office at 125 Front Street and lived at E. 14th Street until 1876. Jonathan still owned the leasehold property at 14th Street at his death. In 1877, Ed moved to the family townhouses at 34 Park Ave.[33] Edward passed away in November 1901 and is buried at Sleepy Hollow Cemetery in Westchester, New York.

When a father obtains significant affluence, the children are often less likely to make their own way in the business world. Frederick retired in 1868 after making a small fortune of his own. Edward retired in 1872 at the age of thirty-five, like his brother. Henry's last year of college was in 1872, when he was awarded an A.M. degree, or Master of Arts as it is commonly referred to today. Tradition has it that he studied law under noted lawyer Theodore Dwight (1822-1892) until weakening eyesight forced him to discontinue his studies.[34] In the 1870s, Henry Sturges enjoyed a life of leisure, sailing from New England to most of the islands of the Caribbean. He sent back a travelogue to his parents that started in Trinidad, writing of emerald green sugar cane fields and factories, mangoes and picturesque palms, the beauty of the Botanical Gardens and enjoying the indigenous cuisine and people. While in Jamaica he lunched at "Kings House" with Lady Musgrave, the wife of the Lord Anthony Musgrave, the English Governor-General there. She had been a friend of Memie's as a young lady.[d] Henry commented, "she is as lovely and unaffected as she was [when] un-married. She showed me Memie's locket which she always wears…"[35]

Henry's sailing adventures in 1874 were aboard the sailing yacht Aroostook. He must have developed a special attachment to that boat as he later owned a sixty-eight-ton, seventy-three-foot schooner (built in 1880) by the same name. The family story is that Henry had to sell the Aroostook to marry, as he could not afford maintenance of both a family and a large yacht. However, in 1896 the New York Yacht Club still listed him as the owner of the Aroostook.[36] He was member #125, and his former brother-in-law, J. Pierpont

---

d Nèe Jeanie Field, daughter of David Dudley Field, a New York lawyer.

Morgan was for many years the Commodore. Henry owned a twenty-eight-foot sloop named the *Mystery* which was docked at the Fairfield/Southport Yacht Club, where he was also a member.[37] He had his own private signal flags, a white pennant with a red border and a cross-like blue anchor on the left half of the pennant, and a red and white sailing flag.[38]

Henry Cady Sturges, c. unk[39] (left),
Henry Sturges Yacht Club Pennant[40] (top), and Sailing Flag[41] (bottom)

With his father and both his brothers retired, there was no actively working family member to mentor him in a business career. Instead, Henry lived off his inheritance and became a gentleman scholar, author, avid yachtsman, horticulturist and civic leader in Fairfield—not working a day in his life. He split his time between 36th Street (his parents' former town house) and the Cottage. Mary Sturges lived with Henry in the New York and Fairfield homes until her death.[42]

He married late, in 1883 at thirty-seven, to nineteen-year-old Sarah Adams MacWhorter. In their travels in 1850, Jonathan and Mary had visited the Adams family in Augusta, Georgia. Their daughter, a friend of Virginia's, married and became Mrs. George MacWhorter, who named her daughter Sarah (Sallie) Adams MacWhorter. Sarah became Henry's wife. Virginia Sturges Osborn sent a congratulatory note to Henry on his impending nuptials in April 1883: "I send you my hearty congratulations on your engagement to dear little Sallie. It will be a great happiness to all to welcome her once more among us...I'm so glad for Mother too, Sallie will be such a bright spot in her life."[43]

Mary Sturges and Abigail D. Sturges, c. 1880s[44]
Mary Sturges, Cottage Library Window Seat, 1890s[45]

Mary Sturges stayed active in multiple charities after Jonathan's death. She was devoted to the Wilson Industrial School for Girls and to another school known as Kitchen Garden Training which was similar to the Wilson mission, both of which she remained a manager until her death.

Later in life, Mary Sturges was an officer of the Society for Decorative Arts in New York. Founded in 1877, its purpose was to educate and train women to make a living producing such things as interior decorations, pattern designs, embroidery and needle work for home decor. Mary was in the forefront of fundraising and ensuring society's support for the school.

In 1880, Mary was a promoter of a sewing circle for young ladies in Fairfield, who were students in the Mill Plain Industrial School (modeled after the Wilson School). The average age of these girls was about eight or nine years old. They spent two hours on a Saturday sewing clothes. For one hour they sewed for their own needs and another hour for charitable purposes. Mrs. Sturges facilitated the distribution of the many pieces they produced to needy children in New York.[46] Mary also hosted the annual graduation procession through her Cottage gardens.

Mary's emphasis on crafts for women was embraced by her granddaughter, Allison Osborn Webb. Allison, daughter of William Church Osborn, married

Vanderbilt Webb, a great-grandson of Cornelius Vanderbilt, and focused her efforts on furthering the art of craft making, both as a livelihood during the Great Depression and as a cultural art form. She founded the Handcraft Cooperative League of America (now American Craft Council), the School for American Crafts (now a college of Rochester Institute of Technology) the Museum of Contemporary Crafts (now Museum of Arts and Design) and the World Crafts Council that supports ethnic craftsmen worldwide.

In the late 1870s, to the end of her life, Mary Sturges was a key founder and benefactor of the Women's Board of Foreign Missions (WBFM), an organization affiliated with the Dutch Reformed Church. She was the first and long-time President (1875-1894), served on the Board of Managers, and paid the entire cost of printing manuals outlining the many missions the WBFM sponsored. There were other missionary organizations in operation associated with the Reformed Church before 1875, but the WBFM merged all operations and encouraged other missions to form. By their first anniversary meeting in 1876, there were already thirty auxiliary societies doing missionary work under the WBFM banner.[47]

In 1878, the WBFM agreed to establish a missionary school in Nagasaki, Japan, and named the school The Jonathan Sturges Seminary, in tribute to Mary and Jonathan's generous support of foreign missionary activities.[48] Due to staffing challenges, the seminary building construction was delayed until 1887, when it opened in Nagasaki with 17 pupils.[49] Besides the boarding school, the Sturges Seminary taught five English classes a day, Bible study and instruction in music and singing. In 1890, attendance had grown to twenty-two pupils, and a YWCA had also formed, and it was still operating when war with Japan broke out in 1941.[50]

Her work done on this earth, Mary Cady Sturges passed away on July 29, 1894, at the Cottage, twenty years after her beloved husband had died. She originally dictated her memoir to Mrs. Mary G. Fulton in 1885, with a small revision made in 1894 just before her death. It has become an oft-referenced historical journal of life in the nineteenth century in New York. Her obituaries spoke of her charitable and substantial life, including this *New York Times* obituary that read in part:

> Their home on Greenwich Street was the headquarters of the Sketch Club. She entertained the art and literary celebrities of the day there. Bryant, Irving, and Willis were among her friends. Columbia College

was on Murray Street when she resided there. Mrs. Sturges remembered the building of the City Hall, the first steam ferryboats to cross the Hudson, and the first railway and telegraph. Her husband's prominence as a merchant brought public men to their home. She knew nearly all the Presidents. Clay, Webster, and Calhoun enjoyed her hospitality. In later years, her guests included Grant, McClellan, Sherman, Burnside, Hancock, and Farragut...Her home in the city, at Park Avenue and Thirty-Sixth street, was the centre of undertakings in various directions, organized by the charitably disposed, with whom she was ever ready to join.[51]

Mary Sturges' memorial service was held in Fairfield on August 1, 1894, at 3:00 with an extra car added to the 1:00 train from Grand Central Depot to carry her many friends.[52] She was buried next to Jonathan in the East Cemetery and her gravestone reads appropriately: "Blessed are the pure at heart, for they shall see God." Henry Sturges wrote an epilogue to her memoir, *Reminiscences of a Long Life*, as it went to press days after her death:

The thousand acts of kindness, love, and charity, which endeared her to everyone, the record of her life work and example, and the triumphant ending, all these need no words of praise. As the pages of these *Reminiscences* were coming from the press, before she could look upon this last work which had given her so much pleasure, she fell asleep. Surely everyone who knew and loved her will place the proper value upon these precious memorials of a Long Life, so grandly good and holy.[53]

In 1905, the Union Seminary and the Woods Memorial Church established the Mrs. Jonathan Sturges Camp for young boys of impoverished circumstances to enjoy a fresh air vacation. A family friend, Mrs. Hugh Auchincloss (former Emma Brewster Jennings of Fairfield), was the Treasurer of the fund and implored: "Help us perpetuate her memory by giving the boys a chance to see the worth of an honest life."[54]

After Mary's death, Henry was the primary resident and owner of the Fairfield Cottage and proudly maintained the gardens. Its gardens were often noted for exceptional landscaping and beautiful flowers. The 1900 Cottage Garden painting, by family friend Mabel Osgood Wright, captures some of that beauty. Henry and Frederick were active with the Horticultural Society of New York. In 1914, they both earned awards from the Society for flower arrangements (prepared by their gardeners).[55]

Mabel Osgood Wright, *Cottage Garden*, c. 1900[56] and
Cottage Front Prior to Paved Road c. 1880.[57]

Henry had an impressive collection of first edition books, many of which were kept in the Cottage book tower that was built as an addition to the house and in an outbuilding called the "carriage house." Most were sold at auction by the Anderson Galleries after his death. He was the author or co-author of multiple books, including:

- Chronologies of The Life and Writings of William Cullen Bryant, With A Bibliography of His Works in Prose and Verse
- The Poetical Works of William Cullen Bryant
- Social and Intellectual Life of Old Fairfield

Henry was a founder of the Fairfield Historical Society and spent so much time there that his buggy horse "Dave" would leave the house and without guidance go straight there—even when Henry wanted to go somewhere else. The Society's primary purpose was to preserve the town's history and the genealogy of the old families. He was also the founder and president of the Fairfield Beach Company.

Henry Cady Sturges passed away at the Cottage in December 1922, in the same room where he was born. Later in life and continuing after his death, he and his family were forced to sell items, such as his rare book collections and artworks, for financial support. He and Sarah had six children; Henry Pemberton, Ann Adams, George MacWhorter, Mary Cady, Sarah MacWhorter, and John Adams. Ann Adams Sturges married the architect Roger Bullard. They had four children, Roger, Henry, Mary and Jonathan. Mary Bullard married Henry Rousseau and their family moved into the Cottage after they were married and raising their children.

About 1977, after Ann Sturges' death, when the Cottage was part of an estate owned by descendants of Henry Cady Sturges, Mary Rousseau received a knock on the door at the Cottage. The visitors, representing the Westport School for Young Artists, expressed an interest in buying the house from the estate. Mary referred them to her uncle, the executor of the estate, but his alarming response revealed a lack of interest in keeping the house in the family. Valuing the family heritage too much to see the home go out of family control or torn down for development, Mary bought the house from the estate. Mary Bullard Rousseau's husband Henry invented and marketed the product Fritos. Before he passed away in 1972, he sold Fritos to Pepsi, ultimately providing the means for Mary to purchase, live in and maintain the house after her husband's death. She enjoyed sharing her memories and welcomed many guests and groups to the Cottage over the years. Mary's whimsical nature, and the Gothic, haunted house look of the home, inspired her to dress up every year as a witch, delighting in welcoming the many trick-or-treaters to the Cottage. Mary Rousseau sadly passed away in 2015, but at this writing her daughter Mary "Polly" Roessler continues to live in and maintain the historic home.

The Jonathan Sturges House is one of twelve National Historic Landmark Houses in the country occupied by descendants of the original family. In 2016, it won the American Institute of Architects (AIA) People's Choice Award as a Connecticut Treasure. Designed and built in 1840 by the noted architect Joseph Collins Wells, a founder of the AIA, additions were built in 1846, 1883 and 1890 as described by the Connecticut Trust for Historic Preservation:

In 1846, the original lean-to attached at the northwest side of the house was demolished and replaced by a two-and-a-half-story three-bay addition, the roofline of which was built over the original ell and extended west. In 1883, a large three-and-a-half-story block (second addition) was attached on the north side of the 1846 addition. The three-bay structure is distinguished by a clapboarded third-floor book tower which rises from a hipped-roof [e] base. The west wing (1890)[f] contains a scullery and several smaller service rooms on the first floor, and chambers on the upper two floors.[58]

The Cottage has over thirty rooms, thirteen fireplaces and eleven staircases. Although it does not have a public tour schedule, the family has been very generous in opening their home for family gatherings, club outings, and for smaller community events such as the annual Mill Plain Neighborhood Improvement Association gathering. Most of the personal correspondence, books, photographs, paintings and other artworks have been sold or donated to museums through the years, but there are still many interesting historic items there.

Developers demolished the Sturges townhomes on Park Avenue in 1954 but the 1840 Cottage has been owned and lived in by direct descendants of the family since it was built, securing the remarkable legacy of Jonathan Sturges. He and his family achieved significant wealth, and they counted among their friends and associates the famously wealthy, including the Morgans, Vanderbilts, Roosevelts and Astors, as well as politicians, renowned artists, writers, and generals. Yet the poor and disadvantaged could not have found a better friend than Jonathan and Mary. Theirs was a remarkable and truly purposeful life.

---

[e] A hipped roof has slopes on all four sides.

[f] Addition built by Northrop Brothers builders of Southport, CT.

About the Author Robin McPhillips

Born and raised in the Seattle, Washington area, Robin graduated from the U.S. Naval Academy, Annapolis, Maryland. Two decades of aerospace logistics and project management followed, as well as retirement from the Naval Reserve at the rank of Captain. Living in Fairfield, Connecticut for twenty-four years, she served as a docent for several years with the Fairfield Museum and History Center and completed a Master's Degree in American Studies from Fairfield University. Her master's capstone project captured the lens through which Fairfield society viewed and treated immigrants at the turn-of-the-century (19th to 20th century). During this research Robin was exposed to Jonathan Sturges, his 1840 Cottage and his extraordinary legacy—the hook was set. Six years later, she proudly presents the story of *Jonathan Sturges—Merchant of Old New York.*

The author is a member of Biographers International (Bio), the Nineteenth-Century Studies Association (NCSA), Organization of American Historians (OAH), Nonfiction Authors Association (NFAA) and the Independent Book Publishers Association (IBPA). When not writing you'll likely find the author on the golf course or tennis court. Robin is married to Tom McPhillips, a fellow Naval Academy graduate. They have two adult children and live on Hilton Head Island, South Carolina.

Appendices

Appendix I

Selected Partial Family Trees Sturges

Sturges/Osborn Genealogy Trees (Part I)

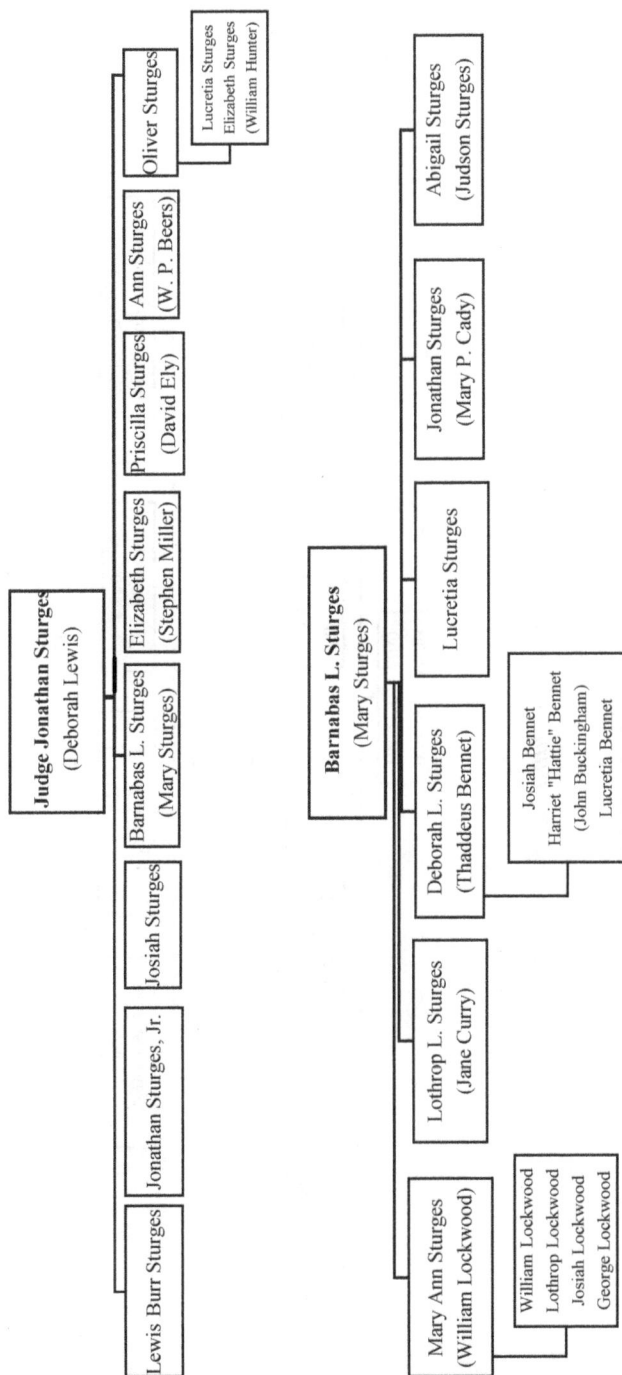

Judge Jonathan Sturges
(Deborah Lewis)

- Lewis Burr Sturges
- Jonathan Sturges, Jr.
- Josiah Sturges
- Barnabas L. Sturges
  (Mary Sturges)
- Elizabeth Sturges
  (Stephen Miller)
- Priscilla Sturges
  (David Ely)
- Ann Sturges
  (W. P. Beers)
- Oliver Sturges
  - Lucretia Sturges
  - Elizabeth Sturges
    (William Hunter)

Barnabas L. Sturges
(Mary Sturges)

- Mary Ann Sturges
  (William Lockwood)
  - William Lockwood
  - Lothrop Lockwood
  - Josiah Lockwood
  - George Lockwood
- Lothrop L. Sturges
  (Jane Curry)
- Deborah L. Sturges
  (Thaddeus Bennet)
  - Josiah Bennet
  - Harriet "Hattie" Bennet
    (John Buckingham)
  - Lucretia Bennet
- Lucretia Sturges
- Jonathan Sturges
  (Mary P. Cady)
- Abigail Sturges
  (Judson Sturges)

Appendix II

Sturges/Osborn Family Genealogy Trees Part II

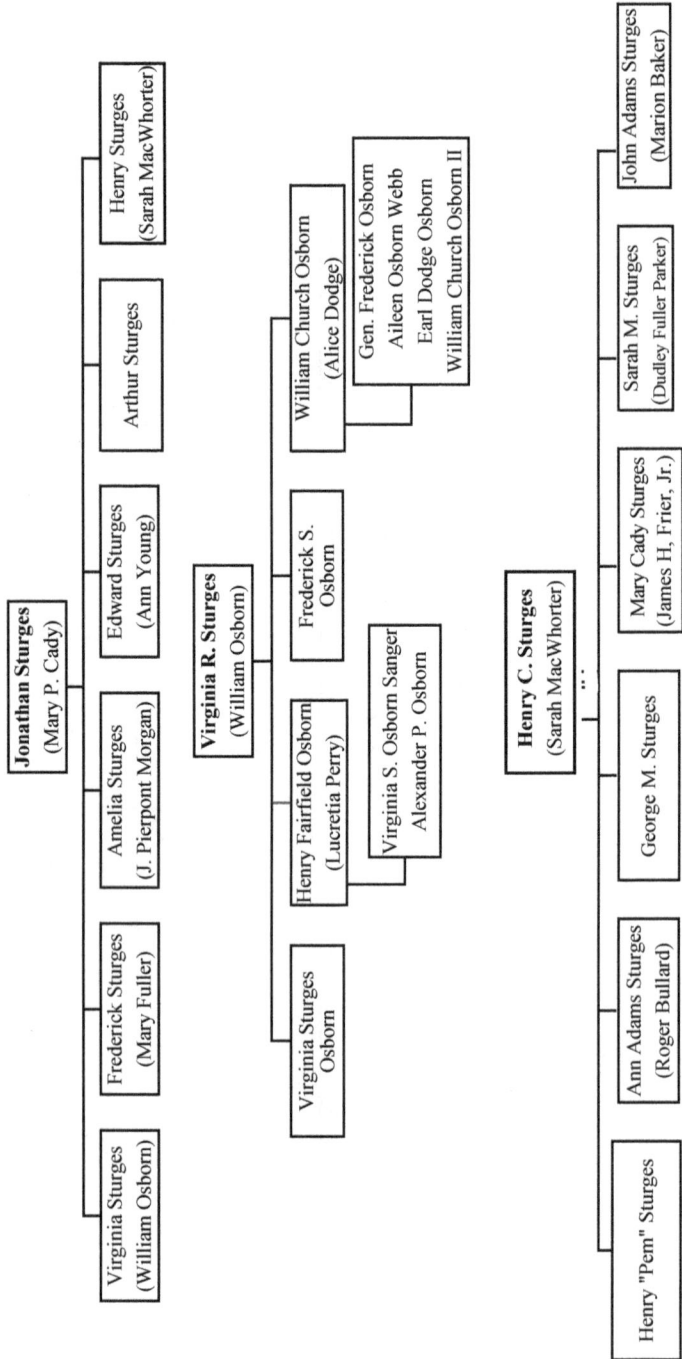

Jonathan Sturges
(Mary P. Cady)

Virginia Sturges
(William Osborn)

Frederick Sturges
(Mary Fuller)

Amelia Sturges
(J. Pierpont Morgan)

Edward Sturges
(Ann Young)

Arthur Sturges

Henry Sturges
(Sarah MacWhorter)

Virginia R. Sturges
(William Osborn)

Virginia Sturges
Osborn

Henry Fairfield Osborn
(Lucretia Perry)

Virginia S. Osborn Sanger
Alexander P. Osborn

Frederick S.
Osborn

William Church Osborn
(Alice Dodge)

Gen. Frederick Osborn
Aileen Osborn Webb
Earl Dodge Osborn
William Church Osborn II

Henry C. Sturges
(Sarah MacWhorter)

Henry "Pem" Sturges

Ann Adams Sturges
(Roger Bullard)

George M. Sturges

Mary Cady Sturges
(James H, Frier, Jr.)

Sarah M. Sturges
(Dudley Fuller Parker)

John Adams Sturges
(Marion Baker)

Rules for Christian MECHANICS, MERCHANTS, &c.

1. I must be industrious, neat, and orderly in my shop or store.
2. I must have order in the general arrangement of my business.
3. I must study economy in all my expenses.
4. I must pledge my purse, my time, and my influence for the preservation of order, intelligence, morality, and religion in the community.
5. I must identify myself with all the interests of the community.
6. I must be temperate in all things—govern my passions and regulate all my appetites.
7. I must be scrupulously honest, and beware of the maxim so common, "No Principle in Trade."
8. I must keep a Debt and Credit account of all my monied transactions, never depending on my memory for the correctness of a single pecuniary matter.
9. I must not feel above my business.
10. I must be true and punctual to all my engagements.
11. I must always begin the day with God, and worship God twice a day in my family, whatever the pressure of business.
12. I must be polite and obliging to my customers
13. I must not urge upon children and the poor such quantities or species of goods and wares as are unsuitable to their judgment and condition in life.
14. I must not encourage lounging about my shop or store.
15. I must not indulge in habits of vain and foolish conversation with my associates.
16. I must not permit rude conduct, nor profane or licentious conversation in my shop or store.
17. I must not permit my shop, or store, to become the repository or dispensary of news, rumors, &c.

18. I must feel the necessity of constantly improving in knowledge and piety.
19. I must feel responsible for the morality and improvement of my clerks and apprentices.
20. I must be the master of my own household, and with a watchful eye guard all its interests.
21. I must be perfectly conscientious in all things—always doing that which is in itself, right, whatever sacrifice I may cost me.
22. I must never do a seemingly small evil to accomplish a seemingly great good.
23. I must not forget that my faults will often be laid to my master's charge.
24. I must not differ with my Christian friends in an angry manner.
25. I must not talk about the failings of others, especially of Christian friends, in their absence.
26. I must live so that all around me may safely follow my example.
27. I must live so as to reprove all sin in all men.
28. I must converse familiarly, frequently, and solemnly with my "hands," shop-mates—clerks—apprentices, and comers-in, on the subject of Religion.
29. I must, if I am a clerk, apprentice, or journeyman, be faithful to the regulations and interests of my employer (so far as they are just and honorable), both in his presence and absence, remembering that God sees me.

American Tract Society, 1830s

Appendix IV

"Lessons From an Old Merchant"

Retirement Address 1868

I wish I had command of language to express to you the emotions which I feel on this occasion. When I consider the kind words you addressed to me in the invitation which has brought us together, and the honorable mention, you have made of me as a man and a merchant, I almost wonder at my sincerity at accepting such an invitation.

If I had not looked beyond my own personality I should have thanked you for your kind courtesy and declined your proffered hospitality, but when I reflected that you might have a double object in conferring this honor upon me, I did not feel at liberty to decline it, unworthy as I felt myself of it. It occurred to me that you might desire an opportunity to discuss that approbation of steady perseverance and watchfulness in business, which I trust I have credit for, with you. It also occurred to me that you desired an opportunity to warn the younger merchants against the prevalent desire to accumulate wealth hastily, thereby endangering the property of their creditors and their own integrity.

If this testimony to me shall prove an incentive to the young business men of this and other communities to greater caution in these respects, I shall feel that a double honor has been conferred upon me. I am not so vain as to suppose that I have not often erred in my judgment as to what was just in my dealings with others; this perfection is not attained by any man. I thank God that I have been so guided as, upon the whole, to meet the approval of such a body of merchants as I now see about me, and I pray that I may still be so guided as not to forfeit their good opinion.

I see around me who are my seniors in business as well as my superiors. I also see those who are younger. I see those who are the successors of honorable men now dead. I do not see any upon whom the stain of dishonor rests.

Such a Jury as this is not often assembled, to pass judgment upon the business career of any man, and a verdict of approval is a rich legacy to leave to one's posterity. You may well have supposed it was not an easy matter to bring my mind to withdraw from active business life. Habits of forty-five years standing cannot be changed at once pleasantly, or perhaps, safely. However, we may theorize upon the subject, it is not such an easy matter as many suppose, for a man who has been forty or fifty years in a prosperous business, to withdraw from it. If he has the feelings of a man, how can he withdraw from all the pleasant business associations which have clustered around him; how can he sever his connection with men who have given him their confidence for twenty, thirty, or forty years; how can he withdraw from those who have looked to him for advice and encouragement, without the deepest feelings of regret. It is a great mistake to suppose that merchants continue in business late in life merely for the purpose of accumulating property.

Perhaps it is providential that I have been let to take this steep, before I arrived at that period of life when my friends would not be willing to incur my displeasure by intimating that the falling powers of my mind rendered it advisable that I should retire.

Many years ago, I knew an upright Judge, who retired from the bench when he was sixty-one. The members of the Bar remonstrated and told him he would be as competent to fill the office when he was seventy, as he was then. His only reply was; 'Gentlemen, if I hold the office until I am seventy, I am afraid I shall think just as you do.' I do not intend, however, to withdraw myself from Front Street entirely, as long as I am able to go there. I intend to retain an office on the old location, where I shall be glad to see my business friends, and to advise with young merchants and clerks when I can be of service to them. Nor is it my intention to lead as idle a life, so long as the power to be useful is continued to me. I have never believed that any man could be happy who lived entirely for himself. It will be a source of great satisfaction to me, if I can feel that I am permitted, to retain the friendship of my old associates and to have the privilege of cooperating with them in various ways for the public good.

But my friends, with all my eagerness to remain young, and with you in the activities of life, I cannot and ought not forget that I am approaching the limit of life as appointed by our Maker, and I prefer to take home to myself the thought so beautifully expressed by Dr. Chalmers, that our life is divided, as the week in to six days or decades of years of preparation for, and engagement in, the activities of life; the second day or decade ought to be the Sabbath of rest and more near contemplation of that, "eternal rest which remaineth for the city of God."

Pardon me gentlemen for talking so much about myself. I have tried to think of something that would interest you, and really, I could not think of anything but myself; this is all owing to the importance you have given me. I cannot talk to you about Finances; you all understand these better than I do. I never was much of a financier; I never could run in debt, without first considering how I was to get out of it, and, besides, the subject has been worn thread-bare.

I cannot talk to you about politics. I never had any genius in that line, and if I had I do not think I could say much that would be satisfactory just now. I do not think it necessary to talk about patriotism, love of the Union, etc.; we have stood shoulder to shoulder in that line and need not glorify ourselves. I cannot talk to you about the action of Congress; I think it more prudent to wait and see what it all means. I cannot talk to you about General Grant. He prefers to speak for himself. I cannot talk to you about yourselves; it would not be considered as in good taste here.

Now, gentlemen, since there is nothing that I can talk about that you do not understand a great deal better than I do, I propose to say a few words for the benefit of the young men outside, and if you approve of what is said, let it be considered as said by the Grand Jury of Merchants now assembled.

One of the first lessons I received was in 1813, when I was eleven years of age. My grandfather had collected a fine flock of merino sheep, with were cherished during the War of 1812-15. I was a shepherd boy whose business was to watch the sheep in the fields. A boy who was more fond of his books than of sheep, was sent with me, but he left the work to me, while he lay in the shade and read his books. I finally complained of this to the old gentleman. I shall never forget his benevolent smile as he replied: "<u>Never you mind; if you watch the sheep, you will have the sheep</u>." I thought to myself what does the old gentleman mean? I don't expect to have any sheep. My aspirations were quite moderate in those days, and a first-rate merino buck was worth $1,000. I could not make out exactly what he meant, but I had great confidence in him, as he was a judge, and had been to Congress in Washington's time: so, I concluded that it was all right, whatever he meant, and went out contentedly with the sheep. After I went back to the field I couldn't get that idea out of my head. Then I thought of my Sunday lesson: "Thou hast been faithful over a few things, will make thee ruler over many things." Then I understood it: "<u>Never you mind who else neglects his duty; be you faithful and you will have your reward</u>." I do not think it will take many lads as long as I did to understand this proverb.

I received my second lesson soon after I came to this city as a clerk to the late Luman Reed. A merchant from Ohio, who knew me, came to purchase goods of Mr. Reed. He expressed his gratification at finding me there and said to me: "You have got a good place. Make yourself so useful that they cannot do without you." I took his meaning quicker than I did the proverb about the sheep. Well, I worked upon these two ideas until Mr. Reed offered me an interest in the business. The first morning after the partnership was announced, James Geery, the old tea merchant called to see me, and said to me: You are all right now: I have one word of advice for you; be careful who you walk the streets with. That was lesson number three.

In this connection I must repeat an anecdote told of the late Robert Lennox. A country merchant came into the store of Mr. Morton, a highly respectable Scotch merchant, to purchase goods. He spoke about credit, references, etc. Mr. Morton said: "I will give you what credit you wish. "But, said the merchant; I am, an entire stranger to you." Mr. Morton replied: "Did I not see you at church with Robert Lennox?" "Yes, I was at church with him.'" 'Well, I will trust any man whom Robert Lennox will take to church with him." I hope these three lessons of watchfulness over the interests of their employers, watchfulness over their partner's interests and their own, after they are joined, followed by intense watchfulness that no black sheep creep into their folds, may be impressed by these anecdotes upon the minds of those for whom they are intended.

One other lesson I feel it very necessary to inculcate is that of patience. With a little patience, most young men will find a position as high as they have fitted themselves to fill. In all the changes which have taken place in my firm since 1822. No partner has been brought in who has not served as a clerk in the establishment. And I now leave my house well organized, prosperous and free from complications, still in the hands of those who have served in it as clerks for a longer or shorter period. I mention this as encouragement to young men to persevere in the faithful performance of their duties."

I feel that it would be unpardonable for me not to allude, before closing, to the kindness which I received in my early business course from some of the noble merchants of those days. While Mr. Reed lived, I never needed a friend or adviser. When he died in 1836, the case was altered, but kind friends stood ready to take his place. All the prominent merchants expressed their sympathy, but I was more particularly indebted to Mr. George Griswold, Mr. Jonathan Goodhue, Mr. Pelatiah Perit and Messrs. Gardiner and Samuel Howland. Each of these came to me within a few days after Mr. Reed's death and said to me:

"You must not think of letting the establishment go down; we do not know how you are left as to Capital, but if you need more than you have, we will furnish it to you." I did not appreciate the offer any less, because I had no occasion to avail myself of it. The confidence then expressed was not withdrawn from me while they lived. It is pleasant to me to mention it now, in the presence of the Sons or successors of each of them. And now, my friends and neighbors, I pray you to excuse the imperfect manner in which I have addressed you, and to accept the warmest thanks for the honor you have conferred upon me.

"A Complimentary Dinner to Jonathan Sturges," 1868, p. 13-21

Appendix V

Jonathan Sturges Art and Sculpture Holdings

Reference Listing

This listing is a compilation of those artworks credited to have been in the collection of Jonathan Sturges. Little documentation was kept by the family over the years as works were sold, donated or distributed to various family members. As a result, the location of most of these items is unknown. However, the digital age has enabled the continuing discovery of items that were once owned by Jonathan Sturges, as well as the location of some of these items. Museum records, art journals, exhibition records, newspaper reports, the *Crayon* art periodical, National Academy of Design records, authoritative books, national artwork databases, auction records, graduate research, family records and other miscellaneous research has been used to compile this table of art items. Where there is a question mark, sources disagre. The effort to add to and update this list will continue as more infor-mation comes to light. The author welcomes inputs to this living document (www.jonathansturges.com).

Table Legend

Known Owners or Locations:

(B) – Museum of Fine Arts Boston; (Bk) – Brooklyn Museum; (Cr) – Currier Museum of Art, Manchester, NH; (CM) – Chrysler Museum, Norfolk, VA; (JPM) – Morgan Library and Museum; (L) – Long Island Museum, Stonybrook; (M) – Metropolitan Museum of Art; (N) – National Gallery of Art; (NYH) – New York Historical Society, Cooperstown; (P) – Private Collection; PF – Family Collection; Wadsworth Atheneum, Hartford, CT

	Year	Painting	Artist or Engraver	Loc
1	1837	View on the Catskill- Early Autumn aka View of the Catskill Mountain	Thomas Cole	M
2	1841	Sunset in the Catskills aka Catskill Creek	Thomas Cole	B
3	1841	Mill Dam on the Catskill Creek	Thomas Cole	Cr
4	1844	View on the Thames	Thomas Cole	B
5	1839	View of the Mountain Pass Called the Notch of the White Mountains	Thomas Cole	N
6	1865	Falls at Catskill (drawing-lithograph)	Thomas Cole	
7	1838	Sketch for the Ohio State Capitol Design	Thomas Cole	N
8	bef. 1867	Faith Holding the Sacramental Chalice	Robert W. Weir	
9		Child's Devotion aka The Child's Evening Prayer	Robert W. Weir	
10	1847	Flower Girl	C. Ingham	M
11		Day Dream	C. Ingham	
12		Bertha	C. Ingham	
13	1843	Stealing Milk aka Caught in the Act	F. Edmonds	
14	1842	The Bashful Cousin	F. Edmonds	N
15		Mischief in the Pantry	F. Edmonds	
16	1841	News Boy	Henry Inman	
17	1855	Woodland Interior	A.B. Durand	B

	Year	Painting	Artist or Engraver	Loc
18	1855	Woodland Interior	A.B. Durand	B
19		A Composition (Landscape)- (2) unnamed landscapes	A.B. Durand	
20	1836	Composition (possibly alt name for View Near Saugerties)	A.B. Durand	
21	1842	Shakespeare's Church at Stratford aka View, Church at Stratford on Avon	A.B. Durand	
22	1842	View in the Valley of the Oberhasle, Switzerland aka Alpine View, Near Meyringen	A.B. Durand	
23	1836	View near Saugerties	A.B. Durand	P
24	1842	Copy of Titian's Graces	A.B. Durand	
25	1840	Copy of Soldier Visiting a Young Woman by Gabriel Metsu	A.B. Durand	
26	1855	In the Woods	A.B. Durand	M
27	1852	God's Judgment Upon Gog	A.B. Durand	CM
28		Portrait of a Turk	A.B. Durand	
29	1855	Forest in the Morning Light**	A.B. Durand	N
30		Music Lesson (copy of Metsu)	A.B. Durand	
31	1842	The Knight and the Lady (copy of Metsu)	A.B. Durand	
32	1841	Group of Children	A.B. Durand	
33	1840	Self-Portrait (after Rembrandt)	A.B. Durand	W
34	1842	Several copies and studies of heads from nature	A.B. Durand	
35		Italian Girl Asleep by the Wayside aka Sleeping Girl/Girl Asleep in a Forest	D. Huntington	
36		The Amanuensis	D. Huntington	
37		Hagar and Ishmael	D. Huntington	
38	1846	Proserpine and Bacchus	Henry Peters Gray	
39	1850	Young Poetess	Henry Peters Gray	
40		Greek Lovers*	Henry Peters Gray	M
41		Hagar and Ishmael	Henry Peters Gray	
42	1836	Farmer's Nooning	William S. Mount	L
43	1842	Ringing the Hog aka Ringing the Pig/Scene in a Long Island Farm-yard	William S. Mount	NYH

*Bought by Mrs. Jonathan Sturges after Jonathan's Death
** Ownership attributed to both Jonathan and Frederick Sturges

	Year	Painting	Artist or Engraver	Loc
44	1851	Who'll turn the Grindstone aka Turning the Grindstone/Axe to Grind/Tardy Scholar	William S. Mount	L
45		Girl and Cottage	William S. Mount	
46		Tropical Landscape	Frederic Edwin Church	
47	1855	The Cordilleras: Sunrise	Frederic Edwin Church	P
48	1870	Arabian Desert aka Landscape South America	Frederic Edwin Church	P
49	1870	Study of Jerusalem	Frederic Edwin Church	
50	1857	View of Amalfi, Bay of Salerno	George Loring Brown	M
51		Hebrew Women Borrowing the Jewels of the Egyptians	John Gadsby Chapman	
52	1843	Spoiling the Egyptians	John Gadsby Chapman	
53		Etruscan Girl	John Gadsby Chapman	
54		Life size study of a donkey's head	John Gadsby Chapman	
55	1849	Copy of Old Couple Reading the Bible by Garrett Dou	John Gadsby Chapman	P
56	1857	Beacon Rock, Newport Harbor**	John F. Kensett	
57	1869/72	Beach at Beverley**	John F. Kensett	N
58	bef. 1861	Landscape (Marine) aka Coastal Landscape ***	John F. Kensett	N
59	1837	View on Lake George**	John Williams Casilear	N
60	1855	Early Autumn	John Williams Casilear	
61		A Bit of the Housatonic	Alfred F. Bunner	PF
62	1863	Sheep	Eugene Verboeckhoven	
63	1858	A Lady (Crayon)	Vincent Colyer	
64	1853	A Landscape (water colors)	Davison Davidson	
65	1871	Marine Landscape	Edward Moran	
66		Landscape	William Hart	
67		Marine Landscape	David Johnson	
68		Landscape	David Johnson	PF
69		Seascape	William Hazeltine	

** Ownership attributed to both Jonathan Sturges and his son Frederick
*** Birthday gift by artist to Amelia Sturges

	Year	Painting	Artist or Engraver	Loc
70		Venetian Scene	possibly Thomas Moran	
71		Landscape with Apple Blossoms	William Russell Smith	
72	1843	Columbus Before the Court of Ferdinand and Isabella	Emmanuel Leutze	Bk
73	1867	Atmospheric Landscape	Hitterzog or Hitterzog	
74	1857	A Boy	Samuel Worcester Rouse	
75	1855	Children and Dog	Benjamin Vautier	
76	1859	Landscape	Hendrick D.K. Van Elten	
77		Unk	William H. Beard	
78		The Cloisters	unk	
79		Five Children in a Doorway Shelling Peanuts	unk	
80		The Disappointed Hunter	unk	
81		Interior painting with old man and woman (probably a copy)	unk	
82	1793	Portrait Dr. William Hartigan	Gilbert Stuart	N
83	1840	Portrait, Jonathan Sturges	A.B. Durand	M
84	1850s	Portrait, Jonathan Sturges	A.B. Durand	
85	1840s	Portrait, John Cady	A.B. Durand	PF
86	1840	Portrait, Virginia & Frederick Sturges	A.B. Durand	PF
87	1840s	Portrait, Amelia & Edward Sturges	A.B. Durand	JPM
88	1836	Portrait, Luman Reed	A.B. Durand	M
89		Portrait, Mother Sturges	A.B. Durand	PF
90		Portrait, Mary Pemberton Cady Sturges	Charles Cromwell Ingham	PF
91		Portrait, Ebenezer Pemberton	unk	PF
92		Portrait, Luther Smith, Soldier of Revolutionary War	unk	PF

	Year	Painting	Artist or Engraver	Loc
		Prints/Engravings/Mezzotints		
1		Copy of an Adriaen van Ostade	unk	
2		Engraving of *Guido's Aurora*	Engr. Raphael Morghan	
3		Engraving of *Angels and Apostles- Antonio de Correggio*	Engr. P. Toschi	
4		Engraving of set of *Correggio's Loves of Jupiter (4)*	Engr. P. Toschi	
5	1787	Engraving of *Gleaners* by Henry William Bunbury	Engr. P. Toschi	
6	1784	Engraving of *Morning Employments* by Henry William Bunbury	Engr. Tomkins	
7		Engraving of Il Guercino Unk title drawn by Toffanelli	Engr. Raphael Morghan	
8	1816	Engraving of *Venus and Adonis* by Francesco Albani (Print #9)	Engr. P. Toschi	
9	1840	Engraving of *Pastoral Scene of Lake Nemi* by Joseph M. W. Turner	Engr. Robert Wallace	
10	bef. 1851	Print- *Lowstoffe Lighthouse* Joseph M. W. Turner Print #23	Printed by James C. Allen	
11	1782	Print- *Achilles Among the Daughters of Lycomedes* by Angelica K. Ulysses	Published by J. Boydell	
12	1826	Lithograph pencil Portrait of Mrs. Ellen Kean, Actress *"Ellen Tree"*	Abraham Wivell	
13	1727	Mezzotint print of *Mrs. Anastasia Robinson* by John Vanderbank	Print by John Fabar the Ygr	
14	1778	Mezzotint print of *Israel Putnam of Continental Forces 1775* by F. J. Wilkinson	Published by C. Shepherd	
15	1735	Mezzotint print of *Richard Van Bleek* by Petrus Johannes (Pieter) Van Bleek	P.J. Van Bleek	
16	1792	*Map/Plan of the City of Wash.* D.C. Andrew Ellicott's rev. of C. L'Enfant original	Engr. Thakara & Vallance	
17	1801	Engraving of *Spirit of Child Arrived in the Presence of the Almighty* by Wm. Peters	Engr. Francesco Bartolozzi	
18		Print of 1700s Baroque hunting scene by Peiters Serwouters	Unk	
19	1825	*Musidora* (owned by HCS at his death) engraving	Engr. A.B. Durand	
20		*Crossing the Brook* engraving (1 of 500 saved by Turner)	Joseph M. W. Turner	
		Sculpture		
1	1850	*Thomas Cole* (Bust)	Henry Kirke Brown	
2	1844	*Washington Allston* (Bust)	Edward Augustus Bracket	M
3	1850	*The Good Angel Conducting the Soul to Heaven*	Henry Kirke Brown	M

Selected Bibliography

Ackerman, William K. *Historical Sketch of the Illinois Central Railroad, Together with a Brief Biographical Record of Its Incorporators and Some of Its Early Officers.* Chicago: Fergus Printing Co., 1890. Google Books.

A Record of the Metropolitan Fair in aid of the United States Sanitary Commission, held at New York in April 1864, US Sanitary Commission. New York: Herd & Houghton, 1867.

Barile, K.S and Barbara Willis (Eds.). *A Woman in a War-Torn Town, The Journal of Jane Howison Beale, 1850-1867.* Fredericksburg: Downing Co., 1979.

Barker, George, "Luman Reed Reminiscence," Luman Reed papers, 1820-1895, Mss Collection (Reed Box Non-circulating), New York Historical Society, New York, NY, 1884.

Becker, Sven, *The Monied Metropolis: New York City and the Consolidation of the American Bourgeoisie, 1850-1896.* New York: Cambridge University Press, 2001.

Bellows, Henry, *An Historical Sketch of the Union League Club-Its Origin, Organization and Work, 1863-1879,* New York: By the Club, 1879.

Bellevue: A Short History of Bellevue Hospital and the Training Schools. Alumni Association of Bellevue: Pension Fund Committee. New York: American Lithographic Co., 1915. The Internet Archive (archive.org).

Bigelow, John, *William Cullen Bryant,* Boston: Houghton-Mifflin Co., 1890.

Bishop, Nathan, L.L.D., ed. *A Memorial Record of the New York Branch of the United States Christian Commission,* New York: John A. Gray & Green, 1866. Internet Archive (archive.org).

Buckingham, Ebenezer, *Solomon Sturges and His Descendants: A Memoir and a Genealogy.* New York: Grafton Press, 1907. The Internet Archive (archive.org).

Bulkley, Jonathan *The Journals of Jonathan Bulkley,* Vol. I, 1802-1826, Vol. II, 1844-1858, Pequot Library, Southport, CT.

Child, Frank Samuel, *An Old New England Town, Sketches of Life, Scenery, Character.* New York: Scribner, 1895.

Clark, Eliot, *History of the National Academy of Design, 1825-1953.* New York: Columbia University Press, 1954.

A Complimentary dinner to Jonathan Sturges, Library of Congress (CT275.S895 C6), 1868. The Internet Archive (archive.org).

Cummings, Thomas S. *Historic Annals of the National Academy of Design.* New York: G.W. Childs, 1861. Google Books.

Cutter, William Richard. *Genealogical and Family History of the State of Connecticut: A Record of the Achievements of Her People in the Making of a Commonwealth and the Founding of a Nation Vol. III.* New York: Lewis Historical Publishing Co., 1911. Internet Archive (archive.org).

Deems, Charles F. "Jonathan Sturges," *Frank Leslie's Sunday Magazine*, V.4, Oct. 1878. HathiTrust.

Durand, John. *The Life and Times of A.B. Durand, 1822-1908.* New York: Charles Scribner & Sons, 1894. HathiTrust.

Farnham, Thomas J. *Fairfield: The History of a Community, 1639-1989.* Fairfield Historical Society. Fairfield: Phoenix Publishing, 1988.

Foshay, Ella M. *Mr. Luman Reed's Picture Gallery.* New York: Harry N. Abrams, Inc., 1990.

"The First Extant Parish Record of Christ Church–Record of Baptism 1785-1806," Fairfield, Connecticut, http://dunhamwilcox.net/ct/christ_ch_fairfield6.htm.

Giles, Dorothy, *A Candle in Her Hand: A Story of the Nursing Schools of Bellevue Hospital* New York: Putnam, 1949. https://babel.hathitrust.org/cgi/pt?id=mdp.39015007154605;view=1up;seq=141.

Hobson, Elizabeth. *Recollections of a Happy Life.* New York: Self Published, 1914.

Hornberger, Eric. *Mrs. Astor's New York: Money and Power in a Gilded Age.* New Haven: Yale University Press, 2002.

Howatt, John K. and Natalie Spassky, et.al., Eds. *19th-century America: Paintings and Sculpture: An Exhibition in-Celebration of One Hundred Years.* April 16-September 7, 1970 Issue 1: "Asher B. Durand, *Kindred Spirits,*" Metropolitan Museum of Art, New York, NY. New York: Graphic Society Limited, 1970. Google Books.

Jonathan Sturges Receipt Book, Jonathan Sturges Papers, American Archives of Art, Smithsonian Institution. ID:16627. Vol. I (1843-1852) & Vol. II (1844-1858). http://www.aaa.si.edu/collections/items/detail/jonathan-sturges-receipt-book-16627.

Jonathan Sturges Papers 1834-1866, American Archives of Art, Smithsonian, ACL-1. Digital Archive.

Kansfield, Mary L. *Letters to Hazel-Ministry within the Woman's Board of Foreign Missions of the Reformed Church of America.* Reformed Church Press. Grand Rapids: William B. Eerdmans Publishing, 2004.

Levine, David B., *Anatomy of a Hospital, Hospital for Special Surgery, 1863-2013,* Hospital for Special Surgery. New York: Print Matters, 2013.

Longworth, David. *Longworth's American Almanac, New York City 1825-26.* New York: David Longworth, 1826. https://archive.org/details/longworthsameric18256long?q= 1825+longworth%27s+almanac.

Lossing, B. J., C.C. Moreau and G.E. Perine, *History of New York City: Embracing an outline sketch of events from 1609 to 1830, and a full account of its development from 1830 to 1884,* Vol. II. New York: Perine Engraving and Publishing, 1884. GoogleBooks.

Nesbitt, George F., Ed., *Banquet Given by the Members of the Union League Club of 1863-1864: To Commemorate the Departure for the Seat of War of the Twentieth Regiment of United States Colored Troops Raised by the Club*. New York: George F. Nesbitt, 1886.

New York Supreme Court Testimony, Nov. 12, 1863, Records of the New York Supreme Court, *The New York and New Haven Railroad against Morris Ketcham and Edward Bement, Survivors of Thos. Rogers impleaded with Robert Schuyler and others*, 1866.

Oschner, Jeffrey Carl, *H.H. Richardson Complete Architectural Works*. Boston: Massachusetts Institute of Technology, 1982.

Osborn Family Papers (OFP), 1832-1836. MS474-Mss Collection (Osborn Non-circulating). New York Historical Society, New York, NY.

Osborn and Dodge Family Papers, 1726-1983. CO537, Manuscripts Division, Department of Rare Books and Special Collections, Princeton University Library, Princeton, New Jersey.

Perry, Kate E., *Ye Old Burying Ground*. Hartford: American Publishing Co. 1882. Internet Archive (archive.org).

Reed and Sturges Account Book 1833-1835, Mss Collection, BV Reed and Sturges Non-circulating. New York Historical Society, New York, NY.

Rousmaniere, John. *The Union League Club, 1863-2013*. Union League Club: New York, N.Y., 2013.

Rousseau, Mary B. *The Jonathan Sturges Cottage : Its Builder, Architect and Family Owners 1840-2007*. Fairfield: Self-published, 2007.

Scoville, Joseph Alfred, ed. Walter Barret, *Old Merchants of New York*, Vol I. New York: Carleton, 1863. Internet Archive (archive.org).

Scoville, Joseph, Walter Barrett ed. *Old Merchants of New York*, Vol. III. Thomas R . Knox: New York, 1885. Internet Archive (archive.org).

Stillé, Charles Janeway *History of the United States Sanitary Commission*. New York: Herd and Houghton, 1868. Internet Archive (archive.org).

Strouse, Jean *Morgan: American Financier*. New York: Random House, 2012.

Schenck, Elizabeth Hubbell *The History of Fairfield, Fairfield County, Connecticut, From the Settlement of the Town in 1639 to 1818*, Vol I. New York: Self Published, 1889. Google Books.

Sturges Family Papers (SFP) 1775-1905. ARC-1218 Pierpont Morgan Library, New York, NY.

Sturges, Jonathan, *Some Reminiscences of the Progress of Art in New York*, for the *Dear Crayon* periodical, undated, ARC 1218, Folder.3.8, SFP, PML.

Sturges, Mary Cady. *Reminiscences of a Long Life*. New York: F.E. Parrish & Co., 1894

Sturges, Virginia, Journal of, 1851-1852, Box 23-24A, OFP, NYHS. Union League Club of New York, "Monthly Meeting Minutes." Union League Club Archives, New York, NY.

United States Sanitary Commission. "Statement of the Object and Missions of the U.S. Sanitary Commission," Document No. 69. New York: William C. Bryant & Co., 1863. The Internet Archive (archive.org).

Endnotes

Citation abbreviations: AS–Arthur Sturges; AmS–Amelia Sturges; CHS–Connecticut Historical Society, Hartford, CT; HCS–Henry Cady Sturges; FS–Frederick Sturges; JS-Jonathan Sturges; MS-Mary Cady Sturges; ODFP-Osborn and Dodge Family Papers; OFP-Osborn Family Papers: JPM-J.P. Morgan; NYHS–New York Historical Society, New York, NY; NYPL–New York Public Library: PML–Pierpont Morgan Library, New York, NY; PUL–Princeton University Library, Princeton, NJ; SFP-Sturges Family Papers; *NYT–New York Times* (New York, NY); VS–Virginia Sturges; VSO–Virginia Sturges Osborn

Acknowledgements

1 Mary Rousseau, Obituary picture, October 2015.
2 Mary Rousseau in library, with Judge Jonathan Sturges gavel, photo by author.

Introduction

1 "Misc.," *Tribute Territorial Enterprise* (Virginia City, NV), December 12, 1874, p. 6.

Chapter 1

1 Cutter, *Genealogical and Family History,* p. 1468.
2 Perry, *Ye Old Burying Ground,* p. 105.
3 Barber, John Warner, *Connecticut Historical Collections, General Collection of Interesting Facts, Traditions, Biographical Sketches, Anecdotes, &c., Relating to the History and Antiquities of Every Town in Connecticut, with Geographical Descriptions,* South view Borough of Southport, (drawing) (Hartford: A. Willard, 1836), p. 361. Google Books.
4 The First Extant Parish Record of Christ Church, Record of Baptisms Fairfield, 1785-1806 http://dunhamwilcox.net/ct/christ_ch_fairfield6.htm (accessed November 7, 2013).
5 Child, *Old New England Town,* p. 223.
6 Ibid, p. 223.
7 Farnham, *Fairfield,* p. 111
8 Barnabas L. Sturges, 1810 United States Federal Census, Fairfield County, Fairfield, CT, digital image, Ancestry.com www.ancestry.com (accessed November 8, 2013).
9 Atwater, Rev. Lyman H., "The Christian Merchant," *New York Observer and Chronicle,* December 24, 1874.
10 A *Complimentary Dinner to Jonathan Sturges,* p. 18.
11 Bulkley, *The Journals of Jonathan Bulkley,* Vol I, p.147.
12 Farnham, *Fairfield,* p. 127.
13 Sturges, *Reminiscences,* p. 12.
14 Daggett, David, *A Serious Remonstrance to the People of Connecticut Against Changing Their Government,* Hartford: Hudson & Goodwin, 1805.
15 Buckingham, *Solomon Sturges,* pg. 24.

Chapter 2

1 Sturges, *Reminiscences*, p. 9-13.
2 Ibid, p. 12.
3 Ibid, p. 12.
4 Ibid, p. 22.
5 Ibid, p. 22.
6 Ibid, p. 26.
7 Ibid, p. 31.
8 Ibid, p. 35.
9 Bulkley, *The Journals of Jonathan Bulkley*, Vol I., p. 138.
10 JS to Lothrop Sturges, February 23, 1817.
11 Sturges, *Reminiscences*, p. 37.
12 Ibid, p. 37.
13 "Obituary," *Titusville (PA) Herald*, September 13, 1872, pg. 1.
14 Child, *Old New England Town*, p. 220.
15 Scoville, *Old Merchants*, Vol I, p. 93-94.
16 "Jonathan Sturgess," *The Steven's Point (WI) Journal*, October 23, 1886, p. 6.
17 Barker, *Luman Reed*, p. 32.
18 Rousseau, *Sturges Cottage*, p. 7.
19 Deems, "Jonathan Sturges," p. 417.
20 Wardley, Rosemary, Erie Canal Map, https://commons.wikimedia.org/wiki/File:Erie-CanalMap.jpg (accessed September 9, 2018). https://commons.wikimedia.org/wiki/Category:Maps_of_the_Erie_Canal#/media/File:ErieCanalMap.jpg
21 Durand, *Life and Times*, p. 105.
22 Scoville, *Old Merchants*, Vol. III, p. 47.

Chapter 3

1 Sturges, *Reminiscences*, p. 81.
2 Longworth, *Almanack, 1825-26*, p. 405.
3 Sturges, *Reminiscences*, p. 92.
4 Bulkley, *The Journals of Jonathan Bulkley*, Vol I, p. 243.
5 Sturges, Reminiscences, p. 100.
6 Longworth, Thomas, *Longworth's American Almanac, New-York Register and City Directory for 1827, (*New York: Seymour Printer, 1827), p. 6.
7 Hemans, Felicia, Records of Women and Other Poems, (Gilly: New York, 1828), p. 321,
8 Sturges, *Reminiscences*, p. 110.
9 *New York, Marriage Newspaper Extracts, 1801-1880 (Barber Collection)* p.97 (database on-line.: Ancestry.com Operations Inc., Provo, UT, USA, 2005: accessed April 12, 2014).
10 Longworth, Thomas, *Longworth's American Almanac, New-York Register and City Directory for 1829.*, (New York: Thomas Longworth, 1829), p. 540.
11 Sturges, *Reminiscences*, p. 125.
12 MS to JS August 18, 1834, ARC-1218, Pt. 4, SFP, PML.
13 Ibid.
14 MS to JS, July 8, 1831, ARC-1218, Pt. 4, SFP, PML.
15 MS to JS, July 12, 1831, ARC-1218, Pt. 4, SFP, PML.
16 Ibid.

17 MS to JS, August 10, 1831, ARC-1218, Pt. 4, SFP, PML.

18 Ibid.

19 MS to JS, July 17, 1834, ARC-1218, Pt. 4, SFP, PML.

20 MS to JS, August 28, 1831, ARC-1218, Pt. 4, SFP, PML.

21 MS to JS, August 31, 1831, ARC-1218, Pt. 4, SFP, PML.

22 MS to JS, Aug 19, 1834, ARC-1218, Pt. 4, SFP, PML.

23 Sturges, *Reminiscences*, p. 128.

24 MS to JS, August 17, 1831, ARC-1218, Pt. 4, SFP, PML.

25 JS to MS, Aug.13, 1838, ARC-1218, Pt. 3, SFP, PML.

26 Sturges, *Reminiscences*, p. 136.

27 Ibid, p. 138.

28 Ibid, p. 138-139.

29 Scientific: "The Cholera Its Symptoms and Moue of Treatment," *Mercury* (New York, NY), Vol. I, Issue 34, August 22, 1832, p. 267.

30 Sturges, *Reminiscences*, p.139-140.

31 Wilford, James Noble, "How Epidemics Shaped the Modern Metropolis," *NYT*, April 15, 2008, p. D4. *NYT* digital archive.

32 Ibid, D4.

33 Scoville, *Old Merchants* Vol. III, p. 50.

34 Ibid, p. 46.

35 Sturges, *Reminiscences*, p.145.

36 Ibid, p. 146-7.

37 Pfieiffer, Judith & Robert C. Burns, *A Guide to the History and Heritage of Pecander Hundred, Newcastle and Frenchtown, Railroad*, Pecander Heritage Area Association http://www.pencaderheritage.org/main/landmarks/phland_p18.html (accessed November 16, 2013).

38 JS to MS, December 19, 1832, New Bern N.C., OFP.

39 Ibid.

40 JS to MS, New Bern/Smithville, N.C., December 17, 1832, OFP.

41 JS to MS, January 8, 1833, ARC 1218, Pt. 3, SFP, PML.

42 MS to JS, December 25, 1832, Box 1, OFP.

43 Sturges, *Reminiscences*, p. 151-155.

Chapter 4

1 Sturges, *Reminiscences*, p. 156.

2 Scoville, *Old Merchants*, Vol. III, p. 49.

3 "Atlantic Garden House" (Burns' Coffee House in 1765.) Broadway/Bowling Green, NYPL Digital Gallery, Image ID: 805534,1856 http://digitalcollections.nypl.org/items/510d47e0-d6b2-a3d9-e040-e00a18064a99#/?zoom=true (accessed November 19, 2013).

4 Sturges, *Reminiscences*, p. 162.

5 Ibid p. 159.

6 Sturges, Jonathan, "Some Reminiscences of the Progress of Art in New York."

7 Harshaw, Tobin, "Artists and Writers in a New World," November 19, 2000, *NYT on the Web*, http://www.nytimes.com/books/00/11/19/bookend/bookend.html, accessed November 20, 2013.

8 Stock Quotes, *Evening Post* (New York, NY), April 8, 1830, p.3.

9 Lossing, Moreau and Perine, p. 506.

10 Jonathan, "Some Reminiscences of the Progress of Art in New York."

11 Huntington, Daniel, 1816-1906. *Asher B. Durand*. Printed for The Century Association, New York: G.P. Putnam's Sons, 1887), p. 43, Hathi Trust.

12 "History, National Academy Museum,"National Academy Museum. http://www. nationalcademy.org/about-us/history/ (accessed November 22, 2013).

13 Clark, Eliot, History of the National Academy of Design, 1825-1953," (Columbia University Press: New York, 1954), p. 39

14 Sturges, Jonathan, "Some Reminiscences of the Progress of Art in New York."

15 Sturges, *Reminiscences*, p. 170.

16 JS to MS, July 25, 1835, OFP.

17 Sturges, *Reminiscences*, p. 126.

18 Luman Reed to JS, June 9, 1834, Boston, ARC-1218, SFP, PML.

19 Asher B. Durand to Mrs. Durand, March 17, 1835, Luman Reed Papers, 1820-1895, MSS Non-Circulating, NYHS, NY.

20 Luman Reed to JS, June 10, 1835, Boston, ARC-1218 SFP, PML.

21 Luman Reed to JS, June 6, 1835, Boston, ARC-1218, SFP, PML.

22 Luman Reed to JS, July 6, 1835, Newburgh, ARC-1218, SFP, PML.

23 Durand, A.B, *Luman Reed*, c. 1835, Accession No. 63.36, Metropolitan Museum of Art, New York, NY.

24 Durand, A.B., *Virginia and Frederick Sturges*, c. 1835, Photograph by Lauren Reeves, 2015

25 Foshay, *Reed's Picture Gallery*, p. 57.

26 Sturges, Jonathan, "Some Reminiscences of the Progress of Art in New York."

27 Foshay, *Reed's Picture Gallery*, p. 57.

28 "Public Meeting of the Citizens- Aug. 27, 1835," *Maryland Gazette* (Annapolis), Sep.3, 1835, p. 2.

29 Luman Reed to JS, June 8, 1835, Boston, SFP, PML.

30 Wilhlem, Kendra, *A Different Cup of Tea: The Culture of Tea in Britain and Sri Lanka,* Tea Comes to England, http://panix.com (accessed May 2014).

31 Reed and Sturges Account Book 1833-1835.

32 McNamara, Robert, "New York's Great Fire of 1835," ThoughtCo http://history 1800s.about.com/od/crimesanddisasters/ss/New-Yorks-Great-Fire.htm (accessed May 2014).

33 Sturges, Reminiscences, p. 163-165.

34 Calyo, Nicolino, *The Great Fire Of New York – Burning Of The Merchants' Exchange December 17, 1835* http://www.boweryboyshistory.com/2016/04/podcast-rewind-great-fire-1835.html (Accessed September 10, 2018).

35 "Humorism." The Free Medical Dictionary, Farlex, Inc. http://medical-dictionary. - the freedictionary.com/Humorism (accessed May 8, 2015).

36 *Sturges, Reminiscences, p. 167.*

37 Barker, Luman Reed, p. 59.

38 JS to MS, July 8, 1838, ARC-1318, Part III, SFP, PML

39 Sturges, Reminiscences, p. 168.40 Ibid, p. 167.

41 "Misc.,"*Alexandria* (VA) *Gazette*, March 12, 1838, p. 2.

42 *The National Bank of Commerce*, (New York: bank published, 1917), p. xviii.

Chapter 5

1 Sturges, Reminiscences, p. 169
2 JS to MS, July 10, 1836, OFP.
3 JS to MS, July 13, 1836 OFP.
4 Ibid, OFP.
5 JS to MS July 14, 1836, OFP.
6 JS to MS Sep. 1, 1836, OFP.
7 JS to MS May 24, 1837, OFP.
8 JS to MS, 18th Sabbath (undated-probably June 1837) Box 1, OFP.
9 JS to MS, July 9, 1838, ARC 1218, SFP, PML.
10 JS to MCS, August 13, 1838, ARC 1218 SFP, PML
11 Ibid.
12 JS to MS, July 11, 1838 abt., ARC 1218, SFP, PML.
13 JS to MS, August 18, 1838 , ARC 1218, SFP, PML
14 Sturges, *Reminiscences*, p.175-178.
15 Ibid.
16 Ibid, p. 177
17 Ibid, p. 178
18 Miner, Marcia, Blog, "Town Leaders Destroy Historic Sturges-Atkinson Cottage, October 2010, http://marciaminersroomwithaview/blogspot.com/2010/10/historic-town-screws-history.htm (accessed September 29, 2014)
19 Jonathan Sturges Cottage, Joseph Wells Architect, c. 1840, Historic Buildings of Connecticut, http://historicbuildingsofconnecticut.com/?p5821 (accessed December 14. 2016).
20 Roseland Cottage, c. 1846, Shutter Stock.com (accessed September 5, 2018).
21 JS to VS, July 29, 1840, Box 14, Osborn and Dodge Family Papers. 22
VS and Elizabeth Cady to JS, July 25, 1840, ARC 1218, SFP, PML.
23 Hornberger, Eric, Mrs. Astor's New York: Money and Power in a Gilded Age, (Yale University Press: New Haven, 2002), p. 240.
24 Sturges, Reminiscences, p. 182.
25 Joseph Wells receipt, Jonathan Sturges Receipt Book, p. 58.
26 Webster, Daniel, Webster On the Currency: Speech of Hon. Daniel Webster At the Merchant's Meeting, In Wall Street, New York, September 28, 1840. (New York: E. French, 1840), Hathi Trust.
27 Asher B. Durand to JS, June 25, 1840, ARC 1218, SFP, PML.
28 Ibid.
29 Durand, Asher B., *Jonathan Sturges*, c. 1840, accession no. 1977.342.1, Metropolitan Museum of Art, New York, NY. http://www.metmuseum.org/collection/the-collection-online/search/10791 (accessed November 14, 2014)
30 Durand, A.B., Amelia and Edward Sturges, c. 1840, FO1, SFP, Image provided by PML.
31 Clark, H. Nichols B., "A Taste for the Netherlands: The Impact of Seventeenth-Century Dutch and Flemish Genre Painting on American Art 1800-1860," American Art Journal, Spring 1982
32 Asher B. Durand to JS, October 17, 1840, ARC 1218, SFP, PML.
33 Kman, Joanna E., ed., Asher B. Durand: American Landscape, (Brooklyn Museum publication, 2007), p. 118.

34 JS to Thomas Cole, March 23, 1837, Thomas Cole Papers, 1821-186, Folder 6, Box 2, Reel ACL-1, Smithsonian Archives of American Art.

35 Cole, Thomas, View on the Catskill—Early Autumn, New York: The Metropolitan Museum of Art, 2000-(August 2009), (ID no. 95.13.3) http://www.metmuseum.org/toah/works-of-art/95.13.3 (accessed November 15, 2015)

36 Transactions of the Apollo Association for the Promotion of the Fine Arts in the United States 1839-1845, (New York: by the Association, 1845), p. 5, Google Books.

37 "The Old Art Union: First Paper," The Art Union, March 1, 1884, Vol . I, No. 3 (New York: Art Union, 1884), p. 56. Internet Archive (archive.org)

38 Transactions of the Apollo Association for the Promotion of the Fine Arts in the United States 1839-1845, Annual Report (New York: by the Association, 1842), p. 31.

39 McElroy, Guy, Facing History: The Black Image in American Art http://courses.ischool.berkeley.edu/i182ac/f04/paint160.html (accessed November 22, 2015).

40 Mount, William Sydney, *Farmers Nooning*, C. 1836, ID no. 15774, The Athenaeum http://www.the-athenaeum.org/art/full.php?ID=15774 (accessed November 22, 2015).

41 Apollo Association Annual Report 1843 (New York: by the Association, 1843), p. 6.

42 Spectator (New York, NY), October 14, 1846, p. 4.

43 *"The Old Art Union: First Paper,"* The Art Union, March 1, 1884, Vol. I, No. 3, (New York Art Union, 1884), p. 61. Internet Archive (archive.org)

44 "Partnership," Commercial Advertiser (New York, NY), February 3, 1841, p. 1.

45 "Partnership," The Evening Post (New York, NY), February 8, 1843, p. 4.

46 "The National Bank of Commerce," NYT, August 9, 1896, p. 20, NYT archive.org.

47 The Evening Post (New York, NY) February 1, 1843, p. 1.

48 Commercial Advertiser (New York, NY), February 9, 1844, Vol. XLVII, p. 3.

49 Sturges, Jonathan, *"Some Reminiscences of the Progress of Art in New York."*

50 Howe, Winifred E., *A History of the Metropolitan Museum of Art, With a Chapter on the the Early Institutions of Art In New York* (New York: Gillis Press, 1913), p. 64. Hathi Trust.

51 "The Reed Gallery," The Evening Post (New York, NY), March 9, 1844, p.2.

52 Durand, Life and Times, p. 128.

53 Gourlie, John H., The Origin and History of the Century (New York: W.C. Bryant & Co., 1856) http://www.centuryarchives.org/publications/origins_and_history.pdf.

54 History of The Century Association, The Century Association Archives Foundation http://www.centuryarchives.org/ead/century_association_records.html (accessed November 22, 2015).

55 Jewitt, Frank, Jr., & Leonard Bacon, Eds., The Century, 1847-1946 (New York: Century Association, 1947), p. 299.

Chapter 6

1 Beach, Moses, *Wealth and the Wealthy Citizens of New York City*, (New York Sun office, 1842) p. 8. HathiTrust.

2 Beach, Moses Yale, *The Wealth and Biography of the Wealthiest Citizens of the city of New York* (*New York Sun* office, 1846), p. 27. HathiTrust.

3 *An Act to Incorporate the New York Mining Company*, Archives of Maryland Online, Session Laws 1844, Chap. 220, Vol. 609, December 1844, p. 156, http://aomol.net/000001/000609/html/am609--156.html

4 Maryland Geological Survey (Baltimore: John Hopkins Press, 1905)–http://www.mount savagehistoricalsociety.org (accessed November 22, 2015).

5 "New York and Harlem Intact for Century," *NYT*, May 25, 1930, *NYT* digital archive.

6 *Acts of Incorporation of the New York and Harlem Railroad, with Statements and Proposals for Preferred Stock 1848*, (New York: G.F. Nesbitt, 1848), p. 3.

7 *Happy Birthday to the New York and Harlem Railroad-180 years!* iridetheharlemline.com, Author unknown, blog editor "Emily,"September 25, 2011 post http://www.iridethe harlem line.com/2011/04/25/happy-birthday-to-the-new-york-harlem-railroad-180-years/ (accessed April 16, 2015).

8 "New York and Harlem Railroad Streetcar" c. 1850s, "The Street Railway of the New York and New Haven Railroad,"June 21, 2013 http://www.iridetheharlemline.com/2013/06/21/ the-treetcars-of-the-new-york-and-harlem-railroad/(accessed September 30, 2013).

9 Jonathan Sturges Testimony, New York and New Haven Rairlroad vs. Morris Ketchum and survivors of Thomas Rogers, New York Supreme Court, April 10, 1866, p. 102

10 VS to Lucretia Sturges, January 3, 1846, ARC 1218, Pt. 8, SFP, PML

11 Whittemore, Henry, *Fulfilment of Three Remarkable Prophecies in the History of the Great Empire State, 1808-1908*, self-published, 1909, p. 75

12 "Short Importation," *Indiana State Sentinel* (Indianapolis, IN), August 19, 1847 http:// chroniclingamerica.loc.gov/lccn/sn82015677/1847-08-19/ed-1/seq-/ (accessed June 16, 2015).

13 *Evansville* (Indiana) *Daily Journal,* July 4, 1848

14 "New York Past, Present and Future," *Spectator* (New York, NY), July 8, 1848, p.1.

15 Jacobs, Warren, "Early Days of the New Haven R.R. in New York," The Railway and Locomotive Historical Society Bulletin, No. 38, October 1935, p. 32, https://www.jstor. org/stable/43517079

16 *First Annual Report of Directors of the Hudson River Railroad to the Stockholders*, June 12, 1848, (New York: Van Norden and King, 1848), p. 10.

Chapter 7

1 Citizens Bank Advertisement, *The Evening Post* (New York, N.Y.), May 15, 1847, p. 3.

2 "Rules for Christian Merchants, Mechanics, &c" American Tract Society, about 1840, LOC, ID 24401200, https://www.loc.gov/resource/rbpe.24401200/ (March 17, 2018).

3 *The Twenty-Second Annual Report of the New York Association for Improving the Condition of the Poor for the Year 1865* (New York: John F. Trow & Co., 1865) p. 2. Google Books.

4 Wilson, James Grant, ed., *Memorial History of the City of New York From its First settlement to the Year 1892, Vol. III, (New York: New York History Co., 1892), p 436.

5 Lamb, Martha J. 1829-1893. *History of the City of New York: Its Origin, Rise, and Progress. 1877-1896*, (New York: A.S. Barnes, 1896), p. 764. HathiTrust.

6 *Aid to Ireland, Report of the General Relief Committee of the City of New York*, Organized February 10th, 1847, (New York: by the Committee, 1847), p. 162.

7 "Special Notice–An Opportunity of Aid to Hungary," *Evening Post* (New York, NY), Dec 18, 1851, p. 3.

8 Jonathan Sturges Receipt Book, pp. 39, 77, 79.

9 "Relief of the Veterans," *Spectator* (New York, NY), July 27, 1848, p. 1.

10 "Asher B. Durand: *Kindred Spirits*" (L.2008.21). New York: The Metropolitan Museum of Art, 2000– [October 2009] http://www.metmuseum.org/toah/works-of-art/L.2008.21 (accessed December 12, 2013).

11 Letter from Mrs. Bryant, April 17, 1849, Bryant Family Association Papers in the Bureau County Historical Society, MSS Letter, Princeton, Illinois. [Ref. from Bryant, William Cullen II, *Poetry and Painting: A Love Affair of Long Ago*, American Quarterly for Winter, 1970, Vol. XXII, no. 4]

12 Howatt & Spassky, et.al., Eds., *19th-century America*, p. 62.

13 Ibid.

14 Durand, Asher B, *Kindred Spirits* (L.2008.21). (New York: The Metropolitan Museum of Art, 2000), [October 2009] http://www.metmuseum.org/toah/images/h2/h2_L.2008.21.jpg (accessed December 12, 2013).

15 Brown, Henry K., *Thomas Cole*, Accession No. 95.8.1 Metropolitan Museum of Art, New York, NY (accessed September 10, 2018).

16 Asher B. Durand, *Kindred Spirits*, Accession No. 2010.106, Crystal Bridges Museum of American Art, Bentonville, Arkansas http://collection.crystalbridges.org:8080/emuseum/view/objects/asitem/search$0040/o/title-asc?t:state:flow=62bde3e5-3353-49d5-9834-fe4a9e42fd32 (accessed June 28, 2014).

17 Keep, Austin Baxter, *History of the New York Society Library* (New York: printed for the trustees by the De Vinne Press, 1908) p. 366. Hathi Trust.

18 "New York Athenaeum," *Evening Post* (New York, NY), April 29, 1850, p. 3.

Chapter 8

1 Sturges, *Reminiscences*, p. 184.

2 Bulkley, *The Journals of Jonathan Bulkley*, Vol. II, p. 15.

3 Survey of federal archives (U.S.), (1941). *Ship registers and enrollments, ship licenses issued to vessels under twenty tons, ship licenses on enrollments issued out of the port of Bristol-Warren, Rhode Island, 1773–1939.* Providence: R. I., The National Archives Project. p. 217. Hathi Trust.

4 Sturges, *Reminiscences*, p. 196.

5 Ibid, p. 200.

6 Harden, William, 1844-1936. *A History of Savannah and South Georgia.* (Chicago: Lewis Publishing Co., 1913) pp. 293 & 310, HathiTrust.

7 Sturges, *Reminiscences*, p. 201.

8 Ibid, p. 193-194.

9 "Arrival of the Swedish Songstress," *Commercial Advertiser* (New York, NY) Sep. 2, 1850, p.2.

10 Sturges, *Reminiscences*, p. 191-2.

11 Mrs. Jenny Lind Goldschmidt, 1850s..

12 Sturges, Virginia, Journal of VS, September.

13 VS to her Aunt Elizabeth, Box 1, OFP.

14 Sturges, Virginia, Journal of VS.

15 Ibid.

Chapter 9

1 Ackerman, *Historical Sketch of Illinois Central Railroad*, p. 17.

2 Lamb, Sean, "Combined route map of the Chicago Central (red) and Illinois Central (blue) railroads in 1996," Illinois Central Corporation 1996 Annual Report, 1997. icrr historical.org https://en.wikipedia.org/w/index.php?title=Illinois_Central_Railroad& oldid=666560185 (accessed June 23, 2015).

3 "Report from the Illinois Journal," *New York Tribune*, February 1, 1850, p. 4.

4 Ackerman, *Historical Sketch of Illinois Central Railroad* p. 20.

5 Sturges, Virginia, Journal of VS.

6 Ackerman, *Historical Sketch of Illinois Central Railroad* p. 79.

7 Ibid, p. 78.

8 Ibid, p. 84

9 Kett, H.F. ed. *The History of Jo Daviess County, Illinois,* (Chicago: H.F. Kett & Co., 1878), p. 546.

10 Alexander, Melissa, "Riding the Rails: The Birth of Restlessness," http://www. ridingthe rails.org/part1 (accessed April 22, 2018).

Chapter 10

1 Mary Cady Sturges, c. Unk.

2 Durand, Asher B., *John Cady,* approx. 1840, Photograph by Lauren Reeves, 2015.

3 Sturges, Virginia, Journal of VS.

4 Slade, William, *Annual Report of the General Agent of the Board of National Popular Education,* 1848, (Cincinnati: Franklin Printing House,1848), p. 28.

5 Warner, Susan (aka Elizabeth Wetherell), *Queechy,* (New York: George P. Putnam, 1852) Google books.

6 VS to her Aunt Elizabeth, May 12, 1852, Osborn Papers, NYHS.

7 Sturges, *Reminiscences,* p. 239.

8 "Instruction," *New York Daily News,* April 5, 1853.

9 *Second Annual Report of the Wilson Industrial School Association for Girls, By-Laws and Regulations,* Article I, (John F. Trow: New York), 1855, p. 8.

10 "The Wilson Industrial School," *NYT,* November 6, 1854, *NYT* digital archive.

11 *Second Annual Report of the Wilson Industrial School Assoc. for Girls,* (New York: John F. Trow, 1855), p.4-7.

12 "The Wilson Industrial School-Preparations for Thanksgiving," *NYT,* December 5, 1864, *NYT* digital archive.

13 Editorial *Mississippi Free Trader* (Natchez, Mississippi), April 28, 1852, p. 1.

14 Ibid, p.1.

15 *Solomon Sturgis* [sic], Bust by Hiram Powers, c.1862, Smithsonian American Art Museum, Object Number 1968.155.49, https://americanart.si.edu/artwork/solomonsturgis-20141 (accessed September 10, 2018).

16 *Harriett Lewis Bennet Buckingham,* c. 1850s, contributed by Elizabeth Negrau, Ancestry. com, database, accessed December 21, 2017.

17 Buckingham, *Solomon Sturges,* p. 25.

18 Bateman, Newton, 1822-1897. *Historical Encyclopedia of Illinois,* (Chicago: Munsell Publishing Co., 1905), p. 512, HathiTrust.

19 "Big Granary," *Sandusky (OH) Register* August 3, 1855, p.2.

20 VS to JS, June 21, 1852, SFP, ARC 1218, Pt. 8, PML.

21 Sturges, Virginia, Journal of VS.

22 *William Henry Osborn,* c. unk, Private Collection.

23 *Virginia Reed Sturges Osborn* c. unk Private Collection.
24 Sturges, *Reminiscences*, p. 204.
25 FS to MS, Richmond, October 1852, Box 1, OFP.
26 VS to Dear Aunt, January 28, 1853, Box 1, OFP.
27 Sturges, *Reminiscences*, p. 206.
28 VS to MS, April 21, 1853, ARC 1218, Pt. 8, SFP, PML.
29 VS to MS, May 21, 1853, ARC 1218, Pt. 8, SFP, PML.
30 FS to JS, Paris, March 13, 1853, ARC-1218, Pt. 5, SFP, PML.
31 Ibid.
32 VS to Jonathan and MS, March 20, 1853, ARC-1218, Pt. 8, SFP, PML.
33 VS to JS, April 28, 1853, ARC-1218, Pt. 8, SFP, PML.
34 Crawford, Thomas, *George Washington Equestrian Monument*, The Virginia State Capitol History Project, 2006-2009 www.vacapitol.org (accessed September 13, 2015).
35 Crawford, Thomas, *The Babes in the Wood* (89.9.4) New York: The Metropolitan Museum of Art, 2000-2018 (Accessed September 10, 2018) https://images.metmuseum.org/CRD/Images/ad/original/DT202043.jpg
36 VS to JS, May 21, 1853, ARC-1218, Pt. 8, SFP, PML.
37 VS to JS, Florence, May 25, 1853, ARC-1218, Pt. 8, SFP, PML.
38 VS to JS, August 26, 1853, ARC-1218, Pt. 8, SFP, PML.
39 VS to JS, April 24, 1853, ARC-1218, Pt. 8, SFP, PML.
40 VS to JS, June 19, 1853, ARC-1218, Pt. 8, SFP, PML.
41 VS to JS, April 21, 1853, ARC-1218, Pt. 8, SFP, PML.
42 VS to JS, August 26, 1853, ARC-1218, Pt. 8, SFP, PML
43 VS to MS, July 1, 1853, ARC-1218, Pt. 8, SFP, PML.
44 VS to JS and MCS, September 2, 1853, SFP, ARC-1218, PML.
45 Sturges, *Reminiscences*, p. 209.
46 VS to MS, August 31, 1853, ARC-1218, SFP, PML.
47 VS to MS, August 28, 1853, ARC-1218, SFP, PML.
48 Kofoid, Charles A. & Prudence W., *Charles L. Tiffany and the House of Tiffany* Tiffany & Co., 1893), p. 19, Internet Archive (archive.org).
49 Elizabeth Cady Invitation to Wedding of Virginia Sturges and William Henry Osborn Box 1, OFP

Chapter 11
1 "The Catastrophe", Norwalk Rail Accident, May 6, 1853, Unk artist, World History Project, https://worldhistoryproject.org/1853/5/6/norwalk-rail-accident.
2 Bulkley, *The Journals of Jonathan Bulkley*, Vol. II, p. 296.
3 JS to MS, Dubuque, October 23, 1853, ARC 1218, Pt. 3, SFP, PML.
4 JS to MS, Chicago, July 11,1852, ARC 1218, Pt.3, SFP, PML.
5 Shaw, Robert, "The Great Schuyler Stock Fraud," Railroad History, No. 141 (Autumn 1979), p. 9. https://www.jstor.org/stable/43520750
6 Jonathan Sturges *New York Supreme Court Testimony*, p. 102
7 Sturges, *Reminiscences*, p. 213-214.
8 Morris Ketchum, *New York Supreme Court Testimony*, p. 88.
9 MS to sister, July 19, 1854, Box 1, OFP.
10 "Two Million Defalcation," *NYT*, September 25, 1854, p.1, *NYT* digital archive.
11 Jonathan Sturges, *New York Supreme Court Testimony*, p. 104.

12 "Astounding Fraud Upon the Stockholders of the New Haven Railroad," *Evening Post* (New York, NY), July 5, 1854, p. 1.

13 "The Case of the New-Haven Railroad," *NYT*, May 21, 1860, *NYT* digital archives.

14 Ackerman, *Historical Sketch of Illinois Central Railroad* p. 99.

15 Andrews, Wayne, "The Vanderbilt Legend: the story of the Vanderbilt family, 1794-1940," Part one (Harcourt, Brace & Co.: New York, 1941), p. 37

16 "Supreme Court," Digitized Records of the New York Supreme Court, 1859, p. 61. Google Books.

17 "State Affairs," *NYT*, January 5, 1855, *NYT* digital archive.

18 Sturges, *Reminiscences*, p. 215.

19 Cummings, *Historic Annals of the National Academy of Design*, p. 242.

20 MS to her sister, July 19, 1854, Box 1, OFP.

Chapter 12

1 Banks, Raymond H., *King of Louisiana 1862-1865 and other Government Work, A Biography of Maj. Gen. Nathaniel Prentice Banks* Biography, privately published, Las Vegas, Nevada, 2005, p.182. Google Books.

2 Ackerman, *Historical Sketch of Illinois Central Railroad*, p. 88.

3 *William Henry Osborn*, Private collection.

4 VSO to JS, New York, May 20, 1857, Box 1, OFP.

5 VSO to JS, Chicago, December 15, 1856, ARC 1218, SFP, PML.

6 VSO to My Dear Aunt, February 17, 1857, Box 1, OFP.

7 VSO to MS, Chicago, February 7, 1857, ARC 1218, SFP, PML.

8 Ackerman, *Historical Sketch of Illinois Central Railroad*, p. 65.

9 Rousmaniere, *The Union League Club*, p. 25.

10 Ibid, p. 25.

11 Sturge, *Reminiscences*, s p. 224.

12 Corlis, Carlton J., *Abraham Lincoln and the Illinois Central Railroad, Main Line of Mid America*, (U.S.:Self Publish),1850, p.14.

13 MS to Mrs. Cady, March 18, 1856, Box 1, OFP, NYHS.

14 Osborne, Rev. J.W., March 1, 1857 Report on activities as Colporteur on Illinois Central Railroad, ARC 1218, Folder 8.11, SFP, PML.

15 Sturges, *Reminiscences*, p. 219.

16 "Inaugural Address of William H. Bissell," *Alton (IL) Weekly Telegraph*, January 15, 1857, p.2.

17 Copy of handwritten draft inscription for plate, Box 14, Osborn and Dodge Papers, PUL; original plate in possession of Osborn family descendants.

Chapter 13

1 Prevost, Victor, Reed and Sturges Warehouse, c. 1855, Public Domain

2 MS to her mother Mrs. Cady, March 18, 1856, Box 1, OFP.

3 Hill, Edwin C., ed., *The Historical Register*, (New York: E.C. Hill, 1922), p. 55, HathiTrust.

4 AmS to MS, July 1856, from Adams, Elaine, "Frederic Edwin Church and the Splendor of Small-Scale Landscapes," California Art Club newsletter, Summer 2006.

5 VSO to MS, Niagara, August 5, 1856, ARC 1218, SFP, PML.

6 AmS to Aunt Lucretia, New York, December 21, 1856, ARC 1218, SFP, PML.

7 VSO to MS, Coblenz on Rhone, July 1, 1853, ARC 1218, Pt. 8, SFP, PML.

8 Advertisement- Dr. Reisig, M.D.-*Evening Post* (New York, NY), April 15, 1850.

9 Giles, *A Candle in Her Hand,* p. 117.

10 Annals of Wing-and-Wing, as transcribed by Anita Prentice, private collection.

11 MS to Sister, Fairfield, July 13, 1858, Box 1, OFP.

12 Durand, *Life and Times of Asher B. Durand,* p. 175.

13 Mount, William Sidney, *Who'll Turn the Grindstone,* c.1851, Unk Newspaper clipping.

14 Durand, Asher B., *God's Judgment Upon Gog,* c. 1852, http://www.the-athenaeum.org/art/detail.php?ID=46620 (accessed January 18, 2018).

15 Durand, Asher B., *In the Woods* c. 1855, (New York: The Metropolitan Museum of Art), © 2000-2017 http://www.metmuseum.org/toah/works-of-art/95.13.1 (accessed January 28, 2018).

Chapter 14

1 Sturges, *Reminiscences,* p. 223.

2 AmS to MS, Fairfield, June 1857, ARC 1218, SFP, PML.

3 Sturges, *Reminiscences,* p. 221.

4 Hoyt, Edwin. P., *House of Morgan,* New York: Dodd, Mead & Co., 1966, p. 105

5 Sturges, *Reminiscences,* p. 223.

6 "New York," *Lebanon (PA) Daily News,* November 21, 1952, p. 19.

7 Sturges, *Reminiscences,* p. 224.

8 Ibid, p. 227.

9 VSO to AS, April 29, 1859, Box 5, Osborn and Dodge Family Papers, PUL.

10 Amelia Sturges (Morgan), Diary 1858, March 9, 1859, ARC 0611, SFP, PML.

11 Sears, Stephen W., *George B. McClellan-The Young Napoleon,* Da Capo Press Inc.: New York, 1988, p. 61.

12 JPM to JS, April 11, 1859, ARC1218, SFP, PML.

13 The British Grand Tour in the 18th Century, *The Grand Tour, Art and Travel 1740-1914,* Indiana University Art Museum, 2009 http://www.iub.edu/~iuam/online_modules/grand_tour/03_map.php?ptID=3 (accessed July 19, 2016).

14 JPM to JS, April 11, 1859, ARC1218, SFP, PML.

15 VSO to AS, April 29, 1859, Box 5, ODFP, PUL.

16 Sturges, *Reminiscences,* p. 230-231.

17 AmS to Aunt Lucretia, May 17, 1859, ARC 1218, Pt. 1, SFP, PML.

18 AmS to Aunt Elizabeth, Jun/July 1859, ARC 1218, Pt. 1, SFP, PML.

19 AmS to Aunt Elizabeth October 15, 1859, ARC 1218, SFP, PML.

20 VSO to AS, April 29, 1859, Fairfield, CO537, Box 5, ODFP, PUL.

21 VSO to AS, July 26, 1859, Fairfield, CO537, Box 5, ODFP, PUL.

22 *The Economist* (London), November 19, 1859, issue 847, p. 1298.

23 JPM to Jim Goodwin, January 19, 1860, MS 75347, Goodwin Family Papers, 1847-1896, CHS.

24 "The Human Side of America's Greatest Financier- J. Pierpont Morgan," *Sunday Herald* (Boston, MA) November 9, 1909, p. 7.Amelia Sturges photograph, 1859,

26 JPM in Paris, Private Collection, about 1859.

27 Sturges, *Reminiscences,* p. 233.

28 VSO to AS, July 26, 1860, Box 5, Osborn and Dodge Family Papers, PUL.

29 AmS to Henry Sturges, September 28, 1860, ARC-1218, SFP, PML.

Chapter 15

1 *Jonathan Sturges*, 1860s photograph, Private Collection.

2 *Official Report of the Great Union Meeting, Held at the Academy of Music, New York, December 19th, 1859*. (New York: Davies & Kent, 1859), p. 6. HathiTrust.

3 "News of the Day," *NYT*, April 26, 1860, *NYT* digital archive.

4 "Baltimore Union Convention-A Platform Adopted," *NYT*, May 11, 1860, *NYT* digital archive.

5 "Notes on the Campaign," *Springfield Daily Republican* (Springfield, IL), November 5, 1860, p. 1.

6 "The Black Republicans of Wall Street: Look on this Picture then on This," *New York Herald*, Nov. 15, 1860, pg. 5. (reprinted from Nov. 5, 1860 *New York Daily Times*)

7 *Address of Union League President John Jay*, Blue Book, Union League Club Archives, New York NY, 1868, p.6.

8 Low, A.A. *Memorial to Congress, Adopted at a Meeting of Citizens at the Rooms of the Chamber of Commerce, Friday, January 18, 1861*, New York, 1861. HathiTrust.

9 MCS to her mother, March 29, 1861, OFP.

10 "Mass Meeting Today in Support of Union," *New York Herald*, April 20, 1861, p. 8.

11 VSO to Lucy Wheeler, May 6, 1861, OFP.

12 Winslow, Homer "Great Union Meeting in Union Square to Support the Government, April 20, 1861, Digital Public Library https://dp.la/item/35d8756fe356a7bce9d06f8cb2a8e88f item/35d8756fe356a7bce9do6f-8cb2a8e88f (Accessed September 11, 2018)

13 "Chamber of Commerce-Letter of Acknowledgement from Mr. Seward," *New York Herald*, May 3, 1861, p.4.

14 Ibid.

15 Coates, Earl J. & Kochan, James, *Art by Troiani, Don, Soldiers in America*, 1754-1865, (Mechanicsburg: Stackpole Books, 1998), p. 134.

16 "*The Seventh Regiment Marching Down Broadway to Embark for the War*," *Harpers Weekly* (New York, NY), May 4, 1861, p.281. Image 831489, https://digitalcollections.nypl.org/items/510d47-e838-a3d9-e00a18064a99

17 Swinton, William, A.M., History of the Seventh Regiment National Guard, State of *New York, During the War of the Rebellion*, (New York: Fields Osgood & Co.), 1870, p. 37, Internet Archive (archive.org).

18 VSO to Lucy Wheeler, May 6, 1861, OFP.

19 VSO to MCS, December 12, 1861, OFP.

20 Lizzie Babcock to her mother Olivia, May 20, 1862, transcript of original.

21 Edward Sturges to MS, August 21, 1962, ARC-1218, SFP, PML.

22 Wingate, George Wood, 1840-1928. *History of the Twenty-Second Regiment of the National Guard of the State of New York: From Its Organization to 1895*, (New York: E. W. Dayton, 1896), p. 13. HathiTrust.

23 Lizzie Babcock to her mother Olivia (sister of Mary Cady Sturges), May 20, 1862.

24 FS to MS, July 6, 1862, ARC-1218, SFP, PML.

25 *Harpers Ferry-Camp Hill,* Harper's Ferry National Park, National Park Service, Historic image, HFNHP Collection. c. unk http://www.nps.gov/resources/place.htm?id=102 (accessed January 7, 2014).

26 Company G, 22d New York State Militia near Harpers Ferry, Va., 1862, Civil War Collection, LOC, c. 1862 http://www.loc.gov/pictures/resource/ppmsca.34576/?co=civwar (accessed January 7, 2014).

27 *History, 22nd New York State Militia, Unit History Project,* New York State Military Museum http://dmna.ny.gov/historic/reghist/civil/infantry/22ndNYSM/22ndNYSM-Main.htm (accessed January 7, 2014).

28 FS to JS, Paris, December 28, 1862, ARC-1218, SFP, PML.

29 Stillé, *History of the United States Sanitary Commission* p. 59.

30 Ibid, p. 63.

31 Ibid, p. 84.

32 "The Sanitary Commission," *Evening Post* (New York, NY), July 1, 1861, p.3.

33 *Statement of the Object and Missions of the U.S. Sanitary Commission,* Documents of the U.S. Sanitary Commission, US Sanitary Commission No. 69, by the Commission, (New York William C. Bryant & Co.,1863), p. 139. Google Books.

34 *Washington, D.C. Field relief wagons and workers of U.S. Sanitary Commission,* April 1865, LC-DIG-cwpb-04159, LOC, 1865 http://www.loc.gov/pictures/item/cwp2003000991/PP/

Chapter 16

1 VSO to Lucy Wheeler, January 31, 1861, Box 1, OFP.

2 AmS to Auntie, February 12, 1861, Box 1, OFP.

3 MS to Mrs. Cady, March 2, 1861, Box 1, OFP.

4 Sturges, *Reminiscences,* p. 234.

5 Strouse, Jean, "J.P. Morgan, National Banker," Lamb, Brian, ed., *Book notes: Stories from American History,* (New York: Public Affairs, 2001), p. 166.

6 "Marriages', *Hartford (CT) Daily Courant,* October 10, 1861.

7 *Pierpont Just Before His Marriage,* Photographs FO1, Archives, ARC-2505, PML.

8 Amelia Sturges Morgan Wedding Dress, C. 1861, Fairfield Museum and History Center display. Photo by Author.

9 Sturges, Reminiscences, p. 234.

10 Marriage to Amelia Sturges, PML, New York, NY http://www.themorgan.org/about/pierpont-morgan-banker/2 (accessed September 8, 2014).

11 J. Pierpont Morgan to JS, Algiers, December 28, 1861, OFP.

12 JS to AS Morgan, March 3, 1862, ARC-1218, SFP, PML.

13 "Announcements," *NYT,* May 2, 1862, *NYT* digital archive.

14 JS to AS Morgan, March 3, 1862, SFP, PML.

15 VSO to Frederick Osborn, March 11, 1862, ARC-1218, SFP, PML.

16 JS to MS, July 7, 1862, SFP, ARC-1218, PML.

17 Pastor (unk) to JS, March 6, 1862, SFP, ARC-1218, PML.

18 William Evans to MS, April 10, 1862, SFP, ARC-1218, PML.

19 Mrs. Goodwin to son James Goodwin, Hartford, January 18, 1862, MS74734 Goodwin Papers, CHS.

20 *"J. Pierpont Morgan Expedition to White Mountains,"* 1863, ARC-2506, PML.

21 Strouse, Morgan: Financier p. 109

22 *Annual Report of the New England Society in the City of New York,* 68th Annual Meeting, V.66-70, 1871-75, (New York: The Society, p. 96). HathiTrust.

23 Croffut, William A. and John M. Morris, *The Military and Civil History of Connecticut During the War of 1861-1865,* (New York: Ledyard Bill, 1868), p.833 (Appendix)

24 "Military," *Boston Evening Transcript,* October 9, 1861, p. 1.

25 *Maimed soldiers and others before office of U.S. Christian Commission, Washington, D.C.* LC-DIG-cwpb-04166 LOC, http://hdl.loc.gov/loc.pnp/pp.print, February 4, 2014

26 A Memorial Record of the New York Branch of the United States Christian Commission, by the Executive Committee, (New York: John A. Gray & Green, 1866), p.11. Google Books. 27 Ibid, p.15.

28 "The Christian Commission," San Francisco Bulletin, December 4, 1863, p. 2.

29 "U.S. Christian Commission-Heroes of Faith During the Civil War," History of the USCC http://www.usccgettysburg.org/history.asp (accessed February 4, 2014).

30 Diary of Henry Cady Sturges, May 12, 1862, SFP, PML.

31 Welland Canals, Canadian Canal Society, http://www.canadiancanalsociety.org/maps/map-welland.html

32 "The Ship Canal Proceedings of the Second Day," Cleveland Morning Leader (OH), June 5, 1863, p. 1

33 "Legislative," New York Daily Reformer (Watertown, NY), February 12, 1864, p. 2.

34 "The Meeting in New York- An Overwhelming Outpouring of the People," Boston (MA) Post, July 17, 1862, p. 2.

35 "Meeting of the War Committee," NYT, August 30, 1862, p. 3, NYT digital archive.

36 "Correspondence National War Committee," Sacramento Daily Union, (Sacramento, CA) October 6, 1862, p.3.

37 "The New York Resolutions," The Boston Herald, July 26, 1862, p. 1.

38 Ibid.

39 "Grocers Regiment," NYT, September 13, 1862, p. 3, NYT digital archive.

40 162nd Infantry Regiment, Civil War, 3rd Regiment, Metropolitan Guard-History http://dmna.ny.gov/historic/reghist/civil/infantry/162ndInf/162ndInfMain.htm (accessed May 19, 2014).

41 "Special Bounty Subscriptions," *NYT,* July 30, 1862, p. 5, *NYT* digital archive.

42 "Chamber of Commerce-Meeting in Relation to the Starvelings' of Great Britain," December 4, 1862, *NYT,* p. 5.

43 "Aid for the Lancashire Operatives," *World,* December 5, 1862, p. 8, Genealogy Bank Archive.

44 "Relief for the Suffering Poor of Ireland," *San Francisco Bulletin* (San Francisco, CA), May 20, 1863, p. 1.

Chapter 17

1 Bellows, *An Historical Sketch of the Union League Club,* 1879, p. 8.

2 Ibid, p. 13.

3 Ibid, p. 20.

4 "The Union: Monster Mass Meeting of Loyal Citizens of New York," *NYT,* March 6, 1863, p. 1, *NYT* digital archive.

5 Bellows, *An Historical Sketch of the Union League Club,* 1879, p. 39.

6 Report of the Executive Committee: Constitution, By-Laws and Roll of Members, Union League Club, July 1864, Club House, Union Square, 1864, p. 6.

7 "The Forgotten Profit," Reprint of *Sunday Gazette Mail* (Charleston, West Virginia), date unk. 1866.

8 Samuel Morehouse to Angeline Morehouse, July 18, 1863, Morehouse Family Papers, Fairfield Museum and History Center, Fairfield, CT.

9 "New York- burning of the Provost Marshall's Office," New York Public Library Digital Collections, Image ID No. b17539717 https://digitalcollections.nypl.org/items/510d47e1-280f-a3d9-e040-e00a18064a99 (accessed May 29, 2017).

10 *New York–The Rioters Dragging Col. O'Brien's Body Through the Street*, Image ID No. b17539717, NYPL Digital Collections. https://digitalcollections.nypl.org/items/510d47e1-2809-a3d9-e040-e00a18064a99 (accessed May 29, 2017).

11 "Report of the Executive Committee Presented at the Annual Meeting," January 13, 1864, Union League Club "Blue Book," Union League Club Archives, New York, NY, p.5.

12 Rousmaniere, *The Union League Club*, p. 47.

13 *Shoe and Leather Reporter*, 1891, Vol. 23, no. 1 (Jan. 1877), p. 661, Hathi Trust.

14 Meeting of Merchants in Behalf of Colored People, *Evening Post* (New York, NY), July 21, 1863, p 1.

15 Ibid.

16 Whitehorne, George, "Report of the Committee of Merchants for the Relief of the Colored People Suffering from the Late Riots in the City of New York," (New York: by the committee, 1863), p. 5 http://www.blackwallstreet.freeservers.com/new%20yor%20 draft%20riot%20of%201863.htm (accessed June 4, 2014).

17 Nesbitt, *Banquet Given by the Members of the Union League Club* p.26.

18 "The Situation," New York Herald (New York, NY), January 16, 1864, p. 4.

19 Garnet, Henry Highland, *A Memorial Discourse*. (Philadelphia: J.M. Wilson, 1865), p. 60, HathiTrust.

20 Nesbitt, *Banquet Given by the Members of the Union League Club*, p. 27

21 Ibid, p. 12.

22 Ibid, p. 15.

23 Bellows, *An Historical Sketch of the Union League Club*, 1879, p. 54.

24 Report of the Executive Committee, Annual Meeting, January 13, 1864, Union League, New York City, p. 11.

25 Rousmaniere, *The Union League Club*, p.88.

26 "Metropolitan Fair," *Centinel of Freedom* (Newark, NJ), February 18, 1864, p. 2.

27 *A Record of the Metropolitan Fair, 1864*, US Sanitary Commission, p. 2.

28 Ibid, p. 3.

29 Goodrich, Frank B., *The Tribute Book: A Record of the Munificence, Self-sacrifice and Patriotism of the American People During the War for the Union....* (New York: Derby & Miller, 1865), p. 244, HathiTrust.

30 "West Wing," LC-USZ62-89872, New York, 1864, LOC, Washington D.C. http://hdl.loc.gov/loc.pnp/cph.3b36242 (accessed June 4, 2015).

31 "The Metropolitan Sanitary Fair- The Art Gallery," *Frank Leslie's Illustrated Newspaper*, Vol. XVIII, No. 447 April 23, 1864, p. 69 https://www.loc.gov/resource/ds.08306/ (accessed June 21, 2017).

32 *Catalogue of the art exhibition at the Metropolitan Sanitary Fair in Aid of the U.S. Sanitary Commission*, By the Metropolitan Fair, (New York: John F. Trow, 1864), Internet Archive (archive.org)

33 Covey, Carl, *The Life Story of J.P. Morgan: A Biography*, (New York: Sturgis & Walton, 1911), p.28.
34 *A Record of the Metropolitan Fair* 1864, US Sanitary Commission, p.239.

Chapter 18

1 *Virginia Osborn*, Private collection.
2 *Frederick Osborn and William Church Osborn*, Private Collection.
3 VSO to MS, September 9, 1862, ARC-1218, Pt. 8, SFP, PML.
4 Ibid.
5 Frederick Sturges to JS, Paris, December 9, 1863, SFP, PML.
6 Frederick Sturges to JS, Paris, December 28, 1863, SFP, PML.
7 *Mary Reed Fuller Sturges*, Private Collection, Unk. Date.
8 Wilson, Mark R., Sturges, *Buckingham and Co.*, Encyclopedia of Chicago, (1820-2000), Chicago Historical Society, 2005 http://www.encyclopedia.chicagohistory.org/pages/2866 .html (accessed January 23, 2014).
9 *Collected Works of Abraham Lincoln*, Vol. 3, Ann Arbor Michigan, 2001 http://quod.lib. umich.edu/l/lincoln/lincoln4?id=4_44_3;note=ptr;rgn=div1;view=trgt (accessed January 24, 2014).
10 Sharps New Model 1859 Rifle, The Horse Soldier, Military Americana sales, Gettysburg, PA 2014 http://www.horsesoldier.com/products/firearms/longarms/5312#sthash.36e7AKBn .dpuf (accessed January 25, 2014).
11 "The City," Daily Illinois State Journal (Springfield, IL), May 30, 1862, p. 3.
12 Daily Illinois State Journal (Springfield, IL), June 6, 1862, p.2.
13 "The City," Daily Illinois State Journal (Springfield, IL), January 23, 1863, p. 3.
14 Lucretia Sturges to MS and JS, Savannah (undated, early 1861), ARC-1218, SFP, PML.
15 AmS to Dear Aunt, August 26, 1850, Box 1, OFP.
16 Beers, Mrs. Fannie A., *Memories*, (Philadelphia: J.B. Lippincott, 1889), p. 12
17 Barile, *Woman in a War-Torn Town*, p. iii.
18 Ibid, p. 53.
19 "Bombardment of Fredericksburg," December 11, 1862, LOC, ID LC-USZ62-108240 (b&w film copy neg.) https://lccn.loc.gov/93509695
20 Barile, *Woman in a War-Torn Town*, p. 87.
21 Ibid, p. 43.
22 Jane Beale to MS, December 12, 1865, OFP.
23 Ibid.
24 Jane Beale to MS, November 22, 1867, OFP.
25 Jane Beale to MS, January 7, 1868, OFP.

Chapter 19

1 Rossiter, Thomas Prichard (1818-1871), Representative *Merchants of America*, Oil on Canvas, Inventory photo, Object No. 1941.239, *Collection of the* NYHS, 1857 http://nyhistory .org/exhibit/merchants-new-york-or-merchants-america (accessed November 2014).
2 Provenance, Lot 315: Thomas Prichard Rossiter (1818-1871) oil on canvas A Study for the Original *Representative Merchants of America*, Invaluable, LLC., https://www.invaluable. co.uk/auction-lot/thomas-prichard-rossiter-1818-1871-oil-on-canv-315-c-b0a4b4abe8# (accessed June 21, 2017)

3 *Spectator* (New York, NY), October 14, 1846, p. 4.

4 Cummings, *Historic Annals of the National* Academy, p.285.

5 *The National Academy of Design, Ceremonies on the Occasion of Laying the Corner-stone, Oct. 21st., 1863. And the Inauguration of the Building, April 27th, 1865,* (New York: Miller & Mathews, 1865), p. 49

6 *National Academy of Design,* New York, c. 1865, LOC, LC-DIG-stereo-1s06878 (digital file from original, front) https://www.loc.gov/resource/stereo.1s06878/ (accessed April 9, 2018)

7 Masiello, Domenick, J., D.O., *History of Homeopathy,* Holistic Family Medicine, LLC, http://www.drmasiello.com/homeopathy/history-of-homeopathy (accessed February 5, 2014).

8 Bradford, Thomas Lindsey, M.D., ed., *Homoeopathic Bibliography of the United States: From the Year 1825 to the Year 1891, inclusive,* (Philadelphia: Boericke and Tafel, 1893), p. 31.

9 Rogers, Naomi, *An Alternative Path: The Making and Remaking of Hahnemann Medical College and Hospital of Philadelphia,* (New Jersey: Rutgers University Press, 1998), p.26.

10 *New York Homeopathic Medical College and Hospital,* c. 1868, Image courtesy of Dr. David Levine, Hospital of Special Surgery, NY, NY

11 *Dr. James Knight Home & Hospital* c. 1860s, image courtesy of Dr. David Levine, Hospital of Special Surgery, New York, NY.

12 Sturges, Jonathan, *The New York Society for the Relief of the Ruptured and Crippled,* Wells (New York: Sackett and Brothers: 1872), p. 6.

13 "Cure of the Crippled," *Norwich Aurora* (Norwich, CT), April 7, 1869, p.1 (reprint from the Evening Post, NY).

14 "Journal of Transactions, 1863-1864, Society for the Relief of the Ruptured and Crippled," Hospital for Special Surgery Archives, New York, NY.

15 Ibid.

16 "Society for the Relief of Crippled Persons," *NYT,* November 10, 1864, *NYT* digital archive.

17 "A Notable Charity," *NYT,* April 3, 1869, p.2, *NYT* digital archive.

18 Sturges, Jonathan, *The New York Society for the Relief of the Ruptured and Crippled,* (Wells, Sackett and Brothers: New York, 1872), p. 9.

19 *Hospital for the Ruptured and Crippled, 42nd St. & Lexington, c. 1870,* Image Courtesy of Dr. David Levine, Hospital of Special Surgery, New York, NY.

20 Levine, David B., MD, *Hospital for Special Surgery, Origin and Early History, First Site: 1863-1870,* (Springer.com:2005), http://www.ncbi.nlm.nih.gov/pmc/articles/PMC2504132/ (accessed February 5, 2014).

21 Levine, *Anatomy of a Hospital,* p. 13.

22 Levine, David B., "The Hospital for the Ruptured and Crippled Entering the 20th Century, 1900-1912" http://www.ncbi.nlm.nih.gov/pmc/articles/PMC2504092/ - (accessed August 22, 2014).

Chapter 20

1 "A Monster National Bank- $50,000,000," *New York Herald* (New York, NY), November 21, 1863, p. 4

2 *Gold Coin Sold since January 1863,* House Executive Doc.84, Serial Set Vol. No. 1381, pgs. 5, 9, 28, 40, 49, 51.

3 "The Rise and Fall of Gold," *NYT,* April 20, 1864, *NYT* digital archive.

4 "News from Washington- The Gold Bill," *NYT*, June 25, 1864, *NYT* digital archive.

5 "The Gold Committee," *New York Daily Tribune* (New York, NY), June 24, 1864, p.1

6 Drabik, West Harlem, City University of New York http://macaulay.cuny.edu/eportfolios/drabik11/transit/subway-overview/ (accessed June 2014).

7 "Underground Railway," *NYT*, March 26, 1864, *NYT* digital archive.

8 "The Underground Railroad; What is required," *NYT*, March 6, 1865, *NYT* dig. archive.

9 Walker, James Blaine, Fifty Years of Rapid Transit, Ch. IV (New York: Law Printing Co., 1918 http://www.nycsubway.org/wiki/Fifty_Years_of_Rapid_Transit_(1918)#Chapter_IV._First_Rapid_Transit_Bill_Passed_by_the_Legislature_and_Vetoed (accessed July 14, 2014).

10 Don Matias Romero, Mexican Minister to United States, 1863, National Archives https://www.archives.gov/research/military/civil-war/photos/184.html (accessed January 4, 2017).

11 *Message from the President of the United States, communicating, in answer to a resolution of the Senate of the 25th ultimo, papers relative to Mexican affairs, William Seward, June 20, 1864.* Referred to the Committee on Foreign Relations. June 29, 1864, Referred to Committee on Printing. January 25, 1865, p. 405. Genealogy Bank.

12 Sherman, William T., *Reply of Maj. Gen. Sherman to the Mayor of Atlanta: And Speeches of Maj. Gen. Hooker, Delivered in the Cities of Brooklyn And New York, Sept. 22, 1864. Letter of Lieut. Gen. Grant,* Union League Club, 1864, p.5. HathiTrust.

13 "Thanksgiving Dinner for Soldiers and Sailors," proclamation flyer, Minutes of Monthly Meetings (Insert), November 1864, Records of the Union League Club, Union League Archives, New York, NY.

14 McClarey, Donald R. and Paul Zunno, *Thanksgiving for the Troops*, "Almost Chosen People: A blog about American History and the Development of a Great Nation" https://almostchosenpeople.wordpress.com/2010/11/26/thanksgiving-for-the-troops -1864/ (accessed June 4, 2014).

15 A History of the Union League Club, Union League Club, New York, NY, 1953 p.47.

16 Military and Naval Asylum, March 2, 1865, 38th Congress, Congressional Globe (Washington: F & J Rives), p. 1287.

17 History of the National Home for Disabled Volunteer Soldiers, National Park Service, U.S. Department of the Interior, Washington, D.C. http://www.nps.gov/nr/travel/veterans_ affairs/History.html (accessed August 6, 2014).

18 Records of the Department of Veterans Affairs, U.S. National Archives and Records Administration, Predecessor Agencies http://www.archives.gov/research/guide-fed-records/ groups/015.html (accessed August 6, 2014).

19 Allen, Col. Ethan, "Deceased Presidents of the Union League Club," Howard, Joseph, Jr., *The Union League Club, Historical and Biographical, 1863-1900*, (New York: J.J. Wohlton, 1900) p. 20 https://archive.org/stream/unionleagueclubhoohowa/unionleagueclubhoo howa_djvu.txt (accessed April 22, 2018)

20 Minutes of Monthly Meetings, November 1864, Records of the Union League Club, Union League Club Archives, New York, NY, p. 176.

21 "Relief for Savannah," Contributions Received the Steamers Rebecca Clyde and Daniel Webster Soon to Sail with Full Cargoes," *NYT*, January 15, 1865, *NYT* digital archive.

22 "The President and the Union League," Evening Star (Washington, D.C.), April 21, 1865, p.3.

23 Bonwill, C.E.H. *Sketch of Lincoln's Funeral in East Room of White House, Frank Leslie's Illustrated* (New York, NY), May 6, 1865, p. 100-101.

24 Brooks, Noah, *Washington in Lincoln's Time* (New York: The Century Co., 1895), p. 262.

25 "THE OBSEQUIES; Removal of the Remains from Washington," *NYT*, April 22, 1865, *NYT* digital archive.

26 Bellows, *An Historical Sketch of the Union League Club*, 1879, p.87.

27 Union League Annual Report "Blue Book," 1866, Union League Club Archives, New York, p. 90.

28 "Greetings to Grant: The Lieut.-General in the Metropolis," *World* (New York, NY), June 8, 1865, p. I

29 "Grant-A Magnificent Reception of the Lieutenant General," p. 1. New York Herald, November 21, 1865, p. 1.

30 Ibid.

Chapter 21

1 *JS to Henry Sturges, February 3, 1860, ARC-1218, SFP, PML.*

2 Frier, Mary Sturges, *Family Memories*, 1979, Fairfield Museum and History Center.

3 VSO to Arthur Sturges, December 6, 1861, ODFP, Box 1, PUL.

4 Arthur Pemberton Sturges, 1860s, Private Collection.

5 "Columbia College," *NYT*, December 22, 1862, *NYT* digital archive.

6 Diary of Arthur Sturges, January 1863, SFP, PML

7 VSO to MS, December 31, 1862, ARC-1218, Pt. 8, SFP, PML.

8 "Anniversary of the Philolexian Society," *NYT*, December 20, 1863, *NYT* digital archive.

9 Cardozo, Ernest A., *A History of the Philolexian Society of Columbia University, from 1802--1902*, Philolexian Society, New York, 1902, p.134.

10 JS to MS, February 12, 1862, ARC-1218, SFP, PML.

11 *Report of Special Committee On Volunteering, Embracing a Complete Statement of Operations In Filling the Quota of the County of New York Under the Call of the President, Dated July 18, 1864, for 500,000 Men*, (New York: W. L. S. Harrison, 1864), p. 454, HathiTrust.

12 AS to Henry Sturges," undated (1865?), ARC-1218, SFP, PML.

13 AmS to AS, October 1860, ARC-1218, SFP, PML.

14 VSO to Grandma (Cady?), July 1, 1866, ARC-1218, SFP, PML.

15 VSO to Dear Aunt, July 1, 1866, ARC-1218, SFP, PML

16 "Died," *New York Tribune* (New York, NY), July 2, 1866, p. 5

17 "Chamber of Commerce-Annual Election of Officers," *NYT*, May 5, 1865, p. 8, *NYT* digital archive.

18 "Local Intelligence-Special Meeting of the Chamber of Commerce," *NYT*, May 12, 1865, p. 2, *NYT* digital archive.

19 "The Ketchum Defalcation," *Evening Post* (New York, NY), September 2, 1865, p. 1.

20 "News," *Daily Milwaukee News*, Mar 22, 1868 p. 4.

21 "The Case of Edward B. Ketchum," *New York Tribune* (New York, NY), March 18, 1868, p.1.

22 "Gov. Fenton's Refusal to Pardon Young Ketchum," *NYT*, March 30, 1868, *NYT* digital archive.

23 "Notice of Dissolution," *NYT*, January 30, 1866, p. 6, *NYT* digital archive.

24 Sturges, *Reminiscences*, p. 236.

25 *The African Repository* (American Colonization Society), No. 6, 1873, p. 8.

Chapter 22

1 *A Complimentary Dinner to Jonathan Sturges*, p. 4.

2 *Ibid*, p. 8.

3 *Ibid*, p. 28.

4 "Words of a Wise Man," Boys and Girls Treasury, *Arthur's Home Magazine*, May 1881, p. 5.

5 "Sound Doctrine," *Lowell (MA) Daily Citizen and News* February 4, 1868, p. 2.

6 "Oldest Business Firms on Front Street," *Evening Post* (New York, NY), August 13, 1869, p. 2.

7 *The Lancaster Intelligencer* (Lancaster, PA), December 8, 1869.

8 Advertisement, *NYT*, April 5, 1865, p. 6, *NYT* digital archive.

9 "The Weekly Underwriter: An Insurance Newspaper," Vol. LXXIX., Saturday, Aug. 1, 1908, (New York: Underwriter Printing and Publishing Co.,1907), p. 79.

10 Advertisement, *New York Tribune*, March 28, 1870, p. 8.

11 Official report of the proceedings of the National Insurance Convention of the United States, compiled by Henry S. Olcott, (New York: Goodsell, 1871), p. 34-37, HathiTrust

12 "Meeting on Behalf of the Indians," *Helena Weekly Herald*, July 16, 1868, p.4.

13 "The Indian Commission-Meeting on Behalf of the Indians at Cooper Institute," *NYT*, June 30, 1868, *NYT* digital archive.

14 Oman, Kerry, "The Beginning of the End of the Indian Peace Commission of 1867-1868," *Great Plains Quarterly*, January 1, 2002 (Winter 2002), p. 35.

15 Burns, Louis F., *The Drum Creek Treaty*, Project Muse http://muse.jhu.edu/chapter/154211 (accessed September 16, 2017).

16 "City Intelligence-The Osage Treaty Swindle," *Commercial Advertiser*, March 3, 1869, p. 4.

17 *Annual Report of the Commission on Indian Affairs to the Secretary of the Interior for the Fiscal Year Ended 1869*, Washington: Government Printing Office, 1870, p. 96.

18 "The Indians-Executive Order Relating to the Indian Commission," *New York Tribune* (New York, NY), June 8, 1869, p. 8.

19 Kessner, Thomas, *New York City and the Men Behind America's Rise to Economic Dominance, 1860-1900*, (New York: Simon & Schuster, 2004), p. 77.

20 Lamb, Albert R. *The Presbyterian Hospital and the Columbia-Presbyterian Medical Center*, 1868-1943, (New York: Columbia University Press, 1955) p.11.

21 Bayless, Pamela, *The YMCA at 150: A History of the YMCA of Greater New York*, (New York: Fordham University Press, 2002), pp. 217-222.

22 "YMCA Building," c. 1869, American Scenery New York City post card, LOC, LC-DIG-stereo-1s07013 http://loc.gov/pictures/resource/stereo.1s07013/ (accessed April 9, 2018).

Chapter 23

1 "Jonathan Sturges," *Boston (MA) Daily Advertiser*, December 1, 1874, p. 4.

2 "The Internal Revenue-Splendid Success of the Measure," *New York Herald* (New York, NY), January 15, 1865, p. 1.

3 "Income Tax-Formation of an Organization to Abolish the Income Tax," *New York Herald* (New York, NY), March 30, 1871, p.4.

4 Ibid.

5 "The Panic-Run On Fourth National Bank," No. 20 Nassau Street, New York, NY (1873), *Frank Leslie's Illustrated*, October 4, 1873, LOC, Call # Illus. in AP2.L52 1873 (Case Y) [P&P], https://www.loc.gov/resource/cph.3a00900/ (Accessed April 9, 2018)

6 "New York Post Office," *NYT*, February 7, 1866, *NYT* digital archive.

7 "The New-York Post Office," *NYT*, June 27, 1868, p. 1, *NYT* digital archive.

8 "City Hall Post Office, New York" c. 1887, Mullen, Chris, Full Table.com New York Photographs, The Albertine Co. http://www.fulltable.com/VTS/n/nny/08.jpg

9 "New Political Organizations Throughout the City," *New York Herald* (New York, NY), February 8, 1864, p. 4.

10 "News," *New York Tribune* (New York NY), March 12, 1864, p.6.

11 "Meeting of the Citizen's Association," *World* (New York, NY), November 30, 1864, p.5, Genealogy Bank.com.

12 *Report of the Council of Hygiene and Public Health of the Citizen's Association of New York Upon the Sanitary Condition of the City*, NYT, June 19, 1865, NYT digital archive.

13 "News," New York Tribune, November 22, 1865, p. 4.

14 "Virtual New York City, Cholera in 1866," The Graduate Center, CUNY, 2001 http://www.virtualny.cuny.edu/cholera/1866/cholera_1866_3new.html (accessed June 2015).

15 "War Against the Ring," *New York Tribune* (New York, NY), September 6, 1871, p. 1.

16 "Reward of the Seventy," *Daily Graphic* (New York, NY), May 23, 1873, p. 3.

17 "Editorial," *NYT*, June 6, 1873, *NYT* digital archive.

18 "Reorganization of the Committee of Seventy," Letters to the Editor, June 6, 1873, *NYT*, p. 5, *NYT* digital archive.

19 "Local Politics–Committee of Seventy," *NYT*, October 22, 1873, *NYT* digital archive.

Chapter 24

1 *Henry Cady Sturges* 1860s, Private Collection.

2 "Columbia College Goodwood Cup," *NYT*, June 13, 1868, *NYT* digital archive.

3 "Columbia College, Presentation of the Goodwood Cup," *Evening Post* (New York, NY), June 13, 1868, p. 2.

4 Kurshan, Virginia, *H.H. Richardson House*, Designation List 352, LP-2141, Landmarks Preservation Commission, March 30, 2004, p.4 http://www.nyc.gov/html/lpc/downloads/pdf/reports/richardson.pdf (accessed February 27, 2014).

5 Ludlow, E.H., *19 Lots for Sale on Murray Hill…*, Advertising map, 1865, Call No. NS12 M10.4.15, NYHS.

6 Oschner, *H.H. Richardson Complete Architectural Works*, p.63.

7 *Jonathan Sturges Parlor* at 40 E. 36th St., Box FO2, ARC 2798, Courtesy of PML. Note: It is unclear whether is picture is from their E. 14th Street home or their 1870s Park Avenue home.

8 Deems, *Jonathan Sturges,* p. 420.

9 "Our Artists at the Paris Exhibition," *Evening Post* (New York, NY), January 23, 1867, p.2.

10 "Innocents Abroad: American Painters at the Exposition Universelle, Paris," *American Art-Journal*, Autumn, 1984, Vol. 16, No. 4 (Kennedy Galleries, Inc.), p. 13 http://www.jstor.org/ stable/1594386 (accessed February 15, 2014).

11 Ibid, p. 19.

12 "History of the Museum, The Metropolitan Museum of Art," http://ww.metmuseum.org/en/about-the-museum/history-of-the-museum/main-building (accessed February 16, 2014).

13 "Meeting of the Officers of the Metropolitan Museum of Art," *NYT*, December 23, 1870, *NYT* digital archive.

14 Bryant, William Cullen, II, *Poetry, Painting- A Love Affair from Long Ago*, American Quarterly, (Johns Hopkins University Press: Winter 1970), p. 864.

15 DePaster, Frederic, *An Address Delivered Before the NYHS, At the Celebration of Its Sixty-Ninth Anniversary*, The New York Historical Society, (New York: by the Society, 1874), p. 5.

16 Sturges, Jonathan, "Some Reminiscences of the Progress of Art in New York."

17 "Died," *NYT*, August 31, 1868, p. 5, *NYT* digital archive.

18 *Jonathan Sturges and Grandchildren*, Osborn and Dodge Family Miscellaneous Photographs, Box 14, Courtesy of PUL.

19 VSO to J. Pierpont Morgan, September 1867, ARC-1218, SFP, PML.

20 Frances Morgan to MS, June 26, 1872, ARC-1218, SFP, PML.

21 Dunwell, Frances, *America's River*, Columbia University Press, NY, 2008, p. 178. Google Books.

22 Griffin, Margaret Porter, Blog: "Pictures that Didn't Make the Book," Garrison, Wing and Wing, 2013, https://amazingbirdcollection.files.wordpress.com/2014/08/wing-wing-may-2013-color.jpg (accessed June 12, 2015).

23 *Virginia Sturges Osborn*, 1860s, Private Collection.

24 Becker, *The Monied Metropolis*, pg. 157.

25 Bigelow, *William Cullen Bryant*, p. 233.

26 Ibid, p. 234.

27 Deems, "Jonathan Sturges," p. 421.

Chapter 25

1 Giles, *A Candle in Her Hand*, p. 64.

2 Hobson, *Recollections of a Happy Life*, p. 80.

3 Giles, *A Candle in Her Hand*, p. 102.

4 Hobson, *Recollections of a Happy Life*, p. 91.

5 Giles, *A Candle in Her Hand*, p. 73.

6 "Florence Nightingale's Letter of Advice to Bellevue," *American Journal of Nursing*, Vol. 11, No. 5, p. 361 http://www.jstor.org/stable/3404989?seq=1 (accessed November 15, 2014).

7 Hobson, *Recollections of a Happy Life*, p. 101.

8 Ibid, p. 104.

9 Ibid, p. 106.

10 Giles, *A Candle in Her Hand*, p. 72.

Chapter 26

1 "Jonathan Sturges," 1874 Obituary, unknown minister author, Fairfield Museum and History Center, Fairfield, CT.

2 MS to JS, July 13, 1834, ARC-1218, SFP, PML.

3 Atwater, Rev. Lyman H., "The Christian Merchant," *New York Observer and Chronicle* (New York, NY), December 24, 1874.

4 Elizabeth Cady to JS, New York, June 1848, ARC-1218, SFP, PML.

5 JS to MS Sturges, July 10, 1836, OFP.

6 VSO to HCS, January 1, 1871, ARC-1218, SFP, PML.

7 Edward Sturges to MS, Baltimore, August 21, 1862, ARC-1218, SFP, PML.

8 VSO to Grandma, Fairfield, July 1, 1866, ARC-1218, SFP, PML.

9 Duff, Alexander, *Proceedings…: Held in New York, May 4th & 5th, 1854,* (New York: Taylor & Hogg, 1854, p. 13, 17, 18, 21 https://play.google.com/books/reader? id=mIkyAQA-AMAAJ&hl=en&pg=GBS.PP1

10 "To the Christians of America", *New York Evangelist,* New York NY, September 14, 1865, p. 14

11 "Temperance Reading-Rooms for Working-Men," *New York Evangelist* (New York, NY), May 30, 1872, p. 4.

12 Brace, Charles L, *The Dangerous Classes of New York,* p. 112 www.munseys.com/disknine/ dany.pdf (accessed October 13, 2014).

13 "New York City Council of Political Reform. Report on Compulsory Education," (New York: *Evening Post* Steam Presses, 1874), p. 12. HathiTrust.

14 Griffis, William Elliot, *Verbeck of Japan: A Citizen of No Country,* (New York: Caxton Press, 1900), p. 154.

15 Wright, Henry Otis, *The Centennial History of the American Bible Society-Vol. I,* (New York: MacMillan Co., 1916), p. 5

16 "National Sabbath Convention," *NYT,* July 11, 1863, *NYT* digital Archive.

17 "The Excise Question-Protest Against the Proposed Amendment-Mass Meeting Tonight," *NYT,* April 8, 1869, p.5, *NYT* digital archive.

18 "The Late Jonathan Sturges," *NYT,* December 3, 1874, *NYT* digital archive.

19 "Protest Sunday theatricals to the Police Commission," *Jacksonville* (FL) *Gazette,* November 28, 1874, p. 1

20 "Sunday Theatricals," *NYT,* December 14, 1874, *NYT* digital archive.

21 Griffin, Margaret Porter, Blog: "The Amazing Bird Collection: Finding Freddie" https:// amazingbirdcollection.wordpress.com/tag/frederick-sturges-osborn/ (accessed June 12, 2015).

22 "Jonathan Sturges," *Evening Post* (New York, NY), December 1, 1874, pg. 3.

Chapter 27

1 Deems, *Jonathan Sturges,* p. 421.

2 "The Sunday Amusement Law," *New York Post* (New York, NY), December 14, 1874, p. 5.

3 "The Funeral of Mr. Sturges," *World* (New York, NY), December 2, 1874, p. 1.

4 "The Last Tributes to Jonathan Sturges," Funeral addresses by Rev. Drs. Hall, Ludlow, et.al, *New York Tribune* (New York, NY), December 2, 1874, p. 5

5 "Jonathan Sturges," *Evening Post* (New York, NY), December 1, 1874, p. 3.

6 Letter from William Sydney Mount, April 4, 1852, Relating a speech he made April 6, 1851, at National Academy of Design Meeting http://longislandmuseum.pastperfect online.com/archive/D1432F6A-A592-42BA-B921-917046014977 (accessed February 14, 2018).

7 "Misc.," *Tribute Territorial Enterprise* (Virginia City, NV), December 12, 1874, p. 6.

8 Secretary of State Hamilton Fish to HCS, Washington, D.C., December 7, 1874.

9 "The Late Jonathan Sturges," *Frank Leslie's Illustrated Newspaper,* December 19, 1874, p. 245.

10 "The Late Jonathan Sturges-The Action of the Union League Club," *New York Herald* (New York, NY), December 1, 1874, p. 7.

11 Wilson, George, ed., *Portrait gallery of the Chamber of Commerce of the state of New-York, catalogue and biographical sketches*, published by the New York Chamber of Commerce, 1890, p. 59.

12 "New York-A Talk About Wills," *Cincinnati Daily Gazette*, December 26, 1874, p.2.

13 "Jonathan Sturges," *The Christian Intelligencer* (New York, NY), December 3, 1874, p.8.

14 "The Late Mayor Havemeyer-Details of his Death," *The Sentinel of Freedom* (Newark, NJ), December 8, 1874.

15 "In Memoriam: C.N.T. (Charles Nocoll Talbot)," November 29, 1874 (New York: Printed for the *Family Circle*, 1875), p. 40. HathiTrust.

16 "Sturges's Will," *New York Daily Tribune* (New York, NY), December 17, 1874, p. 7.

17 "The Late Jonathan Sturges Will," *NYT*, December 14, 1874, *NYT* digital archive.

18 Jane Beale to MS, December 5, 1874, OFP.

19 "Nature and Art-At the Country," *Evening Post* (New York, NY), June 21, 1875, p. 4.

Chapter 28

1 "Co-partnership Notice," *New York Tribune* (New York, NY), January 3, 1872, p. 6.

2 Conant, Charles A., *The Progress of the Empire State: a Work Devoted to the Historical, Financial, Industrial, And Literary Development of New York*, (New York: Progress of the Empire state company, 1913), p. 343 HathiTrust.

3 "The Hermits Letter-Concerning Old Houses," *Troy* (NY) *Daily Times* March 15, 1883, p. 1.

4 Strouse, *Morgan: Financier*, p. 202.

5 Winkler, John K., *Morgan The Magnificent*, (New York: Vanguard Press, 1930), p. 59

6 "As Reopening Nears, Morgan Library Gets a Good Scrubbing," *NYT*, August 8, 1991, *NYT* digital archive.

7 "Sturges Chimes are Installed in Fairfield Church," *Bridgeport Telegram* (Bridgeport, CT), January 1, 1923.

8 Ackerman, *Historical Sketch of Illinois Central Railroad* p. 67.

9 Huntington, Daniel, *Jonathan Sturges*, Oil on canvas, New York Chamber of Commerce Portrait Collection, Courtesy of New York State Museum, Albany, NY.

10 Hobson, *Recollections of a Happy Life*, p. 110.

11 Choate, Joseph, H., "What Florence Nightingale Did for Mankind," *American Journal of Nursing*, Vol. 11, No. 5, February 1911, p.356, https://archive.org/stream/jstor-3404987/3404987#page/n13/mode/2up/search/choate (accessed October 15, 2014).

12 "Sturges Pavilion," *Bellevue: A Short* History, p.26.

13 "Osborn Hall," *Bellevue: A Short History*, p.50.

14 *Bellevue: A Short History*, p.51.

15 *Virginia Osborn*, daughter of William H. and Virginia Sturges Osborn, Private collection.

16 Stain Glass Memorial to Frederick and Virginia Osborn, St. Phillips Church, Garrison, New York, photography by author.

17 Griffin, Margaret Porter, *The Determined Study of a Young Naturalist, Theodore Roosevelt, 1874-1875*, p. 6 http://www.theodoreroosevelt.org/atf/cf/%7B01a413bf-e254-454d-b340-8502d6ea02de%7D/TRA-JOURNAL-2014-SUMMER.PDF (accessed June 12, 2015).

18 Castle Rock, Garrison, NY, Photo in PD, https://www.pinterest.com/pin/28837118236 3935021/, (accessed September 13, 2018)

19 View from Castle Rock balcony, photo by author.

20 "Henry Fairfield Osborn," 1890s, NYHS Library Blog, September 2009, http://blog. nyhistory.org/wp-content/uploads/2013/09/redwoods014.jpg (accessed September 13, 2018).

21 VSO to Fanny Morgan, undated, Box 5, CO537, Osborn and Dodge Family Papers, PUL.

22 "Osborn Gates," *Things to See, Central Park*, 2010, Central Park Conservancy http://www. centralparknyc.org/visit/things-to-see/great-lawn/osborn-gates.html (accessed February 5, 2014).

23 Thatcher, John S., MD and George Woolsey, MD, eds., *Medical and Surgical Report of the Presbyterian Hospital of New York City*, Vol. VIII, December 1908, pp. iii-iv, Google Books.

24 "Hospital Saturday and Sunday," *NYT*, December 20, 1880, *NYT* digital archive.

25 New York City Health and Hospitals Corporation-Bellevue, a timeline of firsts, 1872, https://partner.hpdnyc.org/whalecom81b846a8d7ea6a1bb1b6bf/whalecomo/html/hhc/ bellevue/html/about/history.shtml (accessed June 5, 2014).

26 King, Moses, *Notable New Yorkers*, 1896-1899, (New York: The Orr Press, 1899), p. 18.

27 Sterner, Albert, *Jonathan Sturges* (1865-1911), c. 1912, General Manuscripts Misc. Collection, Princeton University Library.

28 James, Henry, Letter to Henrietta Reubell, Rye, Nov. 12, 1899, as transcribed by Percy Lubbock, University of Adelaide, Australia (Charles Scribner and Sons: 1920).

29 Sterner, Albert, *A Pastel Sketch of Jonathan Sturges*, for his sister Mary Fuller Sturges Chalmers, Graphic Arts Collection GA 2006, 1911 https://graphicarts. princeton.edu/ 2015/06/18/jonathan-sturges (accessed June 6, 2016).

30 "The Early Property Acquisitions," Fairfield University's Ur-History, History of Fairfield University, http://www.faculty.fairfield.edu/jmac/fu/FUrur.htm (accessed March 1, 2014).

31 Sturges Park Deed, Sturges Family File, Fairfield Museum and History Center, Fairfield, CT.

32 "About the Fairfield Museum and History Center's Architecture," Fairfield Museum History Center http://www.fairfieldhistory.org/wp-content/uploads/2011/05/About Architecture.pdf (accessed October 15, 2014).

33 Trow's New York City Directory, Vol. XC, for the year ending May 1,1877, (New York: The Trow City Directory, 1877), p. 1335.

34 Hill, Edwin, C., ed., The Historical Register, (New York: E.C. Hill, 1922), p.55, HathiTrust.

35 HCS to JS, Kingston, April 10, 1874 (est. yr.), Box 1, OFP.

36 *American Yacht List for 1896.* (New York: T. Manning, 1896), p. 67, HathiTrust.

37 *American Yacht List* (New York: T. Manning, 1889), p. 141, HathiTrust.

38 New York Yacht Club: [yearbook]. New York, 1904, p. 35, HathiTrust.

39 Chamberlin, Joshua, L.L.D., Ed., *Universities and Their Sons*, (Harvard, Yale, Princeton, Columbia), V. 5, (Boston: R. Herndon Co.1900), p. 265-256.

40 Henry Sturges private sailing pennant #387, New York Yacht Club Yearbook, 1902. Hathi Trust.

41 Henry Sturges sailing flag. Photo by author.

42 Trow's New York City Directory, Vol. XCII, for the year ending May 1,1879, New York: The Trow City Directory, 1879, p. 1423.

43 VSO to Henry Sturges, April 7, 1883, ARC1218, P.8, SFP, PML.

44 Mary Sturges and Abigail Sturges, c. 1880s, private collection.

45 Mary Cady Sturges, Fairfield Cottage-Library Window Seat, 1890s, Private collection.

46 "Mill Plain," *Southport Times*, January 1, 1880, pg. 1 http://cslib.cdmhost.com/cdm/com poundobject/collection/p15019coll9/id/2721/rec/13 (accessed March 1, 2014).

47 "General News," *Albany Evening Journal* (Albany, NY), May 10, 1876, p.2.

48 Kansfield, Mary L. *Letters to Hazel-Ministry within the Woman's Board of Foreign Missions of the Reformed Church of America*, Reformed Church Press, (Grand Rapids William B. Eerdmans Publishing, 2004), p. 54.

49 Corwin, Edward Tanjore, D.D., *A Manual of the Reformed Church of America (formerly Ref. Prot. Dutch Church, 1628-1902*, 4th Edition, Board of Publication of the Reformed Church, 1902, p. 274.

50 *Sixteenth Annual Report of the Women's Board of Foreign Missions of the Reformed Church in America-For the Year ending April 30, 1890*, (New York: Reformed Church of America, 1890), p. 15.

51 "The Obituary Record-Mrs. Mary Pemberton Sturges," *NYT*, July 31, 1894, p. 5, *NYT* digital archive.

52 "Mortuary Notice," *New York Herald* (New York, NY), July 31, 1894, p. 1.

53 Sturges, *Reminiscences*, p. 246.

54 "A Chance to Do Good: These Boys Need a Helping Hand-Who will give it?" *New York Observer and Chronicle* (New York, NY), July 20, 1905.

55 Nash, George B., ed., *Journal of the Horticultural Society of New York*, Vol. II, No. 1, Published by the Society, (Lancaster: The New Era Printing Co., 1914), p. 39, 72, 106, 107, 170, 174, 226, 229.

56 Wright, Mabel Osgood, "Cottage Garden," c. 1900, *Fairfield Museum Collection*.

57 Everett, William Henry, "Sturges Cottage," c. 1880, *Fairfield Museum Collection*.

58 Jonathan Sturges House, Local Historic Districts and Property Commissions in Connecticut, CT Trust for Historic Preservation http://www.historicdistrictsct.org/district/jonathan-sturges-house (accessed March 1, 2014).

Appendix

1 *Rules for Christian mechanics, merchants &c. n. p. n. d.* Pdf. American Tract Society, 1830s, Library of Congress, https://www.loc.gov/item/rbpe.24401200/. (accessed March 11, 2018).

Index

Page numbers in *italics* indicate an illustration. Page numbers with the suffix 'a' indicate material in the appendices.